American Rubber Workers & Organized Labor

Daniel Nelson

American Rubber Workers
& Organized Labor,
1900-1941

PRINCETON UNIVERSITY PRESS | PRINCETON, NEW JERSEY

CONTENTS

ILLUSTRATIONS

THIS IS A STUDY of opportunity and response—the opportunity for economic and political gain and the response of American rubber workers between 1900 and World War II. The opportunities reflected conditions in and out of the industry; the responses varied but nearly always included efforts to organize. The interplay of these forces culminated in the 1930s when the labor movement, including unions of rubber workers, grew more rapidly than at any other time in the twentieth century and began to confront the challenges of organizational maturity that have dominated the labor history of the last half century.

A central premise of this work, that the rubber workers' behavior reflected the evolution of the industry and the performance of the economy, largely dictated the organization of the material. Most chapters include a summary of economic and other external developments and a description of the workers' activities. The first part is usually brief, the second more expansive. A study of the industry or of the United Rubber Workers alone would undoubtedly strike a different balance. My goal has been to describe the workers' behavior against a background that included the era's most important changes in business, technology, and politics.

The preparation of this study extended over many years and benefited from the expertise and generous assistance of a veritable army of individuals. Of the union veterans who submitted to oral history interviews, John D. House deserves special mention for his helpfulness, unfailing honesty, and courtesy. The others, like Rex D. Murray, Harley Anthony, and nearly a score more, were patient and cooperative. They are frequently cited in the footnotes.

I also benefited from the work of three fine reporters who covered the rubber workers in the 1930s. James S. Jackson, Edward Heinke, and Ray T. Sutliff were masters of their craft who left a rich and varied legacy.

Of the many union officials who helped me obtain materials, several deserve special notice. Ike Gold, former international secretary-treasurer of the URW, gave me unrestricted access to the minutes of the International Executive Board and the correspondence of the International during the 1930s. Robert Strauber, former education director of the International, responded positively to what must have seemed an endless series of requests. The officers of locals 2, 5, 26 and 44 opened their historical records to me. Floyd Gartrell in Los Angeles, James E. Green in Cumberland, Maryland,

and Cecil S. Holmes in Gadsden, Alabama, were particularly generous with their time and advice.

A host of archivists and librarians aided in the search for documents. Lane Moore and his colleagues at the National Archives provided invaluable assistance at an early stage of my research. Marjory J. Garman at the Goodyear Tire & Rubber Company was extremely helpful, as were the professionals at the State Historical Society of Wisconsin, the AFL-CIO, Columbia University, the Firestone Tire & Rubber Company, the New York State School of Industrial and Labor Relations, Catholic University, the Ohio Historical Society, the Franklin D. Roosevelt Library, Western Reserve Historical Society, New York Public Library, Carnegie-Mellon University and the University of Akron. Valerie Johnson and Sara Lorenz, interlibrary loan librarians at the University of Akron, helped me locate widely scattered and often fugitive secondary sources.

Various individuals provided more specialized but no less valuable assistance. Jesse Marquette and Donald L. Winters provided invaluable advice on the use of election statistics. J. Robert Constantine and David A. Shannon helped me locate Marguerite Prevey and Eugene V. Debs materials. Judith Stein provided several clues to the roles, or nonroles, of black rubber workers in the labor movement. Stuart B. Kaufman helped me make sense of the Gompers Papers. Nuala M. Drescher provided materials on the Dunlop union and Robert H. Storey and Terry Copp helped me with the activities of the Canadian locals.

I am especially indebted to Robert H. Zieger, George W. Knepper and John D. House, who read an early draft of the manuscript and saved me from a variety of pitfalls. Sanford Jacoby and Robert Asher also read the pre-Depression chapters and offered many valuable suggestions. They all have my sincere thanks for a job well done. Needless to say, they bear no responsibility for the book's residual flaws.

Generous financial assistance from the University of Akron Faculty Research Committee and the American Philosophical Society greatly aided my work, as did a sabbatical leave in 1980. I am grateful to my colleagues at the University of Akron for their cooperation and assistance.

Garnette Dorsey, Inez Bachman, and especially Mia Hahn typed and retyped various drafts of the manuscript with their customary efficiency, dispatch, and good humor.

My wife Lorraine and my children have borne the rigors of this effort with admirable patience and understanding, for which I am, as always, grateful.

ABBREVIATIONS

ABJ   *Akron Beacon Journal*
AP   *Akron Press*
ATP   *Akron Times Press*
CL   *Cleveland Leader*
IRW   *India Rubber World*
SCLN *Summit County Labor News*
TT   *Trenton Times*
URW   *United Rubber Worker*
WCL   *Wingfoot Clan*

American Rubber Workers & Organized Labor

CHAPTER ONE

Introduction: The Rubber Workers and Organized Labor

THE RELATIONSHIP between American rubber workers and organized labor properly dates from the 1880s, when manufacturers responded to the growth of the market with a series of new technologies—"mass production"—and the labor movement embraced an approach to organization based on the craft and, later, the strategic occupation rather than on the wage earner.[1] For many years these developments were only indirectly related. Mass production created armies of "semiskilled" machine operators who were highly paid and reasonably powerful compared with most factory laborers but who lacked a craft or identifiable occupation. To organize strategic workers in such a setting often meant organizing the entire plant. Uncomfortable with that prospect, the American Federation of Labor and its affiliates concentrated on mining, construction, the services, and small-batch manufacturing. By the turn of the century, when the advent of relatively inexpensive automobiles and electrical machinery created a second generation of mass production industries and more semiskilled machine operators, the divorce of mass production and the labor movement was virtually complete. Appropriately, the long and often rancorous debate between "craft" and "industrial" unionists dated from the same period.[2]

At the turn of the century the rubber industry consisted of more than three hundred small plants that employed a mature, labor-intensive technology to produce footwear, belting, hose, druggists' supplies, and related items. The automobile at first simply added another popular product, the pneumatic tire. Beginning about 1909, however, inventors and engineers introduced innovations in manufacturing techniques that distinguished tires

---

[1] The best study of mass production in a historical context is Alfred D. Chandler, Jr., *The Visible Hand: The Managerial Revolution in American Business* (Cambridge, 1977), pp. 240–83. Also see two quite different but illuminating studies: David A. Hounshell, *From the American System to Mass Production, 1800–1932: The Development of Manufacturing Technology in the United States* (Baltimore, 1984), and Naomi R. Lamoreaux, *The Great Merger Movement in American Business, 1895–1904* (Cambridge, 1985), pp. 14–45. For the labor movement, see Christopher L. Tomlins, "AFL Unions in the 1930's: Their Performance in Historical Perspective," *Journal of American History* 65 (1979): 1021–42.

[2] James O. Morris, *Conflict Within the AFL: A study in Craft Versus Industrial Unionism, 1901–1928* (Ithaca, 1958), pp. 4–42.

from other rubber goods. The central feature of this development, which continued through the 1910s and 1920s, was specialized machinery that increased the speed of manufacture and reduced unit production costs.[3] The boldest of the tire manufacturers fully exploited the new technology and made substantial commitments to crude rubber production and tire marketing; their firms became vertically integrated. The less adventurous simply created large factories and remained single-function manufacturers;[4] unless they found a specialized market niche, they faced an increasingly perilous existence. The many marginal producers who clung to the labor-intensive technology of the turn of the century had even smaller chances of survival.

By the early 1920s, then, the American rubber industry had two major divisions: a tire sector consisting of four big businesses, a handful of large factories, and a few small, marginal firms; and a nontire sector consisting of a few large factories and many small firms. Without a mass production technology, size conferred little or no competitive advantage.[5]

The advent of tire manufacture also transformed the industry's labor force. In contrast to the insecure European immigrants who gave many of the older New England and New Jersey rubber plants a distinctive social cast, brawny farm youths dominated the labor force in the midwestern tire firms. Because the early tire factories used primitive tire-building and curing machines that relied on human energy as much as steam or electrical power, a physical elite was indispensable. The young men who were large and strong enough to qualify earned the wages of skilled workers in other industries. Understandably, they became known for their optimism, self-confidence, and independence. In the 1910s mass production gradually reduced the need for physical stamina, but the simultaneous labor shortage, resulting from the World War I industrial boom, forced manufacturers to look to Appalachia for additional workers. Most of the individuals they recruited shared their predecessors' familiarity with hard physical labor as well as their ambitions and values.[6]

[3] Chandler, *The Visible Hand*, pp. 240–83.

[4] The single function is production; hence a single-function manufacturing firm is not vertically integrated.

[5] The big businesses all produced rubber products besides tires during this period, and two of them, U.S. Rubber and B. F. Goodrich, had substantial nontire operations. The avantages of large size and vertical integration in tire manufacture were comparatively small; in nontire markets they were probably negligible. See Joe S. Bain, *Barriers to New Competition: Their Character and Consequences in Manufacturing Industries* (Cambridge, 1956), pp. 82, 151, 239, 258.

[6] See, for example, John Bodnar, *Workers' World: Kinship, Community, and Protest in an Industrial Society, 1900–1940* (Baltimore, 1982); Tamara Hareven, *Family Time and Industrial Time* (Cambridge, 1983); Ronald D. Eller, *Miners, Millhands, and Mountaineers: Industrialization of the Appalachian South, 1880–1930* (Knoxville, 1982), pp. 9–11.

After 1910 the tire workers profoundly influenced the labor organizations that appeared in the industry. Because the elite was large but unskilled, it spurned traditional craft organization. Because it was ethnically and socially homogeneous in the midwestern plants, the industry leaders, it dominated the labor force. And because most tire employees were involved in mass production operations, they made the distinctive "veto" of machine operators in capital-intensive industry a focus of union activity.[7] During the labor upheavals of the World War I era, the elite shared the leader's mantle with other workers. After 1920, it became the vital element in organizing efforts throughout the industry. Only at the end of the 1930s, when a new combination of demand and technology reduced the importance of the tire workers, did its influence lessen.

Though nearly all employers opposed organization, they tempered their hostility with an appreciation of economic and political conditions. The big businesses, with greater resources and more control over the environment, had more options than the large factories or small plants. In the 1920s they experimented with company unions; in the 1930s they embraced diverse approaches to their employees, ranging from "progressive" to "realistic."[8] Though they were also more subject to political pressures than the non-integrated companies, they soon learned to implement their choices in legally and politically acceptable ways. Moreover, they retained a final option, the ability to move their operations to new, more accommodating sites.

The executives of large factories and small firms, on the other hand, were captive to their environment. Where the local labor movement was weak and public authorities were committed to industrial expansion, employers resolutely resisted organization. Where the labor movement was strong or the elite divided, they were more flexible. Since most of the successful large factories were in the Akron area, a center of union activity, it is hardly surprising that they became known for good relations with their employees in periods of union growth. By the mid-1930s they had become models of accommodation and "mature" industrial relations.[9] Some small firms in or

---

[7] The veto embraced a continuum of activity that included informal efforts to restrict output and technological change, more formal limits on production, and, finally, sit-downs and other demonstrative actions. The veto was common in all industries where the worker controlled the pace of work but took special, subtle and, in the 1930s, especially interesting forms in capital-intensive industry.

[8] Howell John Harris, *The Right to Manage: Industrial Relations Policies of American Business in the 1940s* (Madison, 1982), pp. 32–34.

[9] See Richard A. Lester, *As Unions Mature: An Analysis of the Evolution of American Unionism* (Princeton, 1958), pp. 21–34. In describing the political setting in Akron, I have found Carl V. Harris's *Political Power in Birmingham, 1871–1921* (Knoxville, 1977), pp.

near Boston, New York, and Philadelphia were also cooperative. But most small companies were in isolated communities with little history of organization and a strong sense of the value of low wages. In these settings, union efforts often became prolonged, violent adventures.

Two other familiar influences had a large and demonstrable impact on the rubber workers' behavior. The first was the business cycle, the critical variable in the ebb and flow of the American labor movement in the pre–World War II years.[10] If the industry influenced the character of union activity, the business cycle largely determined its timing. When jobs became plentiful and the future seemed promising, workers organized.[11] There were no exceptions. Conversely, when the economy declined and opportunities were more limited, workers abandoned their unions and remained deaf to outsiders' appeals. The unique feature of the 1930s was not the breakdown of this pattern but the manufacturers' unparalleled loss of self-esteem and public stature, which allowed unions to operate in a comparatively peaceful environment during the years of economic growth, 1933 to 1937. The workers' activities during those years and afterward, when they faced severe challenges, underlined the close association between the health of the economy and the vitality of the labor movement.

The other influence was a variety of pro-union groups from outside the industry. The most important of these, perhaps surprisingly, was the AFL. While most established unions remained oblivious to the 80–90 percent of rubber workers who did not have an identifiable craft, the Federation itself was reasonably active. Under Samuel Gompers and especially William Green, the Ohio miner, politician, and United Mine Workers official who became AFL president in 1924, the AFL became the focal point for most organizing efforts. Its failures were due partly to conditions that Federation officials could not control and partly to shortcomings in their approach. Two flaws stand out: erratic leadership and the failure of Gompers, Green, and their subordinates to recognize tire builders and pit workers as strategic workers in the tire factories. Ultimately it was not Green or his deputies but the leaders of the CIO and another prominent Mine Worker, Allan S. Haywood, who became the external catalysts in the consolidation of the United Rubber Workers. One of the more intriguing features of the rubber work-

---

39–56, 270–85, particularly useful. Like Birmingham, Akron had a distinctive group of industrialists and a larger ''middle'' echelon of merchants and professionals.

[10] The most thorough survey is George Sayers Bain and Farouk Elsheikh, *Union Growth and The Business Cycle: An Econometric Analysis* (Oxford, 1976), pp. 6–22. Also see Lee P. Stepina and Jack Fiorito, ''Toward a Comprehensive Theory of Union Growth and Decline,'' *Industrial Relations* 25 (1986): 248–64, and Barry T. Hirsch and Jon T. Addison, *The Economic Analysis of Unions: New Approaches and Evidence* (Boston, 1986), pp. 54–55.

[11] Economists have used various measures of economic conditions, none of which, it appears, is entirely satisfactory or inherently superior.

ers' experiences in the 1930s was the contrast between the popular images of the rival federations and the behavior of their representatives. In Akron and other rubber manufacturing centers, AFL organizers often seemed irresponsible and unbusinesslike. CIO agents, on the other hand, were unfailingly moderate and cooperative; whatever their personal inclinations, they spoke the language of labor-management harmony and business unionism.

Besides the AFL and CIO, various political activists sought to influence the rubber workers and their organizations. This was a common experience among industrial workers, though the results in this case may have been atypical.[12] The avowed radicals—Socialists and Communists—were colorful but ineffectual. Among the rubber workers their militancy was redundant and their ideas unappealing. The Democrats, on the other hand, were less flamboyant but more successful. By the mid-1930s they could claim the active allegiance of most rubber workers. Their relationship with the URW was more turbulent and inconclusive; before 1940 it had little if any effect on the union's prospects.

Government also played a substantial but ambivalent role in the workers' history. The early New Deal legislation, notably the National Industrial Recovery Act, created a favorable climate for union growth and shaped the rubber workers' response at least as long as William Green and the AFL guided their actions. The Wagner Act of 1935 had a similar effect in the late 1930s. It is more difficult to show that any law or executive action directly advanced the workers' prospects. Ohio Governor James M. Cox had set the stage in 1913 by carefully hedging his assistance to Akron workers during a major strike. The New Dealers of the 1930s similarly operated in accordance with conceptions of public service and professional responsibility that stopped well short of offering meaningful aid.[13]

By 1941 the rubber workers' relationship with organized labor reflected influences that affected a substantial minority of all industrial workers (mass production technology), virtually all workers (the business cycle), and most of the 10 million organized workers (politics, federal government policy, and the labor movement). Their experiences had been similar to those of other industrial workers who had come of age in the 1910s and 1920s and who had witnessed the spread of mass production, the exhilaration of the World War I boom, the anxieties of the 1920s and early 1930s, and the seemingly unique opportunities of the 1930s to do something for themselves.

[12] The best summary of the literature on the role of radicals in the labor movement is Robert H. Zeiger, "Toward the History of the CIO: A Bibliographical Report," *Labor History* 26 (1985): 491–500.

[13] Christopher L. Tomlins, *The State and the Unions: Labor Relations, Law, and the Organized Labor Movement in America, 1880–1960* (Cambridge, 1985), p. 188.

CHAPTER TWO

New Industry, New Workers, 1900–1913

SHE LOOKS OUT from faded drawings and photographs with the fierce determination that was her hallmark. A Canadian who had migrated to Boston as a teenager, Marguerite T. Prevey (1869– ?) became a seamstress and later an optician. In 1901 she and her husband Frank, a jeweler, moved to the fast-growing industrial city of Akron, Ohio, and opened a jewelry and optometry shop on bustling Main Street. Business was good and they bought a large house on High Street, a block from the shop. As they became more prosperous, Marguerite devoted more of her energies to another of her interests, the Socialist Party of America. She became a close personal friend of Eugene Debs, the Socialists' leader and presidential candidate, and made her house his informal Ohio headquarters. In 1908 and 1909 Prevey headed the party's Woman's National Committee. Brimming with indignation, she preached a secular gospel of salvation through political action that was especially appealing to wealthy sympathizers. Ironically, she would find her greatest opportunity virtually in her backyard, among the more humble men and women who worked in the giant rubber plants that dominated the local economy.[1]

ORIGINS OF THE INDUSTRY

The industry that Marguerite Prevey would confront had appeared in the 1830s and developed with little fanfare for three quarters of a century. Traditional histories of the rubber industry are stories of heroic entrepreneurship, particularly that of Charles Goodyear, the tragic figure whose discovery of vulcanization, the process of heating rubber and sulfur to make the rubber stable and elastic, was the foundation of the industry. This emphasis has not been wholly misplaced, for the pioneers dominated the industry on both sides of the Atlantic for a half century. Yet it has tended to obscure the fact that the development of rubber manufacture, like the growth of many

---

[1] The best source on Prevey's early life is a brief biography in a 1912 Socialist party campaign pamphlet that Prof. J. Robert Constantine graciously located for me. Also see Sally M. Miller, "Other Socialists: Native-Born and Immigrant Women in the Socialist Party of America, 1901–1917," *Labor History* 24 (1983): 87–88; Ray Ginger, *The Bending Cross: A Biography of Eugene V. Debs* (New Brunswick, 1949), p. 365; David A. Shannon, *The Socialist Party of America: A History* (New York, 1955), pp. 16–18; Mary Jo Buhle, *Women and American Socialism, 1870–1920* (Urbana, 1981), pp. 150–51.

nineteenth-century industries, simply reflected the potential of crude empirical experimentation and mechanization.[2]

If the origins of the industry were less novel than the founders and their nineteenth-century chroniclers believed, the subsequent history of rubber manufacture was wholly unexceptional. After the 1840s there were no major technical or organizational innovations; "progress resulted from continuous improvements by the practical man."[3] When bales of wild rubber arrived at a factory, workers removed dirt and impurities; milled and "compounded" the rubber by adding sulfur and other chemicals; calendered the mixture into thin sheets, often combined with cotton fabric; cut the sheets into pieces and in the case of boots and shoes assembled the pieces; vulcanized the resulting product; finished it, usually by adding varnish to improve the appearance; and shipped it to wholesalers for resale and distribution. The manufacture of industrial and druggists' products was similar, except for the assembly stage. The work was labor intensive, particularly in the manufacture of footwear, where the hand assembler or "maker" was the central figure in the production process. Together with the uncertain quality of the raw material, intense competition created a hazardous, speculative atmosphere. Manufacturers reacted by setting up informal associations and cartels. Between 1865 and 1892, the history of the rubber boot and shoe industry was largely the history of these anticompetitive combinations.

Finally, in 1892, Charles R. Flint, a wholesale rubber merchant and speculator, merged nine boot and shoe companies into the United States Rubber Company, one of the first of the great horizontal combinations of that era. Other acquisitions in 1893 raised U.S. Rubber's market share to 50 percent, and the purchase in 1898 of the Boston Rubber Shoe Company, the industry leader, boosted U.S. Rubber's output to three quarters of the industry total. In 1898 Flint also engineered the formation of the Rubber Goods Manufacturing Company, a combination of mechanical goods producers that soon embraced half the market and most major producers except for a group of Trenton, New Jersey, firms and the B. F. Goodrich Company of Akron, Ohio. By 1905, when U.S. Rubber acquired a controlling interest in Rubber Goods Manufacturing, it was as large as its new parent.[4]

---

[2] Nancy Paine Norton, "Industrial Pioneer: The Goodyear Metallic Rubber Shoe Company" (Ph.D. diss., Radcliffe College, 1950), pp. 81–83; W. H. Dooley, *A Manual of Shoemaking and Leather and Rubber Products* (Boston, 1912), pp. 231–39; William Woodruff, "Growth of the Rubber Industry of Great Britain and the United States," *Journal of Economic History* 15 (1955): 377.

[3] J. D. Van Slyck, *New England Manufacturers and Manufactories* (Boston, 1879), 1: 323–28, 2: 626–32.

[4] Woodruff, "Growth of the Rubber Industry," pp. 379, 381; Glenn D. Babcock, *History*

Like other architects of late-nineteenth-century combinations, Flint and his associates discovered that mergers provided only a temporary antidote to price competition. Their failure to embrace the "managerial revolution," specifically, to centralize and rationalize production, encouraged manufacturers who had sold out to the trust to form new companies and undercut the inefficient giant. U.S. Rubber's profits declined after 1895 and it paid no dividends from 1900 to 1911. Though it remained the industry leader in boots and shoes and mechanical goods, it continued to decline until the 1920s, when severe losses forced a major overhaul of the company.[5]

Apart from competent management, the success of a rubber boot and shoe factory depended on the cutters' skill and the makers' dexterity. In the nineteenth century, some cutting was done with dies and mallets but most of it "required a sharp knife whipped by a dextrous wrist motion around a tin pattern."[6] Since waste increased costs, capable cutters commanded high wages. In early plants they often worked as inside contractors, managing subordinates and earning piece rates for the group's output. In later years, as dies increasingly superseded hand cutting, they were usually pieceworkers. Makers then assembled the pieces on a last. Since there were thousands of styles and sizes, making required intelligence, speed, and agility. The workday for makers, who were customarily women, ranged from eight to fourteen hours, depending on the individual's ability. In 1849, the Goodyear Metallic Rubber Shoe Company employed men to make boots. This practice spread, presumably because boot making required "strength as well as dexterity."[7]

There were few other skilled workers in boot and shoe plants. To operate washing, compounding, and milling machines required only brief practical experience. One investigator found that 80 percent of the employees in calender departments were unskilled. Vulcanizing was no more demanding—nor was dipping, the process for making rubber gloves, or cold vulcanizing, a related technique. Buffing, vapor curing, rubber reclaiming, rubber cement preparation, and vulcanization by steam process (used for druggists' supplies) required "comparatively little skill."[8]

Employment conditions depended largely on the location of the plant and

---

of the United States Rubber Company: A Case Study in Corporate Management (Bloomington, 1966), pp. 24, 39, 74.

[5] Ibid., pp. 39, 78; Alfred D. Chandler, Jr., *The Visible Hand: The Managerial Revolution in American Business* (Cambridge, 1977), pp. 433–38.

[6] Norton, "Industrial Pioneer," p. 131.

[7] Dooley, *A Manual of Shoemaking*, p. 236.

[8] E. R. Hayhurst, "A Survey of Industrial Health Hazards and Occupational Diseases in Ohio" (Columbus, 1915), p. 211, 225.

the manufacturing process. The early boot and shoe factories were concentrated in New England where textile industry standards prevailed. The Goodyear Metallic Co. of Naugatuck, Connecticut, for example, provided houses, discouraged drinking, and required church attendance. Until the 1890s, many of its workers were part-time farmers. Piecework let them set their own pace and schedule; "shop discipline . . . did not exist."[9] In other respects, the employees' lot was less agreeable. Visitors to mill rooms were shocked to see workers "choking out blue-colored froth from their mouths."[10] An 1886 study by the New Jersey Board of Health reported widespread lead poisoning among rubber workers.[11] Thirty years later naphtha and benzine poisoning, which caused dizziness, nausea, and "naphtha jag," a condition similar to a drunken stupor, were common occupational hazards. One investigator reported that "in one large place each girl averaged 1 day a week off on account of sickness."[12] Less common but more sensational was aniline poisoning, which affected skin pigmentation and produced "blue men" and "blue boys."[13] The longer term dangers of cancer eluded even the most conscientious early-twentieth-century researchers.

Wages and hours varied widely throughout the industry. Skilled employees in Trenton and Akron fared reasonably well, but most rubber workers were less fortunate. Akron workers, for example, averaged $562 in 1909, only slightly less than Detroit auto workers, but women and inexperienced men earned only half or two-thirds of the average. Sherman H. Dalrymple, a fourteen-year-old beginner in 1903, earned ten cents an hour for a sixty-hour week. By 1914 half of all Trenton rubber workers worked less than fifty-four hours per week, but elsewhere Dalrymple's experience was closer to the norm. Three-fifths of the Akron workers labored fifty-four hours or more; all Massachusetts employees worked fifty-four hours, due to the state's maximum hours law; and most Rhode Island workers were on the job between fifty-four and sixty hours a week. Differentials in wages and hours would continue to grow in later years.[14]

[9] Constance McL. Green, *History of Naugatuck, Connecticut* (Naugatuck, 1948), p. 226; Norton, "Industrial Pioneer," pp. 312–13.

[10] D. H. Killeffer, *Banbury, the Master Mixer: A Biography of Fernley H. Banbury* (New York, 1962), p. 93.

[11] Alice Hamilton, "Industrial Poisons used in the Rubber Industry," U.S. Bureau of Labor Statistics, *Bulletin No. 179* (October 1915), p. 61.

[12] Hayhurst, "Industrial Health Hazards," p. 218; Hamilton, "Industrial Poisons," p. 24.

[13] Hamilton, "Industrial Poisons," pp. 57–58.

[14] Kevin Michael Rosswurm, "A Strike in the Rubber City: Rubber Workers, Akron, and the I.W.W., 1913" (M.A. thesis, Kent State University, 1975), p. 15; Sherman H. Dalrymple, interview with Joe Glazer, April 2, 1955, United Rubber Workers Archives, URW offices,

Despite a variety of real or potential worker grievances, organized labor played only a minor role in the industry during the nineteenth century. Apart from a short-lived Knights of Labor organization in the 1880s, unions were local and isolated. They accounted for thirteen of fifty-six industry strikes between 1881 and 1900. Even in Massachusetts, the center of the industry and of labor activism, only a small fraction of employees were involved and no durable organizations emerged.[15]

The economic recovery of the late 1890s and the AFL membership surge of 1898–1903 led to the first important break with this pattern. In towns and cities where the labor movement was active, rubber workers often formed unions. By 1902 they had organized seven AFL federal locals and several locals affiliated with the Allied Metal Mechanics. In Akron, for example, John F. Boyle and nineteen fellow Diamond Rubber employees contacted the Central Labor Union, which arranged a meeting at the Bricklayers' hall and chartered Boyle and his associates as a local of the Metal Mechanics. By the fall of 1902, leaders of the federal and Metal Mechanics locals were confident enough to petition for an international charter, and in November they formed the Amalgamated Rubber Workers Union of North America, an industrial organization that claimed "all persons working at the trade of making rubber goods."[16] The union counted fourteen locals by October 1903. The largest were the Hood Rubber Company local at Watertown, Massachusetts, with 300 boot and shoe workers, including 150 women; the Morgan & Wright (U.S. Rubber) local at Chicago, with 500 bicycle and automobile tire department employees; and the Diamond Rubber local, with 400–500 members from the mechanical goods and tire departments. The most formidable of all was Trenton Local 4, with 800–900 members from nine mechanical goods plants.[17]

As the Amalgamated grew, workers and employers became more militant. There were nineteen strikes between 1901 and 1905, a majority directly or indirectly related to union organizing activity. In January 1903, Morgan & Wright workers struck and won a seniority plan. The following June a union member at Whitehead Brothers in Trenton quit when the man-

---

Akron, Ohio; U.S. Department of Commerce, Bureau of the Census, *Census of Manufactures, 1914* (Washington, 1918), 1:1159, 906, 600, 1375.

[15] Harold S. Roberts, *The Rubber Workers: Labor Organization and Collective Bargaining in the Rubber Industry* (New York, 1944), p. 32.

[16] Ibid., pp. 25–26; Alfred Winslow Jones, *Life, Liberty and Property: A Story of Conflict and a Measurement of Conflicting Rights* (Philadelphia, 1941), p. 74.

[17] Roberts, *Rubber Workers*, p. 28; "The Rubber Trade in Trenton," *IRW* 28 (1903): 312; "News of the American Rubber Trade," *IRW* 27 (1903): 167. Theodore W. Glocker described the Amalgamated as "an unnatural combination of groups of workers having no interest in common" ("Amalgamation of Related Trades in American Unions," *American Economic Review* 5 [1915]: 570).

agement rejected his demand for a wage increase. Other union members then walked out, closing the plant. Insisting that the walkout "was in no sense the work of the union," shop committee members hastily negotiated a settlement. In August a group of nonunion makers at L. Candee & Co. struck when the company introduced a new line of shoes that required more work. When the plant superintendent realized the gravity of the situation, he called the makers in, raised their rates, and served ice cream and cake, supposedly "introducing a new idea in dealing with labor troubles." Shortly afterward union members at Maple Leaf Rubber, near Toronto, struck for a wage increase and union recognition. After ten weeks they acknowledged defeat, agreeing to return as individuals and to "sign new factory regulations."[18]

Most rubber workers who contemplated organizing could expect similar treatment. As the Amalgamated grew, so did the manufacturers' commitment to the open shop. In March 1903, before the Akron local had taken any action, local manufacturers formed an employers' association and pledged to oppose boycotts and strikes. By the fall, Trenton manufacturers were considering similar action. Amalgamated leaders naturally were alarmed. The Amalgamated President, T. J. Edwards, believed that the midwestern employers were the troublemakers. "There exists in the East," he told a reporter, "a perfect understanding between organized labor and the rubber trade."[19]

The Trenton unionists soon tested their "perfect understanding." On December 4, they formally demanded a 10 percent wage increase and sent a union committee to call on each employer. Their reception was distinctly cool. Several manufacturers explained that they feared any concessions would lead to demands for the eight-hour day.[20] Others were more concerned about union power. All of them rejected the union demands. After the workers set a January 25 strike deadline, the Grieb Rubber Company began hiring nonunion men, forcing the Grieb unionists to strike. On January 25, five hundred to six hundred other union members joined them. The local industry was crippled, though only two plants, both in isolated locations outside the city limits, actually closed.

The strike proved to be bitter and prolonged. In an effort to close the plants by mass picketing, strikers gathered daily at the gates to curse and occasionally to assault entering workers. In late January, they followed nonstriker James Hoagland to a nearby shop. "Put the scab out," they de-

---

[18] "News of the American Rubber Trade," *IRW* 27 (1903): 167; "The Rubber Trade in Trenton," *IRW* 28 (1903): 350; "News of the American Rubber Trade," *IRW* 28 (1903): 26; "News of the American Rubber Trade," *IRW* 28 (1903): 60.

[19] "The Rubber Trade in Akron," *IRW* 28 (1903): 62.

[20] *TT*, March 19, 1904.

manded of the shopkeeper. "You don't want to have a ———— rat around your place." The store owner complied, and Hoagland was beaten. As a result of this incident, the police began to arrest aggressive pickets, including local union president Thomas Stanton, who was charged with "assault and vile language."[21] By the end of January, it was clear that militancy and mass action alone would not win the strike.

Besides employer intransigence and police interference, the strikers faced two other obstacles. The first was "the readiness with which the mills could be filled with new hands."[22] When the manufacturers imported experienced workers from the Boston area, the strikers tried to turn them back, even paying return fares in some cases. But more and more outsiders appeared, and many new employees lived in the plants. The strikers' second and ultimately fatal problem was an inadequate treasury. The first strike benefit payment on February 6 nearly exhausted it. The strikers' only hope was to raise money from unions and other sympathizers. President Edwards wrote that he had "tramped night after night and Sundays from union to union, begging for Financial Assistance." He had "sent out printed appeals all over the country," but "the total amount rec'd would not more than pay the cost of printing, postage and car fares."[23] The strikers also staged theatrical shows with varying results. As a last resort, they turned to the AFL. James O'Donovan, secretary-treasurer of the Amalgamated and a prominent Trenton rubber worker, discussed the strike with Federation president Samuel Gompers in early February 1904 and implied afterward that the AFL would supply $3,000 a week. In fact, Gompers sent only an organizer. Edwards pleaded again for help in mid-February. The strike, he explained, was "life or death" for the Amalgamated. "It is a case of must win or bust for the Rubber Workers."[24] Gompers sent another organizer but no funds.

By late February, the strikers were penniless and dispirited. Several accused Amalgamated officers of "grafting." One disillusioned union man wrote that he had had "enough of O'Donovan's bluff" and would return to work "a sadder but wiser man." A major blow came on February 29, when the local's secretary-treasurer quit his post and returned to work. After another month, the one hundred remaining strikers voted to return to work but "were unable to secure employment in any of the plants."[25]

[21] *TT*, Jan. 29, 1904.

[22] *TT*, April 4, 1904.

[23] Thomas J. Edwards to Samuel Gompers, April 5, 1904, American Federation of Labor Papers, Reel 44, State Historical Society of Wisconsin, Madison.

[24] Edwards to Gompers, Feb. 8, 1904, AFL Papers, Reel 44; *TT,* Feb. 1, 4, 1904.

[25] TT, Feb. 29, March 1, 3, 1904; "The Rubber Trade in Trenton," *IRW* 29 (1904): 245; "The Rubber Trade in Trenton," *IRW* 47 (1913): 307.

Other problems beset the Amalgamated in the spring of 1904. A bitter strike at Hood Rubber reduced the membership of Local 3 from eight hundred to fifty-two. Another Massachusetts local collapsed after the International executive board suspended it for favoring a Knights of Labor assembly over an AFL local in a jurisdictional dispute. The Akron local succumbed to the carrot-and-stick tactics of the Diamond Rubber managers, who raised wages, formed an employees' "relief" society, and discharged some union members. The Morgan & Wright local also declined, perhaps for similar reasons.[26]

By the summer of 1904, the Amalgamated was a shadow of its former self. Only five locals were in good standing, six had collapsed and three, including the Trenton and Akron unions, were moribund. The international officers canceled the annual convention. By the end of the year, the Amalgamated could count only 275 members in good standing.[27] Gompers once more sent an organizer. He found his work "mighty tough."[28] By the end of 1905, Gompers's patience and the resources of the Amalgamated were exhausted. It was "ridiculous," Gompers wrote, to have an international union of 50 members.[29] The Federation's executive board revoked the Amalgamated's charter in December 1905.

THE BEGINNING OF TIRE MANUFACTURE

During the next decade, far-reaching changes in the character of the industry made Gompers's decision less important than it must have seemed to Amalgamated veterans. The safety bicycle of the 1880s first created a market for rubber tires, and the emergence of the automobile a decade and a half later greatly expanded that market. By 1905 the manufacture of tires and tubes (for the increasingly common pneumatic tires) surpassed that of all other rubber goods combined.[30] Tires and tubes did not initially require a radically different technology, and many footwear and industrial products manufacturers began to make them. But there were important distinctions. Tires required additional machinery, stronger workers, and a new, more expansive outlook. Relatively few established companies had the resources or the will to make a successful transition. By 1910 leadership in the indus-

[26] Frank McCarthy to Samuel Gompers, March 1, 1905, AFL Papers, Reel 44; Roberts, *Rubber Workers*, pp. 28–29; Jones, *Life, Liberty and Property*, p. 75.

[27] C. E. Akerstrom to Affiliated Unions, August 15, 1904, AFL Papers, Reel 44.

[28] McCarthy to Gompers, June 28, 1905, AFL Papers, Reel 44.

[29] Gompers to Akerstrom, Feb. 3, 1906, AFL Papers, Reel 44.

[30] U.S. Department of Commerce, Bureau of the Census, *Biennial Census of Manufactures, 1921* (Washington, 1924), p. 1172.

try had shifted to a group of vigorous newcomers committed wholly or largely to the tire business.

In tire plants, workers washed, dried, milled, compounded, calendered, and cut rubber, as they did in other plants. Tire builders then constructed the tire on a circular mold, much as the "maker" assembled overshoes on a last. The tire builder stretched the plies over the mold, added the "bead," which held the tire to the rim, and attached the tread. The mold and tire, which could weigh as much as 175 pounds, then went to the curing department for vulcanization. There workers loaded the tires and molds in huge, steam-heated cylindrical containers, often built in recessed "pits." After vulcanization, "pit" workers removed the tires from the molds and sent them to the finishing department for cleaning, wrapping, and shipping.[31]

The basic difference between a rubber shoe and a tire factory was the scale of operations in the assembly department and pit, where 60 percent or more of the employees worked. Unlike the makers, tire builders and pit workers had to be exceptionally strong and rugged. Employers had little choice but to seek a physical elite of tall, heavy, muscular men. To ensure an adequate supply they paid wages in excess of the customary rates for machine operators, including most of those in the rubber industry. It became possible for brawny teenagers to command the wages of skilled, middle-aged men. Hulking, boisterous, and free-spending, tire builders and pit workers became the dominant element in the tire plant labor force.

Because of the importance of the original-equipment market during the first decade of the century, when nearly all automobile purchasers were first-time buyers, tire manufacturers sought locations close to the auto companies. The Great Lakes states gradually became the preferred area for both industries. In 1906 U.S. Rubber moved its Morgan & Wright subsidiary to Detroit to be closer to one concentration of auto firms. Other manufacturers located in Indiana, Ohio, and Wisconsin. By 1910 the largest concentration was in Akron, the midwestern city that had the strongest ties to the pre-auto era rubber industry. At that time the B. F. Goodrich Company was the most successful of the diversified firms. Alone among the major rubber companies, it made hose and mechanical goods, druggists' supplies, footwear, and bicycle and carriage tires in the same sprawling plant. Local capitalists rushed to emulate Goodrich's success, forming more than a dozen rubber companies. In 1912 Goodrich purchased the Diamond Rubber Company, one of the most vigorous of the new tire companies. The Diamond acquisition ensured that Goodrich would continue to play a major role in the tire market.[32]

[31] Snowden B. Redfield, "The Making of Autombile Tires," *American Machinist* 32 (July 29, 1909): 191–97; *WCL*, June 2, 7, 14, 1913, all p. 4, and May 4, 1927, p. 5.

[32] William Franklin Fleming, *America's Match King: Ohio Columbus Barber, 1841–1920*

1. The Firestone tire building room about 1911. Ohio Historical Society.

Of the other Akron companies, two were especially notable. Goodyear
Tire & Rubber Company, founded in 1898, was an extension of the personality of its founder, Frank A. Seiberling. An optimist and speculator,
Seiberling was not daunted by inadequate capital and potentially disastrous
legal battles over carriage tires. By 1900, he was confident enough to hire
Paul W. Litchfield, an MIT graduate who had worked in several eastern
rubber plants, as factory manager. It was an auspicious decision. More than
anyone, Litchfield set the course for the industry in the following years.
The combination of Seiberling's visionary leadership and Litchfield's technical expertise made Goodyear a vigorous competitor. The company con-

(Barberton, 1981), pp. 223–24; Howard Wolf and Ralph Wolf, *Rubber: A Story of Glory and Greed* (New York, 1936), pp. 418–21.

tinued to make bicycle tires and other products, but it was first and foremost an automobile tire producer.

The second firm, even more heavily committed to the tire business, was the Firestone Tire & Rubber Company. Harvey S. Firestone had started his career as a bookkeeper and patent medicine salesman. By the 1890s he was selling rubber carriage tires. In 1900 he began to make auto tires, found a ready market, and overcame problems similar to Seiberling's. In 1907 he contracted to make tires for the Ford Company, establishing a relationship that proved highly profitable for many years. By concentrating on tires, Firestone was in a position to exploit the enormous potential of the auto industry. In 1910 he built the first of the modern tire factories, a massive steel, concrete, and glass structure modeled after Ford's spectacular Highland Park plant. He chose a site approximately a mile south of the Goodrich complex on the city's southern periphery.[33]

The success of Seiberling, Firestone, and other tire manufacturers had a substantial impact on Akron. By 1910 nearly 20,000 of the city's 69,000 residents were employed in sixteen local rubber plants. Wealthy residents eagerly bought the shares of the tire firms, and citizens of all income levels speculated in real estate. Contractors, alert to the rubber workers' comparatively high wages, put up thousands of large, single-family houses south of the downtown commercial district in an arc that extended roughly from the Goodrich complex in the west to the expanding Goodyear plant in the east. After 1910 the arc expanded steadily to the south as the population grew and became more diverse. At the turn of the century, south Akron had had a distinctly central European flavor, reflecting the city's German blue-collar elite. Though the immigrant population continued to grow, native workers fresh from farms in southern Ohio, West Virginia, and Kentucky occupied many of the new houses. Except for conditions in several rundown neighborhoods on the fringes of the downtown area and a small black ghetto in the valley north of the commercial center, the standard of living was relatively high.[34]

At the same time, the ever-increasing demand for tires led manufacturers to enlarge their factories, plan new, better organized facilities, and attack bottlenecks that limited output. In the process they began a course that would ultimately lead them to mass production, which would widen the gap between tire plants and other rubber factories until it became a chasm. The most obvious bottleneck was the tire room, with its crowded rows of building stands and perspiring behemoths. In 1909 Goodyear master mechanic William State devised a massive tire-building machine that im-

---

[33] Alfred Lief, *Harvey Firestone: Free Man of Enterprise* (New York, 1951), pp. 27–93.

[34] "Akron and Vicinity," *India Rubber Review* 13 (Jan. 15, 1913): 21; Theresa S. Haley, "Infant Mortality: Results of a Field Study in Akron, Ohio, Based on Births in One Year," U.S. Department of Labor, *Children's Bureau No. 72* (Washington, 1920), pp. 12, 15.

2. *The State tire building machine, symbol of the beginning of mass production in the rubber industry. Goodyear Tire & Rubber Company Archives.*

proved tire quality and increased the builders' output by five hundred or six hundred percent. Essentially, it extended the worker's capabilities; the machine required the same steps and almost as much strength as the customary stands. By 1912 Goodyear had practically eliminated hand building in the auto tire departments. Firestone, Goodrich, and U.S. Rubber soon launched aggressive efforts to develop their own machines and challenged State's patent. They eventually succeeded in both endeavors. Firestone introduced its machine, similar to State's, in the fall and winter of 1912. By 1915 only the smaller and poorer companies built auto tires by hand.[35]

During the transition period, Seiberling and Litchfield tried to exploit their advantage. They expanded the plant and pushed the foremen to increase output. Still, they sensed that the plant was operating at less than optimum capacity. The way to be certain was to employ an engineering firm to systematize and standardize plant operations. But, as Litchfield recalled, they were "impressed with the importance of time."[36] The State

[35] Alfred Lief, *Harvey Firestone*, p. 114. By 1914 the capital-to-output ratio of the tire plants was the second highest in U.S. industry. (Daniel Creamer, Sergei P. Dobrovolsky, and Israel Borenstein, *Capital in Manufacturing and Mining: Its Formation and Financing* [Princeton, 1960], pp. 265-67.)

[36] Paul W. Litchfield, *Industrial Voyage: My Life as an Industrial Lieutenant* (Garden City, 1954), p. 110.

machines gave them only a temporary advantage; they could not afford the time to evaluate operations properly. So they turned to the tire builders. In February 1912, Litchfield announced a production bonus. Output supposedly rose by 40 percent, and the builders' earnings increased from about $3.50 to $4.50 a day, with some exceptional individuals earning $6.00 or $7.00—two years before Ford's famous $5.00 a day. Critics accused the company of installing the "Taylor Speeding-Up System," a well-known incentive plan based on careful research and prior standardization.[37] Nothing could have been further from the truth. In 1912 Seiberling and the other manufacturers had neither the time nor the expertise to embrace scientific management.

The Goodyear bonus plan nevertheless revealed a willingness to risk controversy and censure. Rubber industry wages created problems for the smaller rubber companies, for other Akron employers, and for city officials and local residents, who had to cope with a growing population of migrants who were responsible for many of the city's social ills. Any move that accelerated the wage spiral would only increase these problems. Seiberling and Litchfield were not oblivious to this prospect. In October they abandoned the bonus plan, despite its positive impact, and created an efficiency department to study production processes.

The Goodyear bonus plan cast in bold relief two other features of the Akron labor force. The first was an escalating turnover rate. High wages drew workers to the rubber plants, but did not make them permanent employees. In January 1912, Goodyear hired 1,405 employees and lost 461; in February, it hired 1,478 and lost 815.[38] A year later Firestone lost an average of 116 workers a day, 5 percent of its labor force.[39] Litchfield complained bitterly that "we are daily hiring a large number of men . . . we know have not the grit and stamina to remain here long enough to learn our processes and earn good wages."[40] The second feature was the plight of several thousand women employees, mostly at Goodrich, who made shoes and industrial goods. Most were immigrant teenagers who lived with parents or relatives. Their wages and opportunities reflected conditions in the low-wage eastern plants and the limited employment possibilities for women in the Akron area. Goodrich female workers started at ten cents an hour for a ten-hour day, but shifted to piecework as soon as they became familiar with the work. The fastest employees earned about two dollars per

[37] Leslie H. Marcy, "800 Per Cent and the Akron Strike," *The International Socialist Review* 13 (1913): 714.

[38] Frank A. Seiberling to Frank W. Rockwell, March 16, 1912. Frank A. Seiberling Papers, Box 14, Ohio Historical Society, Columbus.

[39] Labor Department file, Firestone Archives, Firestone Tire & Rubber Co., Akron, Ohio.

[40] *WCL*, Oct. 1, 1912.

day; less capable workers earned very low wages and left. In extreme cases, individuals earned as little as eighty or ninety cents per week.

The manufacturers' answer to these developments was systematic welfare work, the response of socially conscious employers, especially those like U.S. Rubber with large numbers of women workers. For Seiberling, Litchfield, Firestone, and their colleagues, rapid expansion and high turnover were the functional equivalents of a female labor force. In Litchfield's words, it was necessary "to bridge over" the "increasing gap" between managers and workers and give employees "a fair deal." By 1913 Goodyear had introduced an extensive health and safety program, an employee savings plan, a variety of athletic teams, lunch rooms, theatrical shows, and a plan to help home buyers. These activities were undertaken not "in a paternal or missionary spirit but in a clear-cut man to man fashion."[41] The Firestone approach was similar but not as extensive.

Goodrich, which already had a band, athletic clubs, an insurance society, and a much larger female labor force, held back. The difference was due to Edwin C. Shaw, the Goodrich plant manager. An industry veteran, Shaw strenuously disavowed any measure to "control the conduct of or in any way interfere with the personal liberty of any employee outside of working hours." Workers became "more self-reliant and dependable by means of *instruction* and *advice* than could have possibly resulted from Housing Schemes, lecture courses, entertainments, etc." Any charity "is sooner or later resented," and benefit plans generally constituted "an indefensible system of espionage and negative welfare work." His answers to the social strains of rapid expansion were "clean, safe, wholesome, attractive working conditions," high wages, and, presumably, substantial "instruction and advice."[42]

The rubber workers responded to their environment in three distinct but overlapping ways. The first was to accept the high wages and benefits and overlook the tensions, annoyances, and occasional injustices that accompanied them. The second was to take advantage of the favorable economic climate to organize. Since the turn of the century, Akron had had a vigorous labor movement with more than forty organized crafts and industries. AFL members bargained with employers, tried to regulate the supply of labor, and turned out for parades and other public occasions in brightly colored uniforms, badges of their determination to play a role in civic affairs commensurate with their numbers.[43] Rubber workers could not have been oblivious to their power and élan.

[41] *WCL*, June 1, 1912.
[42] Edwin C. Shaw to W. G. Mather, June 23, 1914, National Civic Federation Papers, Box 112, New York Public Library.
[43] *ABJ*, Sept. 8, 1903.

In the years following the Amalgamated debacle, AFL organizers made several forays into the rubber industry. In 1910, for example, they formed a new Akron local, which soon fell prey to the now-experienced Akron Employers' Association, whose spies infiltrated the Central Labor Union and obtained the local's membership list. The effort quickly collapsed. Workers in the Trenton plants were shrewder or more fortunate. A victorious strike by pottery industry employees in early 1913 inspired a wave of militancy that AFL officials successfully exploited. By mid-February 1913 they had formed locals at Joseph Stokes Co., Luzerne Rubber, and one other plant and had enlisted four hundred members. AFL secretary-treasurer Morrison saw these gains as a prelude to the organization of U.S. Rubber.[44]

To their surprise and annoyance, AFL leaders encountered competition from the Industrial Workers of the World, the loosely organized, flamboyantly radical coalition of dissidents and anti-AFL union activists. The IWW began to organize eastern industrial workers in 1911 and scored a major coup the following spring and summer in the Lawrence, Massachusetts, textile workers strike. After Lawrence, Wobbly influence spread rapidly. By early 1913 IWW organizers were active among rubber workers in Boston, Akron, and Trenton. Their effort in Boston was apparently negligible; in Akron it attracted approximately 150 members; but in Trenton, it produced more substantial results. In the wake of AFL successes in Trenton, Wobbly organizers precipitated walkouts at Acme Rubber and Crescent Belting and Packing in early February 1913. The Acme strike quickly deadlocked; the managers rejected demands for higher wages and shorter hours, and the strikers attacked employees who tried to enter the plant. The Crescent Belting strike followed a different course. By late February, the Wobblies had lost control of the strike to AFL organizers who negotiated an agreement that provided for the reinstatement of the workers at their old rates and the recognition of the union. The company president indicated his strong preference for the AFL.[45]

Akron workers who were neither indifferent nor willing to accept the risk of union membership had a third option. They could support the protest campaigns of local Socialists, part of a movement that briefly gave Ohio the largest bloc of Socialist voters in the country. The Socialists first made a significant showing in the municipal elections of 1911, when their mayoral candidate finished a strong third and they elected two of eight councilmen. They did even better in the city's industrial suburbs, winning mayoral contests in three small communities. In 1912, their presidential candidate,

[44] *ABJ*, March 3, 1913; *TT*, Feb. 4, 11, 17, 1913.

[45] Rosswurm, "Strike in the Rubber City," pp. 42–44; "The Rubber Trade in Boston," *IRW* 47 (1913): 303; "The Rubber Trade in Trenton," *IRW* 47 (1913): 307; *TT*, Feb. 21, 24, 26, 1913.

Debs, placed third in the county, ahead of the incumbent Ohioan William Howard Taft; in the city he trailed Taft by only a hundred votes. The Socialists drew most of their support from the heavily ethnic south Akron neighborhoods that had been Democratic bastions. Their inroads made the Democrats uneasy, despite the local victories of Woodrow Wilson and gubernatorial candidate James M. Cox.[46]

The three responses were not mutually exclusive. Some workers were passive or active depending on the occasion, and many AFL partisans voted for Socialist candidates. The links between the Wobblies and Socialists were even closer. During the summer of 1912, Wobbly orators William D. "Big Bill" Haywood and Elizabeth Gurley Flynn appeared in Akron on behalf of the Lawrence strikers. They encouraged Prevey and other local radicals to foster more Lawrences.

WOBBLIES AND RUBBER WORKERS

By early 1913 Firestone executives were optimistic about their prospects. They had installed tire-building machines and underbid Goodyear for Ford's 1913 original-equipment order, the largest in the tire industry's brief but buoyant history. To make sure that the Ford business was profitable, they ruthlessly cut costs, including piece rates. As a final safeguard, they introduced an innovation that Litchfield embraced only after the bonus incident. Sometime in 1912 the company employed Robert P. Holmes to make stopwatch time studies of the workers. Holmes was one of the hastily trained time study practitioners whom orthodox industrial engineers bemoaned as "fakirs" and destroyers of scientific management. He apparently made no effort to analyze or improve the work. Given the developments of the preceding months, it was unlikely that the tire workers viewed his efforts with equanimity. "Sherlock," as the men called him, promised trouble.

To compound the problem, Firestone officials overlooked one detail in the tire-building department. They were unable to set an informed piece rate because of their lack of experience with the new tire-building machines, so they simply divided the old rate between the machine operators and the tire "finishers," who worked at the stands. They may have warned that the rate would be lowered. For a brief period, however, the builders and finishers were in a position comparable to that of the Goodyear workers during the bonus period. Some of them earned $5.00 to $6.00 a day. In the meantime, Holmes timed several workers with a stopwatch and reported to

[46] Lysle E. Meyer, "Radical Responses to Capitalism in Ohio Before 1913," *Ohio History* 79 (1970): 204–207; Karl H. Grismer, *Akron and Summit County* (Akron, n.d.), p. 372; *AP*, Nov. 6, 1912; *ABJ*, Nov. 2, 1912.

his superiors. On Monday, February 10, Firestone managers posted a new scale, designed to limit the builders' and finishers' earnings to $3.50 a day. By afternoon the fastest men were complaining that they could earn little more than half their original wage. On Tuesday morning, they selected three men to see the superintendent and foreman. The supervisors refused to restore the original rate but proposed a compromise that would allow the best workers to earn $3.50. Some men accepted this offer; other workers balked and demanded the old rate. When the foreman asked them to go home and think about their demands, they refused. The foreman then ordered them out of the plant but offered to reinstate them the following day at the compromise rate. Approximately one hundred fifty workers left.[47]

Many of the builders and finishers remained in the area, milling around the gate. They were joined by workers from other departments who were laid off because of the tire department closing. Uncertain about their next step, some of them went to Rev. William M. Davis, a former rubber worker and AFL member whose nearby congregation included many Firestone employees. Davis offered to speak to the men at the gate. At 5:30 P.M., when the shift changed, Davis, mounted on a box, offered a prayer and urged peaceful protest to a crowd that soon blocked the street. When he finished, workers began to picket the gate. Davis later denied that he had publicly urged a strike, but his appearance encouraged the workers at a critical moment. Ultimately it provided an opening for Prevey and the radicals.[48]

On Wednesday, most of the tire builders and finishers returned to see if the superintendent would restore the old rate. When he refused, many of them left; other workers gradually joined them and the department closed. Among the men who congregated at the gate there was talk of a union. "Now . . . that the ball has been started rolling," one striker told a reporter, "I hope it will see the formation of a rubber worker's union in this city." While three hundred or more of the strikers were gathered in front of the gate, one man, supposedly an IWW member, threw his hat in the air and shouted, " 'Hurrah! We're out.' " He and other Wobblies in the crowd urged the men to meet at Socialist Hall, approximately a mile away. Most of the strikers agreed.[49]

Prevey met the men at the hall. She spoke for fifteen minutes, describing the tactics and the goals of the IWW. She encouraged them to "stick together," warned against "any sort of violence," and insisted that they "must show their colors."[50] To thunderous cheers she urged them to picket and to return later to set up a strike organization. At the evening meeting

[47] *AP*, Feb. 2, 1913; *ABJ*, Feb. 18, 1913.
[48] *AP*, Feb. 12, 1913; *ABJ*, March 6, 1913.
[49] *ABJ*, Feb. 13, 1913.
[50] *AP*, Feb. 17, 1913.

Prevey and Walter Knox, the local IWW organizer, proposed a strike committee representing all the plants and helped recruit pickets. By the time the meeting ended the walkout had become an organized strike, and the Firestone protesters had become the nucleus for an expanded and much more formidable IWW local.

On Thursday the strike became an IWW crusade for all rubber workers regardless of skill and status. At 6:00 A.M. pickets gathered at the Firestone gate with banners that read "We Will Win" and "Be a Winner." After enough workers had joined them to close the tire room, the throng moved to Socialist Hall, where Prevey assured the strikers that "the IWW has been waiting for this and is prepared to meet any situation."[51] Hundreds answered Knox's call to join the IWW local. At noon four hundred strikers marched to the Goodrich plant, only a few blocks from Socialist Hall. They shouted and cheered; one man carried his daughter on his shoulders. As they approached, Goodrich employees gathered at the windows of the six-story buildings. Girls waved from the upper stories. Many Goodrich workers promised to strike at the end of the day. When Goodrich supervisors offered their tire builders and finishers a higher rate, "100 workers . . . laid down their tools and with dinner baskets slung on their arms, marched with cheers and shouts, to strike headquarters." Later that afternoon several hundred Firestone and Goodrich strikers, preceded by fife, drum, and horn players, marched on the Goodyear complex. "Come on boys, and help us along," they urged arriving night shift workers. "Don't go to work tomorrow."[52] By Friday the strike momentum seemed irresistible. When six hundred pickets, with flags and drums, appeared at the Swinehart plant, the employees left en masse. When the Buckeye plant superintendent threatened to fire anyone who left, every tire worker joined the strike. Executives of the Miller Rubber Company agreed to close their plant. During the afternoon the first Goodrich women workers walked out. Strikers pointed to them and "derided the men [for] going to work when the girls were game enough to quit." Many men would "waver a moment, and then join the strikers." Soon only the "older contingents of married men" continued to work.[53]

By the end of the first tumultuous week of demonstrations, the IWW claimed twelve thousand strikers and eight thousand others who refused to cross picket lines or were locked out. The strikers' spirit "permeated the entire town." Crowds of strikers and onlookers milled through the downtown area, cheered pickets, and filled strike meetings to overflowing. Wob-

---

[51] *ABJ*, Feb. 14, 1913.
[52] *AP*, Feb. 14, 15, 20, 1913; *ABJ*, Feb. 14, 1913.
[53] *ABJ*, Feb. 17, 1913; *AP*, Feb. 20, 1913.

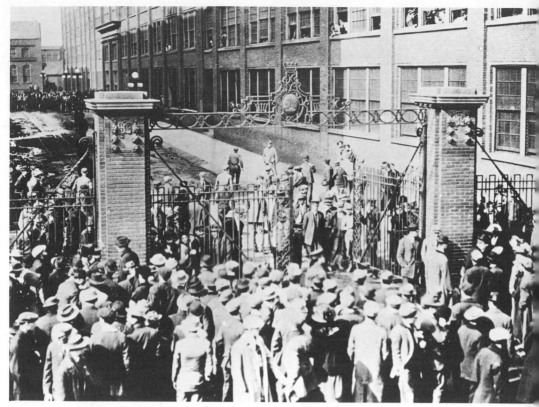

3. Strikers crowd the B. F. Goodrich gate, February 19, 1913. American History Research Center, University of Akron.

blies predicted the Akron strike would be "bigger and more significant" than the Lawrence strike.[54] The euphoria overshadowed any thought of grievances or negotiations. If Prevey had wanted a general strike, she would have had little difficulty paralyzing the city's economy.

Instead she worked to convert the uprising into a rubber workers' union. Her house "was thrown open to the strikers" and became "a hive that hummed twenty hours out of the twenty-four."[55] She recruited speakers and organizers from other cities, became the strikers' principle fund-raiser, and worked closely with the women strikers. Strike opponents who delighted in attacking "outside" agitators acknowledged bitterly that she was the chief thorn in their side. But Prevey may also have been responsible for the strike leaders' first serious miscalculation. Schooled in Debsian gradualism, she viewed the strike as an opportunity for organization rather than

[54] *AP*, Feb. 15, 1913; *Solidarity*, Feb. 22, 1913.
[55] Marcy, "800 Per Cent," p. 712.

as a struggle for immediate material gain. "The ultimate outcome," she told a reporter on February 13, would be a rubber workers' union. [56] By the time she realized the workers did not fully share her perspective, it was too late.

Beginning on February 14 a diverse collection of Wobbly activists responded to Prevey's pleas. Most important was George Speed, IWW national organizer. A genial Californian who strongly opposed violence, Speed helped sustain the strikers' positive public image for the first two weeks of the conflict. William Trautmann, the Wobblies irascible secretary-treasurer, soon joined him. Trautmann's many enemies included most of the other Wobblies who came to Akron. According to one account, his squabbles with Speed severely hurt the strike organization. [57] Arturo Giovannitti, the hero of Lawrence, arrived with Trautmann for a temporary stay, and Haywood, the most exciting of the IWW orators, made two brief appearances. The first was on March 5, long after the strike had peaked. A thousand workers met him at the railroad station and marched with him to the Preveys' house. Thousands more jammed the hall where he was to speak, drowned out other speakers with calls for "Big Bill," and interrupted his forty-five-minute talk with thunderous applause.[58] An outdoor appearance that afternoon and another visit ten days later, when the strike was near collapse, were no less exciting. Among the IWW speakers, Haywood alone had the ability to revive the spirit of the first heady days of the conflict.

Together with the Wobblies, Prevey brought in out-of-town Socialists to bolster the strike organization. From Youngstown she recruited Frank Midney, the editor of a Socialist paper; from Cleveland, William "Red" Bessemer and Carl Bailey, well-known militants; and from Toledo, Josephine Bates, a specialist on women's issues. Despite their political orientation, the Socialists proved to be less politic than the Wobblies. Midney organized an attack on the Goodrich gate, and was arrested and fined. Comparing himself to Jesus, he demanded a prison sentence. The strikers wanted speakers rather than martyrs and paid his fine. Bessemer and Bailey were hardly more helpful. Their speeches were so fiery and provocative that the strikers eventually repudiated them. Bates's most notable contribution was to suggest to her presumably native-born audience that if they did not picket

[56] *AP*, Feb. 13, 1913. Also see Seiberling to H. B. Manton, March 26, 1913, Seiberling Papers, Box 11.

[57] Harold Lord Varney, "The Story of the I.W.W.," *One Big Union Monthly* 2 (April 1920): 46. Also see Melvyn Dubofsky, *We Shall Be All: A History of the Industrial Workers of the World* (Chicago, 1969), pp. 151, 158.

[58] *AP*, March 5, 1913.

with greater verve, the female strikers would find foreign husbands. "Girls do not want to marry milksops," she warned.[59]

With funds that Prevey raised and the assistance of local socialists and a few of the strikers themselves, the outsiders ran a reasonably effective strike organization for nearly a month. By the end of the first week they had a half-dozen secretaries working twelve hours a day enrolling members and collecting the one dollar IWW initiation fee. From February 12 to mid-March they conducted daily rallies and provided daily press releases to the city's three newspapers. They organized pickets, led parades, ran a soup kitchen, supplied food and fuel to strikers' families in emergencies, and persuaded a local charity to create a Girls' Relief Committee to help female strikers who did not live with their parents. Because donations from local unions and merchants were minimal, they depended almost exclusively on Akron Socialists and Prevey's fund-raising efforts.[60]

Prevey found that her most valuable resource was the Goodrich women, who solicited funds in downtown Cleveland and conducted a "house to house" canvass in working-class neighborhoods there. She announced that they would make similar appeals in Pittsburgh, Philadelphia, and other eastern cities, but there is no evidence that they got farther than New Castle, Pennsylvania. Prevey also enlisted Wobblies and Socialists in several cities. Youngstown Socialists staged a benefit at a local theater, and Columbus Wobblies "had kettles on the streets." Pittsburgh radicals also sent funds.[61]

Besides filling Wobbly coffers, these activities spread word of the strike among rubber workers. Wobbly organizers formed new locals at small plants in Barberton and Youngstown, Ohio. Even more encouraging was the prospect of an organization at U.S. Rubber's Mechanical Rubber Goods plant in Cleveland, which employed two thousand five hundred. On February 20, Wobbly organizer Walter Glover spoke to an enthusiastic crowd of five hundred Mechanical Rubber Goods workers. He urged them to organize and demand Akron wages. The Wobblies also foresaw rubber workers' unions in South Bend, Chicago, and New York, and a nationwide rubber industry strike.[62]

The one area in which the outside organizers apparently did not play a decisive role was a crucial one—the formulation of the workers' demands. From the beginning the Wobblies and Socialists insisted that they would leave this activity to the strikers, and the evidence, and results, suggest that they adhered to their laissez-faire approach. After considering various pro-

[59] *ABJ*, Feb. 27, 1913.
[60] *Solidarity*, Feb. 22, 1913; *AP*, March 3, 7, 1913.
[61] *CL*, March 7, 1913; *Solidarity*, March 22, 1913; *AP*, March 10, 1913.
[62] *CL*, Feb. 22, March 6, 1913.

posals, the strikers voted on February 13 to create a committee of representatives from each plant to draw up a list of demands. The names of the committee members were not published and the composition of the committee changed frequently. Still, its assignment was relatively straightforward. The strikers and Wobblies had mentioned several demands: reinstatement, a wage increase, the eight-hour day, abolition of piecework, and recognition of the IWW local. The committee, however, insisted on drafting a detailed wage scale. Members spent endless hours interviewing representatives from different plants and trying to reconcile the workers' conflicting claims. The committee chairman acknowledged that the task was "enormous."[63] It is hardly surprising that the result was unsatisfactory. The committee did not complete the wage scale until the morning of February 21, a few hours before strike leaders were to present it to a mass outdoor meeting for ratification. Encouraged by Speed, who chaired the rally, the strikers accepted the report, including the wage scale, without dissent. As soon as they had had an opportunity to study the document, many of them changed their minds. They complained about inconsistencies and differentials between jobs. A local AFL organizer "laughed" at the strikers' efforts. One historian of the strike concluded that the wage scale demonstrated the strikers' "confusion . . . lack of effective organization and leadership."[64]

The manufacturers' reactions to these events gradually coalesced into a common policy as the extent of the walkout and the character of the protest became apparent. At first Harvey Firestone was surprised and almost apologetic; he may even have authorized a few furtive contacts with the strikers. After several days, however, he and his associates refused to make any statements. Goodyear executives were equally circumspect. Shaw and the Goodrich managers were less discreet. The company's downtown location and large female labor force made it an easy target for the strike leaders, and Shaw's intemperate statements played into the Wobblies' hands. The IWW leaders exploited a threat to move the plant, for example, by parading a live bull in front of the factory. "This is Shaw's bull. Going to move from Akron," read a banner. A cow followed with another sign: "I.W.W. This is no bull."[65]

During the second week of the conflict, the manufacturers apparently agreed to avoid contacts with the press and to act in concert when necessary. Seiberling became their semiofficial representative. Genial and outwardly conciliatory, he was more than a match for Prevey and Speed. His

---

[63] AP, Feb. 19, 1913.

[64] Rosswurm, "Strike in the Rubber City," pp. 59–60; Roberts, Rubber Workers, 50; CL, Feb. 22, 1913.

[65] AP, Feb. 15, 1913; Solidarity, Feb. 22, 1913.

evident good will also encouraged the view that a compromise settlement would eventually end the strike. In fact, as his recently opened private papers show, he had no intention of dealing with the strikers. He wrote that Goodyear would not "yield to pressure . . . from these strikers in any form." He would "beat them completely . . . ."[66] If one of the other large companies had broken ranks, Seiberling might have had to compromise. If the strikers had had greater resources and had handled the wage issue with greater finesse, it is possible that the manufacturers would have felt compelled to offer concessions. But a compromise was not inevitable or even likely, given the manufacturers' resolve and the strikers' meager resources.

The manufacturers signaled their determination in a variety of ways. They erected high wooden fences around unfenced areas of their plants and hired additional guards. Foremen met nonstrikers at the gates and escorted them to their jobs. Employees who crossed the picket line were given their regular wages and free meals, even when there was no work. Company representatives refused to deny that they would hire strikebreakers, though in fact they made no serious effort to replace the strikers.[67]

They also employed detectives to attend the strikers' meetings and infiltrate the IWW union. Acting through the Employers' Association, they engaged Edwin L. Reed & Co., a firm that specialized in industrial espionage. Several of Reed's men undoubtedly served on the wage scale committee. Others apparently won local union offices. For their services Reed charged $3,765, or the daily wages of nearly one thousand one hundred tire builders. Since Akron newspapers printed accounts of the strikers' public meetings, the spies' value was questionable. Even Seiberling later complained that Reed's services had been far too expensive.[68]

When the strikers ratified the wage scale and sent their demands to the manufacturers, Seiberling publicly dismissed all concessions and described the strike as "hopeless."[69] Many of the strikers were shocked. Even experienced union leaders believed the employers were bluffing. Speed and the IWW organizers responded with a call for greater militancy. Both sides prepared for a violent confrontation on Monday, February 24, when Goodyear and Goodrich were to reopen. Yet on Monday only a handful of pickets gathered at the plant gates, and hundreds of strikers reported for work.

[66] Seiberling to C. J. Butler, Feb. 24, 1913, Seiberling Papers, Box 12.

[67] *CL*, Feb. 23, 1913; *AP*, Feb. 17, 18, 1913; *ABJ*, Feb. 18, 1913; "Testimony," p. 65, Firestone Archives; "The Rubber Trade in Akron," *IRW* 47 (April 1, 1913): 365; Rosswurm, "Strike in the Rubber City," p. 15.

[68] H. C. Parsons to Seiberling, April 24, 1913; and Seiberling to Parsons, April 26, 1913, Seiberling Papers, Box 7; Raymond Boryczka and Lorin Lee Cary, *No Strength Without Union: An Illustrated History of Ohio Workers, 1803–1980* (Columbus, 1982), p. 136.

[69] *ABJ*, Feb. 22, 1913.

The manufacturers broke their silence and proclaimed the strike broken. They too were mistaken. The two sides were now deadlocked with no prospect of an immediate settlement.

GOVERNOR COX AND THE AFL

The stalemate provided an opening for two outside groups that would dictate the subsequent course of the strike. Ohio's new, progressive Democratic governor, James M. Cox, and Akron's commercial elite, organized in the chamber of commerce, were both ambivalent about the city's boom and its consequences. The governor, closely allied with the AFL, was uncertain about Akron's army of semiskilled workers and its radical leadership; the merchants agonized over the city's future and the irresponsibility of the manufacturers and workers. They first became linked on February 15, when Republican Mayor Frank Rockwell, the merchants' ally, called Cox and requested troops to keep order. A group from the chamber of commerce arrived at Cox's office at approximately the same time and reiterated Rockwell's demand. Cox flatly refused. His only concession was to send a National Guard observer and the members of the state board of arbitration—Theodore I. Reese, an Episcopalian clergyman; George Lattimer, a manufacturer; and D. H. Sullivan, an AFL organizer.[70]

The board members arrived in Akron on February 15 and immediately met with the manufacturers and strikers. Sullivan and Reese received a warm welcome from Speed and other strike leaders, who canceled all parades and demonstrations for two days to emphasize their reasonableness. The arbitrators were pleased. In the meantime Lattimer conferred with the manufacturers. He was impressed with their accounts of high wages and favorable working conditions. After several days of discussions he concluded that the Akron conflict had been "occasioned by the prosperity which each side believes the other enjoys."[71] The arbitrators' report to Cox echoed this theme. Wages in the rubber plants were already so high, they asserted, that they threatened other local industries. Apart from ridding the city of the IWW, which they recommended, the only obvious antidote was closer "personal contacts" between employers and workers. Lattimer wrote Seiberling that the strikers "are hungry for the human personal touch from your higher officials."[72]

The arbitrators also reported that the dispute had evoked "little civic interest." Reese told the governor that "practically nothing had been done

[70] *AP*, Feb. 14, 15, 1913; *ABJ*, Feb. 15, 17, 1913; *Columbus Evening Dispatch*, Feb. 15, 1913; *Ohio State Journal*, Feb. 18, 1913.

[71] George W. Lattimer to Seiberling, Feb. 28, 1913, Firestone Archives.

[72] Lattimer to Seiberling, Feb. 28, 1913.

by the local and county authorities to prevent trouble."[73] As a result, Cox felt compelled to intervene directly when the manufacturers rejected the strikers' wage scale and a crisis seemed imminent. He summoned the arbitration board to an emergency meeting with State Senator William Green, the newly elected Democratic senate leader, and a United Mine Workers leader. Gathering on early Saturday, February 22, in Cox's office, they discussed the conflict and agreed that Cox should "compel the local authorities to preserve order" and "awaken Akron citizens" to the need for a settlement. If the manufacturers remained intransigent, Green would sponsor a legislative exposé of their exorbitant profits and ruthless labor policies.[74]

After the meeting the arbitrators returned to Akron, and Green, eager to proceed, began to organize support for an investigation. On Tuesday, February 25, he introduced a resolution charging the rubber manufacturers with autocratic labor policies. He insisted that "the time had come to call a halt upon the arrogance of the rubber trust."[75] He was equally determined that the investigating committee reflect this view and apparently tried to enlist Louis D. Brandeis, the prominent Boston attorney, to direct the investigation. Such stories led to speculation about Green's motives. Seiberling and others hostile to the Senate inquiry saw it as a Democratic or AFL conspiracy and had little doubt about its punitive character.[76]

In the meantime the arbitrators implemented other features of the plan. They urged prominent citizens to demand negotiations, and the sheriff to hire extra officers. On Thursday morning, February 27, they met the chairman of the strikers' executive committee, H. E. Pollock, a Goodyear tire builder, and then the full committee of fifteen. In the afternoon they conferred with Shaw and other executives. By evening they had concluded a modest deal. Firestone, Shaw, Seiberling, and managers of the Miller, Buckeye, and Swinehart plants agreed to take back their employees, "to consider any grievances and to treat with them in a fair spirit."[77] Pollock and the executive committee simultaneously banned Bessemer and Bailey from speaking at meetings and rallies. Clearly a "spirit of compromise was abroad."[78] On Friday the arbitrators returned to Columbus to report to Cox. They believed that the Senate probe, coupled with the emergence of mod-

[73] *Columbus Evening Dispatch*, Feb. 21, 1913. Also see *AP*, Feb. 18, 1913.

[74] *AP*, Feb. 19, 20, 22, 1913; *Ohio State Journal*, Feb. 20, 23, 1913; *CL*, Feb. 20, 23, 1913; *Columbus Evening Dispatch*, Feb. 27, 1913.

[75] *Columbus Evening Dispatch*, Feb. 25, 1913. Also see *CL*, Feb. 26, 1913; *Ohio State Journal*, Feb. 25, 1913.

[76] *Columbus Evening Dispatch*, Feb. 26, 1913; *Ohio State Journal*, Feb. 25, 1913; *ABJ*, Feb. 25, 1913; Marcy, "800 Per Cent," p. 720; Seiberling to Manton, March 26, 1913, Seiberling Papers, Box 11.

[77] *CL*, Feb. 28, 1913.

[78] *ABJ*, Feb. 28, 1913.

erate strike leaders, would ensure a satisfactory settlement in the near future.

Their efforts were closely related to an AFL campaign to supplant the IWW, reminiscent of AFL initiatives in Little Falls, New York, and Lawrence, and more recently in Trenton. Federation leaders had plans for a rubber industry campaign later in 1913, but the Wobblies forced their hand. They reacted by sending Cal Wyatt, who had headed the Little Falls and Lawrence efforts, two Ohio organizers, and John L. Lewis, a young Iowan of unusual promise.[79] Arriving on February 17, Wyatt attacked the Wobblies and urged rubber workers to abandon the IWW. His behavior appalled many strikers. When Wobbly orators asked, "Will you stick with us boys?" they received a resounding vote of confidence from the strikers. Wyatt's problems multiplied when he presented his plan, which included a national rubber workers' union—"one solid compact union"—to the Central Labor Union on February 18. After a "hot three-hour debate," the Akron unionists voted to aid the strikers, tolerate the IWW, and postpone all recruiting until the strike was over. Their "universal desire" was to "win the strike."[80] Wyatt had no choice but to retreat. For the next few days he confined himself to discouraging sympathy strikes by craft groups that had contracts with local employers. On February 24 he revived his original idea and won grudging CLU approval for a rubber workers' union. Yet by the end of the month he had recruited only 310 members. Wobbly counterattacks were partly to blame, but the overriding factor was the arbitrators' inability to wring more substantial concessions from the manufacturers, who had no more intention of dealing with the AFL than the IWW. Despite its apparent respectability and political influence, the AFL could offer the strikers little more than the IWW.[81]

Cox's intervention had another effect that did influence the outcome of the conflict. The arbitrators' appeals, coupled with the threat of violence and the decline of business, encouraged the chamber of commerce to renew its effort to resolve the strike. By February 21 there was widespread talk of a "vigilance committee" to prevent street violence. That evening, after Seiberling had rejected the wage scale, twenty prominent citizens, mostly chamber of commerce members, called on Rev. George P. Atwater, an

[79] Robert E. Snyder, "Women, Wobblies, and Workers' Rights: The 1912 Textile Strike in Little Falls, New York," in Joseph R. Conlin, ed., *At The Point of Production: The Local History of the I.W.W.* (Westport, 1981), pp. 39–40; Melvyn Dubofsky and Warren Van Tine, *John L. Lewis: A Biography* (New York, 1977) pp. 26–30; Roy Wortman, "The I.W.W. and the Akron Rubber Strike," in Conlin, *At The Point of Production*, p. 54.

[80] *AP*, Feb. 19, 1913.

[81] *Columbus Evening Dispatch*, Feb. 25, 1913; *Ohio State Journal*, Feb. 25, 1913; *ABJ*, Feb. 22, 27, 1913; *AP*, Feb. 27, 1913; Gompers to Cal Wyatt, Feb. 27, 1913, AFL Papers, Reel 172; Seiberling to Manton, March 26, 1913.

Episcopalian minister and civic leader, and asked him to preside over the formation of such an organization. Atwater agreed to convene a larger citizens meeting the next day. That gathering of about three hundred formed a Citizens' Welfare League (CWL) and named Atwater president. Other officers were merchants, public officials, and clergymen. The CWL attracted five thousand recruits in the next twenty-four hours.[82]

Many of these individuals had publicly opposed the IWW or the strike. One officer, the chamber of commerce president, had urged Cox to send the National Guard and would later serve as the manufacturers' attorney. A priest who was active in the CWL supposedly threatened to excommunicate parishioners who joined the IWW. According to one account, the entire membership of the local YMCA, which had disavowed the strike, joined the CWL. Yet these individuals were not as representative of the organization as partisans of both sides later charged. Atwater had good relations with organized labor and was determined to be evenhanded. Many other CWL members considered themselves neutral; a minority favored the strikers. The dominant sentiment among them was the desirability of peace. The CWL drew from the middle strata of society, which favored, perhaps contradictorily, economic growth and social stability. Whatever their personal convictions about labor disputes, CWL members would support any activity that promised to hasten the return of normality.[83]

For the next week these sentiments led the CWL to back the governor's initiatives. Atwater endorsed the efforts of the arbitration board and praised the February 27 bargain between the manufacturers and strikers. On the twenty-eighth, the CWL executive committee released a statement attacking the IWW and urging a return to work. This statement drew the wrath of the organization's treasurer, who took it as an antilabor statement. It was a natural mistake. As long as the governor's agents were active, most CWL members remained neutral. When the strike did not end, their anti-Wobbly, antistrike inclinations became more pronounced. After February 28 the CWL increasingly aligned with the manufacturers.[84]

DECLINE AND COLLAPSE

The Governor's strategy, the AFL campaign, and the work of the CWL were far less harmful to the strikers' prospects than a series of self-inflicted blows

[82] *ABJ*, Feb. 21, 24, 1913; *AP*, Feb. 24, 1913.

[83] Marcy, "800 Per Cent," p. 713; Varney, "Story of the I.W.W.," p. 45; Litchfield, *Industrial Voyage*, p. 131; *AP*, Feb. 24, 1913. Atwater recalled that the CWL was a "neutral body" that "seemed to be hostile to the workmen" because of its opposition to the IWW (George Parkin Atwater, *Annals of a Parish* [Akron, 1928], p. 16).

[84] *CL*, Feb. 27 1913; *AP*, March 4, 1913.

that wracked the strike organization in late February and early March. The most catastrophic of these is the hardest to explain. Despite their idealistic statements about the strikers' role and their apparent failure to control the wage scale deliberations, Prevey and Speed made little effort to foster a cadre of local leaders. In fact, they continued to preempt most leadership opportunities and made only minimal efforts to involve the strikers. Whether factionalism, poor judgment, or more subtle psychological factors accounted for this course, the immediate effect was to create a vacuum that H. E. Pollock, the chairman of the strikers' executive committee, quickly filled.

Pollock was a young, articulate, and attractive figure. As a strike leader, he adopted a consistently moderate approach. On April 27 he engineered the expulsion of Bessemer and Bailey. Several days afterward, he revised the strikers' demands and omitted the ill-conceived wage scale in favor of an across-the-board increase. Pollock later insisted that the strike organization was only affiliated "in a way, not entirely" with the IWW.[85] He seems to have envisioned an independent, moderate, industrial union. Wyatt probably saw him as a promising leader for his AFL local. Yet like many coworkers, Pollock wanted wealth as well as power, a goal that only the manufacturers could satisfy. A contact was easy to arrange. Each evening after the strikers' executive board meeting, Pollock would give his sister the minutes to type. The sister, a stenographer in Seiberling's office, would make one copy for the strikers and another for Seiberling and the Reed operatives. Pollock also was seen in the presence of company agents.[86]

On March 1, when Green and the other state senators opened their hearings at the Portage Hotel, Pollock was the first witness. To a packed room that included Seiberling, Firestone, Shaw, Prevey, and the Wobbly leaders, Pollock insisted that he had no personal grievances. When pressed by an incredulous Green, he acknowledged that poor materials often prevented him from working as fast as he desired. Otherwise, he had no complaints. By the end of his testimony Pollock had wrecked Green's plans for an exposé. Prevey and the strike leaders were outraged. Three days later, after a belated investigation, the Wobblies forced his resignation from the executive committee on charges of spying. To a shocked audience of strikers Bessemer characterized Pollock as a "traitor, a Benedict Arnold."[87] For many strikers, already impoverished, Pollock's apostasy was the last straw.

Subsequent sessions of the Green committee hearings were hardly more

---

[85] *ABJ*, Feb. 28, 1913; Strikers Central Strike Committee to Rubber Manufacturers of Akron, March 3, 1913, Seiberling Papers, Box 4; "Testimony," p. 79.

[86] *ABJ*, March 5, 1913.

[87] *ABJ*, March 5, 1913.

helpful. Prevey and the Wobblies made little effort to prepare other witnesses, who were as unimpressive as Pollock was sensational. A parade of workers said almost nothing about "speedups," blacklists, and discrimination. Their most common complaint was that the factories were unsanitary. Several of the Goodrich women raised eyebrows with accounts of scandalously low wages and unpleasant working conditions. Too often, however, they exaggerated their plight or added sensational charges that raised doubts about their credibility. Claims that a Goodrich foreman demanded "kisses and hugs" from female employees and that the company manufactured "immoral" rubber products brought indignant replies from a host of supervisors.[88]

In contrast, the manufacturers were well-rehearsed and knowledgeable. Firestone and Seiberling discussed their humble beginnings and early struggles; they implied that any rubber worker might tread a similar path. Firestone refuted the strikers' most consistent charge with detailed and enthusiastic descriptions of washrooms, showers, and other sanitary facilities. Shaw was the last and best rehearsed of the prominent witnesses. He described the company's generosity to accident victims and plans for a pension system. The women's wages, he explained, were essentially a philanthropy. A mandatory minimum wage would simply force the firing of marginally competent workers.[89]

Green soon realized that his plans had miscarried. By the second week of March he was ready to admit failure and insisted that only witnesses with new information could testify. The hearings ended on a note of disappointment. Contrary to Green's expectations, he and his colleagues "discovered that the Akron rubber workers have been well paid as a class and that few grievances exist."[90] Only one of Green's original objectives remained. The committee's report, published a month after the strike ended, blamed the iww for the turmoil that had paralyzed Akron. Otherwise, Seiberling summarized the senators' conclusions when he wrote that they found only "trifling" problems and "no just cause for the strike."[91]

The failure of the Senate probe to sustain the governor's plans broke the back of the strike. As early as March 3, hundreds of former strikers crossed the picket lines to apply for work. During the following days the rush continued. The strikers seemed to have "lost hope of success."[92] By March 14 nearly fifteen thousand employees were at work and the number of strikers had declined to approximately three thousand.

[88] *ABJ*, March 24, 1913; *AP*, March 24, 1913.

[89] *ABJ*, March 7, 24, 1913.

[90] *ABJ*, March 13, 21, 1913.

[91] Seiberling to Manton, March 26, 1913, Seiberling Papers, Box 11.

[92] *ABJ*, March 7, 1913; *CL*, March 8, 1913.

This was only one of several Wobbly setbacks in early March. In Paterson, New Jersey, a police crackdown on pickets supplied the coup de grâce to the famous silk workers strike. In Trenton the police used similar tactics to prevent the Wobblies from sustaining the Acme Rubber strike. With Wobbly activities curtailed, Acme executives were able to employ new workers. Under these conditions even the AFL locals withered. When Joseph Stokes employees struck over the discharge of a dozen union members, the Trenton police arrested the president of the local for threatening nonstrikers and forcibly removed five women who conducted an impromptu sit-down in the plant. Despite support from other Trenton unions, the strikers returned without concessions and without a union. By April, the Trenton unions were in disarray. In Boston, several Wobbly-inspired strikes and a riot at a Milford, Massachusetts, plant on March 3 produced similar results.[93]

Even more decisive was the defeat of the Cleveland rubber workers, who began a walkout on March 4 in sympathy with the Akron strikers. The movement spread through the plant and surprised the Wobblies as much as the company. Walter Glover returned to head the strike organization but was never able to control the workers. On March 5, a striker fired a pistol into the house of another worker, precipitating a near riot. Two days later, when the company brought women workers to the plant in taxis, a woman striker with a basket of bricks "ran along close behind" hurling missiles "with the regularity of a machine gun."[94] The vehicles were wrecked. On March 8, twenty strikers attacked an employee who was escorting a group of women to the plant. Later that day, a mob of one thousand tried to rescue a striker who had been arrested, and the police charged with drawn revolvers. Glover pleaded for peace but was shouted down. The disorders continued until March 11, when the plant manager announced that he had hired replacements for the strikers. Faced with unemployment and ever larger contingents of mounted police, the strikers lost their courage. On March 12 and 13, they "besieged" the employment office. Glover brought in other Wobblies from Akron but to no avail. On March 14, the remaining union members voted to end the strike and return to their jobs. The plant gates were "thronged" with applicants. "Many were crying and declaring they were sorry they had joined the walkout."[95]

The collapse of Wobbly efforts in Trenton, Boston, and Cleveland foreshadowed the more prolonged decline of the Akron strike. As the back-to-

---

[93] *TT*, March 14, 20, 27, April 1, 1913; "The Rubber Trade in Boston," *IRW* 47 (1913); 368; Steve Golin, "Defeat Becomes Disaster: The Paterson Strike of 1913 and the Decline of the I.W.W.," *Labor History* 24 (1983): 223–25.

[94] *CL*, March 8, 1913.

[95] *CL*, March 11, 15, 1913.

4. Wobbly pickets, March, 1913. American History Research Center.

work movement grew, the mass uprising of mid-February degenerated into a desperate rearguard action by a handful of militants. The eclipse of the strike moderates, the reemergence of Bessemer and Bailey in the wake of the Pollock scandal, and the arrival of IWW extremists Jack White, Matilda Rabinowitz, and various "anarchists," also changed the internal balance of the strike group. Increasingly, the focus of the strikers' activities became the workers who had returned to their jobs. This conflict, pitting the manufacturers, city fathers, the CWL, and former strikers against a hard core of IWW militants, dominated later accounts of the strike.

The first serious incident occurred on March 7, when Frank Midney "delivered a fiery address and wrought the men up to a pitch of excitement." As the strikers left the hall, Prevey and a man waving an American flag led a procession of about six hundred to the Goodrich plant and began "chain" picketing in a huge circle on both sides of the street. The police told the marchers that they could not block traffic or march in front of the gate, and Prevey agreed to stay on the sidewalks. But others continued to cross and soon there was a rush for the gate. The sheriff ordered his deputies to push the strikers back, and when that failed, to "wade in and get busy, if you don't want to lose your jobs." As the officers attacked, some strikers threw bricks and stones; others fought with their fists. Many of the spectators who had gathered along the street tried to escape, adding to the panic. Prevey remained in the center of the melee. A witness reported that she was "one of the most conspicuous on the firing line. . . . She knocked the hat from

one officer's head and dared him to fight.''[96] In the meantime the flag car-
rier received a "sounding wallop" and fell to the ground. Without his
standard to rally them, the strikers wavered, retreated, and then ran. Striker
leaders hurried back to their headquarters to draft a protest to Governor
Cox.

The next day they were back. At the 11:30 A.M. shift change, about three
hundred fifty strikers tried to prevent Goodrich workers from entering the
plant. Again they confronted club-wielding officers. When the battle was
over, "unconscious strikers were piled like sardines into patrol wagons."[97]
Afterward, the Wobbly moderates scored a final victory when a strikers'
committee publicly censured White and urged demonstrators to avoid violence. On Monday, March 10, two hundred strikers gathered outside the
Goodrich plant but were more subdued. When the officers forced them
back, they shouted insults but did not attack.[98]

On Tuesday the restraints failed. Inflammatory addresses by White, Bailey, and others attracted as many as eight hundred demonstrators. This time
the protestors surprised the police by marching past Goodrich to the Firestone plant, where they paraded and jeered at Firestone employees. When
a streetcar filled with workers stopped at the gate, a woman striker pulled
one of the men from the car and other strikers attacked him. A policeman
was about to fire on them when the sheriff and a large force of deputies
intervened. The strikers then returned to Socialist Hall where Bailey tried
to speak to a crowd outside the hall. The police arrested him, touching off
the most dramatic clash of the entire strike. Strikers and police battled amid
thousands of onlookers and homeward-bound clerks and shoppers. For half
an hour the police, "unable to tell strikers from bystanders, used their clubs
on both." When a striker shot at one of the officers, the police returned the
fire while pedestrians dove for cover. Remarkably, no one was hit. Police
arrested twenty members of the crowd.[99]

That evening the mayor, sheriff, and civic leaders, including Atwater,
met to make plans for ending the disorder. The sheriff issued a proclama-
tion banning parades and demonstrations and calling for additional deputies. Atwater volunteered hundreds of CWL members. The sheriff issued
them clubs and yellow ribbons and assigned them to patrol the streets
around the plants in automobiles. He may also have forced some Wobbly
activists to leave town.[100]

The strikers were demoralized. When White tried to organize a demon-

---

[96] *CL*, March 8, 1913; *ABJ*, March 8, 1913.

[97] *CL*, March 9, 1913.

[98] *AP*, March 10, 1913.

[99] *ABJ*, March 12, 1913; *AP*, March 12, 1913.

[100] *CL*, March 13, 1913; *AP*, March 13, 1913; Hugh Allen, *The House of Goodyear: Fifty Years of Men and Industry* (Akron, 1949), 173; Wortman, "The I.W.W.," p. 54.

stration Wednesday morning, he received only hostile responses. Speed
finally persuaded about four hundred strikers to walk casually "without
appearing to parade" to the Goodrich plant. There they confronted every
city policeman and scores of deputies. The officers kept them away from
the gate and later ordered them to leave the area. There was no violence, to
the disappointment of hundreds of eager spectators.[101] Haywood returned
the following day for what proved to be the last major demonstration of the
strike. Again he led a crowd from the railroad station to the Preveys' house
and spoke to a large and enthusiastic audience. In the afternoon he addressed five thousand men and women in Perkins Park, adjacent to the
houses of several manufacturers as well as that of John Brown, the nineteenth-century abolitionist. Standing near a statue of Brown, he compared
the strikers with the slaves Brown tried to free. Afterward the crowd dispersed quietly. When one thousand five hundred workers tried to march
back downtown, they met a police cordon and disbanded without incident.[102]

For all practical purposes the strike ended that afternoon at the Brown
statue. During the following week there were only a few isolated incidents
of Wobbly "guerrilla" activity. On March 22 Speed acknowledged that
fewer than five hundred strikers remained and that the conflict would formally end as soon as the Green committee finished its work. On March 30,
140 strikers voted to end the conflict. Fifty-eight remained opposed.[103]

Why did the strike and the union collapse? In recent years historians have
singled out the CWL and the AFL for special attention, arguing that an Es-
tablishment conspiracy undermined the alliance between the radicals and
the workers. The charges against the CWL obscure the position of the city's
merchants and professionals as "middlemen," committed to peace and stability and wary of both the manufacturers and workers. If, as one Wobbly
recalled, the formation of the CWL was "the thing that discouraged the men
most," it was because that event suggested growing public impatience with
the dispute and the Wobblies. The AFL, on the other hand, unquestionably
conspired against the Wobblies, though its principal successes were in Columbus, not Akron.[104]

There was, of course, another classic factor in the failure of the strike.
As the prostrike *Akron Press* explained, the strike demonstrated "one ab-
solute truth: Akron's rubber companies propose to continue the use of un-

----

[101] *AP*, March 13, 1913; Also see the inaccurate report in Varney, "Story of the I.W.W.,"
p. 45.

[102] *AP*, March 15, 1913.

[103] *ABJ*, March 22, 31, 1913.

[104] Roberts, *Rubber Workers*, pp. 77-78; Rosswurm, "Strike in the Rubber City," p. 94;
ABJ, March 22, 1913.

organized labor in their shops at whatever cost.''[105] Though the manufacturers could not prevent the workers from organizing or leaving their jobs, they could control the length of the strike and influence the outcome. They decided, perhaps incorrectly, that the costs of curtailed operations and labor spies would be lower than the costs of an agreement and wage concessions. Yet by the standards of their contemporaries, including the Trenton and Cleveland rubber manufacturers, they were comparatively reasonable. Disarmed by the initial moderation of Wobbly leaders like Speed, the lukewarm support of the community, and the machinations of Cox and the AFL, they pursued a wary course.

Worker disunity probably played a larger part in the strike outcome than the actions of the manufacturers or community leaders. Seiberling, who should have known, asserted that ''the greatest factor in keeping order and holding the I.W.W.'' was the ''influence of the Catholic Church.''[106] Some of the Wobblies, in their less noble moments, sounded a similar theme. ''You are weak,'' White charged at the last striker meeting. ''You thought it was a holiday instead of a serious proposition.''[107] Governor Cox, presumably reflecting the opinions of the arbitrators, also characterized the strike as a ''picnic jaunt.''[108] Yet relatively few of the strikers were Catholics, and the length of the dispute attested to their seriousness. Given the absence of clear-cut goals, strong leadership, and relief funds, the workers can hardly be faulted for disunity. If they viewed the conflict as a ''picnic,'' it was a picnic largely without food or drink.

Finally, there were the radicals. The Green committee, AFL partisans, and many local citizens blamed them for the defeat. In Green's words the Wobblies, ''instead of helping the striking employees . . . did them much injury.''[109] Green may have been right in one sense. Prevey and the Wobblies, wedded to preconceived ideas about the oppressive nature of industrial work, dissipated their most valuable asset, the rubber workers' desire for still higher wages. They understood the plight of the women workers but could not fathom the complaints of the tire builders. Their management of the strike was no more astute. It was little wonder that many strikers finally concluded that they could do more for themselves as individuals (and perhaps as Socialist voters) than as union members.

Judging from the events of the immediate poststrike period, the ''failure'' of the strike was probably less important than most of the participants imagined. It unquestionably hurt the IWW in the rubber industry, the Mid-

---

[105] *AP*, March 17, 1913.
[106] Seiberling to Manton, March 28, 1913, Seiberling Papers, Box 11.
[107] *ABJ*, March 31, 1913.
[108] James M. Cox, *Journey Through My Years* (New York, 1946), p. 217.
[109] *ABJ*, April 18, 1913.

west, and manufacturing generally. The exposure of several Akron Wobblies as spies and the looting of the local's treasury after the conflict added
to the Wobblies' woes. The Socialists, on the other hand, enjoyed an immediate surge of support. In a special election in April 1913, and in the
November local elections, Akron voters divided along Socialist and anti-
Socialist lines. In November the radicals won four of eight ward council
seats, all in south and east Akron. The Socialist candidate for mayor finished a close second to the incumbent.[110]

What of the workers? Tire builders on average probably lost $150 or
more in wages, and the other employees a lesser amount—no small penalty
considering their annual income was $1,000 or less. Some strikers also lost
their jobs. Wobbly threats of sabotage and various incidents of suspected
sabotage during the strike made employers wary of reemploying strike
leaders. Employment agents interviewed returning workers and turned
away individuals who had signed strike manifestos or had been arrested.
Of 115 men and women who were identified in newspaper accounts as
strikers, only 15 appear in the 1913 city directory as rubber workers. For
less conspicuous strikers, the hardships of the strike period were short-
lived. The economic boom continued; within two years the strikers' "unrealistic" wage scale had become unrealistically low. For the rest of the
decade, labor shortages and skyrocketing wages characterized Akron industry.[111]

The boom also eased the manufacturers' burden. Litchfield computed his
company's immediate strike loss at $21,000. When the conflict ended, he
awarded two weeks' paid vacation to each of one thousand seven hundred
employees who had worked continuously through the strike period, adding
$68,000 to the total. Even that was relatively inconsequential. In late
March, as the strike was ending, a disastrous storm flooded the Goodyear
plant. The cost of cleaning up afterward was $96,000. Presumably the di-
rect costs of the strike to Firestone and the smaller companies that had
closed, and to Goodrich, which had been the scene of most of the violence
and disruptions, were higher. Yet they were hardly crippling. Firestone had
no difficulty meeting its commitments to Ford, and the other firms flourished in the aftermath of the strike. In economic terms, the strike was simply another of the obstacles that confronted managers in the 1910s.[112]

Its long-term impact was more subtle. The manufacturers became more

---

[110] Varney, "The Story of I.W.W.," p. 46; Dubofsky, *We Shall Be All*, p. 287; Joseph R.
Conlin, *Big Bill Haywood and the Radical Union Movement* (Syracuse, 1969), pp. 139–46;
Wortman, "The I.W.W.," pp. 55–56; *ABJ*, Nov. 11, 1913.

[111] Seiberling to Manton, March 26, 1913, Seiberling Papers, Box 11; *AP*, Feb. 26, 1913;
"The Rubber Trade in Akron," *IRW* 47 (1913): 366; *ABJ*, March 24, 1913.

[112] P. W. Litchfield to Seiberling, June 24, 1913, Seiberling Papers, Box 11.

wary of labor organizations and more sensitive to their workers. The result of this combination was a new determination to manage their employees. Seiberling, as usual, captured their mood. He wrote in April 1913 that "It rather looks as though . . . all of us have to do some pretty hard thinking on matters sociological for the next few years."[113] Their "hard thinking" produced a series of notable personnel innovations. Whether it had any effect on the workers' interest in organizing and their willingness to act is less certain.

[113] Seiberling to Gorton W. Allen, April 24, 1913, Seiberling Papers, Box 4.

CHAPTER THREE

Innovations, 1913–1920

IN LATE MARCH 1913, as the Green committee concluded its work and the Wobblies pondered their future, a devastating flood struck the Midwest. The destruction in Akron was most severe on the city's east side, where the swollen Little Cuyahoga River inundated factories, commercial buildings, and houses. The toll at Goodyear would have been even higher except for the vigorous actions of a young employee, Clifton Slusser (1889–1949). Donning old clothes and hip boots, Slusser worked day and night to unclog drains, remove debris, and repair machinery. Four days after the disaster, the plant resumed operations. Seiberling and Litchfield were elated; Slusser had "won his spurs."[1] It was one of many triumphs for Slusser, who came to epitomize the upwardly mobile rubber workers. Raised in nearby Massillon, he had left school at eleven, and had become a rubber worker at eighteen and an assistant to the Goodyear plant superintendent at twenty-three.[2] After 1913 he helped to extend the new capital-intensive technology and recruit an expanded physical elite. As P. W. Litchfield's favored lieutenant, he was as responsible as anyone for the milieu in which other workers would operate for nearly two decades.

EXPANSION OF THE TIRE INDUSTRY

Between 1910 and 1920, the small, close-knit world of the nineteenth-century rubber manufacturer gave way to a new and different environment, better symbolized by State's tire-building machine than the maker's last, by bustling Akron rather than sedate Boston, and by Slusser and Litchfield rather than the rubber merchants or U.S. Rubber executives. Two major stimuli accounted for the change. The first was the growth of the automobile industry. Between 1908, when inexpensive automobiles first appeared, and 1913, auto production increased nearly eightfold and auto registrations sextupled. Between 1913 and 1920, automobile production quintupled and registrations grew from 1.1 million to 8.1 million. Truck and bus production, which had been negligible in 1913, also increased phenomenally; by

---

[1] Hugh Allen, *The House of Goodyear: Fifty Years of Men and Industry* (Akron, 1949), p. 121.

[2] "Clifton Slusser, General Superintendent," *IRW* 62 (1920): 795; Edwin J. Thomas interview with author, Aug. 6, 1982.

1920, every ninth motor vehicle was a truck. All of these new cars and trucks required multiple sets of tires. Automobiles used an average of five pneumatic tires and tubes per year at a cost of at least one hundred dollars and often two hundred dollars or more. Truck tires, nearly all solid rubber, were twice as durable but three times as expensive. As a result, the growth of the tire market was the "great outstanding" feature of the decade.[3]

The second stimulus was temporary but no less profound. The outbreak of world war in 1914 stimulated an industrial boom in the U.S. that continued through the first half of 1920. During these frenzied years rubber manufacturers made footwear, raincoats, truck tires, gas masks, dirigibles, and other equipment for the U.S. and Allied governments.[4] They also confronted an inflationary price spiral that undermined the discipline of the market and the scientific management systems that had swept through industry during the early 1910s. Most of all, they faced a severe labor shortage. After a mild recession during the winter of 1914–1915, due in part to the disruption of the international economy, the cutoff of European immigration and the war boom created a seller's market for labor. Steel, munitions, and rubber companies quickly bid up the price of unskilled labor and profoundly changed the lives and outlook of American workers.

One measure of the new environment was a proliferation of rubber firms. Since the turn of the century the auto boom had enticed aspiring entrepreneurs; the overlapping auto and war booms eliminated the last inhibitions. Between 1910 and 1920 the number of rubber firms of all types increased from 301 to 477; the number of tire and tube makers rose from 95 to more than 200. Many more mechanical goods and footwear companies established tire departments, including seven of the Trenton companies and Hood Rubber, the largest footware maker. Two important foreign firms, Michelin and Dunlop, established or expanded American plants. Production managers and superintendents who aspired to greater wealth and status found ready investors for new companies.[5]

The new manufacturers soon discovered that the allure of easy profits disguised a harsh reality. Far from an easy road to wealth, the industry demanded boldness, commitment, and tenacity. The successful firms of the 1910s, most of which dated from the turn of the century or before, all followed a similar pattern. They expanded rapidly, borrowed heavily, spent

[3] See A. Staines Manders, ed., *Who's Who in the Rubber World* (London, 1914): U.S. Department of Commerce, Bureau of the Census, *Historical Statistics of the United States, Colonial Times to 1957* (Washington, 1960), p. 462; "The Year 1916 in Review," *IRW* 55 (1917): 189.

[4] "The Rubber Trade in Boston," *IRW* 53 (1916): 190.

[5] U.S. Department of Commerce, Bureau of the Census, *Census of Manufacturers, 1919* (Washington, 1923), p. 192; "The Rubber Trade in New Jersey," *IRW* 60 (1919): 606.

their money on improved manufacturing processes and integrated backward to secure raw material supplies. By the end of the decade their preeminence was clear. The one important addition during the decade was General Tire & Rubber, an Akron firm formed in 1916 by Michael O'Neil, the city's most prominent merchant, his son William, a Firestone sales representative, and several key Firestone and Goodyear production executives. Relatively few of the other new firms had a significant market share; most of them disappeared in the 1920s. The Trenton firms went back to their original businesses; Dunlop and Hood continued as marginal producers; and Michelin abandoned the American market in 1926.[6]

Even the better-established companies faced many perils. The fates of the four largest manufacturers are illustrative. U.S. Rubber and B. F. Goodrich were the behemoths of the pre-auto age. Both were full-line companies, with major stakes in mechanical goods, footwear, and tires, and substantial marketing departments. U.S. Rubber's subsidiaries produced 21 percent of the country's original-equipment tires in 1915 and probably a comparable share of replacement tires. Goodrich was the largest of the Akron companies, though its share of the tire market was probably smaller than Goodyear's by 1915. Goodyear and Firestone were conspicuous examples of the specialist tire firms that appeared with the auto age.[7]

Though all four companies expanded rapidly in the 1910s and embraced the new technology, the two older companies traded places with the newer firms. Despite record sales and profits and much stronger performances than most new firms, U.S. Rubber and Goodrich lost substantial ground to Goodyear and Firestone. U.S. Rubber suffered the greatest decline. As the company's share of the tire market decreased, President Samuel Colt reacted forcefully. He concentrated auto tire production in Detroit and Hartford, truck tire production in Providence, and bicycle and motorcycle tire production in Indianapolis. To run the tire division he hired J. Newton Gunn, a pioneer of the scientific management movement, and in an unmistakable challenge to the Akron manufacturers, authorized a vast new plant in Detroit. But these steps were not enough. U.S. Rubber was unable to regain its lost ground. By 1920 it produced only 9.5 percent of original-equipment tires and 7.6 percent of replacement tires.[8]

Goodrich, on the other hand, had a comparatively simple, centralized

---

[6] "The Rubber Trade in Akron," *IRW* 53 (1916): 308; Dennis J. O'Neil, *A Whale of A Territory: The Story of Bill O'Neil* (New York, 1966), pp. 45–69.

[7] Glenn D. Babcock, *History of the United States Rubber Company: A Case Study in Corporate Management* (Bloomington, 1966), pp. 210, 212; "The Rubber Trade in Akron," *IRW* 55 (1917): 222.

[8] Babcock, *History of United States Rubber*, p. 212; *U.S. Rubber News* 3 (Jan. 1917): 18; "President J. Newton Gunn," *IRW* 53 (1915): 132.

management structure but lacked strong leadership. Edwin C. Shaw, its most vigorous executive, increasingly devoted his time to civic and philanthropic activities while department heads ran the company. By late 1916, Goodrich could boast of fifty-eight buildings and nearly a hundred acres of factory space, but it remained a rabbit warren of disjointed parts rather than an integrated manufacturing complex. Like U.S. Rubber, its achievements were impressive only when isolated from those of the rest of the industry.[9]

Goodyear and Firestone, on the other hand, were ideally suited to the conditions of the 1910s. Seiberling and Harvey Firestone were daring entrepreneurs, and Litchfield was the industry's most innovative production manager. Already committed to tires, expansion, mass production, and aggressive management, they easily outdistanced their competitors. Goodyear led the way. Seiberling gave full reign to his speculative instincts and Litchfield indulged his dreams of an ideal factory. In 1914 Goodyear's market share was approximately the same as U.S. Rubber's; six years later it was more than three times greater. Though the company was dangerously overextended, it had achieved preeminence in the tire industry. Firestone grew almost as rapidly. Family controlled and highly centralized, it probably passed both U.S. Rubber and Goodrich in tire production by 1920.[10]

After 1914 technological leadership was "the most important factor . . . in the concentration of tire manufacturing in Akron."[11] Firestone's 1910 plant had been the first of the modern tire factories. In 1917 the company added a second—a massive seven-story steel-and-concrete structure with windows so large that it seemed to have glass walls.[12] Until 1915 the Goodyear complex grew by accretion as the company expanded east along Market Street. Then Litchfield developed a systematic expansion plan whose centerpiece was a vast new seven-story structure south of the main plant. Modeled after the Firestone plant, it was "laid out to permit a more efficient movement of materials in process."[13] Altogether, the Goodyear additions of 1915–1917 nearly equaled the size of the entire Goodrich complex.

These impressive steel-and-glass structures were symbols of an outburst of inventive activity that simultaneously changed the character of tires and

[9] "The Rubber Trade in Akron," *IRW* 55 (1916): 97.

[10] Goodyear Tire & Rubber Company, *Annual Report to Stockholders, 1935* (Akron, 1935), p. 20; Alfred Lief, *The Firestone Story: A History of the Firestone Tire & Rubber Company* (New York, 1951), p. 114.

[11] John Dean Gaffey, *The Productivity of Labor in the Rubber Tire Manufacturing Industry* (New York, 1940), pp. 153–54.

[12] See "Hunkin-Conkey Construction Company" (Cleveland, n.d.), pp. 37, 42–43: Richard Lansburgh, *Industrial Management* (New York, 1923), p. 132.

[13] Allen, *The House of Goodyear*, p. 107.

tire production. Major breakthroughs included the introduction of "straight-sided" tires, which were easier to change than conventional "clincher" tires, and cotton "cord," which superseded conventional "square woven" fabric in tire plies. Cord tires reduced the motorist's tire cost per mile by 50 percent and helped reduce sales per vehicle from five to four tires between 1916 and the early 1920s. The tire manufacturers began to confront the paradox that would haunt them in later years: product improvements that reduced, rather than increased, the demand for tires.[14]

Of greater importance to the industry's labor history was the accelerating revolution in production techniques. Like other mass production technologies, the tire-making processes introduced after 1910 increased the ratio of capital, energy, materials, and managers to labor. In most cases they began, like the State tire-building machine, as solutions to a particular bottleneck in the manufacturing sequence. But each new machine or engineering change, introduced in the expectation of reduced unit production costs, demanded more mechanization, reorganization, and investment. This process continued for more than a decade and transformed the tire factory and its labor force. Of the specific features of the new technology, none had a greater impact than the Banbury mixer, invented by Fernly H. Banbury and patented in 1916. Banbury's machine, which mixed rubber and chemical additives in an enclosed compartment rather than in an open mill, permitted more precise and uniform operations, faster speeds, and greater control over the temperature of the milling process. It also eliminated the dust that choked mill workers. Only with an internal mixer could "the intimate and thorough incorporation of carbon black and chemicals . . . be accomplished efficiently without allowing the material to come into contact with the workman's skin."[15]

Generally, however, mass production in the tire industry resulted from an inconspicuous process of adjustment and innovation rather than notable inventions. Because of this gradual development, and because it was possible to make money during the war boom with obsolete equipment and labor-intensive methods, the new technology evoked comparatively little comment until the 1920s (it is examined in detail in the following chapter). By the late 1910s, however, the die was cast. The structure of the industry and the fate of the vast majority of firms that did not embrace mass production and its concomitant, vertical integration, were apparent by 1920. By that date the new machinery was too expensive, the competition too severe, and the profits too meager for the laggards to catch up.

Because mass production depended on a series of discrete, interrelated

[14] WCL, Feb. 6, 1935, p. 3; Henry C. Pearson, Pneumatic Tires (New York, 1922), p. 230.

[15] D. H. Killeffer, Banbury, the Master Mixer: A Biography of Fernley H. Banbury (New York, 1962), p. 92. Also see Alfred D. Chandler, Jr., The Visible Hand: The Managerial Revolution in American Business (Cambridge, 1977), pp. 240–83.

steps and a host of individual decisions, tire manufacturers simultaneously embraced the principles and techniques of scientific management. Henry Pearson, publisher of the *India Rubber World*, the industry's leading trade journal and a close and sympathetic observer of contemporary Taylorism, was a bridge between the consultants and the tire makers. At U.S. Rubber, J. Newton Gunn provided an additional, direct link. Most firms also employed outside consultants. At all companies the boom created powerful incentives to emphasize systematic procedures, line and staff distinctions, explicit standards, and managerial controls.

By the end of the decade most manufacturers had introduced a variety of management systems and controls. Goodyear had installed a factory cost-accounting system in 1907. After the 1912 bonus episode, Litchfield employed J. L. Sydnor, an industrial engineer who had worked for Harrington Emerson, the prominent efficiency expert, to introduce time studies.[16] In 1913 his operation became an Efficiency Department within the larger Labor Department. By 1916 Goodrich had established an "operating committee" to "coordinate" production and bring the executives "in closer touch" with the employees.[17] In 1919 Goodrich introduced the Bedaux incentive wage plan, which offered workers higher pay for additional output. In 1913 Firestone created an "Industrial Service" or personnel department, and in 1919, a production control department.[18]

All of the large firms substantially curbed the powers of the foremen. They did this indirectly by adopting elaborate production-control systems, or directly by transferring specific functions to staff experts. Some companies tried to compensate by elevating the foremen's status. U.S. Rubber introduced annual foremen's conferences in its footwear and tire divisions in 1919. Ostensibly the men met to discuss technical problems, but most of the meetings were banquets and social affairs designed to help the foremen adjust to the "passing" of "old style" supervision.[19]

Besides systematic operations, mass production depended on a carefully regulated flow of raw materials to the manufacturing site. For rubber manufacturers this meant even greater anxiety over the availability of crude rubber. Until 1912, 90 percent of the world's crude rubber came from trees that grew wild in the vast Amazon basin. As demand grew, the Brazilian merchants who controlled the trade were unable to expand output and prices rose. In response, U.S. manufacturers built reclaiming factories and British merchants developed plantations in southeast Asia that were able to

[16] *WCL*, Feb. 20, 1935.

[17] "The Rubber Trade in Akron," *IRW* 55 (1916): 163.

[18] Lief, *The Firestone Story*, pp. 71, 111; L. P. Alford, ed., *Management's Handbook* (New York, 1924), pp. 696, 698.

[19] "The Rubber Trade in Massachusetts," *IRW* 61 (1920): 312. Also see "Rubber Factory Foremanship," *IRW* 61 (1919): 145.

produce a superior crude rubber at approximately one quarter the cost of wild rubber. The first plantations were highly profitable, stimulating a planting boom that transformed the economy and society of Malaya. By 1920 Malayan and other East Asian plantations produced 90 percent of all crude rubber.

Manufacturers soon realized they were as dependent on the British as they had been on the Brazilians. In 1910 U.S. Rubber had obtained a vast tract on the island of Sumatra in the Netherlands East Indies. After 1914, when production began, this operation became the largest and most successful American-run plantation; for years it was U.S. Rubber's most profitable subsidiary. In 1917 Goodyear bought twenty thousand acres in Sumatra and Firestone began a search for a similar tract.[20]

Cotton, the other essential commodity, presumably posed no such difficulties. The cotton textile industry was large and manufacturers were accustomed to making specialized fabrics for customers. But the rapid growth of the tire market created temporary shortages and volatile prices, especially after the introduction of the cord tire, which required scarce long-staple cotton. After 1915 rubber manufacturers found that cotton, not rubber, was their most serious problem. Their response was similar. Goodyear and U.S. Rubber bought mills in 1917; other companies followed in 1918. The Mason Tire & Rubber Co., a small Kent, Ohio, concern, built the first Ohio mill in 1919. Litchfield went one step further. He purchased thirty thousand acres of Arizona desert in early 1918 and embarked on a crash program to grow cotton. By 1920 all the large tire firms had become vertically integrated big businesses. In the process they had also widened the already formidable gap in technique, outlook, and costs between big and small firms.[21]

A NEW LABOR FORCE

The other major obstacle to expansion and profitability was the labor force. Until 1915, high wages, liberal benefit programs, and occasional newspaper advertising attracted an ever-increasing number of workers. After 1915, the growth of the industry, together with competition from other war busi-

[20] Barbara Weinstein, *The Amazon Rubber Boom, 1850–1920* (Stanford, 1983), pp. 71, 166, 213–15; Randolph R. Resor, "Rubber in Brazil: Dominance and Collapse, 1876–1945," *Business History Review* 51 (1977), pp. 350, 357; James C. Jackson, *Planters and Speculators: Chinese and European Agricultural Enterprise in Malaya, 1786–1921* (Kuala Lumpur, 1968), pp. 244–45; Babcock, *History of United States Rubber*, p. 88.

[21] "New Developments of the Mason Tire and Rubber Co.," *IRW* 61 (1919), p. 172; Paul W. Litchfield, *Industrial Voyage: My Life as an Industrial Lieutenant* (Garden City, 1954), pp. 160–61. Textile production subsequently became a source of substantial savings and a barrier to aspiring manufacturers (see Joe S. Bain, *Barriers to New Competition: Their Character and Consequences in Manufacturing* [Cambridge, 1956], p. 258).

5. *Shift change at Goodyear about 1919. Goodyear Tire & Rubber Company Archives.*

nesses and the army, demanded a more formal, systematic approach, equivalent to the strategy of vertical integration. The new methods helped raise employment in the industry from 74,000 to 159,000 between 1914 and 1919; in tires and tubes the total rose from 50,000 to 120,000, and in the Akron plants, from a high of 19,818 in 1914 to a high of 70,188 in 1919, just prior to peaking at 73,490 in April 1920.[22] They also put the rubber manufacturers in the forefront of the nascent personnel movement.

By 1915 it was apparent that there were really two labor problems: a

---

[22] U.S. Department of Commerce, Bureau of the Census, *Biennial Census of Manufactures, 1921* (Washington, 1924), p. 1172; Federal Housing Administration, ''Akron, Ohio, Housing Market Analysis'' (Washington, 1938), pp. 218–20.

shortage of workers and a spiraling turnover rate. The first was the result of a temporary imbalance of supply and demand. In the prewar years eastern manufacturers had typically hired young immigrant women, who started as teenagers and returned as the demands of marriage and child rearing permitted, working alongside their mothers or daughters. The only persistent difficulty was a shortage of skilled workers, particularly cutters. By mid-1915 new problems began to appear. As wages rose, many employees opted to work less. Others became more critical, refusing, for example, to take the heavier jobs. The cutoff of European immigration in 1914 and the appearance of alternative employment opportunities simultaneously reduced the supply of potential recruits. By 1916 it was hard to find employees "of even mediocre ability while expert rubber workers have become almost priceless." Newspaper advertising did not help; only generous wage increases and recruiting bonuses ensured an adequate supply of workers.[23]

In the midwestern tire plants the problem was more severe and the solution less obvious. Since the turn of the century, employment at the Akron plants had been highly cyclical, with busy seasons in the spring and late fall followed by layoffs. In 1914, the first year for which data are available, the peak was one third higher than the trough; five thousand jobs were filled and lost. News that the plants were hiring, usually in early February, brought a "rush for positions."[24] In the summer of 1915, however, the jobs did not disappear. The spring rush continued into the fall season. Employment in December, typically the low month, was 80 percent higher than in December 1914 and set a new record. Growth was uninterrupted through 1916 and the first half of 1917. By the summer of 1917, there were thirty thousand more rubber workers in the Akron area than in the best month of 1914, and rubber industry employment had risen from 53 to 67 percent of local industrial employment.[25] Still, the supply was inadequate. To fill so many jobs employers had to offer ever higher wages and find new types of workers.

One possibility was to hire more women. After 1915, manufacturers employed them for all positions that did not require strenuous work, including many jobs in the tire departments. By 1920, Goodyear had approximately six thousand female employees, more than any of the rubber shoe manufacturers except Hood. Besides filling most jobs in the mechanical goods, balloon, and gas mask departments, they became electric-truck drivers, time clerks, inspectors, and stockroom attendants. In the tire departments they washed rubber, prepared tire beads, cut plies, finished tires, and made

[23] "The Rubber Trade in Rhode Island," *IRW* 55 (1917): 289; Constance McL. Green, *History of Naugatuck, Connecticut* (Naugatuck, 1949), p. 223.

[24] *ABJ*, Feb. 2, 1914.

[25] FHA, "Akron, Ohio, Housing," p. 218.

tubes. At U.S. Rubber's Detroit plant, they cut treads, made patches for repair kits, stamped sizes on inner tubes, packed and inspected tires and, using a special "lifting jack," built small-sized tires. At the Fisk plant they made tubes and finished tires.[26]

Employers generally were pleased with the results. The women learned their tasks quickly and earned as much as the men. Dressed in khaki blouses and bloomers, standard attire in the Akron plants, or in variations such as "womanalls . . . a feminized pattern of overalls with a bloomerized effect," they easily adjusted to the new regimen. Some employers foresaw a time when, with labor-saving machines and special tools like the lifting jack, they might displace the industry's physical elite.[27]

In the Midwest there was another, equally promising source of workers. Akron lay on the northern edge of a vast area of marginal farms and underemployed workers. By 1914, men from southeastern Ohio, southwestern Pennsylvania, and West Virginia appeared regularly for the spring and fall rush seasons. Only a modest additional effort was necessary to tap the huge Appalachian population reservoir and produce one of the most notable phases of the war-induced exodus that embraced more than a half million whites and nearly as many blacks. Akron became the "capital of West Virginia," the fastest growing city in the country and qualitatively a much different community from the small industrial city of 1910 or even 1913. Southern migrants would henceforth play a major role in the labor history of the industry.[28]

Recruiting the young people of Appalachia was surprisingly easy. With real wages rising rapidly after 1917, most manufacturers simply advertised positions in West Virginia or Kentucky newspapers, as they had advertised in Ohio papers and continued to advertise in big-city papers for skilled workers. Goodyear ads, for example, appeared in the Huntington, West Virginia, *Herald Dispatch* during much of March and April 1918. Other companies' notices appeared in Wheeling and other northern West Virginia papers at the same time.[29]

The focus of this effort was southeastern Ohio and the area of north central West Virginia extending approximately from Parkersburg to Charles-

[26] "Some Labor Problems in the Rubber Industry," *IRW* 62 (1920): 413; "War News of the Rubber Industry," *IRW* 59 (1918): 6; "War News of the Rubber Industry," *IRW* 59 (1918): 645.

[27] "War News of the Rubber Industry," *IRW* 59 (1918): 645.

[28] Jack Temple Kirby, "The Southern Exodus, 1910–1960: A Primer for Historians," *Journal of Southern History* 49 (1983): 594; Gavin Wright, *Old South, New South: Revolutions in the Southern Economy Since the Civil War* (New York, 1986), pp. 203–204.

[29] *Huntington Herald Dispatch*, March–April, 1918; Alfred Winslow Jones, *Life, Liberty, and Property: A Story of Conflict and A Measurement of Conflicting Rights* (Philadelphia, 1941), pp. 61–62.

ton. Potential employees could reach Akron by train or automobile within a day at modest cost. Though Akron residents often called them "hillbillies" and "snakes," most of them were farm youths from the valleys of northern West Virginia. Their backgrounds were indistinguishable from those of the Ohio and Pennsylvania natives who delighted in jokes about West Virginia mountaineers. A study of West Virginia migrants found that 28 percent had been farmers, 19 percent, lumberjacks and sawmill workers; 14 percent, railroad employees, 12 percent, gas and oil field workers; and smaller proportions, teachers, factory workers, and coal miners.[30]

Whatever their origins, tens of thousands of young people made the trek. The recollections of a handful of migrants suggest that the supply was usually equal to the demand. Employment offices were often filled to overflowing, and the first prerequisite for a job was the patience to wait for hours in a queue. During the period of the draft, from August 1917 to November 1918, when more than eight thousand Akron rubber workers enlisted or were conscripted and a larger number of prospective employees were diverted before making the journey to the "Rubber City," the lines disappeared. Employers redoubled their efforts to entice women and launched more ambitious recruiting forays into the South. If the war had lasted into 1919, well-organized, extensive efforts might have been necessary.[31]

The effectiveness of the employers' methods is apparent from the persistence of various biases in the recruitment process. Except during the draft period, Akron manufacturers were wary of immigrants, especially those from non-English-speaking countries. All of the Akron companies sponsored Americanization programs, individually at first, and then under the auspices of the public school system. It was one of their few cooperative ventures. Most executives, however, were more concerned about the east Europeans' ability to do precise, fast-paced work than their suspect loyalties. They relegated them to dirty, heavy jobs such as opening and washing bales of crude rubber, where they labored shoulder to shoulder with six hundred to seven hundred black workers who had found their way to the rubber plants by 1919. These practices created minor but noticeable differences in the labor force by the end of the decade. Goodrich had the largest number of East Europeans and aliens, Goodyear the smallest. Goodyear probably had the largest number of black workers.[32]

---

[30] Roberta Lieberman, "Appalachian Migrants to Akron, Ohio" (seminar paper, University of Akron, 1972), p. 8.

[31] Ralph Turner, interview with author, May 10, 1976; Jack O. Abshire, interview with author, Nov. 15, 1972; "The Rubber Trade in Akron," *IRW* 57 (1918): 236.

[32] "Study of Methods of Americanization," March 13, 1919, David Saposs Papers, Box 21, State Historical Society of Wisconsin, Madison; Howard Wolf and Ralph Wolf, *Rubber:*

Even when the supply of applicants was adequate, employers still faced the related problem of retaining the workers they had hired. Before the war boom they had made little effort to reduce labor turnover, either because they viewed it as a safety valve for discontent or hesitated to interfere with the foremen's most cherished powers. In the New England plants high turnover enabled many women to combine work with domestic responsibilities. In the tire plants it reflected the seasonal pattern of demand and the arduous character of tire building and curing. Firestone payroll records, which indicate a 5 percent daily turnover rate, may well have been representative of the industry after 1915. In the footwear plants of U.S. Rubber, turnover ranged from 50 percent per year to over 200 percent. It was much higher in the mechanical goods and tire factories.[33] Akron employees were particularly mobile; they could choose from a dozen plants, all of which were eager to hire additional employees. The record of Goodrich employee Joe Jenks is suggestive of the result:

6/20/11, he was hired [at B. F. Goodrich]. Discharged August 20, 1913. . . . On 1/16/14, he was rehired and worked one day and did not return. On 1/21/14 . . . he was rehired and on 6/1/18, he was dropped.—absent; no report. On 6/21/18 . . . the Company received a request from Goodyear for information concerning his work while at Goodrich. Then on 10/14/18 he was rehired in the Goodrich, and on 7/20/20, was again dropped for no report.[34]

In 1920 Goodyear officials compiled the first comprehensive figures. The company had an average payroll of 18,968 but had hired 27,568 individuals and had fired, laid off, or otherwise lost 45,793. The average was misleading because employment had peaked at 33,000 in the spring and plunged to 10,000 in the fall with the onset of the postwar recession. Because so many workers quit or were fired for reasons that had nothing to do with the recession, the company was able to reduce its labor force by approximately 23,000 with only 8,000 layoffs.[35]

It is not surprising, then, that rubber company executives, like those in other industries, "discovered" turnover and began to view employee mobility differently. Spurred by labor shortages in 1917–1918 and the rising crescendo of unrest in the war industries, they reconsidered the economic

---

A Story of Glory and Greed (New York, 1936), p. 436; Harvey S. Firestone, *Men and Rubber* (Garden City, 1926), p. 137.

[33] Babcock, *History of United States Rubber*, pp. 158–59.

[34] Minutes, Meeting with Management, April 27, 1939, Local 5 Archives, Local 5 Offices, Akron, Ohio.

[35] Goodyear Tire & Rubber Co. "Statement to the Fact-Finding Board, Nov. 25, 1935," Federal Mediation and Conciliation Service Papers, RG 280, File 182/1,010, National Archives.

and social advantages of career employment. Between 1914 and 1920 most of them embraced features of systematic personnel management.[36]

Of the large firms, Goodyear was the most aggressive. Litchfield had created the Goodyear Labor Department in 1910 to manage the relief association, an employee restaurant, and a company hospital. He soon gave it the additional task of hiring new employees and, in 1913, of reviewing discharges, resolving grievances, and conducting time and motion studies, an unusual combination. Personnel work became a feature of his larger plan to establish checks and balances between the line and staff and to maintain a competitive atmosphere in the plant. Promising young executives customarily served a term as personnel manager in the 1910s and 1920s.

In 1912 the company added a major housing program. As south Akron rents rose and congestion and living conditions worsened, Seiberling, already a prominent real estate speculator, became interested in a company-sponsored housing project. Goodyear's directors, including Litchfield, were at first skeptical about the cost and "anything savoring of paternalism."[37] Seiberling, confident of the economic soundness of the plan, bought a large tract of hilly, undeveloped land east of the plant and won the support of Litchfield and the others for "Goodyear Heights." The company laid out the area, built model houses and an athletic complex called Seiberling Field and offered discount mortgages. The Goodyear architects, Mann & McNeille, designed "English cottage"–style houses indistinguishable, except for their compact size, from the Tudor-style houses of executives that were rising on the city's fashionable west side. Goodyear began to sell houses and lots at cost in May 1913. One hundred fifty-three houses were finished by late 1915, 300 were completed by the following spring, and 800 were ready by the end of 1916 when the company opened a second large allotment. Cliff Slusser, newly married, became the first president of the Goodyear Heights Improvement Association. By 1920, four thousand Goodyear employees and their families lived in the Heights.[38]

The events of 1913 inspired another novel venture. Impressed with the company's losses due to the absence of small groups of strikers and the flooding of a few departments, Litchfield decided to form an elite corps of workers, carefully trained to tackle any problem in any department. In April he announced the formation of a "Flying Squadron" with Slusser in charge. Slusser "hand picked" individuals "who would not go very far out

---

[36] Daniel Nelson, *Managers and Workers: Origins of the New Factory System* (Madison, 1975), pp. 148–56; Sanford M. Jacoby, *Employing Bureaucracy: Managers, Unions, and the Transformation of Work in American History, 1900–1945* (New York, 1985), pp. 133–65.

[37] Allen, *House of Goodyear*, p. 170.

[38] "Financing an Industrial Village," *IRW* 56 (1917): 450; *WCL*, Jan. 1, 8, 1916, Feb. 10, 1920.

of their way to avoid trouble." A "slurring remark" was "apt to be answered with a punch in the jaw."[39] There must have been many sore jaws at first. Foremen were hostile because squadron men reported on them. Workers suspected that the squadron's real purpose was to break strikes.[40] Yet Litchfield was pleased with the squadron and the atmosphere it created. He organized a second class for prospective squadron men in early 1914, and an Engineering Squadron, consisting of skilled mechanics, in 1915.

To reassure the foremen, who had lost much of their traditional authority, Litchfield launched a Safety First campaign in late 1913 and gave them a central role in reducing accidents. A "battalion" of 115 supervisors "look[ed] for hazards." Apparently they did not have to look far, because the injury rate declined by 50 percent in the next four months.[41] Litchfield added a foremen's training course in 1914. Its title, suggestive of the new era in Goodyear operations, was "Organization and Management." Many supervisors also benefited from Goodyear Heights and the introduction of paid vacations for blue-collar workers with five years of service in 1914.[42]

In the following years of accelerated growth and tight labor markets, Goodyear greatly extended its personnel activities. In 1915 it provided free life insurance to members of the Relief Association; in 1916, a pension plan; and in 1918, a stock-purchase plan. By 1920, an "Industrial University," with "courses all the way from grade school to college," enrolled five thousand seven hundred students. By that time, the company had completed Goodyear Hall, a block-long, six-story building with an auditorium, classrooms, and the largest gymnasium in the state. Goodyear teams, including "Silents" composed of deaf mutes, competed vigorously in a variety of sports, and "Field Days" at Seiberling Field attracted crowds of forty thousand in 1916 and fifty thousand in 1918.[43]

Litchfield's most important postwar initiative was the Industrial Assembly, destined to be one of the most durable American company unions. During the 1913 strike, he had written that "Goodyear will always be an open shop."[44] Since at least 1916 one Goodyear Labor Department official had devoted full time to grievances, and the department manager handled special cases and appeals. As far as Litchfield was concerned, these measures eliminated the possibility of another strike. His real goal was more ambitious. In 1917 he wrote that Labor Department officials "must invade

[39] Allen, *House of Goodyear*, pp. 188–89.

[40] Goodyear, "Statement to the Fact-Finding Board."

[41] *WCL*, Nov. 8, 1913, Sept. 14, 1914; "The Rubber Trade in Akron," *IRW* 49 (1914): 188.

[42] *WCL*, Sept. 14, 1914.

[43] *WCL*, Jan. 29, Sept. 9, Oct. 1, 1916; "News of the American Rubber Industry," *IRW* 59 (1918): 37; Litchfield, *Industrial Voyage*, p. 182.

[44] *WCL*, March 15, 1913.

6. The opening of Goodyear Hall in 1919. Goodyear Tire & Rubber Company Archives.

the department of the foreman,'' and later that he had sought ''to give the employees a voice in management.''[45] His intention was to make the workers more active, not to keep them quiet. The Industrial Assembly would identify the best workers and enlist them in the operation of the enterprise. This ''squadron'' of the rank and file would be a logical extension of the Flying Squadron.

In April 1919 Litchfield organized a Council of Industrial Relations, consisting of the labor manager, several foremen, and eight elected workers, to study the possibility of a workers' organization. There was no shortage of models; company unionism had gradually emerged from the welfare movement, had become a surrogate for trade unionism in 1918 when the National War Labor Board required many manufacturers to introduce collective bargaining, and was spreading rapidly as an antidote to the unrest and radicalism of the postwar period. The Goodyear council studied the plans of Youngstown Sheet & Tube and Printz-Biederman, among others. With Litchfield's prompting, it adopted a plan based on the U.S. Consti-

[45] *WCL*, June 16, 1917.

tution. An elected House and Senate would legislate for the plant; bills passed by both houses would go to the plant manager for acceptance or veto. In the case of a veto, the House and Senate could appeal to the Goodyear Board of Directors. Representatives had to have one year of service; senators, five. The plan was completed in mid-June and approved by 93 percent of Goodyear employees in a special election.[46] Workers elected representatives and senators in early July. Some executives feared they would select "young men, radicals and men of foreign influences." Instead they chose older, experienced men, nearly all native-born. Litchfield boasted that the Industrial Assembly was as "typically American" as any "legislative body anywhere in this country."[47] It met for the first time on July 8, 1919.

Three months earlier Litchfield had had an unusual opportunity to compare notes with other innovative employers. In early 1919 a group of prominent big-business executives organized a Special Conference Committee to study labor and personnel problems. They asked Seiberling to participate, and he and Litchfield met the heads of du Pont, General Electric, Standard Oil of New Jersey, Standard Oil of Indiana, Westinghouse, Bethlehem Steel, International Harvester, General Motors, and Irving National Bank on April 2. A joint statement, drafted by the respective labor and personnel managers, endorsed corporate personnel departments, centralized personnel work, collective bargaining "regardless of union or nonunion affiliations," Americanization activities, and educational, medical, and safety programs. A manifesto of the conservative approach to personnel work, which emphasized employee benefits and minimal interference with the line managers, it must have seemed bland and uninteresting to Goodyear officials.[48]

In the meantime Firestone began a similar program. In late 1913 the company introduced an Industrial Service Department that hired and fired and conducted "Safety First" work. In 1916 it added an employee stock-purchase plan and appropriated $1 million for group life insurance. It also provided medical services, classes in sign language for its growing corps of deaf workers, and "female investigators" to assist female employees.

---

[46] WCL, June 7, 1919; Litchfield, Industrial Voyage, pp. 183–84; Allen, House of Goodyear, p. 183; Daniel Nelson, "The Company Union Movement, 1900–1937: A Reexamination," Business History Review 56 (1982): 339–45.

[47] Litchfield to Seiberling and G. M. Stadelman, May 3, 1921, Goodyear Archives.

[48] "Report of the Special Conference Committee," July 15, 1920, Goodyear Archives. Also see Robert Ozanne, A Century of Labor-Management Relations at McCormick and International Harvester (Madison, 1967), p. 158; Jacoby, Employing Bureaucracy, pp. 183–89.

Its glee clubs, bands, and athletic teams were a match for any in the industry.[49]

Though Firestone dismissed company unionism in favor of "a right-down rugged honesty," the influence of the Goodyear program was apparent in the development of Firestone Park, a model residential community that opened in October 1916. Though any dwelling, no matter how flimsy or unappealing, would attract buyers, Harvey Firestone insisted on a development as pleasing as Goodyear Heights. The company bought 525 acres (later increased to 1,000) and employed Alling S. DeForest, the Rochester, New York, architect who had designed Firestone's west Akron estate, to lay out the streets and public areas. Winding boulevards, a park, and space for churches and schools, all arranged in an outline of the company's logo, made Firestone Park an attractive replica of Goodyear Heights. Within a year 600 houses, purchased by Firestone employees with small down payments, graced the area. The company spent almost $3 million on "employee happiness," as the company's historian later wrote, with every expectation of recouping the investment.[50]

Firestone also became a leader in Americanization work, thanks to the aggressive direction of one of its personnel managers, E. C. Vermillion. Vermillion soon doubled attendance at the company's English classes and so impressed Akron school board officials that they recruited him to preside over a citywide effort to fulfill their pledge: "Akron, a One Language City in 1921."[51] Vermillion developed a plan that encompassed all the city's industries and promised to be "a model for the whole country." By the end of 1919 he and his assistants had enrolled more than two thousand students; by mid-1920 the total was four thousand two hundred students.[52]

Edwin C. Shaw, the veteran Goodrich manager, might condemn Litchfield's "welfare work," but he gradually embraced many of its "business like" and "sensible" features. By 1914 he had centralized hiring and other employee services in an Industrial Relations Department. Indulging a pet interest, he introduced an "elaborate department of safety and hygiene."[53]

[49] Firestone Tire & Rubber Co. to J. M. Van Hensen, Aug. 26, 1914 and R. E. Lee to W. G. Mather, July 20, 1914, in Lief, *The Firestone Story*, p. 83; J. W. Thomas to Harvey S. Firestone, March 3, 1917, Firestone Archives, Firestone Tire and Rubber Co., Akron, Ohio.

[50] Board of Directors Minutes, Firestone Tire & Rubber Co., Dec. 4, 1915, Firestone Archives; "The Firestone Park Land Co." (1923), Firestone Archives. Also see Frederick M. Davenport, "Treating Men White in Akron Town," *The Outlook* 126 (1920): 408–409, 411; Lief, *The Firestone Story*, pp. 81–82.

[51] J. C. Reich to J. W. Thomas, Jan. 8, 1919, and Ernest P. Wiles to Harvey S. Firestone, Aug. 14, 1919, Firestone Archives.

[52] "The Rubber Trade in Akron," *IRW* 61 (1920): 240; "The Rubber Trade in Akron," *IRW* 62 (1920): 754; L. A. Gredys to W. R. Murphy, Nov. 17, 1919, Firestone Archives.

[53] "The Rubber Trade in Akron," *IRW* 50 (1914): 485.

By mid-1916 he had added athletic fields and an athletic association with a full-time director. The company operated a summer resort for women, a clubhouse for single men, a Housing Bureau to help employees buy homes on the installment plan, and a Bureau of Education, which enrolled more than one thousand five hundred employees in 1918. The local YMCA later recruited the Goodrich education director to conduct a "broader" program aimed at the "colored young men of Akron."[54] Goodrich executives introduced a stock-purchase plan in 1920 but dismissed a company union as unwanted and unnecessary.

At U.S. Rubber, which remained at its base a collection of small, semi-autonomous factories, career employment and personnel management were even more closely associated with the war crisis. Before 1915 several of the footwear subsidiaries had built company houses, and the Mechanical Rubber Goods Company had a welfare committee that administered libraries, gymnasiums, and a savings plan, but the others relied on informal contacts and inertia. Myron H. Clark, the head of U.S. Rubber's footwear division, introduced centralized hiring offices at boot and shoe plants in the mid-1910s. The other division managers would have nothing to do with his radical move.[55]

The war boom, however, necessitated major changes. At the National India Rubber footwear subsidiary in Bristol, Rhode Island, employment doubled to three thousand seven hundred, competent workers became hard to retain, and the close-knit atmosphere of earlier years disappeared. In response, company executives introduced an extensive but traditional welfare program, including a hospital, a restaurant, an employee boarding house, a nursery for employees' children, a grocery store, and a dental clinic. Executives organized a company band and military drills for women.[56] Revere Rubber introduced an extensive safety campaign and "special welfare work . . . for the girl employees."[57] Converse Rubber bought a boarding house, and even Morgan & Wright hired a matron "to make the women feel as much at home as possible."[58]

U.S. Rubber's corporate executives gradually became aware of the im-

[54] "The Rubber Trade in Akron," *IRW* 55 (1916): 36; "The Rubber Trade in Ohio," *IRW* 60 (1919): 579; "The Rubber Trade in Akron," *IRW* 62 (1920): 677; "The Rubber Trade in Ohio," *IRW* 60 (1919): 387.

[55] "News of the American Rubber Trade," *IRW* 49 (1914): 255; Babcock, *History of United States Rubber*, p. 156.

[56] "The Rubber Trade in Rhode Island," *IRW* 52 (1915): 617; "The Rubber Trade In Rhode Island," *IRW* 54 (1916): 435; "The Rubber Trade in Rhode Island," *IRW* 58 (1918): 432; "The Rubber Trade in Rhode Island," *IRW* 59 (1919): 211.

[57] "The Rubber Trade in Rhode Island," *IRW* 54 (1916): 435.

[58] "War News of the Rubber Industry," *IRW* 59 (1918): 6; "The Rubber Trade in Massachusetts," *IRW* 61 (1919): 175.

portance of personnel work. In 1916 they introduced a company-wide safety program and in 1917, an old-age pension plan. In 1918, Charles Seger, Colt's successor, decided that a more vigorous, coordinated effort was necessary and hired Cyrus S. Ching, a gangling Canadian who had acquired a reputation as a shrewd manager of unionized employees at the Boston Elevated Railway Co. Ching had recently completed the famous personnel management course taught by Ordway Tead and Henry Metcalf and was filled with missionary zeal. He spent most of 1919 visiting U.S. Rubber plants and explaining what he had learned. His most difficult task was to persuade the executives to centralize hiring and firing. It was a "delicate job," and he made only modest progress until late 1919, when Seger sent him to Montreal to resolve a strike at one of the Canadian subsidiaries. Ching negotiated a compromise that ended the walkout and established his credibility. As his influence grew, Ching promoted measures to cut turnover and train foremen in more subtle leadership styles. He organized conferences of doctors, nurses, and employment managers from the subsidiaries and encouraged them to exchange ideas, develop a professional interest in their work, and look to him for advancement. By 1920, when he acquired the title of "supervisor" of industrial relations, U.S. Rubber's personnel programs bore a striking resemblance to those of the fast-growing Akron companies.[59]

The capstone of Ching's postwar program was the "Factory Councils" that he introduced into most of U.S. Rubber's footwear plants in 1919. He opted for a relatively common postwar approach; elected employee representatives and management representatives would confer in a council. The Council, in turn, would appoint standing committees to coordinate plant activities and resolve grievances that individual representatives were unable to settle. Trade unionists often argued that such plans fragmented the labor force and neglected important issues like wages. Ching would have replied that he had no intention of creating a replica of a conventional union. His goal was not collective bargaining but "the fullest possible use of the ideas and energies of the workers in the conduct of industry."[60] The company's official description of the councils emphasized that their "chief function" was not to deal with grievances but "to take up, constructively, ideas and suggestions which will contribute toward better and more eco-

[59] Cyrus S. Ching, Oral History Memoir, 1: 55, Columbia University; "The Rubber Trade in Rhode Island," *IRW* 61 (1920): 311; Babcock, *History of United States Rubber*, pp. 156–60.

[60] Quoted in Babcock, *History of United States Rubber*, p. 159. Also see U.S. Rubber Co., "Industrial Relations Activities of the United States Rubber Company, 1922" (New York, 1922)," pp. 38–40, Archives Organization File, Box 75, Labor-Management Documentation Center, Cornell University.

nomical methods of production, better working conditions, and better co-operation."[61]

For personnel managers like Ching, the company union was a logical extension of centralized hiring and dismissal procedures, employee training, promotion and layoff policies, and welfare work. Its target was the power of the foremen over employees. Line supervisors and foremen saw the factory councils for what they were and often opposed them. Ching succeeded in the footwear division because Myron Clark was highly sympathetic. He made no progress at all in the other divisions. Tire-plant managers, led by C. J. Butler, the skeptical head of the big Morgan & Wright subsidiary, strongly opposed company unions, and J. Newton Gunn backed the managers.[62]

Other rubber manufacturers, facing similar problems, adopted various features of systematic personnel management after 1914. By 1917 thirty-six of seventy-eight firms that responded to a poll reported that they had created employment offices to hire and fire employees, a practice unknown except in the largest plants before 1915. Thirty-six also had safety programs; twenty-nine offered insurance benefits; twenty-one had some type of welfare work; twenty had lunchrooms; eighteen offered financial bonuses; and seven provided housing.[63]

Two examples are illustrative of the experiences of the larger firms. In 1915 Fisk Rubber executives introduced a series of benefits for their largely male labor force, including an employee newspaper, an elaborate thirty-acre athletic field, and the Red Tops, which became one of the era's premier baseball squads.[64] At the same time Hood Rubber executives employed R. S. Quimby, a surgeon and industrial health pioneer, to preside over a welfare program for a rapidly growing but predominantly female labor force. By 1919 Quimby managed an elaborate hospital, a safety program, and life and health insurance plans. His department conducted Americanization activities, operated a restaurant, published the *Hood Arrow*, and employed matrons to "see that all the sanitary rules are enforced."[65] Quimby and his assistant, S. Jane Williams, became prominent figures in the employment management movement, but their standing at Hood is less certain. Presumably they acquired some control over hiring, firing, and other personnel functions, but it is unlikely they ever attained the influence of a Cliff Slusser or Cy Ching.

[61] U.S. Rubber, "Industrial Relations Activities," p. 41.

[62] Ching, Oral History, 1: 67.

[63] "Americanization Activities in Rubber Mills," *IRW* 56 (1917): 711.

[64] "News of the American Rubber Trade," *IRW* 53 (1916): 186.

[65] "Welfare Work in a Modern Shoe Factory," *IRW* 53 (1916): 189. Also see "The Rubber Trade in Boston," *IRW* 56 (1917): 672; "The Rubber Trade in Boston," *IRW* 56 (1917): 740.

WARTIME UNIONS

The boom was also a stimulus to the labor movement, which became larger, more aggressive, and more politically conscious than at any time since the 1880s. Total union membership in the U.S. rose from 2.5 million in 1915 to at least 5 million in 1920, and included many employees of large factories and big businesses that had been considered immune to organization. Rubber workers, like other factory employees, formed unions, demanded improvements in wages and hours, and conducted numerous strikes. Their behavior underlined the vulnerability of large firms and the limited value of personnel work as a hedge against organization. Their achievements, on the other hand, were modest and short-lived. Too often they were unable to enlist outside assistance or to hold the allegiance of the tire-building and -curing elite.

The best-known organizing efforts and strikes of the war period occurred in the eastern plants. By mid-1915 the Trenton tire workers had organized a federal labor union and were holding mass meetings. In October a number of men and girls at the Globe and Essex plants walked out to protest low wages, unsanitary conditions, and discrimination against union members. The manufacturers replaced them with new employees, including the wives of foremen and company officials. For more than a month the strikers picketed the plant, interfering with the movement of supplies and workers and prompting federal government mediators to intervene. Government authorities arranged a settlement that satisfied many of the workers' demands and undercut the "outside agitators" who were active in Trenton.[66] Although Essex executives refused to discharge employees they had hired during the strike, business was so good that everyone who wanted to return was rehired. This incident, and strikes in other Trenton industries, prompted employers to form the Rubber Manufacturers' Association of Trenton, supposedly to promote cooperation with their employees. The association included every Trenton rubber company and made union activities much more difficult. By mid-1918 the Trenton manufacturers were determined not "to tolerate labor trouble" despite the shortage of workers. They "summarily settled" several disputes.[67]

In Boston and New York, raincoat workers organized and struck in 1915 and 1917. Taking advantage of the war boom and government contracts,

[66] "The Rubber Trade in Trenton," *IRW* 53 (1915): 140. Also see Harold S. Roberts, *The Rubber Workers: Labor Organization and Collective Bargaining in the Rubber Industry* (New York, 1944), p. 82.

[67] "The Rubber Trade in New Jersey," *IRW* 53 (1916): 374; "The Rubber Trade in Trenton," *IRW* 58 (1918): 622.

they were able to win wage increases that kept their wages in line with consumer prices.[68]

Fisk Tire workers also organized successfully. In early 1916 they struck for the eight-hour day, extra pay for overtime work, and recognition of their union, an AFL federal local. The head of the Massachusetts state board of arbitration finally arranged a settlement. Company officials agreed to eight-hour shifts and overtime pay. Although they refused to recognize the union, they agreed to discuss grievances with union representatives. Since "all the departments [are] unionized, this arrangement is tantamount to recognition of the union."[69]

Of all the rubber workers, however, the New England footwear employees most closely fit the model of the rebellious war worker. Boom conditions, news about high-paying jobs in munitions centers like Bridgeport, and the reluctance of employers to raise wages precipitated periodic upheavals in the normally placid Rhode Island and Massachusetts factories. In early 1916, tennis shoe workers at the Millville, Massachusetts, U.S. Rubber plant struck for higher piece rates. They were paid off and discharged while the nonstriking employees received a "voluntary and unexpected" wage increase. When seven hundred workers at the nearby Woonsocket, Rhode Island, U.S. Rubber plant struck for a similar raise, they too were successful.[70] In June, Revere Rubber employees struck for shorter hours and higher pay. They remained out for more than two months but won only a modest wage increase and a company pledge to deal with union representatives in the future.[71] In the fall, workers at Woonsocket and at National India Rubber in Bristol, Rhode Island, struck for higher pay. The strikers succeeded in closing the huge Bristol plant. However, the "firmness of the police and the severity of the court" gradually undermined the strike. In late November, Rhode Island rubber manufacturers announced a 10 percent "emergency" wage increase for all employees that convinced the strikers to return to their benches.[72]

To the surprise and embarrassment of the Colt family, National India Rubber remained a center of labor unrest. In 1917 and early 1918, an "Allied Workers Union" recruited many Italian and Portuguese employees. In

[68] Roberts, *Rubber Workers*, p. 83; "The Rubber Trade in Boston," *IRW* 53 (1915): 31.

[69] "The Rubber Trade in Boston," *IRW* (1916): 498.

[70] "The Rubber Trade in Rhode Island," *IRW* 54 (1916): 499. Also see Paul Buhle, "Italian-American Radicals and Labor in Rhode Island, 1905–1930," in Herbert G. Gutman and Donald H. Bell, eds., *The New England Working Class and the New Labor History* (Urbana and Chicago, 1987), pp. 285–88.

[71] "The Rubber Trade in Boston," *IRW* 54 (1916): 680.

[72] "The Rubber Trade in Rhode Island," *IRW* 55 (1916): 164; State of Rhode Island, *Report of Commissioner of Labor made to the General Assembly for the years 1916–1917 to 1918–1919* (Providence, 1921), pp. 132, 145–46.

March 1918, it struck briefly for a wage increase and in May demanded the discharge of several supervisors and all nonunion workers. Company executives refused, and when military officers warned the union leaders not to interfere with war production, the union withdrew its demands. National India executives subsequently organized a special police force to curb the union. On at least one occasion these officers thwarted a walkout of union workers. The plant superintendent simultaneously dismissed those "active as agitators and leaders in the trouble."[73] But neither he nor the plant police could prevent a strike in mid-July. Demanding a 25 percent wage increase and the abolition of the plant's bonus wage plan, the strikers were able to close the mill and recruit sympathizers in the Woonsocket and Millville plants. After three days, five thousand five hundred employees were involved.[74]

Despite intense pressures, some strikers held out for as long as two months. On July 19 federal agents in Bristol arrested and temporarily held sixty-nine strikers who did not have draft cards. Later at a strike meeting in Woonsocket, they berated the workers for disrupting production and not taking their complaints to the War Labor Board. The strikers still refused to go back. When National India executives reopened the plant in mid-August, a group of Portuguese workers attacked the returning employees with tools.[75] The plant reopened peacefully ten days later. In Woonsocket and Millville the strike continued until mid-September, when the managers agreed to increase wages and operate restaurants and stores in the plants to help the workers combat inflation.

In August 1919 two thousand eight hundred Naugatuck, Connecticut, boot and rubber reclaiming workers organized as a local of the International Boot and Shoe Workers and called the first strike in the history of that venerable manufacturing center. After a month and a half they returned with a modest increase and union recognition.[76]

The most tumultuous rubber workers' strike of the war period closed the National India plant in May and June 1920. The dispute began when a group of employees demanded higher wages and began to picket. Soon they had closed the plant. Three weeks later a confrontation of guards and strikers led the governor to order the National Guard to Bristol. With the soldiers present, National India executives decided to reopen. At first they were unsuccessful, but gradually the employees began to return and the strike finally ended without a settlement.[77]

[73] "The Rubber Trade in Rhode Island," *IRW* 58 (1918): 580; "The Rubber Trade in Rhode Island," IRW 58 (1918): 621.

[74] *Providence Evening Bulletin*, July 19, 1918.

[75] *Report of Commissioner of Labor*, p. 187; "The Rubber Trade in Rhode Island," *IRW* 58 (1918): 740; "The Rubber Trade in Rhode Island," *IRW* 59 (1918): 45.

[76] Green, *Naugatuck*, p. 235–37.

[77] Roberts, *Rubber Workers,* p. 89.

In the eastern plants, then, the war boom produced the kinds of behavior characteristic of industry generally. Full employment, inflation, Wilsonian idealism, and foreign and domestic radicalism were stimuli. Except in Trenton and the Bristol-Woonsocket area, the plant was the focal point for union activism. The organizations that appeared between 1915 and 1920 were local, independent industrial unions, led by local men and women. The Allied Workers of Rhode Island was the only organization that became important enough to receive public notice, and it, like most of the local unions, had foundered by mid-1920. Apart from a few strike victories, the major influence of the wartime unions was indirect: they forced employers to devote more attention to labor problems and probably reinforced the movements toward personnel management, and, at U.S. Rubber, company unionism.

In Akron the economic and political forces that stimulated organization elsewhere created opportunities that AFL leaders quickly exploited. By June 1916, Central Labor Union leaders were appealing for outside organizers. With AFL help, they were able to organize most skilled construction workers, make inroads among service employees, and enlist many factory craftsmen. Their most dramatic successes were among metal trades workers. The local lodge of the International Association of Machinists grew from thirty-five members in late 1915 to more than one thousand five hundred by the summer of 1916, including nearly eight hundred skilled rubber workers. For the next three years they and the streetcar employees would give Akron employers and residents a strong taste of wartime labor militancy.[78]

In late August 1916, the Machinists demanded an eight-hour day, a wage increase, time and a half for overtime, and double time for Sunday work. The rubber companies, which set de facto standards for all the city's plants, refused to negotiate. When Firestone discharged the members of the union negotiating committee, the Machinists struck. Eight hundred union members walked out on August 28; between five and six hundred more followed them on August 29. Ultimately, twenty plants were affected. Several firms made immediate concessions that brought the men back.[79]

Conceding that the eight-hour day would soon become the industry standard, the other manufacturers were almost as accommodating. On September 5, Goodrich managers agreed to introduce the eight-hour day by January 1, and the Machinists voted to return. Other employers soon made similar offers. At Firestone and Goodyear, executives "made difficulties about reinstating the men" and the strikers remained out for several more

[78] *The People* 15 (June 23, 1916): 1; "What Our Organizers Are Doing," *American Federationist* 24–26 (1917–19).

[79] "Report of Organizer M. J. Mahon," *Machinists' Monthly Journal* 28 (1916): 1011; *AP*, Aug. 28, 29, 1916.

days.[80] When the Firestone superintendent refused to rehire the men whose firing precipitated the walkout, they "stepped aside" and got jobs elsewhere in order to permit the other workers to return. Goodyear finally reinstated its machinists. Union members considered the settlement a victory, all the more satisfying because of the fate of the rubber workers three years before. Akron became a forty-eight-hour city. "Don't come here with the intention of working long hours and overtime," warned an organizer. "The overtime hog here is dead."[81]

The Machinists demonstrated their power again in January 1918, when a dispute arose at the Miller Tire Company. Miller paid only time and a quarter for overtime, a practice that hurt the men's pride more than their earnings. When a new foreman "bitterly opposed to labor organizations" brought the unrest to a head by firing the local union president, the workers appealed to company executives Jacob and William Pfeiffer. Receiving no satisfaction, they asked the mayor to intervene "in order to avoid curtailment of war supplies." Mayor I. S. Myers asked the Labor Department to send a mediator while the AFL appealed to the War Department. The mediator had no more success with the Pfeiffers, who were the "most obstinate" employers he had ever encountered. Frustrated, the Miller Machinists struck and halted most machine repairs for two weeks. In apparent desperation the Pfeiffers agreed to raise overtime pay, rehire the discharged man, and fire the obnoxious foreman.[82] However, they refused to meet the union committee or to sign an agreement. The Machinists decided that they had won enough. Since the workers were "a new organized body of men who are little educated in the labor movement," they "felt it best to accept this verbal proposition and keep their ranks solid . . . and further organize."[83]

Akron unions were not always so successful. When streetcar operators struck for a wage increase in November 1917, the rubber companies responded by organizing fleets of trucks to carry employees to the plants. On the first morning of the strike, the trucks moved thirty thousand people in two hours, virtually duplicating streetcar service. The rubber factories operated on schedule, but small downtown businesses were hurt. After a week

[80] *ABJ*, Sept. 5, 1916.

[81] "Report of Organizer M. J. Mahon," *Machinists' Monthly Journal* 28 (1916): 1012; ibid. 29 (1917): 611. There is no evidence that the skilled employees encouraged other rubber workers to organize. For an illuminating discussion that may explain this apparent shortcoming, see Cecelia Bucki, "Dilution and Craft Tradition: Munitions Workers in Bridgeport, Connecticut, 1915–19," in Gutman and Bell, *The New England Working Class*, pp. 137–56.

[82] *The People* 17 (Jan. 25, 1918): 1; Mark J. Crawford to Secretary of Labor, Jan. 23, 1918, Federal Mediation and Conciliation Service Papers, RG 280, File 33/939.

[83] J. H. Steinhauser to Mark L. Crawford, Feb. 22, 1918, FMCS Papers, RG 280, File 33/939. Also see *The People* 17 (Feb. 1, 1918): 1.

the strikers settled for half of what they had demanded. Two and a half years later, when the car men struck again, the department stores joined the rubber companies in operating trucks. The extra vehicles caused tie-ups on major streets but reduced the effectiveness of the strike and encouraged the workers to settle.[84]

Union organizers were even less successful when they attempted to recruit rubber workers. Between 1916 and 1918, small groups at Firestone, Goodyear, Falls Rubber, and Kelly-Springfield, among others, struck to protest grievances but made no effort to organize permanently. Many rubber workers seemed oblivious to the labor movement. In 1916 the CLU attracted twenty thousand to its Labor Day picnic at Silver Lake, while the Goodyear Field Day attracted forty thousand.[85] Still, the giant plants remained a tempting target. In October 1917, local and national AFL officials launched another effort to organize the Akron workers. Cal Wyatt returned with renewed optimism. He explained that the "negligible results" of past campaigns had been due to the seasonal character of the industry and long lines of job seekers at the gates. Now the war had eliminated those obstacles and the employers had created "pronounced unrest." It was an established fact, he argued, that "unless a man is competent and performs his work in a skilled and speedy manner, his services are of no value to the companies and his discharge follows."[86] By mid-November Wyatt had attracted enough of a following to begin a series of public meetings.

The AFL campaign culminated in mid-January 1918, when Wyatt formed a federal labor union. Rubber workers overflowed the CLU hall to hear Wyatt emphasize "patriotic duty, loyalty to government and peaceful methods." He and the other speakers "were applauded many times during the reference to the patriotism of the working class." His announcement that President Samuel Gompers would visit Akron also elicited "great applause from the crowds." He indicated that the new union would enlist men and women, would not "exclude any nationality," and would be the basis for a new national rubber workers' union. To encourage workers to join, he promised to have a mass meeting every Monday afternoon until March.[87]

On the following Monday the crowd did not fill the hall, supposedly because "more men were working on war orders." Speeches by Wyatt, the president of the CLU, and business agents of the Electrical Workers and Carpenters did not evoke the wild cheers of the week before. Wyatt indicated that AFL secretary-treasurer Frank Morrison might appear in two

[84] *ABJ*, Nov. 11, 12, 1917; July 6, 16, 1920; "The Rubber Trade in Akron," *IRW* 57 (1917): 172.

[85] *AP*, Sept. 5, 1916.

[86] *The People* 16 (Oct. 12, 1917): 1; ibid. 17 (Nov. 9, 1917): 1; ibid. (April 12, 1918): 1.

[87] Ibid. 17 (Jan. 25, 1918): 1.

weeks, and that Gompers would speak at some unspecified later date. The meetings continued for several weeks, apparently with smaller and smaller crowds and no outside speakers. Federation organizers acknowledged that the campaign was "heavily handicapped." In late February, Wyatt left Akron again in frustration.[88]

A month later, sixty Goodyear tire builders struck to protest a piece-rate reduction. The walkout spread to other departments, ultimately affecting six hundred or seven hundred workers. CLU leaders wired the AFL to send Wyatt or another organizer but got no response. They organized "several unsuccessful meetings." After a Labor Department mediator failed to secure any concessions, the strikers returned at the reduced rate. The federal local was not mentioned in contemporary accounts of the strike or of the workers' efforts to obtain assistance.[89]

Even the Machinists had trouble by mid-1918. In May they announced their "greatest organizing campaign ever" with the slogan, "Get the Hun in America."[90] Their goal was to recruit every eligible worker, including women, who were promised equal pay. By August they claimed 90 percent of the city's machinists. Apparently their employers were less impressed this time. They flatly refused to increase wages and discharged several union leaders. The Machinists appealed to the War Labor Board, which had not yet considered the case when it disbanded in December 1918. The Machinists renewed their demands in early 1919 and eventually called a citywide strike. On August 22, 60–70 percent of the city's machinists, including nearly one thousand from Goodyear and Firestone, walked out. Again the manufacturers refused to negotiate. After two weeks of inactivity and limited support from other unions, the machinists returned to their jobs. By mid-September the strike had collapsed.[91]

At Goodyear an Industrial Assembly committee took charge of rehiring the machinists. "The method of interviewing the machinists is that of a typical law court." Men who had not played important roles in the strike were interviewed in groups and rehired after promising to take their complaints to the assembly. Others accused of participating in "street quarrels with the men who remained on the job," threatening nonstrikers, or "being an agitator, Bolsheviki or radical" were considered "with the utmost care and deliberation." Each man was "given a chance to show that he is now willing to go back to work." As a consequence, all but "a very small per-

[88] Ibid. 17 (Feb. 1, 1918): 1; ibid. (March 1, 1918): 1; "What Our Organizers Are Doing," *American Federationist* 25 (1918): 154.

[89] *The People* 17 (April 12, 1918): 1; ibid. (April 26, 1918): 1; *AP*, March 28, 1918.

[90] *The People* 17 (May 24, 1918): 1.

[91] *ABJ*, Aug. 22, 1919.

cent'' of the strikers were rehired. Like other rubber workers, the machinists had learned that strikes ''are unnecessary and out of date.''[92]

The Machinists' defeat, the failure of the streetcar workers in early 1920, and the onset of the postwar recession the following summer brought union organizing efforts to a halt. By 1921 the Akron labor movement had suffered its most serious setback since the 1890s. Yet the experiences of the World War I years had one important long-term consequence: the creation of a coterie of local activists who were impressed with the potential of a rubber workers' union. For leadership, these men looked to Samuel L. Newman, the Machinists' business agent from 1918 to 1923, and Wilmer Tate, his assistant. Newman, Tate, and their allies remained a tenuous but enduring link between the labor movement and the rubber workers.

There was at least one other effort to organize the Akron rubber workers before the postwar recession completed the work of the anti-union employers. The IWW local, sustained by a handful of members who escaped the manufacturers' blacklists, had operated surreptitiously after the collapse of the 1913 strike. The revelation that several of its officers had been agents of a Cleveland detective agency limited its credibility and appeal for several years. By 1917, however, the Wobblies had gained enough adherents to warrant a government raid. Two other raids followed in 1919. By July 1920 a ''newly reorganized'' IWW local claimed three thousand members. Supposedly the fastest growing Wobbly union in Ohio, it declined with equal speed, leaving no record after the summer of 1920.[93]

Why did Akron rubber workers, in contrast with the eastern workers and the Akron craft groups, demonstrate so little of the cohesiveness they had exhibited in 1913? Given the employers' seemingly insatiable demand for labor, tire builders and pit workers had little reason to fear reprisals or to behave differently from the skilled workers. Patriotism or recollections of 1913 hardly explain the meager success of the AFL. Personnel work did not deter the skilled workers from organizing. A conclusive answer may be impossible, but it is likely that real wage gains of approximately thirty percent between 1917 and 1920, the introduction of the eight-hour day, tensions between the skilled and semi-skilled, and several factors peculiar to the Akron environment persuaded most tire builders, pit workers, and others that they could best advance their interests as unorganized individuals.

One of those factors was a marked decline in living conditions. Conges-

[92] *WCL*, Oct. 23, 1919. Also see *WCL*, Oct. 11, 1919.

[93] S. L. Pannel, ''Special Report 920,'' July 3, 1920, and Bliss Morton, ''Report,'' July 31, 1920, Federal Bureau of Investigation Papers, RG 65, Reel 647, National Archives; *ABJ*. Feb. 7, 1914; Kevin Michael Rosswurm, ''A Strike in the Rubber City: Rubber Workers, Akron, and the I.W.W., 1913'' (M.A. thesis, Kent State University, 1975), pp. 92–93, 103.

tion, poor housing, crime, and other social ills were characteristic of the war-boom towns, including Bristol and Trenton, but Akron was a special case. Besides the "high cost of living," residents suffered from a housing shortage that experts estimated at twenty thousand houses in 1920.[94] Some workers gave up their jobs because they could not find adequate accommodations. Others lived in shacks or even tents during the summer months. A cost-of-living survey prepared by the local Bureau of Municipal Research concluded that Akron renters paid one quarter more than the average worker.[95] "Exorbitant rents," wrote one rubber worker, "tend to curb our patriotism."[96] Seiberling and Firestone impressed architects and reformers with their model communities, but local contractors provided a more practical solution to the housing shortage. They crowded thousands of six-room frame houses (suitable for large families or boarders) on small lots or in the backyards of older homes. Most of the new houses were of "single construction in which sheathing reinforcement is absent, so that lack of paint is likely to result in very rapid deterioration within a few years."[97] The city was slow to pave streets and enforce sanitation ordinances. A journalist estimated that ten million empty tin cans littered streets, alleys, and the few vacant areas that remained.[98] A Goodyear executive observed that "men come here because they feel it is a place to make money and forget about . . . pleasant conditions and surroundings."[99]

The effects of the boom were most evident in the south Akron neighborhoods. Table 1 summarizes the transformation of the area bounded by Crosier, Grant, and Brown streets, halfway between the Goodrich and Good-

TABLE 1. Crosier Neighborhood, South Akron

			Occupations (Percentage)			
	Homes	Workers	Rubber	Craft	Other Industrial	Common Labor
1913	108	110	34	16	34	6
1920	353	331	53	15	19	4

Source: Akron Official City Directories for the years cited.

[94] "The Rubber Trade in Akron," IRW 53 (1916): 250; "The Rubber Trade in Akron," IRW 62 (1920): 525. Also see George W. Knepper, Akron: City at the Summit (Akron, 1981), pp. 101–105.

[95] Akron Bureau of Municipal Research, Reports, 1920 (Akron, 1920), pp. 30, 33.

[96] "Reports of Our Organizers," Machinists' Monthly Journal 29 (1917): 611.

[97] FHA, "Akron, Ohio, Housing," p. 132.

[98] Edward Mott Woolley, "Akron: Standing Room Only," McClure's, July 1917, p. 14.

[99] Warren A. Emery to Walter V. Bingham, Oct. 19, 1921, Walter V. Bingham Papers, Box 2, Carnegie-Mellon University, Pittsburgh.

year plants. At the time of the 1913 strike, this neighborhood was on the city's southern periphery. Its unpretentious but inexpensive houses enabled residents to live comfortably, with room for vegetable gardens, chickens, and cows. During the next seven years the building boom and the conversion of single-family houses into apartments tripled the area's population. By 1920, 93 percent of the inhabitants were newcomers; only twenty-three of the families who had lived in the neighborhood in 1913 remained. Along Grant Street, the major north-south artery, shops occupied the ground floors of many houses. Most residents were now rubber workers and a majority were renters. Traffic, street noise, and refuse had become serious disamenities.

Those who sought to escape their cramped and often inhospitable surroundings faced other difficulties. The Bureau of Municipal Research found that Akron workers spent twice as much as the average American worker for recreation "because of the limited opportunities afforded by Akron for free or inexpensive recreation such as parks, playgrounds, and free band concerts."[100] Saloons, gambling halls, poolrooms, and brothels flourished. In 1918 city officials felt compelled to establish a venereal disease clinic to cope with a public health menace that had reached epidemic proportions. The clinic treated more that one thousand five hundred victims, or nearly 1 percent of the population, in its first year.[101]

A second, related factor that probably influenced the fate of the local labor movement was the marked change in the character of the rubber industry labor force. Although it is dangerous to generalize about a group that ranged from 15,000 in 1914 to 73,000 in 1920 (and to 20,000 in 1921) and was highly mobile, several points seem clear. In 1910 the Akron population of 69,000 was 55 percent native, 44 percent immigrant, and 1 percent black. By 1920 the population of 208,000 was 60 percent native, 37 percent immigrant, and nearly 3 percent black.[102] Because of the city's rapid growth, the 5-percent change in the native-born population represented 87,000 individuals, enough men and women to account for nearly all of the additional rubber workers. Given the employers' recruitment and Americanization policies, it is likely that the rubber workers as a group became younger, less experienced, ethnically and culturally more homogeneous, and more likely to be impressed with the immediate benefits of a job in a rubber plant.

The immigrant population, while declining, also changed. In 1910 it was

[100] Akron Bureau of Municipal Research, *Reports, 1920*, p. 31.

[101] Ibid., p. 65.

[102] U.S. Department of Commerce, Bureau of the Census, *Thirteenth Census of the U.S.* (Washington, 1913), 3, *Population, 1910*, p. 418; *Fourteenth Census of the U.S.* (Washington, 1920), 3, *Population, 1920*, p. 797.

overwhelmingly central European. Hungarians and Germans accounted for half of Akron's foreign-born residents and nearly half of the native-born children of immigrant parents. In 1920 the Hungarians and Germans were only a quarter of the foreign-born total. The British and Irish share also fell, from 19 to 12 percent, while the proportions of Italians, Greeks, Russians, and Austrians had all doubled or nearly doubled. Many of the new ethnics lived and worked differently. The Italian community, which became the largest and most identifiable local immigrant group of the 1920s, spurned south Akron for North Hill, an area isolated from the rubber plants by a deep valley that was not bridged until the early 1920s. The city directories for 1919 and 1920 report few rubber workers on North Hill. The other nationalities are harder to trace, but directory listings for south Akron neighborhoods suggest that they, too, gravitated to construction, retailing, and service jobs. The city's black population, which grew more rapidly than any of the European ethnic groups and led all Ohio cities in percentage increase, had a similar experience. A few hundred found positions in the rubber plants, but the majority became service workers or day laborers.[103]

These changes substantially altered the fabric of working-class life. The clubs, societies, and churches that had served as social and intellectual centers since the turn of the century became less prominent. The saloons that had enlivened most south and east Akron neighborhoods also disappeared with the advent of prohibition. The new workers brought their own institutions. The number of Roman Catholic churches increased from six to eleven, and the number of Baptist churches rose from five to eleven. In 1913 Akron had had no Eastern Orthodox churches; in 1920, it had seven.

The effects of these changes on the union potential may be implied from the fate of the local Socialist movement. In the early 1910s, worker militancy had gone hand in hand with the rise of the Socialists in local politics. AFL leaders worked with Prevey, workers ran on the Socialist ticket, and the south Akron neighborhoods provided most of the Socialists' votes. In 1913 the labor-radical alliance came within two thousand votes of controlling the city government. Given the rapid increase in factory employment, the fears of Republicans and Democrats of an eventual Socialist triumph seemed well grounded. In fact, the Socialist tide receded as quickly as it had risen. In 1915, the Socialist mayoral candidate's share of the greatly enlarged electorate fell from 29 to 25 percent, and he ran a poor third. The Socialist councilmen elected in 1913 lost to Democratic candidates in the south Akron wards and to Republicans in the downtown and near west Akron wards. The Socialists' totals increased, but not as much as their oppo-

[103] *Thirteenth Census,* 3: 418; *Fourteenth Census,* 3: 797; Spurgeon Bell, Ralph J. Watkins, and Others, *Industrial and Commercial Ohio* (Columbus, 1928), 1: 149.

nents'. Judging from the neighborhoods that supported the Socialists and the continuing tie between the Central Labor Union and the radicals, it is likely that the Socialists, like the unions, maintained their hold on older workers and recruited additional skilled employees, but failed to attract the semiskilled and unskilled workers, native and foreign-born, who flooded the city.[104]

After 1915 the significance of the Socialist decline is harder to assess. In 1917 the Socialist mayoral candidate received less than 17 percent of the total vote. He was less well known than his predecessor and the party was divided nationally over the war. Most of the defectors probably voted for I. S. Myers, the Democratic candidate, who had ties to organized labor and had promised not to enforce laws against gambling and prostitution. Many rubber workers supposedly favored a "wide open town."[105] The Socialists never again mounted a serious challenge. Like the unionists, they found that conditions that might have favored them were in fact decidedly hostile.

Marguerite Prevey's career after 1917 symbolized the radicals' fate. A signer and prominent supporter of the July 1917 St. Louis Manifesto, which opposed the war and split the national Socialist movement into pro-war and antiwar factions, she became an increasingly vociferous critic of American involvement. In June 1918, she presided over the Canton, Ohio, rally that led to Eugene V. Debs's trial and imprisonment. She provided his bond and was one of his closest confidants during the trial.[106]

In March 1919, Prevey's house was Debs's last stopping place before he reported to prison. When a story appeared in local newspapers that city officials would not allow him to speak in Akron, Prevey "put on her bonnet . . . and took a bee line for the Mayor's office." In "two minutes" she had won a retraction from Myers. "No bluff goes with Marguerite," Debs reported.[107] During Debs's stay, other prominent radicals, including John Reed and James Larkin, an Irish revolutionary, also visited her house. After Reed and Larkin left, Prevey predicted that if Debs were jailed, "the country will wake up to find it is in the throes of a revolution. . . . There will be so many acts of violence that the jails will be unable to hold the participants. I'm not afraid of whatever may come."[108]

---

[104] *ABJ*, Nov. 3, 1915; *The People* 16 (May 4, 1917): 1.

[105] *ABJ*, Nov. 7, 1917.

[106] Ray Ginger, *The Bending Cross: A Biography of Eugene V. Debs* (New Brunswick, 1949), pp. 378–92; Nick Salvatore, *Eugene V. Debs, Citizen and Socialist* (Urbana, 1982), pp. 294.

[107] Eugene V. Debs to Theodore Debs, March 23, 1919, Eugene V. Debs Papers, microfilm copy.

[108] "Report of Special Agent Garrison," March 28, 1919, Department of Justice Papers, RG 60, File 200724, National Archives.

Later, she joined Reed and other left-wing Socialists in forming the Communist Labor Party. Indicted with other CLP members in January 1920 under the Illinois criminal syndicalism act, she was "kidnapped" by Ohio police, taken to Chicago, and sentenced to a brief prison term.[109] On her release she remained active in Communist party affairs and ministered to the imprisoned Debs. Her marriage had broken up in 1917, probably because of the growing controversy around her (Frank, more attuned to the opportunities of the war period, became a Ford dealer), and she sold her house to Frank Seiberling, who erected an office building on the site. After 1920 she lived in her summer house at Portage Lakes, south of Akron, with Charles Baker, a prominent Ohio socialist who had been imprisoned during the war and was active in the Communist Labor Party. Together they operated a modest bookstore.

Throughout this period, Prevey was oblivious to the rubber workers. She recounted her experiences during the 1913 strike to the state Socialist convention in June 1919, but drew no parallels between 1913 and 1919. She worked briefly as a CLP organizer among southern Ohio coal miners but not among the rubber workers. She was not acquainted with Newman, Tate, or the other Machinists. Her few surviving letters provide no clue that she was aware of the Wobbly resurgence. Apparently she no longer viewed the rubber workers as agents of change in industry or society.[110]

By the end of the decade, then, the relationship between the rubber workers and organized labor was no clearer than it had been in 1913. The manufacturers had developed new links to their employees; the radicals had lost their foothold in the industry. The workers, far more numerous than in 1913, were no less interested in doing something for themselves. For some, the best approach seemed to lie in career employment, for others, in rapid job changes. Neither approach foreclosed union affiliation. If the boom had continued beyond 1920, it is conceivable that new organizations might have appeared. As it was, the recession and the continuing technological revolution in the industry changed the nature of the workers' opportunity and the subsequent pattern of organization.

[109] Charles Baker, "Strangling American Workers!" *The Toiler Educational Leaflet* (ca. 1920), FBI Papers, RG 65, Reel 647.

[110] John S. Menefee, "Report," July 8, 1919, FBI Papers, RG 65, Reel 647; Marguerite Prevey to Eugene V. Debs, Nov. 17, 1921, Debs Papers.

CHAPTER FOUR

Maturity, 1920–1929

ALTHOUGH HE NEVER made a tire, a boot, a balloon, or a surgeon's glove, Wilmer Tate (1885–1944) had much in common with the midwestern rubber workers of the 1910s. Born in rural Illinois and raised in northern Iowa, he farmed alongside his father until he was thirty, when he followed thousands of other rural workers to the war-boom towns. He arrived in Akron with a wife and four children in 1915 and found a job at International Harvester and later at the Imperial Electric Company. By 1919 he had become a machinist and the owner of a large, unattractive frame house on Beardsley Street south of Crosier Street. Like many of his neighbors, he rented part of the house to a rubber worker. And like most Akron machinists, he joined the International Association of Machinists and participated in the 1919 strike. By 1920 he was a close friend of business agent Sam Newman and a part-time organizer, known for his fiery rhetoric. Then disaster struck. Tate lost his job and house in the postwar recession and was informally blacklisted because of his union ties. He spent most of the next decade as a municipal worker, and he and his family moved permanently down the socioeconomic scale. Yet these experiences only made him more vocal. As corresponding secretary and guiding spirit of the CLU in the 1920s, he kept alive the memory of the wartime campaigns and the dream of a rubber workers' union.[1]

THE POSTWAR RECESSION AND AFTER

The recession of 1920–1921 initiated a painful adjustment process that continued through the decade and gave the rubber industry the "profitless prosperity" and "dog eat dog" competition that Howard and Ralph Wolf emphasized in their *Rubber: The Glory and the Greed* (1936). The casualties included the boom atmosphere, the tight labor market, and the wage increases that had made Akron and other rubber manufacturing centers meccas for upwardly mobile workers. Other things did not change. The power of the largest firms continued to grow as they performed more steps in the manufacture and sale of their products. The pace of product improvement continued, and the rate of productivity advance was almost identical to that

[1] Carl A. Tate, interview with author, Aug. 8, 1984.

of the 1910s. Nor did anyone question the desirability of mass production, scientific management, or career employees. Most personnel programs survived the recession and became more elaborate in the ensuing period of labor surplus. The manufacturers' hostility to union activity also remained a constant.

Accustomed to boom conditions, most manufacturers did not treat the buoyant business climate of 1918–1920 as a novelty. They continued to borrow, to build, and to hire new employees. In Akron, rubber industry employment rose from forty thousand at the end of the war to seventy-three thousand in April 1920, when the boom reached its peak. Even a break in commodity prices and the cancellation of some orders in mid-1920 did not have much effect. In July, when total employment had fallen to fifty-eight thousand, Litchfield announced that the "low-water mark" had been reached and that the future was bright.[2] A prominent Akron banker reassured local citizens that "the depression will come and go without leaving any failures in its wake."[3] A confident Harvey Firestone took his family to England for the summer. Yet business continued to worsen. By winter the "little slump" had become the most severe downturn since the 1890s, by some measures the most severe recession in American history.[4]

The immediate crisis forced manufacturers to cut production and reduce their debts. For the highly leveraged, vertically integrated tire makers, this was a novel, painful experience. Goodyear had large stocks of rubber and cotton that it intended to pay for with the proceeds of tire sales. When raw materials prices and sales declined simultaneously, the company was left with huge debts and no cash. By the end of 1920 it was illiquid, insolvent, and at the mercy of the investment banking firm of Dillon Read, which provided a much-needed loan in exchange for operating control and a high annual fee. The Seiberling brothers formally resigned in May 1921, their fortunes depleted and their Goodyear stock temporarily worthless. A few months later they bought the bankrupt Portage Rubber Company plant in Barberton and inaugurated the Seiberling Rubber Company. Thanks to their contacts and a new commitment to conservative finance, Seiberling became one of a handful of successful large factories. At the same time, Frank Seiberling became the leader of a prolonged campaign to wrest control of Goodyear from its "absentee" bankers and overthrow P. W. Litchfield, who had taken advantage of the stockholders' eclipse to pursue his dreams.

The plight of the other large manufacturers was less traumatic. Through

---

[2] *ABJ*, July 29, 1920.

[3] "The Rubber Trade in Ohio," *IRW* 62 (1920): 677.

[4] See Charles P. Kindleberger, *The World in Depression, 1929–1939* (Berkeley and Los Angeles, 1973), pp. 32–33.

drastic retrenchment and new financing, Goodrich narrowly avoided bankruptcy and reorganization. Harvey Firestone rushed back from England in September 1920 to direct a ruthless liquidation that obviated the need for long-term borrowing. His decisive action made Firestone the industry's low-cost producer and price leader in the 1920s. U.S. Rubber's Charles Seger was likewise able to avoid large additions to the company's long-term debt. The smaller manufacturers, with relatively little inventory, generally fared better. About 10 percent of the nation's tire companies went out of business during the recession.[5]

Apart from Seiberling and approximately one hundred Akron millionaires who were reduced to more modest circumstances, the burden of the recession fell largely on the rubber workers. Between July and December 1920, all of the jobs created in the Akron plants since 1915 disappeared as employment fell from 73,500 to 19,600. Goodyear abolished 28,000 positions and Firestone, 15,000. Goodyear foremen conducted a "man by man appraisal" in an effort to save the best workers. By early 1921 the eight-hour day had become "a thing of the past"; all tire plants worked one ten-hour shift.[6] In south Akron, Goodyear Heights, and Firestone Park, the results were devastating. Of the 343 families in the Crosier Street neighborhood in 1920, 171 had left by 1922. Forty-seven moved to other addresses in the city—like the Tates, perhaps, to cheaper, rented dwellings—and 124 disappeared. Unable to find new renters, the 172 families that remained made the best of their de facto single-family houses and onerous mortgage payments.[7] They were not alone. All night-shift employees in Trenton lost their jobs, as did four thousand National India workers in Bristol. By January 1921, ten thousand U.S. Rubber employees were out of work in Rhode Island alone.[8] Fisk Tire adopted a three-day workweek in order "to find partial employment for as many operatives as possible."[9]

[5] Frank Robert Chalk, "The United States and the International Struggle for Rubber, 1914–1941" (Ph.D. diss., University of Wisconsin, 1970), p. 43; Glenn D. Babcock, *History of the United States Rubber Company: A Case Study in Corporate Management* (Bloomington, 1966), p. 161.

[6] Goodyear Tire & Rubber Co., "Statement to the Fact-Finding Board, Nov. 30, 1935," Federal Mediation and Conciliation Service Papers, RG 280, File 182/1010, National Archives; Paul W. Litchfield, *Industrial Voyage: My Life As an Industrial Lieutenant* (Garden City, 1954), p. 202; Directors' Minutes, Firestone Tire & Rubber Co., Firestone Archives, Firestone Tire & Rubber Co., Akron, Ohio; United States Rubber Co., "Industrial Relations Activities of the United States Rubber Co., 1922" (New York, 1922), p. 16, in Archives Organization File, Box 75, (Labor-Management Documentation Center, Cornell University); "The Rubber Trade in Ohio," *IRW* 63 (1921): 448.

[7] *Akron Official City Directory, 1922* (Akron, 1922).

[8] "The Rubber Trade in Rhode Island," *IRW* 63 (1921): 358; "The Rubber Trade in Rhode Island," *IRW* 63 (1921): 446.

[9] "The Rubber Trade in Massachusetts," *IRW* 63 (1921): 277.

This share-the-work arrangement was one of the few features of the career employment plans of the 1910s that remained in effect during the recession.

The impact of the American recession extended around the world. In East Asia, crude rubber prices collapsed just as the vast new areas planted in 1913 were maturing. By 1921 only the best-run plantations showed a profit; the rest entered the era of straitened circumstances and narrowed outlooks that W. Somerset Maugham captured in his stories of the East. The British government responded with the so-called Stevenson Plan to restrict rubber production. The plan, which operated from 1922 to 1928, led to wild price fluctuations, which severely hurt the smaller, weaker tire makers. A total of 133 firms, mostly small non-Akron companies formed during the war boom, failed between 1922 and 1929.

Among larger companies, the Stevenson Plan encouraged efforts to neutralize the British initiative. In the early 1920s Harvey Firestone led a campaign for an American rubber cartel that enlisted Commerce Secretary Herbert Hoover. After a spectacular price rise in 1925, the other manufacturers joined him in a private buyers' pool that provided the coup de grâce to the Stevenson Plan. In the meantime the large firms integrated backward more vigorously. U.S. Rubber and Goodyear expanded their Sumatran holdings, Firestone bought a huge tract in Liberia, and the Ford Motor Company began to develop a rubber plantation in Brazil. Only Goodrich among the major producers continued to depend wholly on outside suppliers. By 1930 U.S. Rubber produced one-third of its rubber, and Goodyear, perhaps one-fifth. Firestone's Liberian plantations did not make a substantial contribution until the mid-1930s. Ford's Brazilian experiment was a costly failure.[10]

One other consequence of the recession, the managerial upheaval at Goodyear, also had far-reaching implications for the industry. By removing the Seiberlings and subordinating the stockholders' interest, the Dillon Read plan created a managerial vacuum that Litchfield quickly filled. The new president, Edward Wilmer, was an outsider whose prime objective was to safeguard the bankers' investments. He brought in new men to manage the company's finances but otherwise did not interfere with day-to-day operations. Litchfield was pleasantly surprised when he found Wilmer skeptical "but . . . not unfriendly" to personnel work.[11] As a result, the Goodyear personnel programs weathered the recession better than most Goodyear employees.

[10] Charles R. Whittlesey, *Government Control of Crude Rubber* (Princeton, 1931), p. 137; Chalk, "International Struggle for Rubber," pp. 55–56; Mira Wilkins, *The Maturing of Multinational Enterprise: American Business Abroad from 1914 to 1970* (Cambridge, 1974), p. 99; Randolph R. Resor, "Rubber in Brazil: Dominance and Collapse, 1876–1945," *Business History Review* 51 (1977): 363.

[11] Litchfield, *Industrial Voyage*, p. 208.

By 1922 Goodyear was profitable again and Wilmer turned over most of his duties to the company's marketing head, George Stadelman, who became president in 1923. Stadelman died three years later and Litchfield succeeded him. Though the internecine warfare among Goodyear stockholders went on for years, the "clash between financial and industrial thinking," which Wilmer's arrival had signaled, was over.[12]

Litchfield's first goal was to select a group of key subordinates. He sought "young men, steeped in the Goodyear tradition of hard-driving, concerted action."[13] Clifton Slusser topped his list. In 1919 Litchfield had appointed Slusser to manage the company's new Los Angeles plant. In 1921 he recalled him to help cut manufacturing costs and then put him in charge of the factory staff departments. In 1926 he appointed him vice-president for manufacturing, a notable coup for the thirty-seven-year-old executive. (Slusser's success was not without personal costs. He became an alcoholic, though his drinking did not become widely known until the 1930s.) Litchfield chose equally youthful men to head sales and finance and promoted inexperienced, promising executives to top positions. Edwin J. Thomas, the most important of these men, became personnel director in 1926 at the age of twenty-seven. By the end of the decade Litchfield had gathered around him a group of managers who embodied his conceptions of vigor and success.

Litchfield simultaneously forced a new era of competition on the industry. The crisis of 1920 and the decline in the growth of auto and truck production in the mid-1920s demanded a new business strategy. Firestone and Seiberling proposed a defensive posture based on stable market shares and higher unit profits. Litchfield rejected their approach in favor of continued expansion; if Goodyear's growth could not come from an expanding market, it would have to come from the market shares of other manufacturers. As the company's finances improved, he committed himself to expansion and greater integration. The other manufacturers had little choice but to follow.

In the 1920s Goodyear became the leading U.S. manufacturer of tire cord. Besides mills in Killingly, Connecticut, and Los Angeles that dated from the 1910s, it acquired a New Bedford mill in 1924 and another in Passaic in 1926. When Litchfield discovered that the Passaic mill was losing money because of high wages, he closed it and moved the machinery to Cedartown, Georgia. That move was so successful that Goodyear purchased another plant at Cartersville, Georgia, and built a large mill at Rockmart, Georgia, in 1929. It operated company towns at all three sites and

[12] Ibid., p. 201.
[13] Ibid., p. 214.

*7. Goodyear president Paul W. Litchfield (second from left) and vice-president
Clifton Slusser (on Litchfield's left) receive the first tire made in Gadsden, June,
1929. Goodyear Tire & Rubber Company Archives.*

introduced many of the benefit and recreational programs that were available to Akron workers.[14]

The other manufacturers soon bought additional plants of their own. Firestone purchased three Massachusetts mills—at Fall River in 1924, New Bedford in 1927, and Newburyport in 1929. U.S. Rubber acquired a mill at Winnsboro, North Carolina, in 1921, and Goodrich built a mill in Silvertown, Georgia, in 1928.

In December 1928, Litchfield announced his most controversial step, a new tire plant in Gadsden, Alabama. Though Goodyear, Goodrich, and Firestone had all built Los Angeles factories since World War I, their moves reflected the area's rapid growth and isolation from midwestern manufacturing centers. Gadsden's only advantage was a labor-cost differential. There were fewer drivers in the South than in other regions, and most raw material costs were at least as high as in Akron. Gadsden city officials offered land, a construction loan, and low taxes, but their concessions were only marginally more liberal than the inducements Akron officials were prepared to offer. Litchfield insisted that labor costs were not the

[14] Hugh Allen, *The House of Goodyear: Fifty Years of Men and Industry* (Akron, 1949), pp. 357–58.

key and that Akron would not suffer. Whether he was truthful or not, the specter of "decentralization" appeared. Never again would it entirely disappear.[15]

The Gadsden plant was a feature of Litchfield's boldest initiative, a cost-plus manufacturing contract with Sears Roebuck that assured Goodyear "unquestioned leadership in the tire business" and Sears a major role in the replacement market. Initiated in 1926, the arrangement was renewed in 1928 on condition that Goodyear build the Gadsden factory, and in 1931 after Goodyear offered various financial concessions.[16] By providing Sears with tires at less than wholesale prices, the contracts devastated the independent retailers, including those with whom Goodyear dealt. In 1922 independent retailers sold 98 percent of all tires; in 1928, 85 percent; and in 1934, only 58 percent. More than thirty-five thousand of them failed between 1926 and 1929. Other manufacturers soon established similar ties with Montgomery Ward, Western Auto, and the petroleum companies. Firestone introduced a chain of retail stores to ensure its position in the replacement market, an innovation that the other major companies, including Goodyear, soon copied. The Goodyear-Sears tie was the "most important reason" for the manufacturers' meager profits in the 1920s.[17]

To this atmosphere of upheaval and conflict, scientists and engineers added other potent irritants—changes in products and manufacturing processes that made the factory a microcosm of the marketplace. In the 1920s the larger tire firms completed their transition to mass production. Given the intensity of competition in the industry, the principal beneficiaries were motorists. The victims included stockholders, less imaginative or affluent manufacturers, and the workers. Already buffeted by recession and diminishing employment opportunities, tire workers faced unrelenting pressures to work faster and more effectively. While their efforts were well rewarded in the short term, they had even less reason than the manufacturers and dealers to look upon their age as a time of easy and complacent prosperity.

"Better tires," as Litchfield recalled, "came out of the 1921 depression."[18] Straight-sided, high-pressure cord tires, dominant by the early 1920s, gave way to low-pressure balloon cord tires after 1924. Because of this change, other advances in compounding and tire design, and an ever-increasing number of paved roads, a tire made in 1930 was good for about

---

[15] See *ABJ*, Oct. 31, 1928.

[16] Howard Wolf and Ralph Wolf, *Rubber: A Story of Glory and Greed* (New York, 1936), pp. 472–73; Boris Emmet and John E. Jeuck, *Catalogues and Counters: A History of Sears, Roebuck and Company* (Chicago, 1950), pp. 389–90; Michael French, "Structural Change and Competition in the United States Tire Industry, 1920–1937," *Business History Review* 60 (1986): 39.

[17] Lloyd G. Reynolds, "Competition in the Rubber-Tire Industry," *American Economic Review* 28 (1938): 461.

[18] Litchfield, *Industrial Voyage*, p. 209.

15,000 miles of driving, three times the 1920 average. The average motorist of 1920 bought three replacement tires at $45 each; in 1930 he bought two new tires at an average of $15 each. Tire costs fell from about $3.50 per 1,000 miles to about $.65 per 1,000 miles. Motorists responded by driving more miles at higher speeds, saving the industry from an even more drastic reorganization.[19]

Scientists and engineers also reduced manufacturing costs by redesigning machines and production processes. Their achievements sustained the industry's position on the frontier of technical advance and created additional disadvantages for small and weak firms. The most notable breakthrough occurred between 1917 and 1919, when Ernest Hopkinson, a patent attorney at U.S. Rubber, invented a "flat-band" tire-building machine that soon superseded the "core" machine for auto tire building. With the Hopkinson machine, the builder assembled the tire on a circular drum. The completed carcass was cylindrical; it acquired its characteristic appearance in the curing process. The flat-band method eliminated many opportunities for judgment and error; the work became "completely standardized" and could be done "very rapidly." Most important, it did not require "any particular strength on the part of the tire builder." The physical elite, the most distinctive element of the industry's labor force, became dispensable in the auto tire rooms.[20]

In 1930–1931 U. S. Rubber executives carried this process one step further. They employed a group of consultants to devise a tire assembly line. After months of experimentation, the consultants built a circular turntable equipped with ten single-function machines. This "merry-go-round" greatly increased the output of the ten operators and eliminated much of the skill that remained in the tire builder's job. "Merry-go-round" employees could learn their jobs in a week or ten days as opposed to the six weeks to six months necessary to learn how to operate a flat-band machine. However, the new machines were uneconomical on the short production runs characteristic of the industry and therefore of limited value. Apparently, no other tire manufacturer installed a merry-go-round until the late 1930s, though some tried to introduce the "principle" of sequential assembly.[21]

With these exceptions the technological changes of the 1910s and 1920s

[19] Wolf and Wolf, *Rubber*, p. 466; John Dean Gaffey, *The Productivity of Labor in the Rubber Tire Manufacturing Industry* (New York, 1940); Ralph William Frank, "The Rubber Industry in the Akron-Barberton Area: A Study of the Factors Related to Its Development, Distribution, and Localization" (Ph.D. diss., Northwestern University, 1952), p. 144.

[20] Boris Stern, "Labor Productivity in the Automobile Tire Industry," U.S. Bureau of Labor Statistics, *Bulletin No. 585* (July 1933): 50–51.

[21] Babcock, *History of United States Rubber*, pp. 292–95; Stern, "Labor Productivity," p. 52; Gaffey, *Productivity of Labor*, p. 91.

8. The Goodyear "pit." Curing tires before the advent of the watchcase
vulcanizer. Goodyear Tire & Rubber Company Archives.

usually affected the simplest functions and least-skilled jobs. "The outstanding characteristic of all tire plants, small and large alike," wrote Boris
Stern after a detailed study of six factories, "is the effective utilization of
all types of conveyors." By the mid-1920s, they linked every step from the
crude-rubber warehouse to the tire storeroom. The immediate effects were
a "great reduction in the labor force as well as a very large increase in the
average man-hour output of the plant." In one case the installation of a
conveyor between the curing and final inspection departments reduced the
labor force in those departments by one-third. The truckers were the most
obvious casualties, but the conveyor made it possible to dispense with some
of the inspectors as well.[22]

In virtually every department, machines made the work faster, simpler,
and less labor intensive. In preparatory work, for example, the introduction
of machines that extruded a continuous rubber tube ready for compounding
resulted in a "very large displacement of labor." In one plant 80 percent
of the employees became redundant. In the mill rooms of the plants Stern
studied, Banbury mixers had displaced 40–60 percent of the employees. In
the tire rooms, the flat-band machine revolutionized the assembly process
but machinery also radically changed the preparation of wire beads and the
rubber strips (chafers, cushions, breakers) that helped cushion and protect
the tire. In bead making, "the transition . . . has been exceedingly rapid"

[22] Stern, "Labor Productivity," p. 61.

and workers "are rapidly being displaced by various labor saving devices." According to Stern, an even larger displacement had occurred in the manufacture of chafers, cushions, and breakers.[23]

In the curing room, the most notable new machine was the "watchcase" vulcanizer. The traditional method was to load twenty-five to forty tires, each in a separate mold, into a "pot heater." With the new machine, each tire went into a separate "watchcase." In one case the watchcase machines reduced the labor force from 208 to 15.

Pot heaters (4 lines of vulcanizers curing 18,000 tires per day):

Gang leaders	12
Pressmen	20
Loaders and unloaders	44
Tire removers	16
Tire placers (into molds)	12
Other workers and helpers	104
TOTAL	*208*

Watchcase vulcanizers (battery of vulcanizers curing 7,500 tires per day):

Pressmen	12
Helpers	3
TOTAL	*15*

Output per worker was 86.5 and 600, respectively. Despite this disparity, the "enormous expense involved in completely scrapping the old equipment" slowed the introduction of watchcase vulcanizers. In 1933 the transition was "far from being even halfway completed."[24]

Inner tube manufacture also changed with the substitution of the "molded" tube process for the "mandrel" process. Molded tubes required less labor and were cured in circular molds that eliminated seams. Stern reported an increase in output per worker of 100 percent in one plant.[25]

As factories became more integrated and machinelike, they also became more dependent on human initiative. The transition to mass production entailed large risks; the new capital-intensive technology paid off in greatly reduced costs only if the machines were fully utilized. Conversely, delays and interruptions were more costly than in old-fashioned plants. Executives had little choice but to depend more on management systems and acknowledge the enhanced power of the machine operators.

Goodyear was the leader in industrial engineering techniques during the postwar decade. By 1920 the Efficiency Department set individual piece

[23] Ibid., pp. 39–42, 49–50.
[24] Ibid., pp. 59–60.
[25] Ibid., p. 70.

rates for 81 percent of the production employees and group rates for others who worked in "pools." Goodyear policy was to "eliminate wherever possible pool operations so each employee is entirely dependent on himself."[26] Rate setters used conventional stopwatch studies. Hugh Allen reported that they worked in the open in an effort to get "an accurate measurement of a fair day's accomplishment . . . by an average good man." Slusser "insisted on a full day's work, but it had to be a fair day's work as well."[27]

Once the time study men had gathered their data, Goodyear officials tried to set a rate that would reward skill and effort, preserve equity between various jobs, and retain the best workers. In 1919 they introduced a formula that assigned weights to "unpleasant or dangerous job conditions," the "strenuousness" of the task, and the time required to learn it. In 1920, representatives from Efficiency and the Industrial Assembly devised a more elaborate system. They identified twelve variables—"heat, danger, dust, fumes, noise, effect on body, effect on clothes, application, monotony, responsibility, time to develop the average experienced man," and "strenuousness." Time study clerks were to obtain information "from those best informed of actual conditions" and then compare each "step in a job" with "similar elements of other operations."[28] Individual workers who were dissatisfied could appeal to the supervisor or the Industrial Assembly. Still, time studies and the company's policy of cutting rates when earnings exceeded 110 percent of the predicted wage or "base rate" remained the sources of most wage grievances in the 1920s and 1930s. Rate cuts, condemned by time study theoreticians but dictated by economic reality, preserved the association between time study and rate cutting that dated from the appearance of the nefarious "Sherlock" Holmes.

Given the competitive pressures of the 1920s, most of the other tire companies adopted similar techniques. Goodrich executives, for example, employed the Bedaux Company to install an incentive wage system in the Akron plant and then in other Goodrich factories. In other plants there were efforts to eliminate machine-paced jobs, which restricted the fastest workers, in favor of time studies and incentive wages.[29]

Though systematic comparisons are impossible, the evidence that has survived suggests a pattern consistent with Stern's data and the Goodyear example. Where mass production and scientific management were intro-

---

[26] Fact-Finding Board, "Findings and Recommendations of the Board," FMCS Papers, RG 280, File 182/1010, pp. 29–30. Also see "President's Annual Report to the Board of Directors," Dec. 31, 1921, Goodyear Papers.

[27] Allen, *House of Goodyear*, p. 182.

[28] "Proposed Zoning of Piece Work Operations," Oct. 1, 1920, Goodyear Papers.

[29] Stern, "Labor Productivity," p. 25.

duced, the laborers disappeared, the work became less strenuous, and the pace increased. Slusser quipped in the early 1930s that "all jobs are white collared in comparison with '21.'"[30] A better measure of that phenomenon was the growth of the female labor force, which had been decimated in 1920 but increased to nearly 20 percent of the total in the Akron plants by 1930. By that time the tire-building and -curing rooms were the only remaining exclusively male preserves.

In contrast, the rubber footwear and mechanical goods factories were placid industrial backwaters. There were twenty-two footwear plants in 1929, the same number as in 1899. Employment grew slowly but steadily until 1925, then stabilized and remained almost constant for the rest of the decade. The number of mechanical goods firms and employees grew by about 50 percent during the decade, reflecting the start of a boom in industrial rubber products that would sustain many firms through the depressed years of the 1930s. Yet the statistics disguise the continued decline of U.S. Rubber, the largest employer of both footwear and mechanical goods workers, and the growth of employment in small industrial products firms, mostly in the Midwest.

U.S. Rubber's managerial problems dated from its origins as a turn-of-the-century trust but worsened rapidly in the 1920s. In 1926 U.S. Rubber fell behind Goodyear in total sales (it had lost its leading share of the tire market in the late 1910s). By the end of the decade it was a distant second. The company lost money in 1926, 1928, and 1929, much to the distress of the du Pont family, which had bought a majority interest in 1927 on the assumption that the 1926 performance was atypical. The decline was most glaring in the tire division. Seger and J. Newton Gunn never worked well together and the latter resigned in 1923. Seger then tried to run the tire division himself, with disastrous results. A survey at the end of the decade reported a shocking state of disorganization. The performance of the footwear division was little better. In the 1920s, U.S. Rubber still operated nearly all the plants of the original combination and made little effort to improve technology. Labor costs were more than one-third higher in U.S. Rubber plants than in the footwear industry as a whole.[31]

During the late 1910s and 1920s, some of the plant executives introduced piecemeal improvements. In 1917, the manager of the Naugatuck, Connecticut, plant had employed Frank B. Gilbreth, the prominent industrial engineer, to conduct motion studies and improve operations in the millroom. Gilbreth's work led to "important changes in equipment and meth-

---

[30] Text of Local 18282 Conference with Goodyear, March 20, 1935, National Labor Relations Board Papers, RG 25, Box 15, File 333, National Archives.

[31] Babcock, *History of United States Rubber*, pp. 222, 226, 289.

ods."[32] The Naugatuck managers also introduced "making teams" of specialist workers in the assembly rooms, a step toward assembly line operations.[33] Officials of the American Rubber Company in Cambridge, Massachusetts, installed a conveyor that moved shoe lasts while each worker performed a single, specialized assignment. Executives at Mishawaka Woolen and Rubber installed conveyors, rigorous production and inventory controls, and punch card machines to keep records of orders and invoices. Walter H. Norton, manager of the Lycoming Rubber Company, introduced an extensive efficiency plan that included inventory controls, time and motion studies, and improved layouts. Sanford E. Thompson, a prominent engineer, reported the introduction of production control plans, route charts, job analyses, and time studies in several plants.[34]

When Francis B. Davis succeeded Seger in 1929, he authorized a sweeping reorganization of the footwear division. By 1932 U.S. Rubber had closed eleven factories and had concentrated footwear production at Naugatuck and Mishawaka. Norton, the new Naugatuck manager, installed the machinery and methods he and other executives had experimented with in the 1920s. Most notable was an assembly line that increased the speed of production and obliterated the skills of the aristocratic boot makers. Production quintupled with little additional investment and unit costs declined by 50 percent. The Naugatuck plant was probably the industry's low-cost producer by the early 1930s. The price of success was the elimination of thousands of workers, including many veteran employees who had been part of the U.S. Rubber "family" for decades. Because of the company's dire financial condition, they received little or no compensation.[35] Employees in the Naugatuck area enjoyed greater security, but they worked under very different circumstances. The old regime in the rubber footwear industry disappeared quickly and dramatically in the early 1930s.

The story of U.S. Rubber's mechanical goods operations is similar. After considerable study, Davis's engineers decided to concentrate mechanical goods production at Passaic and to close the other five plants. By the mid-1930s they had created a smaller but more efficient division, ready to take advantage of the resurgent demand for industrial products.

[32] Ibid., p. 130. Frank B. Gilbreth to Lillian M. Gilbreth, Jan. 30, 1922, Frank B. Gilbreth Papers, Box 6, Purdue University, West Lafayette, Indiana.

[33] Constance McL. Green, *History of Naugatuck, Connecticut* (Naugatuck, 1948), p. 226.

[34] Babcock, *History of United States Rubber*, pp. 223–25, 228, 297–98; Sanford E. Thompson and Willard E. Freeland, "Saving Through Management in Rubber Industry," *Management and Administration* 9 (May 1925): 2–3.

[35] Babcock, *History of United States Rubber*, pp. 302, 369. Green, *Naugatuck*, pp. 255–56. However, some workers moved to Naugatuck, and others, at the Hartford tire plant, received generous settlements ("Bonuses Paid by a Rubber Factory to Discharged Workers," *Monthly Labor Review* 29 [1929]: 118).

WORKERS IN THE 1920S

The recession, the consolidation of the tire industry, the extension of mass production, and the rescue of U.S. Rubber were major influences on wages and working conditions during the 1920s. The collapse of 1920 provoked widespread wage cutting, though the decline in living costs offset most of the loss. In Akron, real wages actually rose in 1921.[36] As economic conditions improved, wages and earnings rose. Most tire companies also returned to the eight-hour day in 1922 and introduced the five-and-a-half-day week in the following years. What was missing was the boom atmosphere and the opportunities that had accompanied it. Wages rose more slowly after 1921, and a substantial wage differential continued to distinguish Goodyear, Firestone, Goodrich, and U.S. Rubber from the other plants. For tire workers of the 1920s, bigger was unquestionably better.

Employment conditions, together with the migrant networks established in the 1910s, sustained the flow of southern farmers to Akron in the 1920s. Goodyear, Firestone, and Goodrich, which accounted for most of the new jobs in the industry after 1921, became increasingly selective, though the nature of their selectivity is difficult to gauge. Often it had a distinctly traditional flavor. At least in the early 1920s, employment managers continued to favor applicants with large muscles and thick calluses. Interviews customarily began with the demand: "Let's see your hands."[37] For those who could pass the initial test, ultimate success or failure depended on the needs of the day and the whims of the employment official. At times, novices were favored. At others, such as the period in 1922 after Kelly-Springfield closed its Akron plant, experienced workers received preference.[38] To the workers, at least, there was no rhyme or reason to the hiring process. Some applicants were lucky; others were not.

The workers' sense of powerlessness was strongest when rumors spread that the rubber companies were recruiting in Appalachia. Despite frequent company disclaimers and promises to "discourage a floating population," the rumors were common and in some cases accurate.[39] In May 1922, the manufacturers called for one thousand new workers, despite a backlog of one thousand three hundred names on the lists of the state employment office, explaining that the unwanted applicants were either physically unfit or unskilled for the available jobs. Many workers asked whether that was

[36] Amy Maher, *Ohio Wage Earners in the Manufacture of Rubber Products, 1914–1928* (Toledo, 1930), pp. 34, 38.

[37] Los Angeles rubber workers report similar experiences. Lee Springer, interview with author, Aug. 15, 1977.

[38] Oliver H. Bosley, interview with author, Oct. 23, 1973.

[39] *ABJ*, Jan. 4, 1921.

true "or is it a method to insure a surplus of labor?" One discouraged job seeker had "seen experienced men turned down by the scores."[40] Stories of " men from other states. . . being hired" while "we Akron men are left stranded" persisted through the decade. By common agreement, such practices were "a rotten deal." Whether the outsiders were enticed or not, they severely burdened local charitable agencies and exacerbated tensions between local residents and transients.[41]

Nearly all potential rubber workers sooner or later confronted Lou Hannah, the legendary Firestone hiring boss. A man of the old school, crusty, profane, and shrewd, Hannah left vivid memories. "That guy knew everything . . . when it came to hiring people, he knew."[42] "He was pretty smart. He never forgot your name . . . and he could pretty well tell whether a guy wanted to work or not."[43] Walter Kriebel, newly arrived from southern Ohio in 1925, recalled his interview.

He said "What you been doing?" I said, "Well, I been off working on a sawmill." He said, "That hard work?" I said "Yes that's hard work." He said "Let me see your hands." And I stuck them in his face just like a couple of bear paws and he kind of looked at them and said, "I got a good job for you."[44]

Hannah's old-fashioned methods could not obscure the fact that the personnel experts had substantially eroded the foremen's powers. One man, hired at Goodyear in 1925, recalled that his new foreman at first refused to accept him. "Hell," the supervisor explained, "we got men laid off here with two years service," and sent him back to the employment office. The perplexed worker found himself in the middle of a tug of war between line and staff managers, though the outcome was only briefly in doubt. When he told the personnel manager what had happened, the manager ordered him back to the original department with instructions to "put this guy to work."[45]

The attack on turnover, which had provoked so many innovations in the 1910s, became moderately more successful in the 1920s. Data from U.S. Rubber and Goodyear show a pronounced decline in layoffs, the traditional bane of rubber workers. At U.S. Rubber they rose to 80 percent of total separations between July and December 1920 as business declined. By the summer of 1921, when the recession ended, they were only one-third of

[40] *ABJ*, May 1, 1922.

[41] *ABJ*, May 4, 1926, Jan. 13, 1928, July 22, 1924, Jan. 29, 1925, July 11, 1925.

[42] Oliver H. Bosley interview.

[43] Walter Kriebel, interview with author, Sept. 19, 1972; also Rex Murray, interview with author, Sept. 19, 1972; Jack O. Abshire, interview with author, Nov. 15, 1972.

[44] Walter Kriebel interview.

[45] John D. House, interviews with author, April 15, May 1, 1973.

the total. During the next year and a half, they ranged from one-third to less than one-tenth of all separations.[46] The Goodyear data, which cover a longer period, reveal a similar pattern. Boris Stern's study provides an additional measure of the effect of personnel management. His statistics for three small companies in 1926 and 1929 indicate far greater instability than at Goodyear, though the beginning of the Depression had an adverse effect on Goodyear and two of the three small companies.[47]

The U.S. Rubber data provide another illustration of the role of management in the decline of labor turnover. Litchfield and Slusser directly controlled the destiny of most Goodyear employees, while Ching could only advise. As a result, personnel practices at U.S. Rubber varied widely, depending on the local manager's receptivity to the Ching program. In 1922 total turnover in the footwear plants ranged from 28 to 170 percent; in the mechanical goods plants, from 6 to 225 percent, and in the tire plants, from 104 to 157 percent. Layoffs ranged from zero to 80 percent of all separations. Compared with Goodyear, eight of fourteen footwear plants, eight of nine mechanical goods plants, and one of four tire plants (significantly, the Morgan & Wright plant in Detroit) had better layoff records.[48] The relatively favorable performance of most of the footwear plants partly reflects the close relationship between Ching and the footwear executives, just as the relatively unfavorable performance of the tire plants underlines Ching's difficulties there.

The most striking feature of the data for both companies, however, is the pattern of quits or voluntary departures, which accounted for at least two-thirds of the variation in the turnover rate in every year after 1921. The trend is unmistakable: when times were bad and employment possibilities were limited, as in 1921 and 1929, workers kept their jobs; when conditions improved, they became more adventurous. John D. House's oral history memoir provides an illustration of the behavior of many Goodyear employees in the mid-1920s. In early 1926 he and other tire builders walked out over a piece-rate reduction. Most of the men returned the next day but he went to Firestone, where Hannah hired him and he started to work the following night.

But with that one night I began to suspect that things there weren't as good as they might be. So I hedged a little bit. I called up the Goodyear and told them I was ill and I worked another night out at the Firestone and was sleeping when a fellow from Goodyear came to the house and inquired about my health. And of course I

[46] U.S. Rubber, ''Industrial Relations Activities.''
[47] Stern, ''Labor Productivity,'' p. 36.
[48] U.S. Rubber, ''Industrial Relations Activities.''

did look seedy and convinced him that I was ill but that I was improving and would be back within a day or so.[49]

After another night at Firestone he returned to Goodyear.

In the aggregate, the results of this process were staggering. Between 1921 and the end of 1929, Goodyear hired 87,525 workers to maintain a labor force that never exceeded 18, 766 and averaged only 12,995. From the recession low of 1921, the company added about 10,000 jobs; the rest of the "new" employees were replacements for those who quit or were laid off. When 87,525 is multiplied by 2 or 3 to account for the other Akron firms, the fluidity of the local labor market is apparent.[50] Nor was Akron atypical. In 1922, when turnover at Morgan & Wright was 104 percent, U.S. Rubber executives considered that figure "very good indeed" because the average for Detroit industries was 150–200 percent.[51] It is also clear why confrontations with Hannah and other employment executives are among the rubber workers' most vivid recollections.

Despite continued lip service to the goal of "regularization," Akron employers probably lost little sleep over the comparatively meager results of their career employment programs. Technological change had reduced their dependence on the physical elite, and the consolidation of the industry provided a steady supply of experienced workers. As long as they retained a few thousand career employees in key positions, the costs of high employee turnover were negligible. In the 1930s, when limited employment opportunities revived the workers' interest in job security, they would rue the day they had introduced the idea of permanency.

The failure of career employment was only one example of the clash between the new order in the industry and the independence of the rubber workers. Management efforts to realize the potential of the new technology led to frequent conflicts over production standards and wages. Here, for example, is the recollection of Oliver H. Bosley, a Firestone tire builder.

The tire builders set up a limit [on production] and they wouldn't go over that limit regardless of what the company did. . . . [The managers] threatened to fire people. They threatened to do everything but [the tire builders] wouldn't go over the limit. . . . When I got to making out, they said, "Now, don't you make over a certain amount."

We had the limit because we didn't want the company to make a race track out of the place. . . . I could have made more money, but I worked hard enough.[52]

[49] John D. House interviews.
[50] Goodyear, "Statement to the Fact-Finding Board." Goodyear employment ranged from a low of 7,300 in 1921 to a high of 18,800 in 1929, and total employment in the Akron plants ranged from 19,500 to 58,200.
[51] U.S. Rubber, "Labor Relations Activities."
[52] Bosley interview.

Goodrich and Goodyear workers make similar statements. Ralph Clark, an Ohioan who worked in the new Firestone plant in Los Angeles, summarized the consensus when he recalled that "everybody had it in their mind that you gotta hold this down."[53] There is also agreement that supervisors knew of the limits and tolerated, even encouraged, them. After all, if production varied greatly from worker to worker, they, as well as the workers, would look bad.

The workers' recollections make it equally clear that their primary concern was not mass production or scientific management but the hoary tradition of piece-rate cuts. Most employers acknowledged that they cut rates when the worker's earnings exceeded the base rate by an unacceptable margin, usually 10 percent or more. E. C. Cowdrick, a veteran industry observer, reported that Goodyear managers cut rates "even when the increase was due to the effort of the men themselves." He believed that the cuts "nullified much of the effect of the other excellent policies of the management."[54] If the rubber workers had been highly skilled, they might have resisted through a union or an informal bargaining arrangement. Since they were not, they relied on their ability to compromise the potential of the new technology. For mass production workers, this "veto" could be as effective as the strongest union.

The question, then, is not why workers restricted production but why employers did not take their new management systems more seriously. Historians have been far too intrigued with the romance of "workers' control" and too little concerned with the actual practice of scientific management. By the 1920s Taylorism had produced observable differences in purchasing, accounting, marketing, and other business functions, but in the more pedestrian realm of the incentive wage, a strange amalgam of superficial innovation and traditionalism prevailed. Stanley Mathewson's study of manufacturing plants at the end of the decade suggested that the practice of the tire plants was indeed the practice of much of midwestern industry.[55] Managers spent large sums to install and maintain incentive wage plans, but made little effort to come to grips with their meaning. Why did they worry about paying higher wages for even higher production? Why did they settle for 110 percent when, for a small increase in pay, 120 or 130 percent was feasible?

There are several possible answers. They might have been concerned

[53] Ralph Clark, interview with author, Aug. 16, 1977.

[54] E. S. Cowdrick Memo, July 16, 1936, Special Conference Committee Records, in U.S. Senate, Subcommittee of the Committee on Education and Labor, *Hearings*, 76th Cong., 1st sess. (Washington, 1939), 17071.

[55] Stanley B. Mathewson, *Restriction of Output Among Unorganized Workers* (New York, 1931).

about the effects of an even more frantic pace on their employees' health or morale, or about unduly raising expectations, as they had in 1913. They might also have been victimized by the supervisors, industrial engineers, and clerks who administered the management systems. These individuals, nearly all dedicated career employees, were concerned primarily with maintaining their precarious toehold on the ladder that raised them above the rubber workers. They preferred employees who were steady and predictable, and they depended on periodic time studies and mechanical innovations to increase output and productivity. They, too, were part of an informal web of understandings that favored the status quo. Creatures of scientific management, they found it too dangerous to embrace without reservation.

WORKERS' ORGANIZATIONS

In his respected *The Rubber Workers* (1944), Harold S. Roberts dismissed the postwar decade as a barren period of omnipotent employers and cowed workers when "there were no serious efforts to organize."[56] He then turned to the 1930s, and the "serious efforts" of the New Deal years. His approach tells more about the values and assumptions of liberal historians in the 1940s and 1950s than it does about the workers or the industry. A more careful examination of the postwar decade suggests substantial continuity between the 1910s and 1920s and, indeed, the 1920s and 1930s. There were no fewer "serious" efforts to organize after 1921 than before. Nor did the pattern of stimulus and response change; aspiring organizers of the 1920s continued to operate in the shadow of Marguerite Prevey and Sam Newman. Among the rubber workers, "normalcy" implied continuity, not reaction.

The tire workers' organizing activities occurred principally in three overlapping efforts that spanned the years 1921–1929. The first, by conventional trade unionists in 1922 and 1923, was a continuation of earlier efforts to enlist the Akron rubber workers in AFL organizations. From the unionists' perspective, the future looked no less bright than it had in 1913 and 1919. Jobs were relatively plentiful, workers showed signs of restlessness, and local union veterans were eager to help. Newman, president of the Central Labor Union from 1920 to 1922, and Tate, his right-hand man, were as fiery as Prevey and as orthodox as Cal Wyatt. They faced formidable obstacles but their prospects were bright enough to warrant a substantial investment of time and money.

[56] Harold S. Roberts, *The Rubber Workers: Labor Organization and Collective Bargaining in the Rubber Industry* (New York, 1944), p. 87.

The most encouraging development of 1922 was the revival of worker militancy. As the pool of unemployed rubber workers shrank and the turnover rate increased, worker resistance to the manufacturers' economy moves also grew. It was no accident that reports of new recruiting efforts coincided with the first strikes. Between May and December 1922, there were five strikes at Akron area tire plants, the last of which evoked memories of 1913. There were four additional strikes in the early months of 1923. In seven of the nine cases, the immediate cause was a piece-rate cut; in several, the cuts also symbolized more substantial changes in production methods, as they had at Firestone in 1913. Given the relative shortage of experienced workers, the strikers often succeeded. Thus Goodrich tube workers, who struck in May 1922, when the company reintroduced the eight-hour day but did not increase their rates, won a modest increase.[57] Firestone tire builders, who struck because a wage increase was not as large as the increase awarded lesser employees, won similar concessions. Mason Tire employees, who struck when the company introduced an incentive wage, went back to work in return for a rate adjustment.[58]

The most important of the strikes began at Goodrich on December 26, when the company implemented a rate cut for "band" builders, the men who prepared plies for the tire builders. The workers had used a long Christmas weekend to plan their response. As many as 100 first-shift workers walked out, and others from the second and third shifts joined them. When a committee visited the Goodrich employment manager, he agreed to reinstate them but not to revoke the rate cut. The men refused to go back. On December 29 many tire builders also walked out, raising the number of strikers to 600. Together they met at the CLU hall to adopt resolutions and select leaders. Afterward their representatives "emphatically declared" that their only goals were reinstatement and restoration of the old rates. Their informal organization was "not affiliated in any way, nor will it be."[59] Nevertheless they continued to meet at the CLU hall, to demand negotiations, and to prepare picket signs and placards.

During the first week of January, the Goodrich strike began to evoke memories of 1913. On January 4, 500 men marched from the CLU hall to the Goodrich gate. They carried large banners: "Big Strike On, Cord Tire Department, B. F. Goodrich Co." Their enthusiasm probably peaked the next day when strike leaders reported 750 to 770 men out, some for as long

---

[57] *AP*, May 27, 1922; *ABJ*, May 30, 1922. Alfred W. Jones reports an abortive 1921 AFL effort to organize a rubber workers' union. I have found no other evidence of this activity (Alfred Winslow Jones, *Life, Liberty, and Property: A Story of Conflict and a Measurement of Conflicting Rights* [Philadelphia, 1941], p. 79).

[58] *AP*, May 29, 1922; *ABJ*, May 31, 1922, March 7, 1923.

[59] *AP*, Dec. 29, 1922.

as ten days. Thereafter their demonstrations were less spirited, and some of the men began to drift back. By January 15 only 200 strikers still held out.[60]

Although the Goodrich strikers failed to enlist other workers or to win concessions, they raised the hopes of Akron labor leaders. On January 13, CLU leaders distributed handbills announcing a mass meeting the next day to organize an AFL union. Newman acknowledged that the Goodrich strike "virtually started the rubber factory discussion." On January 14, he, AFL organizer T. J. Conboy, and various local figures spoke for nearly four hours to an enthusiastic audience of approximately 500. Afterward they enlisted approximately 200 members and Newman announced that he would seek an AFL charter and hold weekly rallies. Conboy pledged to remain until the union was firmly established. The only sour note came the next day when the Goodrich strikers voted to return at the new, lower rate. Their leaders explained that the majority of strikers "opposed . . . the union move."[61]

In the following weeks the AFL campaign gradually stagnated. The weekly rally attracted 800 rubber workers on January 21, and a "fair-sized" crowd on January 28, but when Max S. Hayes, a well-known Cleveland labor leader, spoke on February 25, only 250 listeners appeared.[62] Conboy remained through January; after that, Akron CLU leaders were left to direct the campaign. Scattered newspaper references suggest that Newman spent much of his time in Cleveland, pleading for organizers and financial support. His task at home was no easier. He had to answer critics who argued that he would precipitate a 1913-style conflict, that rubber workers were not union-minded, and that the AFL was obsolete. His reply, that a union would "prevent another 1913 . . . standardize the industry, make the workers more permanent," and "create greater civic pride" was in vain.[63] By March, the campaign was dead.

The manufacturers added the coup de grâce. On February 18, Goodyear announced a 10 percent bonus to "cut down turnover." Firestone made an identical adjustment, which "virtually amounts to an increase in pay."[64] Goodrich, Miller, Mohawk, and other companies introduced bonuses the following day. Newman took credit for the bonus, but most rubber workers were too busy celebrating to listen. At Firestone their "spirit" immediately became "much better."[65] The following summer, when the busy season

[60] *ABJ*, Jan. 5, 12, 15, 1923.
[61] *ABJ*, Jan. 15, 1923.
[62] See *ABJ*, Jan. 22, 26, 29, 1923.
[63] *ABJ*, Feb. 14, 1923. Also see *ABJ*, Jan. 24, 27, 29, Feb. 10, 14, 1924.
[64] *ABJ*, Feb. 19, 1923.
[65] C. L. Smith to W. W. Benner, Feb. 22, 1923, Firestone Papers.

was over and the union was dead and the workers' "spirit" was less important, the manufacturers canceled the bonuses. In the meantime, the Akron Employers' Association mounted a campaign to identify union members. Aware of this effort, Newman and Tate kept the membership lists and initiation fees in the Locomotive Engineers Bank in Cleveland. When the union collapsed and Newman left to join the Machinists' International staff, he turned the money and records over to other local AFL officials. "Consequently, before six months had passed, many of those who had signed application cards were fired from their jobs . . . and the money all spent."[66]

After the spring of 1923, Tate and his allies faced even greater obstacles. As the city's machinery industry declined, the Machinists and other metal workers' organizations lost their former prominence and the building trades unions increasingly dominated the local labor movement. Construction union leaders were primarily interested in providing opportunities for their own members, which meant establishing contacts with the rubber companies. Sometime in the mid-1920s they struck a deal; they agreed to resist efforts to organize the rubber workers in exchange for the employment of union men on factory construction projects. In the mid-1930s Cliff Slusser recalled that he had gotten along "peaceably" with Frank Patino, business agent of the Bricklayers, "and no one knew when he came in or when he left or how many times he had been here."[67] Nearly forty years later, Patino still boasted of his relationship with Slusser, though he denied any deal.[68] In 1929 when Tate and James McCartan, a prewar Socialist and Typographical Union activist, proposed to launch another campaign to organize the rubber workers, Patino and the building trades leaders were uninterested. By that time the relationship between the AFL and the rubber workers, always uncertain and frequently unhappy, had resulted in a de facto divorce that would keep them apart for the foreseeable future.

The second effort to organize rubber workers was political and began, like the prewar Socialist movement, in the south Akron neighborhoods where the legacy of the boom was a continuing source of turmoil. Of various lingering problems, the plight of the schools was probably most critical. As the young rubber workers married and started families, Akron's student population exploded. It quintupled between 1910 and 1930, creating "endless problems in financing, staffing and housing the evergrowing

[66] United Rubber Workers of America, *Twenty Years of Effective Service to Our Members, Community, Country* (Akron, 1956), p. 5.

[67] Text of Local 18282 Conference with Goodyear, April 16, 1935, FMCS Papers, RG 280, File 195/335. Also see Roberts, *Rubber Workers*, p. 87; James S. Jackson, interview with author, Oct. 5, 1973. The "deal" did not include the California plants (see *Los Angeles Times*, Oct. 28, 1929; *ATP*, July 26, 1926).

[68] Frank Patino, interview with author, Dec. 18, 1973.

number of school age children."[69] And while overcrowding was common in all parts of the city, it was most severe in south Akron, where the largely Protestant working class depended on the public school system. The school board built eight elementary schools and three high schools between 1910 and 1920, but the necessity of building in all parts of the expanding city minimized the effect in any given area. South Akron residents began to see themselves as victims of west Akron's economic elite, who dominated the school board, and north Akron's Catholics, who were indifferent to the public school system. Gradually they realized that if they acted in concert they could outnumber their opponents. The school issue became the key to the political mobilization of the rubber workers in the 1920s.

The agency that organized the rubber workers was the Ku Klux Klan, which appeared in 1921 in the midst of the school conflict and dominated the city's political life until 1926. The Klan's appeal in Akron, as in other cities swollen by large numbers of southern migrants, was cultural; it attracted Goodrich and Goodyear employees, prounion and anti-union workers, Republicans and Democrats, Methodists and Baptists, the relatively well-to-do and the poor. In Akron, like other cities, "the typical Klansman was decent, hardworking and patriotic." Most Klan activists were anti-immigrant, antiblack, and, more demonstrably, anti-Catholic, but "never once resorted to violence" to attain their objectives.[70] They sought a larger political and cultural role for south Akron, a larger share of the school budget, and public acknowledgment of their social ethic—prayers and Bible readings in schools, enforcement of vice laws, and restrictions on Sunday business and public entertainment.

The leaders of the south Akron rebellion were rarely the rubber workers themselves. Joseph B. Hanan, the most able and influential Klan leader, was assistant office manager at B. F. Goodrich. Kyle Ross, the most outspoken Klan politician, was an executive at a small manufacturing firm. Ernest E. Zesiger, a prominent Klan backer, was a lawyer and former officer of the Carpenters' union and the CLU. Klan representatives elected or appointed to the school board included a butcher, a realtor, a lawyer, a mortician, and the wives of a dentist and a streetcar conductor. Another

[69] John Lee Maples, "The Akron, Ohio Ku Klux Klan, 1921–1928" (M.A. thesis, The University of Akron, 1974), p. 11; George W. Knepper, *Akron, City at the Summit* (Akron, 1981), p. 119.

[70] Maples, "Akron Klan," p. 111. Also see Kenneth T. Jackson, *The Ku Klux Klan in the City, 1915–1930* (New York, 1967), p. 238; Ronald E. Marec, "The Fiery Cross: A History of the Ku Klux Klan in Ohio, 1920–1930" (M.A. thesis, Kent State University, 1967), p. 56. John T. Walker and other scholars have recently documented the movement of many native-born Socialists into the Klan in the 1920's. Very likely this happened in Akron, too, though fragmentary evidence suggests that most Socialists were immigrants, whereas most Klan members were native-born newcomers.

school board member with Klan backing was an auto dealer. Their common bond was an association with the rubber workers. The merchants' stores were in south or east Akron, often in their houses. The lawyers' offices were in declining commercial neighborhoods. Though well-known to their neighbors, these men had little influence in the chamber of commerce or bar association. In 1923 and 1924, as the Klan's political might became apparent, many local politicians also joined. The mayor, sheriff, county prosecutor, clerk of courts, two of three county commissioners, and several city council members, including Ross, were reputed Klansmen. Dow Harter, the area's chief federal prohibition agent and later its New Deal congressman, was also a member.[71]

These men orchestrated a continuous series of parades, demonstrations, and cross burnings designed to impress local residents with their might and unity. The Klan approach to public holidays was symptomatic of their general approach. Before 1913 the CLU-sponsored Labor Day parade had been a high point of the civic year for south Akron residents. During the boom years, however, competing celebrations had gradually eclipsed the CLU parade. In 1922, for example, the rubber companies' athletic programs and a mass meeting of Italian societies highlighted the city's festivities. The Klan soon reclaimed Labor Day for south Akron. Massive parades through downtown streets in 1925 and 1926, with thousands of Klansmen in full regalia, overshadowed all other activities and recalled the formidable parades of costumed workers a quarter century before. At the July 4 rally in 1925, a national Klan official announced that the Akron organization was the largest local Klan body in the country, with fifty-two thousand members. None of the ten thousand or more men and women who had gathered to cheer him disputed his arithmetic.[72]

Important though public demonstrations were to rank-and-file morale, Klan leaders devoted most of their energy to less public endeavors. In November 1923, a secretive Klan campaign elected three members to the school board; a few months later Klansmen arranged the appointment of a fourth member, giving them a majority. For the next two years the Klan representatives ran the board; they provided additional funds for south Akron projects and appointed a Klansman as superintendent. School board politics became heated, and the division between south Akron and the rest of the city became sharper. The city council, similarly reflecting Klan influence, banned Sunday dancing and debated a ban on all Sunday commercial activity. With the help of a large and mysterious band of part-time deputies,

[71] Maples, "Akron Klan," p. 111.

[72] *ABJ*, Sept. 5, 1922; Maples, "Akron Klan," pp. 36, 101. Ronald Marec writes that Summit and Franklin counties both had over fifty thousand members ("Fiery Cross," p. 77).

the sheriff curbed gambling and traffic law violations. Hooded men presented sympathetic ministers with large donations and school principals with Bibles.[73]

The Klan's bumptious style, its association with violence and crime elsewhere, and its threat to the social and political status quo attracted a growing legion of opponents. In 1921, when it first appeared, the city's leading newspaper, the *Akron Beacon Journal*, attacked it for its secrecy and intimidating tactics. City officials were also critical at first. In the spring of 1922, when the Klan first sought to hold mass public rallies, leaders of the Universal Negro Improvement Association and the NAACP protested strongly, and the executive secretary of the black YMCA secured an injunction preventing the Klan from using the local armory. Rev. John J. Sculler of St. Vincent's Church, the city's Irish Catholic congregation, and Rev. Lloyd C. Douglas of the First Congregational Church, a liberal congregation of mostly west Akron residents, also attacked the Klan.[74] However, as the Klan became more powerful, its potential victims adopted a lower profile. A January 1923 anti-Klan rally, organized by an Italian businessman, attracted only a handful of participants.

Thereafter the opposition had a strongly west Akron flavor. Its leaders, like the Klan leaders, were merchants, lawyers, ministers, and their wives, but they were prominent storekeepers, distinguished attorneys, and ministers of elite churches. Their offices were downtown, and their customers and clients lived around them. On example illustrates the difference. M. C. Heminger, a well-known Klansman, and Wendell L. Willkie, a leading Klan opponent, lived within one hundred yards of each other on Beck Street in west Akron. Heminger had a flourishing south Akron real estate business, an office on South Main Street, and many rubber-worker customers, while Willkie, the 1925 president of the city bar association, had a downtown office, big-business clients, and little or no contact with rubber workers.[75] A handful of shrewd Republican politicians also opposed the Klan, but rubber industry executives did not. Like the immigrants, Catholics, and blacks, they had good reasons for maintaining a discreet silence.

A confrontation between Klan and anti-Klan activists on the eve of the 1925 school board elections highlighted these divisions. An October 29 rally sponsored by the Nonpolitical Public School League, the anti-Klan organization, attracted a large Klan contingent. When E. W. Brouse, a prominent attorney, accused the state Klan organization of corruption and

[73] Maples, "Akron Klan," pp. 41–42.

[74] *ABJ*, Sept. 1, 1921; Marec, "Fiery Cross," pp. 23–24.

[75] See Ellsworth Barnard, *Wendell Willkie: Fighter for Freedom* (Marquette, 1966), pp. 66–67; Mary Earhart Dillon, *Wendell Willkie* (Philadelphia, 1952), p. 32; Steve Neal, *Dark Horse: A Biography of Wendell Willkie* (New York, 1984), p. 21.

criminal acts, Klan supporters responded with jeers and shouts of "That's a lie!" Reverend Douglas followed Brouse. Peace and social harmony, he argued, depended on "neighborliness and friendship . . . and as long as one group tries to control the schools for all groups, there will never be any of this friendliness." Despite boos, Douglas continued: "The city of Akron is sick. It is full of personal prejudices, hatred and narrowness. Akron is the biggest little town in the country." His charges evoked a crescendo of boos, jeers, and cries of "Get rid of him," "Get him out of here." Observers feared a riot.[76] Douglas had struck a raw nerve. Parochial, insecure, and sensitive to slights by their economic or social betters, Klan members saw in the urbane, snobbish minister a symbol of the forces that thwarted and exploited them.

South Akron Klan members soon found themselves on the defensive. Their strident, simplistic message and heavy-handed tactics frightened or offended many residents who had been initially sympathetic. Klan candidates lost by large margins in the 1925 elections. Hanan resigned his post shortly thereafter, leaving a void that was never filled. Scandals involving the Klan in other states and a power struggle in the Ohio hierarchy disillusioned others. In late 1926 a dissident group of perhaps three thousand five hundred withdrew from the Akron Klan.[77] By late 1927 the local organization was bankrupt. In 1928 it ceased to function, and rubber workers and their cultural allies again found themselves without a public advocate.

The third organizational effort among the rubber workers provided the most important rebuttal to the image of worker docility in the 1920s. Goodyear's Industrial Assembly and U.S. Rubber's Factory Councils, introduced in 1919, were formidable organizations of rubber workers. They symbolized the potential of the company union movement and illuminated the obstacles that impeded and gradually defeated the liberal thrust of personnel work. In many cases the most formidable barrier was the hostility of line executives who disliked upstarts like Cyrus Ching. They also resented the demands that company unionism imposed on them and feared that it would open the door to an outside, adversarial union. At U.S. Rubber, they retained sufficient power to limit Ching's work. As a result some U.S. Rubber plants still did not have company unions at the end of the decade. Even in the footwear division, where resistance was minimal, the Factory Councils do not seem to have had any influence on the massive consolidation that cost thousands of workers their jobs.[78] Goodyear was

[76] *ABJ*, Oct. 30, 1925.

[77] Maples, "Akron Klan," p. 102.

[78] See Cyrus S. Ching, *Review and Reflection: A Half Century of Labor Relations* (New York, 1953), p. 34; Cyrus S. Ching, Oral History Memoir, vol. 1, Columbia University; George Froelich, interview with author, Jan. 11, 1978.

different. Litchfield's towering presence, his careful recruitment of subordinates, and his policy of shifting executives between line and staff jobs, as well as the company's highly centralized organization, foreclosed the possibility of managerial sabotage. But if there were no challenges from "above," were there threats from "below" in the form of apathy, mistrust, or rebellion? Could Goodyear managers maintain an organization of workers known for their transiency and individualism?

The first real test of the Industrial Assembly came during the winter of 1920–1921, as the company lunged toward bankruptcy and layoffs mounted. Despite highly publicized "achievements," the assembly still bore an uncomfortable resemblance to the hundreds of company unions formed after World War I to stifle trade unionism and political radicalism. Its role in the 1919 Machinists' strike in particular was controversial. One worker inadvertently condemned the assembly when he admitted that he had "not heard the suggestion of strike action on the part of anybody here since the Industrial Relations Plan was started."[79] Given this background, the assembly's role during the recession would be a crucial test of its credibility. Litchfield was not oblivious to this fact. He kept in touch with Assembly leaders, encouraged the House and Senate to discuss retrenchment policies, and urged the representatives to do what they could to mitigate the workers' plight. Such measures, by themselves, probably would have been insufficient. The experiences of other company unions suggest that only a tradition of benevolence and consultation, and a willingness by executives to observe this tradition during the recession, permitted them to emerge unscathed.[80] Goodyear passed this crucial test.

During the latter months of 1920, assembly members devoted most of their time to the crisis. They proposed a layoff plan that emphasized the retention of workers with houses and families. Litchfield vetoed the bill on the ground that it did not consider merit or service. On reconsideration, the assembly members agreed. Later they asked that foremen and assembly representatives jointly determine who would go. Litchfield approved this proposal. The assembly played a similar role when the company cut wages. It approved the reductions in return for promises of "a check on the new scale to prevent injustice . . . [and] give every Goodyearite a square deal." Goodyear executives agreed to allow assembly committees to "review all existing classifications of rates" and to defer any hiring until current employees were on a five-and-a-half day week.[81] In March 1921, as the recov-

[79] See C. A. Cadd to U.S. Department of Labor, Nov. 27, 1935, FMCS Papers, RG 280, File 195/335; WCL, Sept. 24, 1929.

[80] Daniel Nelson, "The Company Union Movement, 1900–1937: A Reexamination," Business History Review 56 (1982): 335–57.

[81] WCL, Oct. 19, 1920, Nov. 23, 1920, Jan. 11, 1921.

9. The Industrial Assembly election of September, 1920. Goodyear Tire & Rubber Company Archives.

ery began, the assembly won company approval for shift assignments by seniority. When Goodyear again cut wages in March and September, the assembly sought to ensure that "no injustice was done," after narrowly rejecting stronger action.[82]

The Industrial Assembly thus fared far better than most company unions and most Goodyear employees. Not only did it survive, but won improved working conditions for the remaining employees. In early 1922, the assembly demanded, and Litchfield agreed to, a small wage increase. As a result, the five thousand to six thousand workers who had not been laid off emerged from the recession with relatively high wages, lucrative fringe benefits, shop floor preferences reminiscent of trade union contracts, and an organization that had almost instant access to any executive. Not surprisingly, the assembly and the veteran workers became closely identified. The Industrial Assembly became in effect a "union" of the oldest and most experienced Goodyear employees. By trade union standards, it was an "industrial" organization; by any other measure it was an elite body.

The following months of unrest and turmoil in the Akron plants posed more challenges for the assembly. Tensions that resulted in strikes at the other plants took the form of conflict within the Industrial Assembly. In the

[82] *WCL*, March 30, 1921, April 12, 1921; *ABJ*, Sept. 7, 1921.

October 1922 elections, all six incumbent senators and nine of seventeen incumbent representatives lost. The new assembly, led by Tracy Douglas in the Senate and Aubrey Hoofman in the House, demanded a 15-percent wage increase. Litchfield vetoed the resolution in early January, at the time of the Goodrich strike and the nascent AFL campaign, apparently on the assumption that assembly representatives trusted him "to do the right thing."[83] He soon discovered his mistake. After "considerable debate" the Senate voted 13 to 4 to override the veto; the House tally was equally lopsided. The Goodyear directors affirmed the veto, but only after considerable publicity and embarrassment. Assuming that the workers were somehow misinformed, Litchfield ordered an elaborate study of wages and living costs in Akron and elsewhere to substantiate his conclusion that a wage increase was "not justifiable." Again he miscalculated. The representatives listened to his report and then voted to raise the minimum wage from $4.00 to $5.00 per day for men and from $2.80 to $3.50 per day for women. Realizing at last that conditions had changed since 1921 and that Goodyear employees were no less sensitive to wages and living costs than other rubber workers, Litchfield retreated. He ordered a 10-percent increase, disguised as a temporary attendance bonus, setting off the chain reaction that helped undermine the AFL campaign.[84]

It is impossible to know whether the AFL effort, which undoubtedly affected the actions of the other companies, also influenced his decision. Most likely the assembly troubled him far more than the AFL. Goodyear had had no strikes in 1922, and any AFL-oriented group must have been small, secretive, and intimidated. The rebellion of the Industrial Assembly, on the other hand, was a serious threat, not because Douglas, Hoofman, and the others were likely to join the AFL, but because their persistent agitation threatened to break the links between managers and workers that were the raison d'être of the assembly. An alienated company union was no more useful than an AFL local. For the work of the assembly to proceed, it was necessary to make concessions, as it had been in 1921.

Litchfield concluded from this experience that his original plan for the Industrial Assembly had been defective. In 1919 he had envisioned the assembly as a forum that would address the challenges of industry from the same perspective that he did. In practice, however, assembly members devoted their attention to details or to issues like the wage question that threatened to undermine the organization. The solution, Litchfield concluded, was to immerse the assembly in the details of running the plant. Such a reorganization would enable the representatives to do what they understood

---

[83] *WCL*, Oct. 11, 1922, Nov. 8, 1922.
[84] *ABJ*, Jan. 9, Feb. 3, 7, 1923.

and at the same time avoid problems like the wage dispute. Litchfield authorized a joint House-Senate committee to study the internal operations of other company unions. Assembly representatives visited the White Motor and American Multigraph plants in Cleveland, the Pennsylvania Railroad shops in Pittsburgh and Altoona, and the Bethlehem Steel complex in Bethlehem. Apparently they did not visit any U.S. Rubber plants.[85] Their conclusions were embodied in a bill, which Litchfield approved, establishing a series of committees with labor and management representatives. After November 1923, each Senate district had a committee composed of six assembly representatives and six management representatives. Joint general committees on wages, working conditions, safety, and welfare considered issues that were not settled at the district level. A Joint Conference Committee served as a committee of last resort. Ordinarily the assembly would not debate an issue until the appropriate committee had considered it. The committee system served as a "clearinghouse" for grievances and made foremen and other low-level line and staff managers an "integral" part of the assembly. Henceforth there would be no surprises.[86]

The reforms were an immediate success. Assembly representatives became more self-confident and Goodyear executives learned more about "what's on the worker's mind" than they wanted to know. A typical district meeting considered a piece-rate allowance for defective materials, the ratio of mill workers to calender workers, a dispute over piece rates and seniority, a request for new time studies, the company's hospitalization policy, streetcar service around the plant, complaints about ventilation in the compounding room, local milk prices, and a proposal to transfer all aliens to the night shift. The discussions were often heated.[87]

As the assembly became more active, it also became more costly. Besides the policy discussions noted above, there were 373 grievance cases in 1924 and 448 in 1925. In 1919, worker representatives averaged 900 hours per month on assembly work. In 1925 they averaged 2,860 hours per month, or nearly 25 percent of each representative's workday. The management representatives spent almost as many hours and became severely burdened. Seeing no end in sight, Litchfield intervened in December 1925. He ordered the assembly to operate on a budget and refused to pay for more than 1,500 hours per month, or half the time spent on assembly business in 1925. Assembly leaders acquiesced after Slusser assured them that the 1,500-hour limit was flexible.[88]

[85] "Fourth Assembly 1922–23," p. 3, Industrial Assembly File, Goodyear Archives.

[86] Ibid.; "Memorandum, Sept. 9, 1935," NLRB Papers, RG 25, Box 15, File 333; Allen, *The House of Goodyear*, p. 185.

[87] See statement by E. S. Cowdrick in U.S. Senate, *Hearings*, p. 17071; *WCL*, Feb. 27, May 21, 1924.

[88] *WCL*, Jan. 20, 1925, Feb. 17, 1926.

The decision not to fight the curb seems to have been part of a deal that assembly activists, led by Hoofman, hoped to strike with Litchfield. Surmising that Litchfield would feel compelled to make some compensating concession to keep the good will of the assembly, Hoofman pushed through a bill calling for a 12.5 percent wage increase as soon as the House and Senate had approved the 1,500-hour limit. Litchfield responded with a veto, citing the high wages of Goodyear employees and the tumultuous international situation arising from the Stevenson Plan. The veto outraged the assembly leaders, who felt betrayed. They passed the wage bill again and reopened the budget issue. When Litchfield refused to reconsider the budget, the House voted to adjourn "until the management conceded [a] more satisfactory and flexible time budget." It also moved to impeach representatives who defied the adjournment.[89] For two weeks the House waged the only recorded company union "strike" of the decade. After repeated management assurances that the assembly would not be curbed and that wages would be raised as rubber prices stabilized, House leaders agreed to resume their deliberations. Litchfield appeared before a joint session in early March to offer assurances of cooperation and to remind the representatives of their many advantages. The crisis passed and the assembly resumed its normal functions, though the incident was not forgotten. In October, Goodyear workers defeated six of eight incumbent Senators, replacing several of them with more independent House members. The activists responsible for the "strike" easily won reelection.[90]

The turmoil also encouraged several assembly leaders to embark on a bold new enterprise. Hoofman, Senator Luther R. Davis, former Senate president Tracy Douglas, and possibly others began to meet privately to plan a new organization that would be modeled after the assembly but free from management interference. Davis summarized their perspective:

[The Industrial Assembly] is not the "Judge and Jury" at all but is meant to give the workers someone who can carry their grievances to those in authority. . . . In every case, however, the final say is vested in the Goodyear management and not the Assembly. If [anyone] tells you this is not the case, then he is working for his own benefit and not yours.[91]

Hoofman resigned from Goodyear in the spring of 1926 to devote full time to the union.

At first the organization met secretly. As the membership grew, the leaders became bolder. In August, Hoofman, Davis, and "several hundred" workers met at a south Akron park to inaugurate the Meliorate Club. They

---

[89] "Seventh Assembly 1925–26," pp. 4–5, Industrial Assembly File, Goodyear Archives; *WCL*, Feb. 10, 1926; *ABJ*, Feb. 10, 1926.

[90] *WCL*, March 10, 1923, Oct. 13, 1926.

[91] *WCL*, Oct. 6, 1926.

elected Davis president and disavowed any ties to the AFL or other unions. For several months, the Meliorate Club published an occasional newspaper and became reasonably well known to the rubber workers. It apparently made no effort to bargain or to play any substantive role in the plants.[92] Alfred Winslow Jones later estimated its peak membership at three thousand, and Harold S. Roberts, still later, at six thousand, but both figures appear greatly exaggerated.[93] The one incident in the club's history that attracted public attention involved twenty-three individuals, and newspaper accounts suggest that they nearly filled the organization's headquarters. Included were five or six Goodyear employees; the others were either white-collar workers or transients.[94]

Whatever its membership, the clashing ambitions of Hoofman and Davis, who continued to serve in the assembly and to agitate for higher wages, and the inevitable problems of translating disaffection into a successful organization, soon wrecked the Meliorate Club. By late 1926 Davis and Hoofman headed rival factions that devoted their energies to fighting each other. The Hoofman group later charged that a Cleveland Communist had gained Davis's ear and was "boring from within" to create a Communist union. The issue, in Hoofman's words, was "Americanism against Communism."[95] In December the "Conservatives" took control of the organization and expelled Davis and his followers. On January 8, 1927, after rallying the majority of the members to his side, Davis and his group seized the headquarters. Hoofman and his allies counterattacked the next morning; the ensuing melee destroyed the office, sent Douglas and another man to the hospital, and led to the arrest of all the participants. This *opéra bouffe* discredited the organization and reinforced longstanding worker suspicions about labor organizers. When Goodyear laid off the men who were arrested and later fired one of them, the seeming "futility" of organization "was apparent."[96]

After 1926 the assembly operated smoothly and, by most accounts, effectively. The decline of the AFL, the collapse of the Meliorate Club, and the perfection of the district committee system all contributed to the more placid atmosphere. Slusser's shrewd management was also a factor. He recognized that he and the other executives had to devote long hours to the assembly if it was to meet their objective of inspiring a "feeling of confi-

[92] John D. House, interview with author, April 15, 1973; N. H. Eagle, interview with author, March 14, 1974; H. L. Lloyd, interview with author, Sept. 16, 1985.

[93] Jones, *Life, Liberty, and Property*, p. 80; Roberts, *Rubber Workers*, p. 87.

[94] *ATP*, Jan. 10, 1927; *ABJ*, Jan. 10, 1927.

[95] *ABJ*, Jan. 12, 1927.

[96] House interview; *ABJ*, Jan. 1, 1927, Aug. 31, 1927.

dence'' in the company.[97] He also had to ensure that it ''won'' concessions for the workers. Management representatives encouraged the assembly to promote a hospital insurance plan and more liberal pensions. By the end of the decade Slusser and his staff believed they had succeeded. The Sears contracts, based on an assumption of ever-increasing manufacturing efficiency, were more tangible evidence of this sentiment.

Most rubber workers were also satisfied. By the standards they used—essentially the business unionist's standards of wages, hours, benefits, and working conditions—their situation was good and improving.[98] Thanks to the assembly, the management was accessible, responsive, and reasonably flexible. Charles Skinner, an assembly representative who would later become an officer of the CIO local, summarized the feelings of many Goodyear employees when he recalled that he ''had no fault to find. We did a lot of good. Yeah, did all right.''[99]

Apart from the immediate benefits and costs that dominated the assessments of workers and managers, there were other effects of the assembly operation that were equally important but less apparent. The joint committees inevitably created a larger role for the staff specialists—the personnel administrators, time study experts, engineers, and others—at the expense of the foremen. Though the committee system was supposed to involve first-line supervisors in grievance discussions, it soon became an elaborate appeals system for aggrieved workers—in effect, a reminder of how little power the supervisors had. The assembly thus extended the managerial innovations of the 1910s and the work of the Flying Squadron. The foremen, not Wilmer Tate and his AFL colleagues, were the principal casualties.

The assembly created even more profound divisions among the production employees. From the beginning it had favored career employees over short-term and transient workers. The 1920–1921 recession, by temporarily eliminating the latter, widened the gap. There was no hard-and-fast boundary; and since the veterans depended on the votes of transient workers and knew that their constituents would show no compunction about dismissing them if they somehow failed, the distinction remained muted. Still, by the end of the decade the assembly had created a new cultural and social entity: a substantial minority of workers whose values included sta-

[97] *WCL*, Nov. 6, 1929.

[98] There were two brief strikes in 1926 and 1927 confined to a single department for one day or less (Goodyear, ''Statement to Fact-Finding Board,'' FMCS Papers, RG 280, File 195/ 336).

[99] C. L. Skinner, interview with author, April 23, 1976. William M. Leiserson, a prominent labor economist with close ties to the AFL, reported to Litchfield after visiting the plant that ''you are very much on the right track'' (William M. Leiserson to P. W. Litchfield, June 15, 1923, William M. Leiserson Papers, Box 15, State Historical Society of Wisconsin, Madison).

ble employment, home ownership, community involvement, and institutional loyalty. Numbering perhaps four thousand to six thousand, they were a tangible measure of the influence of the Goodyear personnel program and, in particular, the assembly. By 1929 neither Tate nor the south Akron merchants who led the Klan could count a tenth as many followers.

In retrospect, then, the most notable feature of the postwar decade was not the quiescence of the rubber workers, but the variety of labor organizations that flourished during that era. The union pioneers of the 1930s would not be novices to organized collective activity. In building their organizations, choosing tactics, and setting goals, they would be able to draw upon a broad range of personal experiences. The appeal of their unions would depend in large measure on the degree to which they had mastered the lessons of the past. Directly or indirectly, Marguerite Prevey, Clifton Slusser, and Wilmer Tate would all play major roles in the most ambitious of the rubber workers' efforts to do something for themselves.

CHAPTER FIVE

Depression and Revival, 1929–1934

A TALL MAN with wavy, thinning hair and a quick smile, he looked more like an insurance agent than a rubber worker, and even less like the stereotypic labor organizer. Yet Rex D. Murray (1908–1985) was representative of the men and women who created the United Rubber Workers of America, the most formidable of the pre-World War II rubber workers' unions. Born in Ripley, West Virginia, Murray began work at the Wheeling Steel Company at fourteen. Four years later he visited his brother and sister, who had migrated to Akron during the boom years. They urged him to stay.[1] After several jobs, Murray found his niche at General Tire, where he worked in the tube room and then in the pit. Competent and popular, he kept his job during the Depression and joined veteran workers to form AFL Federal Labor Union 18323 in the summer of 1933. As the local president in 1933–1934, he faced far different challenges than most of the men who had headed rubber workers' organizations in earlier years. Given the climate of the 1930s, survival was not an issue for the General Tire local, nor was the allegiance of most of the workers. Murray had the luxury of defining the ends and means of a successful organization.

ECONOMIC COLLAPSE

The devastating Depression that began in 1929 adversely affected most groups involved in the manufacture and sale of rubber products. In East Asia, the collapse of crude rubber prices to 10 percent of their 1929 level forced the repatriation of thousands of displaced Indian and Chinese workers.[2] In the U.S., the decline in economic activity bankrupted dozens of manufacturers, including well-known firms like Fisk and Kelly-Springfield; destroyed thousands of tire dealers; and wrecked the careers of tens of thousands of able-bodied workers. The travail of the retailers and workers was especially alarming. Their plight meant that everyone, no matter how successful, was vulnerable. More than any other development, it spurred attacks on competition and demands for a cartel of domestic firms.

[1] Rex Murray, interviews with author, Sept. 19, Oct. 7, 1972; URWA, *Souvenir Program of the Second Annual Convention, United Rubber Workers, Sept. 12, 1937* (Akron, 1937), p. 30.

[2] P. T. Bauer, *The Rubber Industry: A Study in Competition and Monopoly* (Cambridge, 1948), p. 15.

The experiences of the major manufacturers varied, depending largely on their pre-Depression circumstances. U.S. Rubber faced the greatest uncertainty; President Francis B. Davis's rejuvenation program was in its infancy when the Depression struck, and for three years the company skirted bankruptcy. While continuing to consolidate footware and mechanical goods production, Davis embarked on a bold and controversial plan to increase tire sales. He offered to supply 50 percent of all General Motors' original-equipment tires at a price below his current costs. Success and possibly survival would depend on manufacturing economies and a revival of the automobile market. When the contract went into effect in 1931, neither development seemed very likely.[3]

In 1929, Goodrich executives had embarked on a disastrous diversification program. They acquired Hood Rubber in order to jettison their unprofitable Akron footwear operations, and Miller Rubber to add to their line of druggists' sundries and toys. The Hood acquisition was especially damaging. It saddled Goodrich with excess capacity and hurt the company "severely" in the early 1930s.[4] Goodrich's technical expertise and relatively strong production management saved it from the fate of U.S. Rubber, but only narrowly. After 1929 the fate of the Akron complex and the jobs of its thousands of employees were always in doubt.

In contrast, Goodyear and Firestone remained relatively strong. Their dependence on tires was, on the whole, a source of strength. Between 1929 and 1933 all U.S. manufactures declined by 37 percent; auto production fell by 64 percent, and tire manufacture, by 34 percent.[5] Goodyear lost money in 1932, due to the collapse of rubber prices, but otherwise was profitable. Despite continued turmoil among Goodyear stockholders, Litchfield remained firmly in control. Firestone's performance was even more impressive. Not only was it profitable every year of the Depression, but its financial performance actually improved. Through cautious management, rigid economies, and the expansion of its retail chain, it earned a larger profit per tire than any other manufacturer. With abundant resources and centralized management, it was ready to take advantage of the recovery. The better-managed large factories, like General Tire and Seiberling, also fared reasonably well.

[3] Glenn Babcock, *History of United States Rubber: A Case Study in Corporate Management* (Bloomington, 1966), pp. 305–307; "U.S. Rubber I: The Corporate State," *Fortune*, Feb. 1934, pp. 52–55, 124–27. U.S. Rubber also acquired the Samson Rubber Company of Los Angeles and the Gillette Rubber Company of Eau Claire, Wisconsin, in 1931 to produce tires for Montgomery Ward.

[4] B. F. Goodrich Co., *Annual Report, 1929* (Akron, 1929), p. 5; *ABJ*, Aug. 31, 1932.

[5] Federal Housing Administration, *Akron, Ohio, Housing Market Analysis* (Washington, 1938), p. 206.

The rubber workers were less fortunate than most of the employers. Substantial layoffs began in the fall of 1929 and continued intermittently for three years. Total employment in the Akron plants declined from a pre-Depression peak of 58,188 in June 1929, to a low of 27,377 in March 1933, a drop of 53 percent. A more realistic comparison, between the average for 1928, the industry's most profitable year, and March 1932, to March 1933, its most depressed period, reduces the toll to 43 percent, equal to the fall in manufacturing employment in Ohio and less than the 48 percent reduction in tire and tube employment in the U.S. during the same period.[6] However measured, the total was not a static figure. Most individuals who remained in the labor force worked for at least a few months every year. Until 1932, the Depression merely exaggerated the seasonal pattern of industry employment. In 1932 and early 1933, it severely distorted that pattern. In the neighborhood south of Crosier Street, the number of residents with occupations listed in the city directory fell by 21 percent between 1929 and 1933. The number of houses with boarders or apartments declined by 60 percent. The greatest losses were among rubber workers, craft workers, and small business proprietors. The number of laborers doubled.[7]

Even workers who kept their jobs suffered severely due to reductions in working hours. Prompted by President Hoover's Emergency Committee on Employment, many manufacturers adopted share-the-work policies in 1930 and 1931, in effect substituting underemployment for layoffs. In July 1930, before the national campaign got underway, Litchfield introduced a plan to "rotate employment." With vivid recollections of the distress of 1921, he proposed to lay off each worker every eighth week until production increased. The Industrial Assembly concurred. In the following months, as the economy deteriorated, the ratio fell to every seventh week, every sixth week, and every fifth week. By November Goodyear had adopted the four-day week, but even that was not enough. In near desperation Litchfield reduced the workday to six hours. The six-hour day was "not to be construed as a permanent proposition at Goodyear." It was "only a temporary measure."[8] And indeed, in December Litchfield restored the eight-hour day in anticipation of the usual spring season. But as economic conditions worsened in 1931, Goodyear returned to the six-hour day and extended it to the Los Angeles and Gadsden plants. Several of the smaller companies

---

[6] Ibid., pp. 223–24. For the tire and tube industry, the low was 39,000 in March 1933. Also see "Estimated Employment," Federal Mediation and Conciliation Service Papers, RG 280, File 195/335, National Archives; Jurgen Kocka, *White Collar Workers in America 1890–1940: A Social-Political History in International Perspective* (Beverly Hills, 1980), p. 195.

[7] See *Akron Official City Directory, 1928* (Akron, 1928); *Akron, Cuyahoga Falls, and Barberton Official City Directory, 1933* (Akron, 1933).

[8] *WCL*, July 23, Oct. 15, 1930.

went to six-hour shifts in 1931; Firestone and General Tire followed in late 1932, and Goodrich, in early 1933. Firestone and Goodrich also introduced six-hour days in their Los Angeles tire plants, and U.S. Rubber in its Detroit factory.[9]

While the six-hour day was an ad hoc response to the Depression, it was consistent with Litchfield's larger goals. One of these was social and humanitarian. The "problem of unemployment," he confided, was "underlying all other ills," creating a "spirit of dejection and disillusionment." Shorter hours might alleviate some of the psychological distress.[10] A second goal was to maintain a cadre of experienced employees, as he had done in 1920–1921. Despite an occasional note of despair, Litchfield's basic position was that "bad times will clear the deck for good times again."[11] He intended to take maximum advantage of the revival, as he had in 1922, and knowledgeable, disciplined workers were essential to that strategy.

In later years a major controversy developed over a third possible goal, the "speedup." Labor productivity increased rapidly in the tire industry between 1929 and 1933, in part because of aggressive production management. Litchfield wrote in late 1932 that the six-hour day might increase efficiency "if we were in a position to push production."[12] He later changed his mind about the six-hour day, but other manufacturers found a silver lining in the dark cloud of work sharing. The superintendent of the India Tire Co. reported that the six-hour day cut labor costs by more than 8 percent. Workers on six-hour shifts did not have to pace themselves or rest. And their desire to restore lost income replaced any thought of a "veto" of more stringent production standards.[13]

Whatever the exact connection between the six-hour day and productivity increases, rubber workers soon came to believe that the shorter day inspired speedups and "rawhiding." After a month of informal talks with Akron workers, a Goodrich agent summarized their views:

"They just run the life out of a man," so runs the explanation—You daren't lose a minute.—"No time to eat—or go to the wash room—unless you lose produc-

[9] WCL, Dec. 10, 1930; J. E. Lorentz to Charles E. Baldwin, July 7, 1932, FMCS Papers, RG 280, File 195/335; John D. House, "To the Honorable Members of the Fact-Finding Board," FMCS Papers, RG 280, File 195/335.

[10] Paul W. Litchfield to Ralph M. Easley, Jan. 18, 1933, National Civic Federation Papers, Box 73, New York Public Library. Also see Paul W. Litchfield, "The President Talks to the Men" (Akron, 1935); E. J. Thomas, interview with author, Aug. 6, 1982.

[11] WCL, Jan. 28, 1931.

[12] Quoted in "Findings and Recommendations of the Fact-Finding Board," FMCS Papers, RG 280, File 182/1010. Also see John Dean Gaffey, *The Productivity of Labor in the Rubber Tire Manufacturing Industry* (New York, 1940), p. 118.

[13] Lorentz to Baldwin, July 7, 1932, FMCS Papers, RG 280, File 195/335.

tion.''—In summer, men in the pit fall like flies. Frequent descriptions are also given of the tragic change from the time when a fellow made three or four tires an hour and enjoyed life.[14]

Regardless of the motive, the principal effect of work sharing was to emphasize the severity of the Depression. Akron rubber workers who kept their jobs earned, on average, 37 percent less between March 1932 and March 1933 than they had in 1928 ($1,046 vs. $1,672). Goodyear incomes decreased slightly more ($1,066 vs. $1,751). In the tire industry as a whole, the decline was 37 percent.[15] The particularly difficult months of 1932 and early 1933 made the psychological burden even greater. Forty years later, industry veterans recalled a man who spent twenty cents on carfare to collect a fifteen-cent paycheck.[16] Most rubber workers were able to feed their families and avoid the indignity of the dole, but they had no money for home repairs, automobiles, or vacations. Their enforced economies caused painful contractions in Akron and a host of other cities and towns.

The Depression experience also brought the tradition of frequent job changes to an abrupt end. Personnel work had reduced the toll; the Depression had a far greater effect. In 1929, 37.5 percent of Goodyear employees quit their jobs; in 1930 only 10.2 percent left, while in 1931 the number fell to 9.5 percent, and in 1932, to 5.9 percent. At the trough of the Depression in February 1932, 235 workers quit and 29 were hired, presumably to fill critical vacancies.[17] As the number of de facto career employees grew, workers came to think of themselves as Goodyear or Firestone employees. Gradually the labor force at each factory began to acquire a collective personality that would influence its subsequent history.[18]

Most rubber workers reacted to the Depression with bewilderment and resignation. A handful joined the unemployed leagues and councils and agitated for public financial relief. An even smaller group, by most reports drawn from the ranks of supervisors and skilled workers, joined the Communist party. Virtually no one turned to organized labor, despite the AFL's demands for public works and shorter hours. Given the circumstances, the odds of a successful union were no greater than the odds of a new factory.[19]

[14] Whiting Williams to T. G. Graham, Oct. 14, 1934, Whiting Williams Papers, Box 4, Folder 1, Western Reserve Historical Society Library, Cleveland.

[15] ''Findings and Recommendations.''

[16] Harley C. Anthony, interview with author, April 11, 1972.

[17] Goodyear, ''Statement to the Fact-Finding Board,'' Nov. 30, 1935, FMCS Papers, RG 280, File 195/335.

[18] Williams to Graham, Oct. 19, 1934, Williams Papers, Box 4, Folder 1.

[19] Wilmer Tate to John Brophy, Feb. 18, 1936, Congress of Industrial Organizations Papers, Catholic University, Washington.

The one major incident of labor conflict during the period emphasized the unions' limited potential. U.S. Rubber's Mishawaka subsidiary had been relatively unaffected by the company's plight until 1930, when the management introduced time studies, an incentive wage plan, and a new, more competitive environment. A simultaneous collapse of the footwear market due to the Depression and a mild winter reinforced the sense of change. Instead of laying off employees, the Mishawaka managers followed the precedent of the tire manufacturers and reduced hours. Many workers, however, mistakenly associated their losses with the incentive plan. By the spring of 1931, a substantial dissident group had organized an independent union. When the company fired several activists in late May, seventy workers in the cutting room walked out. The strike spread; by May 19, virtually all of the two thousand four hundred employees were out and the plant closed.[20]

For three weeks the deadlock continued. Given the economic outlook, many observers feared mass discharges or the importation of strikebreakers. Unknown to them, Cyrus Ching had arrived in mid-May and was working behind the scenes to promote a settlement without seeming to interfere. Speaking for the management, he refused to deal with the union or scrap the incentive system, but offered to rehire the strikers and create a factory council. For two weeks a government counciliator tried to persuade the strikers to return to work on this basis. Aiding him was AFL organizer Paul Smith, who had won the support of the local union leaders. The opposition included a Communist faction consisting of several hundred Belgian and Italian workers. By early June, Ching, the conciliator, and Smith had the upper hand. After a formal agreement between the local managers and Smith, the strikers voted to return by a 5 to 1 margin. Their only substantive achievement was the Factory Council.[21]

The strike "victory" produced only disappointment and bitterness. The managers refused to take the Factory Council seriously and their intransigence sustained the Communist group, which attacked the union officers for "selling out" and provoked at least one violent clash. In July 1931, the conciliator narrowly averted another strike. In September, he reported that the Mishawaka managers were "sitting on a powder keg." The workers were "so bitter at the treatment they are receiving from the management"

[20] Babcock, *History of United States Rubber*, pp. 369–70; David Brody, *Workers in Industrial America: Essays on the Twentieth-Century Struggle* (New York, 1980), pp. 74–76; C.S. Ching to U.S. Department of Labor, June 25, 1931, FMCS Papers, RG 280, File 172/6272; *South Bend News-Times*, June 9, 1931.

[21] Robert Pilkington to H. L. Kerwin, May 21, 1931, FMCS Papers, RG 280, File 172/6272; *South Bend News-Times*, June 7, 1931.

that another strike was virtually inevitable.[22] Six months later he noted that if business were better the workers would strike, and in May 1932, that if they were assured of AFL benefits, the plant would not "run an hour."[23] When the strike finally came, in July 1932, only nine hundred workers participated, and they returned to work after three days. After this fiasco the union quickly declined. By the end of 1932, only the Factory Council remained.

THE AFL REEMERGES

By that time nearly everyone in the industry agreed that some form of government intervention was necessary. The manufacturers urged publicly sanctioned "cooperation," small business proprietors wanted restraints on competition, and the AFL called for shorter hours and public works. Though their prescriptions were different and often incompatible, their consensus on the desirability of government action was a critical first step in the rise of a new and formidable union movement among the rubber workers.

The National Industrial Recovery Act, which Congress passed in May 1933, underlined the mood of desperation. The act embodied the ideas of business leaders, leftist planners, and trade unionists. It provided for the suspension of antitrust laws, the drafting of cartel-like "codes of fair competition," and the introduction of minimum wages, maximum hours, and restrictions on child labor. In addition, Section 7a guaranteed workers the right to organize and bargain with employers. Among rubber manufacturers, the New Deal program spurred an intense conflict over the character of the new more "restrained" and "civilized" competition. From July to December 1933, the tire-code drafting committee debated issues such as price differentials and private-label production. Led by Frank Seiberling, the smaller manufacturers bitterly fought the marketing tactics of the large companies. The code that finally emerged was "compromised" and "emasculated" and inspired little confidence that price wars and "profitless" production would end. The deliberations of the retail tire dealers were even more rancorous and did not result in an agreement until May 1934. By comparison, there was relatively little conflict over the labor provisions of the tire or rubber products code. The NIRA labor reforms paled beside the more pressing problems of prices and production limits.[24]

---

[22] Employees' Committee Meeting Minutes, 1931, FMCS Papers, RG 280, File 172/6272; Pilkington to Kerwin, July 9, Sept. 30, Oct. 13, 1931, FMCS Papers, RG 280, File 172/6272.

[23] Pilkington to Kerwin, May 19, 1932, FMCS Papers, RG 280, File 172/6272.

[24] See Ellis W. Hawley, *The New Deal and The Problem of Monopoly* (Princeton, 1967), p. 35; Robert F. Himmelberg, *The Origins of the National Recovery Administration: Business,*

While the manufacturers fought over the codes, the news from the shop floor was surprisingly positive. The most important development of the spring of 1933 was not the New Deal, the codes, or Section 7a, but an upturn in the business cycle. The long-awaited recovery began in March. In the tire industry, payrolls more than doubled between March and July as average hours rose from 24.2 to 42 per week and employment increased from 39,000 to 59,100. All of the increase in hours and more than half of the new employees antedated the NIRA, not to mention the rubber industry codes. In Akron, where most of the expansion occurred, the rubber companies hired 8,000 additional workers between March and June and 6,000 more between June and August. Goodyear alone hired 2,500 employees in May and nearly 2,000 in June. These gains erased the employment losses of the preceding three years. Newly reemployed workers paid old bills, made long-deferred purchases, and took a new interest in organized labor. If the NIRA preoccupied employers and at least temporarily neutralized their hostility to organization, the recovery made it possible for workers to reconsider the appeals of the AFL.[25]

In late June, AFL leaders launched the first major organizing campaign of the decade. On June 25 Secretary-Treasurer Frank Morrison told reporters that Section 7a presented "a great opportunity" to organize rubber, automobile, coal, and steel workers in "Ohio and nearby states."[26] Two days later, Akron CLU President Frank Patino announced a rubber workers' meeting for June 30 at the Akron Armory. He acknowledged that the effort was "actually guided by the A. F. of L. in Washington" and that a "spokesman" from Washington would "assume charge."[27] Helping him plan details were the local Federation organizer, W. H. Wilson, CLU secretary Wilmer Tate, and the business agents of the Electricians, Plumbers, and Barbers. Tate distributed handbills at the tire plants and predicted an overflow crowd.

The Armory meeting was at best a mixed success. The Washington

---

Government, and the Trade Association Issue, 1921–1933 (New York, 1976), pp. 181–212; G. S. Earseman, "History of the Code of Fair Competition for the Rubber Tire Manufacturing Industry," National Recovery Administration Papers, RG 9, Box 7600, pp. 18, 21, National Archives.

[25] Geoffrey H. Moore, ed., Business Cycle Indicators (Princeton, 1961), 1: 121; Goodyear, "Statement to Fact-Finding Board," FMCS Papers, RG 280, File 195/335. For Akron business conditions see Federal Reserve Bank of Cleveland, The Monthly Business Review 12–15 (1930–1933).

[26] ABJ, June 26, 1933; James O. Morris, Conflict Within the AFL: A Study of Craft Versus Industrial Unionism, 1901–1938 (Ithaca, 1958), p. 152; Craig Lawrence Phelan, "William Green and the Limits of Christian Idealism: The AFL Years, 1925–1952" (Ph.D. diss., Ohio State University, 1982), pp. 127–30.

[27] ABJ, June 27, 1933.

"spokesman" never arrived, and Tate must have been moderately disappointed at the crowd of two thousand that half filled the auditorium. Patino opened the session and explained that any organization would be directed by the AFL. He then introduced organizer Paul Smith to a chorus of "applause, cheers and whistles." Smith blamed industry for the Depression and read Section 7a. He promised local union charters and an organizer if the men responded. "It's up to you to put it through," he declared, noting that a rubber workers' union would be "patterned after the United Mine Workers" and include all employees making rubber products. Tate, who followed him, invited his listeners to sign AFL pledge cards. By the following day, he reported eight hundred pledges. Several days later the CLU formally requested federal labor union charters and an organizer.[28]

The June 30 rally subsequently became part of the legend of rubber worker activism, thanks to the Communist novelist Ruth McKenny, whose *Industrial Valley* (1939) supposedly recounted the activities of Akron workers during this period. Like most of McKenny's accounts, her description of the rally is more fiction than fact. She claimed that Tate and James McCartan, the only other AFL figure remotely sympathetic to leftist causes, independently organized the rally, paid the armory rental fee by selling the CLU account in a closed bank, and attracted a mob of five thousand rubber workers. Using McKenny as a source, Irving Bernstein wrote in *Turbulent Years* (1970) that "Section 7A hit Akron like a bolt of lightning. . . . The rubber workers needed no prodding from the AFL to organize. They flocked into the union."[29]

The June 30 rally did have one effect that McKenny and Bernstein might have profitably explored. Though it attracted only about 5 percent of Akron's rubber workers, it brought together most of the men who would guide the Akron labor movement for the next decade. Most of them had been farm youths; a minority were the sons of coal miners or railroad workers and had had some contact with organized labor. A majority, like Rex Murray, had arrived in the early or mid-1920s, had found jobs in tire-building or -curing departments, and had become members of the industry's now obsolescent physical elite. Like other veterans of the Akron plants, they were confident, ambitious, and independent. What distinguished them from their co-workers was the ability to inspire confidence among fellow workers and a fierce antiauthoritarianism. "I just didn't feel I was going to be a doormat and be walked on," recalled Walter Kriebel, a soft-spoken

[28] *ABJ*, June 28, 29, 30, July 1, 4, 1933; *ATP*, July 1, 2, 1933.

[29] Ruth McKenny, *Industrial Valley* (New York, 1939), pp. 96–99; Irving Bernstein, *Turbulent Years: A History of the American Worker 1933–1941* (Boston, 1970), pp. 98, 99.

Ohioan who was to be the first president of the Firestone local.[30] Irritants that would have led them to change jobs in the 1920s produced only bitterness in the early 1930s. The economic revival brought these grievances to the surface; the AFL initiative gave them an outlet.

During the following weeks these men created the most substantial "outside" union since 1913. After the armory meeting, Harley C. Anthony and Frederick W. Phillips, Goodrich tire builders, got application cards from the CLU and "stood at the gate and passed them out to anyone who reached for one."[31] Another Goodrich tire builder, Sherman H. Dalrymple, "signed up dozens and dozens of people."[32] Kriebel, Oliver H. Bosley, and a handful of other Firestone tire builders began to meet after work. "We started talking about the union," Bosley recalled, "and I said, 'How long are we going to sit idly by?' People began to organize so that you couldn't write applications fast enough."[33] About the same time, Goodyear veteran Tracy Douglas met millroom worker John "Dutch" Kumpel at the plant gate. "Hey Dutch, how about joining the rubber workers union?" Douglas asked. "Well, sure, that's what we need," Kumpel replied.[34] Kumpel, Douglas, John D. House, and others enlisted hundreds of Goodyear employees. Murray played a similar role, as did H. R. "Whitey" Lloyd and N. Ḥ. "Harry" Eagle, two Mohawk tire builders. As more workers signed, enthusiasm spread. Occasionally someone recalled that "Back in '13 . . . they just fired them right and left." "Well," the activists replied, "if we get fired, we get fired." In fact, nothing happened. "Nobody was being fired. That was the thing that we were watching for all the time. Nobody was being fired."[35] By August it was too late. The unions were a fait accompli.

The workers' response caught the AFL off guard. Patino, Tate, and the business agents did what they could but they were soon immersed in campaigns of their own. Everyone agreed that the special organizer Washington had promised was a necessity. Everyone, that is, except AFL president William Green. His correspondence contains no hint of a plan to send an organizer to Akron before mid-July. When Coleman Claherty, the man he eventually appointed, submitted an application for employment, Green re-

[30] Walter Kriebel, interview with author, Sept. 19, 1972. Also see Daniel Nelson, "The Leadership of the United Rubber Workers," *Detroit in Perspective* 5 (1981): 21–30; Melvyn Dubofsky, "Not so Turbulent Years: Another Look at the American 1930's," *Amerikastudien* 24 (1979): 16–17.

[31] Harley C. Anthony interview.

[32] Sherman H. Dalrymple, interview with Joe Glazer, April 2, 1955.

[33] Oliver H. Bosley, interview with author, Oct. 23, 1973.

[34] John Kumpel, interview with author, Oct. 25, 1972.

[35] Walter Kriebel interview; Oliver H. Bosley interview.

plied that the Federation had no work for him. When Green finally hired Claherty, on July 14, he assigned him to William Collins, who was in charge of AFL efforts in the auto industry. "Perhaps you can give special attention to the organization of automobile workers in Cleveland," Green wrote. Claherty was to help in Akron and "vicinity" as well.[36] Ten days later Claherty went to Akron and found, perhaps to his surprise, thousands of willing recruits. In August he won Green's approval to concentrate on the rubber industry and became one of only five organizers with an industrial rather than a geographical assignment. By the end of August Green and Claherty had done a complete about-face and made Akron the focal point of the Federation's industrial organizing effort.

Claherty was "the old type of craft unionist . . . with white hair and . . . an Irish complexion."[37] In his late fifties when he came to Akron, Claherty was a union veteran. As president of a Cleveland Blacksmiths' local and secretary of the Cleveland Metal Trades Council, he had come to the attention of AFL leaders and won their trust. He had less in common with the rubber workers, and still less with the zealots who were emerging as leaders of the Akron locals. "He worked for Bill Green; he had a job . . . and he had to follow orders," recalled one activist.[38] "He could get up and rabble rouse . . . but he couldn't negotiate worth a darn," added another veteran of the period.[39]

Nevertheless, Claherty presided over one of the most successful membership campaigns in AFL history. By the fall there were four large Akron locals and nine others that were large by conventional union standards. With minimal investment and remarkable speed, the AFL had added twenty-three thousand members. Claherty helped the locals elect officers and write bylaws. The Goodrich local, with seven thousand five hundred members, elected Dalrymple president, Phillips financial secretary, Anthony recording secretary, and George "Bob" Roberts chairman of the executive board. The Goodyear local, with six thousand six hundred members, elected Douglas president by a plurality; when Claherty insisted on a new election, the members turned to House instead. Clark Culver, another tire builder, was elected secretary-treasurer, and Everett White, a strapping pit worker, recording secretary. The Firestone local, five thousand strong, elected Kriebel president and Bosley secretary. The General local, with more than a thousand members, selected Murray. Locals at Seiberling, Mohawk, American Hard Rubber, and India Tire claimed more than

[36] William Green to Coleman Claherty, July 14, 1933, AFL Papers, Green Files, State Historical Society of Wisconsin, Madison.

[37] James S. Jackson, interview with author, Oct. 5, 1973.

[38] John D. House, interviews with author, April 15, May 1, 1973.

[39] John Kumpel interview.

three hundred members each. The India local was the first to achieve 100 percent membership.[40]

The new activism soon spread to other groups of workers. Spurred by aggressive leaders like Tate, whom Claherty added to the AFL staff, and John Shuff of the Movie Projectionists, Akron craft unions tripled their membership in 1933. The Machinists had the largest gain, nearly one thousand members. Twenty new organizations also appeared, including a Teamsters local that had nearly two thousand members by July 1934. The Street Railway Employees, Gas Station Attendants, Retail Clerks, Hotel and Restaurant Workers, and other service workers' unions also registered impressive gains, in many cases because union members demanded "to be served by union attendants."[41] By the summer of 1934, AFL unions outside the rubber industry could claim more than seven thousand members, a sevenfold increase since June 1933. Rather than a bastion of the "open shop," Akron was on its way to becoming the nation's most highly unionized major city.

As the unions grew, opposition quickly disappeared. The managers of a leading theater, a bakery, and the city's largest independent grocery chain resisted at first, but made peace with the labor movement by the end of 1933. The change among the middle stratum of merchants and professionals is apparent from the pages of the CLU's *Summit County Labor News*. In late 1933 most *Labor News* advertisers were restaurants, clothing stores, used car dealerships, bowling alleys, and other small businesses. Sears, with an ad for auto batteries, was the only important exception. By the following spring *Labor News* advertisers included utilities, grocery chains (most notably the chain that had originally fought the unions), breweries, new car agencies, and the city's larger clothing stores.[42] Organized labor had achieved an unaccustomed respectability.

Union leaders also challenged the city's traditional social arbiters. By staging theatrical shows, athletic contests, picnics, and dances, they competed with fraternal lodges, theaters, ballrooms, and amusement parks. Indirectly they challenged the churches, for Sunday was the only day when all members were available for meetings. Once more, their potential rivals adapted quickly. Theater and dance hall operators offered their buildings to the locals rent-free for special occasions. An amusement park proprietor forced his employees to organize so he could proclaim his park "100 percent union."[43] Ministers and priests were unfailingly cordial. The local

---

[40] "Memorandum," National Labor Relations Board Papers, RG 25, Box 275, National Archives.

[41] Tate to Brophy, Feb. 18, 1936, CIO Papers.

[42] *SCLN*, Nov. 24, 1933, May 18, 1934.

[43] *SCLN*, March 30, 1934

newspapers hired labor reporters; local radio stations solicited union business; and the administrators of the municipal university acquired a sudden enthusiasm for labor economics.

The newspapers record an endless succession of union social affairs, from giant summer picnics to weekly shows and dances featuring the "most popular hillbilly singers," and "radio acts."[44] Interunion baseball games and boxing matches attracted huge crowds. The larger locals, led by Goodrich, sponsored elaborate intramural athletic programs. More formal gatherings featured politically ambitious attorneys or colorful personalities like "General" Jacob Coxey, the ancient free silver crusader, or William "Red" Bessemer, the 1913 strike leader. Union wives and some women workers formed a Union Buyers Club to oppose discounting by low-wage, nonunion retailers. A cooperative society attracted a modest following; university classes in labor economics and industrial relations were less popular, and Communist or Trotskyist discussion meetings, even less so. Despite the aura of social innovation that surrounded the post-1933 labor movement, the unions made no effort to change the tastes of their constituents. "The labor movement culture" of the mid-1930s was distinctive only because of its occupational basis.[45]

Although recovery and the NIRA encouraged organizing efforts throughout the industry, rubber workers in other communities lacked the collective power, status, and comparative wealth of the Akron workers. Many of them owed their jobs to low wages and primitive working conditions. By mid-1934 there were twenty-two non-Akron FLUs, but they accounted for only 30 percent of the industry's union membership.[46] Ten locals, with most of the members, were composed of tire workers. The other twelve nontire locals were small and isolated. New England, still the center of footware manufacture, had only one nontire local. A large, independent Trenton local collapsed after the officers absconded with the treasury.

In early July 1933, Ed Barnes and several other truck-tire builders at the Los Angeles Firestone plant called an organizational meeting at a baseball field in Lynnwood, California. Twenty-five men attended. A second meeting, held in a barn, attracted workers from Firestone, Goodrich, Goodyear, and Samson, the U.S. Rubber plant. A single union was chartered and a thousand members enrolled. In 1934 the FLU divided into separate plant

[44] SCLN, Nov. 24, Dec. 29, 1933, June 22, 1934.

[45] Alfred W. Jones, Life, Liberty, and Property: A Story of Conflict and a Measurement of Conflicting Rights (Philadelphia, 1941), p. 67; Elizabeth Fones-Wolf, "Industrial Unionism and Labor Movement Culture in Depression-Era Philadelphia," Pennsylvania Magazine of History and Biography 109 (1985): 3–26.

[46] Harold S. Roberts, The Rubber Workers: Labor Organization and Collective Bargaining in the Rubber Industry (New York, 1944), p. 94.

*10. Thomas J. Burns, leader of
the eastern rubber workers and
United Rubber Workers vice-
president. United Rubber
Workers Archives.*

locals. The Firestone union, initially the largest, elected Barnes president.[47]
The Samson organization, second in size, chose Herbert W. Wilson, a
"big, strapping . . . rough, tough" North Carolinian who worked in the
pit.[48] Goodrich workers elected Leslie Preston, an old-time Wobbly who
often began his remarks with "Well, now, in Portland in 1908," to the
distress of the young tire workers. "Why in the hell don't he shut up about
Portland," they asked.[49] James Martin, a Kansan who worked in the pit,
soon succeeded him. Floyd Gartrell, an Ohioan who had followed Goodrich to Los Angeles, was elected treasurer, and Frank Grillo, another trans-
planted Ohioan, secretary. The Goodyear local was much smaller and
weaker than the other three.

In other areas the pattern was similar. The Fisk local owed its existence
largely to Thomas J. Burns, one of the most important and controversial
figures to emerge from the maelstrom of 1933. A tube-room worker, Burns
called the first meeting, recruited most of the members, and served as the
local president and a part-time AFL organizer. Burns was "a kind of bustling . . . personality that rubbed some people the wrong way."[50] Another

---

[47] Edward Barnes, interview with author, Dec. 14, 1977.
[48] George Crawford, interview with author, Aug. 17, 1977.
[49] Floyd Gartrell, interview with author, Aug. 15, 1977.
[50] James S. Jackson interview.

colleague recalls him as a "braggadocio type of guy."[51] Aggressive and belligerent, he frightened Fisk workers more than their bosses did. To save the workers' jobs at the bankrupt company, he emphasized discipline and restraint. He settled a strike in July 1933 and deterred others in the following months while building the union. By 1935 he had made the Fisk local "the best union in Chicopee."[52]

Three other important eastern locals appeared during the summer of 1933. At the Boston Woven Hose Co. in Cambridge, Massachusetts, union activists recruited six hundred of the eight hundred employees and created the largest organization of mechanical goods workers. Their leader was Salvatore Camelio, a charismatic Italian immigrant who dabbled in Socialist politics. At Pennsylvania Rubber, in Jeanette, bicycle-tire builders led by John Dent and John Marchiando called an organizational meeting after an AFL rally. They had no difficulty persuading the workers to join. By 1934 the Pennsylvania local was among the strongest in the industry.[53] At Kelly-Springfield in Cumberland, Maryland, tire builders and pit workers looked to the AFL with a sense of desperation. The company was near failure. While Akron and Los Angeles tire builders talked boldly of asserting their rights, Kelly workers merely hoped to save their jobs.

The only substantial southern local was at Goodyear's Gadsden plant. Led by E. L. Gray, a burly tire builder, the Goodyear activists claimed five hundred of the plant's seven hundred employees by the summer of 1934.

One other group played a significant role in the burgeoning union movement. The Akron plants had nearly three thousand maintenance, construction, and service workers with identifiable trades. Their presence raised serious and potentially embarrassing questions about the jurisdictional claims of other unions. Green told Claherty that if he found employees who "clearly come under the jurisdiction of some International Union, we can arrange for a transfer."[54] But as Claherty soon discovered, the solution was not that simple. Many craft workers identified with their fellow workers or objected to the higher initiation fees and dues of the established unions. Instead of the FLUs' two-to-four-dollar initiation fee and dollar-a-month dues, the Electrical Workers, for example, charged ten to twenty-five dollars to join and monthly dues of three dollars.[55] Equally serious was a widespread suspicion, based on pre-Depression experiences, that the older or-

[51] Harmon Splitter, interview with author, Aug. 16, 1977.

[52] Emile Mayotte, interview with author, Jan. 11, 1978.

[53] John Marchiando, interview with author, Dec. 22, 1977.

[54] Green to Claherty, Aug. 23, 1933, AFL Papers, Green Files; Morris, *Conflict Within the AFL*, pp. 152–53.

[55] Minutes, Jan. 15, 1934, Feb. 19, 1934, International Brotherhood of Electrical Workers, Local 690, Archives of American History, University of Akron.

ganizations were not really interested in the rubber workers. When Green, under pressure from the internationals, directed the CLU and the FLUS to proceed with the transfer, Claherty proceeded cautiously. The order, however, "created a lot of dissension."[56] By the summer of 1934 1,300 rubber workers had transferred to the Machinists; 216, to the Electrical Workers; 125, to the Sheet Metal Workers; 112, to the Teamsters; and lesser numbers, to other unions, but at least 700 refused to switch.

The transfer issue sparked the first serious challenge to Claherty and the AFL. By the fall of 1933 many rubber workers had been paying dues for four or five months. The locals had had only minimal contact with the employers, and Claherty seemed willing to rely on the National Recovery Administration's National Labor Board to wring concessions from the industry. In the larger plants company unions competed for members. For many activists, the transfer issue was the last straw. Luther L. Callahan, a prominent Goodrich worker, wrote, for example, that the workers "are fast losing faith in the A. F. of L. . . . The locals are beginning to go backward instead of forward."[57] Other observers suggested that former United Mine Workers members, hostile to any hint of craft unionism, exaggerated the discontent. In any case, a small group of aggressive local leaders exploited the dissatisfaction to propose a different course. In the Akron area, Fred Phillips, financial secretary of the Goodrich local, was the rebels' leader. Articulate and ambitious, Phillips had served as the unions' representative at the rubber industry code hearings and had impressed Green. The AFL president even suggested that Claherty hire him as an assistant. Claherty, however, was more wary; he chose the equally fluent but more dutiful Bob Roberts instead. Phillips found a kindred spirit in Clark Culver, the financial secretary of the Goodyear local. Outside Akron, Burns was the most important rebel. Fred S. Galloway, an officer of the U.S. Rubber local in Indianapolis, was the other major figure in the uprising.[58]

In mid-November Galloway issued a call for a late December meeting of local union representatives in Indianapolis to consider the formation of a national rubber workers' union. His intention was apparently to force the AFL to authorize an international, but the implication of his invitation was clear: if the Federation failed to act, the rubber workers would form an independent union. Unaware that anything had been afoot, Green was distressed. Claherty, equally surprised, saw the meeting as a personal affront. Since the Akron locals would be critical to any new organization, he persuaded the local FLU officers only to appoint observers and to oppose any

[56] John D. House interviews.

[57] L. L. Callahan to John L. Lewis, Dec. 7, 1933, AFL Papers, Green Files.

[58] Green to Claherty, Nov. 13, 1983, AFL Papers, Green Files; Anthony interview; *ABJ*, Dec. 21, 1933.

decisive action in Indianapolis. Two of the observers, Murray and Thomas Pinegar, a Goodrich worker, had reservations about a break with the AFL and the third, Phillips, only favored an independent union if it were based in Akron. Culver was apparently the only Akron man pledged to immediate action. Pleading the need to visit a sick mother, he secretly went to Indianapolis. He also stopped dues payments to the AFL in order to provide funds for the new organization.[59]

At Indianapolis Burns and Galloway played leading roles. They "took the position that we would have an international union . . . in or out of the A. F. of L."[60] Since only thirteen locals sent representatives and the Akron delegates were not authorized to act, the convention adopted a resolution calling an Akron convention for January 20. Phillips called on Green to "keep the faith . . . [and] endorse this convention."[61] Burns and Galloway came to Akron to pressure the Akron locals.

Their actions precipitated a showdown. Green refused to endorse the Akron convention and Claherty went from local to local attacking the rebels. Arguing that the move for an international was premature, he "asked them not to give up what they have gained to satisfy a few ambitious individuals."[62] The climax to the controversy occurred at the Goodrich local meeting on January 7, 1934. Burns and Galloway spoke for the convention; Claherty followed them, making "a terrific speech. His face was so red it looked like it was going to bleed."[63] At the end he demanded a vote "as to how many members were going to stick with Phillips and [how many] were going to stick with the American Federation of Labor."[64] The members voted for the AFL. Having won this test Claherty insisted on Phillips' removal. He dismissed Culver the same day and formally expelled both men from the AFL. Burns and Galloway were not punished, apparently because of their local standing. Claherty then indefinitely postponed the convention. His actions were "a dramatic display of the power of the national organization."[65]

Green professed to be surprised at the entire episode. "I just cannot understand for the life of me why Mr. Culver and Mr. Phillips have assumed such an attitude toward you and the American Federation of Labor," he

---

[59] Green to Callahan, Dec. 21, 1933, AFL Papers, Green Files; Minutes, Executive Board, Local 18282, Local 2 Archives, Local 2 Offices, Akron, Ohio; *ABJ*, Dec. 27, 1933; House interviews.

[60] Rex Murray interviews.

[61] Phillips to Green, Jan. 6, 1934, AFL Papers, Green Files.

[62] *ABJ*, Jan. 6, 1934.

[63] Anthony interview.

[64] Minutes, Local 18319, Jan. 7, 1934, Local 2 Archives.

[65] *ABJ*, Jan. 8, 1934.

wrote Claherty.[66] A Washington protest meeting of FLU leaders from other industries on the same day should have provided more insight.

THE ADVENT OF COLLECTIVE BARGAINING

Whatever their opinions of Green, Claherty, and the AFL, rubber workers realized that their foremost challenge was to show that they could make a difference in the plant. This test took different forms. In Akron the Big Three companies presented special opportunities and problems. They were so visible and so closely identified with the NIRA that traditional anti-union policies would have provoked a major scandal; the New Deal program severely restricted their options. But their comparatively enlightened policies also limited the unions' potential. High wages, the six-hour day, good working conditions, generous benefits, and neutrality toward the AFL eliminated most sources of discord. The workers' most obvious grievance was the Depression, not their employers' activities. In other cities and especially in nontire plants, the spirit of the recovery effort was less pervasive. Most employers had little interest in personnel work or public relations and rejected the doctrines of Litchfield, Firestone, and Ching as fatuous or self-indulgent. They paid low wages and cut costs wherever possible. The unions' potential was enormous, providing they could survive.

Akron unionists faced a unique situation in 1933 and early 1934 as recovery reduced the workers' distress and the NIRA put the employers on their best behavior. Besides permitting the largely uncontested organization of their plants, the Akron manufacturers granted wage increases of 10 percent in June 1933, 7.5 percent in August and September, and 10 percent in February 1934.[67] They continued to support the Akron Employers' Association, but their most direct challenge to the unions was the formation of company unions. In the fall of 1933, Goodrich, Firestone, and General Tire created employee representation plans, and Goodyear introduced Industrial Assemblies in all its plants. While these "unions" bore only a superficial resemblance to the original Industrial Assembly or to U.S. Rubber's Factory Councils, they were an alternative to the unproven AFL organizations. Like many other new industrial unions, the Akron FLUs were challenged rather than attacked.

The implications of these developments were apparent in Claherty's relations with two Akron manufacturers. Almost from the moment of his arrival, he faced the prospect of a strike at India Tire, a small, marginal firm in suburban Mogadore. The India employees were poorly paid by Ak-

[66] Green to Claherty, Jan. 22, 1934, AFL Papers, Green Files.
[67] Goodyear, "Statement to Fact-Finding Board," FMCS Papers, RG 280, File 195/336.

ron standards, resentful, and eager to strike. Claherty kept them in check through the summer and fall and negotiated the first tire industry contract for them in February 1934. But he was unable to improve their wages relative to those paid by the big companies, and they remained dissatisfied. In April 1934, they struck for four weeks and won a pay raise. At Claherty's urging the management also adopted the union label and advertised its tires as the only union-made tires. Most buyers were unimpressed and business continued to decline.[68] Claherty and the FLU leaders had foolishly hailed the 1934 agreement as a breakthrough and a model for the industry. After February, they bore the opprobrium of the company's decline.

AFL relations with Goodrich were also complex and unsatisfying. In August 1933, Green reported that as a result of contacts with Goodrich executives, "the management of the Goodrich Company is not fundamentally hostile to the American Federation of Labor."[69] A few months later the company invited Spenser Miller, Jr., the AFL education director, to discuss the Federation's role in the recovery program with two hundred Goodrich executives. When Dalrymple and the local union officers asked for a conference, Vice-President T. G. Graham received them "very cordially" and supplied information that helped them set up grievance committees. Yet Graham's cordiality had limits. He wrote privately that a well-managed company could "challenge" and "defeat" the AFL because the unions "have not been prepared with competent leaders to take care of their tremendous increase in activities."[70] In a free and fair competition he believed he would win.

In October 1933, Graham introduced the Goodrich Cooperative Plan. He had had little faith in company unionism, but saw it as part of his larger plan. "I believe," he wrote, "that industry with the right viewpoint can train men more rapidly for Employee Representation work than can the A. F. of L."[71] Under the Goodrich plan, employees would elect departmental representatives to work with the management. Unresolved issues could be appealed to the president and board of directors. Representatives would receive fifteen dollars per month, and officers, more. As a letter to the employees explained, it was a "simple, workable" approach.[72] Factory workers elected representatives in late October, and office workers chose theirs in February 1934. Claherty ordered union members not to vote and

---

[68] Green to Claherty, July 28, 1933, May 3, 1934, and A. M. Shaffer to Green, April 20, 1934, AFL Papers, Reel 141; *ABJ*, Feb. 23, 1934.

[69] Green to Claherty, Aug. 24, 1933, AFL Papers, Green Files.

[70] Graham to Williams, Feb. 15, 1935, Williams Papers, Box 1, Folder 4.

[71] Ibid.

[72] "The Goodrich Cooperative Plan," Oct. 3, 1935; P. Montgomery to Workers, Oct. 3, 1933, Local 5 Archives, Local 5 offices, Akron, Ohio.

apparently many did not. Others cast blank ballots or voted for union men. Approximately half of the successful candidates were AFL members. Dalrymple and the local leaders soon ordered union members to resign their positions. In December they expelled those who refused. Thereafter the Cooperative Plan and the union were separate, competitive organizations.[73]

As Graham acknowledged, the plan's most important function was to identify grievances and eliminate them before the union could act. By March 1934, it claimed more than twenty improvements, including a minimum daily wage and an appeal policy for discharged workers. It had also resolved many individual grievances. Yet it did not immediately fulfill Graham's expectations. Many Goodrich supervisors apparently did not have the "right viewpoint." Some of them punished workers for submitting grievances; others were "over-hesitant about disciplining workers." Management representatives on the Wage and Welfare committees gave the workers "more information about the company" than they gave the foremen. By far the most serious obstacle, however, was the questionable legitimacy of the plan. One close observer found most employees lukewarm or completely "unsold." They believed that "all [the representatives] get is what the Company wants to give 'em." Their "universal" reaction was that "as long as the Representatives get paid by the Company, what can you expect?"[74] The Cooperative Plan might undermine the union, but it was unlikely to supersede it.

The other company unions formed in 1933 were similar in structure and operation. The Firestone Employees' Conference Plan, created in mid-October, provided for departmental representation, an elaborate grievance procedure, and a "Board of Arbitration." The employee representatives won a liberalized insurance plan and a seniority system that covered layoffs, transfers, and shift changes. The FLU ordered its members to resign from the conference plan and suspended forty-six who refused.[75]

The General Tire organization was more explicitly anti-union. When company vice-president Charles Jahant announced the formation of an Employees' Joint Council in August 1933, he promised that it would do more than the union. During the following months he announced various "concessions" at joint council meetings, including an improved group insurance plan and a generous vacation allowance. Jahant's insistence that

[73] Resolutions, Nov. 5, 1933, Local 5 Archives; Minutes, Executive Board, Local 18319, Local 5 Archives.

[74] Memo from Welfare Committee, Tire Division, March 23, 1934, Local 5 Archives; Williams to Graham, Oct. 14, 1934, Williams Papers, Box 4, Folder 1.

[75] "Constitution of Employees' Conference Plan, Oct. 14, 1933," and "Information for Firestone Employees," Feb. 1936, Firestone Archives, Firestone Tire & Rubber Co., Akron, Ohio; SCLN, June 15, 1934.

his relations with the joint council satisfied Section 7a infuriated Murray and the local union leaders.[76]

At Goodyear, the Industrial Assembly initially coexisted with the FLU. A large number of senators and representatives joined the union, and many assembly candidates in the September 1933 elections were AFL members. Like the Goodrich and Firestone employees, they saw the two groups as complementary workers' organizations. Union leaders were more skeptical, and Goodyear managers tried to tip the balance toward the assembly. By increasing the pay of assembly members, they were able to retain the allegiance of a majority of Goodyear employees with leadership experience. When wary union officers asked assembly representatives to resign, only one man—House—gave up his assembly post. The others cast their lot, sometimes reluctantly, with the assembly. Most notable was William Cash, a senator and union member who would remain a prominent assembly figure. In August 1934, the union officially banned participation in the assembly.[77]

Confident that the assembly insulated them from any serious threat, Goodyear executives fired four activists, including Clark Culver, in July 1933. Claherty immediately contacted Green, who taught the executives a lesson in the new politics of industrial relations. Green arranged for Culver and another discharged man to present their cases to various government officials, after which NRA and Labor Department representatives descended on Goodyear. "I gave special consideration to these cases," Green boasted.[78] In late August Slusser reluctantly agreed to reinstate the men. Several weeks later, when Culver asked for a leave of absence to attend the AFL convention and his supervisor threatened to discharge him, the union again appealed to Washington. A National Labor Board official gave Litchfield a tongue-lashing and Slusser subsequently "discovered" a provision in the factory manual that permitted leaves. Thereafter Goodyear executives were more circumspect. They tried to undermine the union but never actually dismissed workers for union activity. The FLU leaders were surprised.[79]

Outside of Akron, relations between organized rubber workers and their

[76] "From Employees of the General Tire & Rubber Co.," FMCS Papers, RG 280, File 176/446; Minutes of the Joint Council, Feb. 13, March 14, 1934, NLRB Papers, RG 25, Box 3, File 70.

[77] House interviews; Minutes, Executive Board, Local 18282, Aug. 24, 1934, Local 2 Archives.

[78] Green to Claherty, Aug. 29, 1933, AFL Papers, Green Files.

[79] H. D. Friel to H. L. Kerwin, Aug. 27, 1933, FMCS Papers, RG 280, File 176/304; John D. Moore, Memorandum, Oct. 2, 1933, and Denlinger to William M. Leiserson, Oct. 2, 1933, National Labor Board Correspondence, NLRB Papers, RG 25.

employers more closely resembled the traditional pattern of confrontation and resistance. In relatively isolated and hostile settings, company unions were far less common; strikes, firings, and beatings were more frequent; and government intervention was almost wholly ineffectual. The casualties were high by Akron standards. In many cases the workers' only hope was outside assistance.

Tire workers faced a variety of hostile pressures. Gray and the Gadsden officers, for example, were optimistic about their prospects until an August 1933 layoff of eighty-four veteran employees, including many union activists, emphasized their peril.[80] Kelly-Springfield unionists had a similar experience in early June 1934, when the company furloughed most of the local officers, all veteran workers, on the pretext of creating more work for experienced employees. Bob Roberts eventually persuaded the Kelly managers to reinstate the union officers and to consider prior service in the future. Yet the company soon violated the understanding, and relations between the FLU and the plant managers continued to deteriorate in the following months. When the company, bankrupt and in the process of reorganization, made sweeping layoffs in early 1935 without regard to seniority, the workers were ready to strike. The issue was not the layoffs per se, but the credibility of the union. "If we don't get seniority rights at the Kelly Tire Plant quick," one officer wrote to William Green, "we are lost."[81]

The histories of the Los Angeles FLUS were more varied. Samson executives discouraged organization but did not actively interfere, presumably because of Ching's subtle influence. Indeed, the plant manager often seemed "almost happy" to have the union and willingly discussed grievances and other problems. In return the union "didn't agitate."[82] Goodrich managers relied on a company union, fear of reprisals, and industrial espionage to keep the local at bay. Though the company union commanded no more support than it did in Akron, it enabled the company to counter union claims that it alone represented the employees. Goodrich executives used threats of discharges in much the same way. They obeyed the letter of the law but did not discourage suspicions that they would resort to underhanded tactics. As a result, many members carried their membership buttons "in their pockets." Only a handful dared "to stick their necks out."[83] Frank Grillo was one of the latter. In early 1934 he announced with characteristic bravado that he would attend an NRA

---

[80] Local 18372 Minutes, Feb. 10, 24, April 1, 14, 1934, Local 12 File, United Rubber Workers Archives, URW offices, Akron, Ohio.

[81] H. T. Wilson to William Green, May 2, 1935, AFL Papers, Local 19007 Correspondence.

[82] George Crawford interview.

[83] Floyd Gartrell interview.

meeting during working hours. When he refused to heed the foreman's warnings, the supervisor fired him. The union could do nothing. Firestone manager C. L. Smith used threats, promises, and reprisals, including selective discharges, to undermine the union. In the words of Floyd Gartrell, the Firestone workers were "hot to trot and Firestone cooled them off."[84] Just the threat of reprisals was apparently sufficient to contain the union impulse at Goodyear. The local survived but its future remained uncertain.

At most small midwestern tire companies, tension and conflict between the locals and plant officials were the rule. Workers at Cooper Tire in Findlay, Ohio, encountered continuous opposition.[85] Pharis Tire unionists faced a hostile employer and a company union modeled after U.S. Rubber's Factory Councils. In late October 1933, the company fired three union members who were poor workers, and the local prepared to strike. When Labor Department conciliators persuaded the plant manager to reemploy two of the men, union leaders took advantage of the "victory" to demand recognition. Pharis officials refused, and the workers struck in April 1934. After a week the company granted a wage increase and a written contract, the second in the industry.[86]

FLU leaders at Mansfield Tire & Rubber, in Mansfield, Ohio, organized nearly seven hundred of the plant's eight hundred production employees and demanded action on a variety of grievances. They claimed the plant manager had "high-hatted them and had neglected to adjust small difficulties."[87] Their unhappiness came to the surface in March 1934, when the superintendent discharged Edna McGale, a tube worker. McGale's strident defense of the union among the largely nonunion women employees, including a warning that the union would "shoot them" if they tried to work during a strike, made her an unpopular figure. After more than a month of unsuccessful appeals, the Mansfield local began an unconventional protest. As a company document reported on May 15, tire builders "since that time [May 9] have reported for work but have refused to work and have remained idle."[88] Perplexed at what may have been the industry's first sitdown, company executives made no effort to expel the workers. On May 15 union members also began to picket the plant and block the gates. Three days later the company president agreed to begin negotiations and to make

[84] Ibid. Also Edward Barnes interview.

[85] J. G. Hughes to G. B. Roberts, Jan. 31, 1934, URW Archives.

[86] N. S. Clark, "Pharis Rubber Company, Newark, Ohio," n.d., NLRB Papers, RG 25, Box 8, Case 174; *SCLN*, March 24, Aug. 17, 1934.

[87] N. S. Clark, "Report on Mansfield Tire & Rubber Co. Controversy," May 21, 1934; Clark, memo, July 16, 1934, NLRB Papers, RG 25, Box 9, File 201.

[88] "Mansfield Tire & Rubber Co. vs. Federal Labor Union 18384, May 15, 1934," URW Archives.

any pay increases retroactive. The workers called off the strike and returned to work. In the following weeks, union-management conferences resolved many issues. One exception was the McGale firing, which the company refused to reconsider.

In the nontire plants ordinary union members, not the militants, were the issue. As a veteran worker at Sun Rubber in Barberton, Ohio, reported: "The boss has been riding me every day since I have starte[d] this union. He told me 10 days ago that I ought to go back to Pennsylvania and get some brains knock[ed] in my head."[89] In many cases the reprimand was less conditional. One discharged worker reported that he thought he "was safe and that Mr. White [the superintendent] was trying to run a bluff on me but I found out different."[90] An activist at the Johnson Rubber Co. in Middlefield, Ohio, received a message from "a friend": "The goddam storekeepers have a bucket of tar and some feathers. They want to catch you som[e] night from work."[91] Though the exact toll of union members is unknown, its magnitude is suggested by the experiences of four Ohio locals.

Soon after a group of workers at the Eagle Rubber Co. in Ashland, Ohio, formed an FLU, H. R. Gill, the company president, laid off the local officers. When he refused to meet a union committee, approximately 50 of the company's 180 employees struck and appealed to the regional labor board. They received favorable rulings from the Cleveland and National Labor Boards, but Gill still refused to have any contact with the AFL or to pay any attention to the government proceedings. To the strikers, the powerlessness of the labor movement and the government came as a surprise. John Bauman, the union secretary, reported to Roberts in January 1934 that "the fellows come to my house and hound me on the streets. . . . They cuss you and Claherty . . . the A. F. of L., the U.S. government, and I suppose to my back, me too. I can't blame them much."[92]

The Eagle strikers' plight became more severe as the labor board proceedings dragged on. Some union members finally went back to their jobs; others found new work. Gill told Bauman that if he had to rehire the strikers he would find another excuse to fire them. The Akron locals provided financial aid, but without some hope of success the union gradually disintegrated. By late 1934 Bauman was desperate. "If you can . . . do anything to hasten a settlement . . . for Heaven's sake do it," he implored Roberts.[93] By the end of the year the Eagle union had disappeared, together with an-

[89] Carl Page affidavit, ca. Oct. 1933, URW Archives.
[90] C. O. Thornberry to G. B. Roberts, Oct. 30, 1934, URW Archives.
[91] "A friend" to Lee Lane, n.d., URW Archives.
[92] John Bauman to G. B. Roberts, Jan. 17, 1934, URW Archives.
[93] Bauman to Roberts, Nov. 1, 1934, URW Archives.

other local at the neighboring Faultless Rubber Company. Ashland workers seemingly had learned that the New Deal and the AFL had little to offer besides hardship and lost opportunities.

Rubber workers at the Ohio Rubber Co. in Willoughby, Ohio, faced similar difficulties. Employment at the firm doubled to nine hundred as demand revived for the company's principal product, auto running boards, and NIRA restrictions cut the workweek from fifty-six to thirty-five hours. A federal labor union, organized in July 1933, attracted a large but "restless" membership. Led by veteran workers, the union struck for recognition in September. After several weeks the management agreed to recognize the union, and the employees went back to work. Shortly afterward, Ohio Rubber formed a company union and laid off many FLU members. The local turned to Claherty, who appealed to the regional labor board in vain. The local avoided the fate of the Eagle unionists only because it commanded the support of a large number of the employees and had an unusual leader in Charles Lanning, the local president. The son of an Ohio United Mine Workers official, Lanning had been the president of a UMW local in the 1920s and brought to Ohio Rubber a comparative wealth of experience and skill.[94]

When rubber workers at Aetna Rubber Co. in Ashtabula, Ohio, organized in September 1933, company president S. T. Campbell could not decide whether to discharge them or befriend them. He did both. Rounds of discharges, reinstatements, and promises of recognition, punctuated by a ten-day strike in October, followed. After a brief respite, Campbell began a new round of attacks in early 1934. "The situation is very urgent," an anguished union secretary reported. "We are facing the entire eradication of our labor union in this factory."[95] When Campbell arbitrarily discharged fifty workers on March 19, the 450 remaining FLU members struck. The conflict was exceptionally bitter. Campbell persuaded the police to arrest many pickets and on April 5 personally led an attack on the picket line. In the bloody clash that followed, he was among the injured. When federal conciliators finally arranged a conference, Campbell conceded everything the union asked, then reverted to his anti-union posture when work resumed. By late 1934 the union was no better established than it had been a year before.[96]

Union-management relations at the Barr Rubber Company of Sandusky,

[94] E. E. Potts to Green, Aug. 2, 1933, AFL Papers, Green Files; *Souvenir Program*, pp. 32, 34.

[95] H. F. Forsythe to Robert F. Wagner, Jan. 27, 1934, NLRB Papers, RG 25, Box 1, Case 6.

[96] "In the Matter of the Aetna Rubber Company," Nov. 21, 1934, FMCS Papers, RG 280, File 176/756.

Ohio, were no less troubled. When the company fired several union activists in February 1934, the FLU struck. Four days later government conciliators worked out a compromise that provided for reinstatements and a no-strike pledge. The management nevertheless continued to discharge union members and hire nonunion workers; the union charged that forty members were fired in two months. After a hearing on March 27, the regional labor board called for the rehiring of ten employees within two weeks. The next day Barr executives fired another union worker and union members walked out. The strike lasted 190 days, longer than any other in the industry during that turbulent year.[97]

The second Barr walkout was as bitter as the second Aetna strike. Picket line violence, together with the workers' violation of the no-strike pledge, turned local citizens against the union. Ralph Lind, executive secretary of the Cleveland Labor Board, privately called for the AFL and the city's "substantial citizens" to "crack down."[98] In late May the National Labor Board ordered an end to the strike, the retention of all nonstrikers, and the discharge of strikers who had been involved in violence. Union leaders rejected the decision and continued to picket. W. H. Wilson, whom Claherty assigned to the dispute, was caught in the middle. When he defended the strike, he was accused of rabble rousing; when he urged the union to compromise, he was hooted down. Finally, after more attacks on nonstrikers, Wilson persuaded the strikers to capitulate and accept a contract based on the NLB ruling. Ninety-five strikers were rehired immediately and others were placed on a preferential hiring list. The company agreed to meet union representatives "from time to time" and to consider seniority in making layoffs.[99]

CONFLICT AT GENERAL TIRE

During the spring and summer of 1934, the spark of industrial turmoil that Congress had ignited and the AFL fanned became an inferno. Not since the heady days of 1919 and 1920 had Americans witnessed a comparable phenomenon. The San Francisco dock strike, the Minneapolis Teamsters strike, the Toledo Auto-Lite strike, and the nationwide textile strike (which included beatings and the forceable expulsion of union members at Goodyear's Georgia mills) were the best known of dozens of conflicts that set

[97] "In the Matter of Barr Rubber Company and United Rubber Workers Union No. 19075," June 21, 1934, NLRB Papers, RG 25 Box 2, Case 108.

[98] Ralph A. Lind to W. H. Wilson, April 25, 1934, NLRB Papers, RG 25, Box 2, Case 108; *Sandusky Register*, July 17, 1934.

[99] *Sandusky Register*, July 17, 1934; "Conversation with Wilson, Dorn, Frohman," July 17, 1934, and "Agreement," NLRB Papers, RG 25, Box 2, Case 108.

back the recovery program and, directly or indirectly, the labor movement. In recent years historians have argued that the union troubles of 1934 curbed the power of rank-and-file workers and permitted discredited labor bosses like John L. Lewis to regain much of their authority. Thereafter, they suggest, organized labor was more disciplined, more authoritarian, and more dependent on government for its growth.[100]

The rubber workers provide only partial support for this view. They were as "undisciplined" as other novice unionists and as vulnerable, as their experiences at Ashtabula and Sandusky demonstrated. But their reaction was different. By the spring of 1934 most FLU leaders, including those who had opposed the Indianapolis rebels, blamed Claherty and the AFL for their problems and began to consider a more independent and militant course. The change was first apparent at General Tire, where Murray and the FLU leaders became embroiled in a major conflict with the company. The General Tire dispute, which has received virtually no attention in accounts of the turmoil of 1934, was as much a harbinger of the future as any of the strike defeats of that spring.

Two comparatively minor grievances fueled the conflict. General Tire wage rates were marginally lower than those of the Big Three, and General Tire executives maintained the pretense that the Employees' Joint Council represented the employees. For Murray these were not trivial issues. The challenge for Akron union activists was not survival, but viability. Mass discharges were not a threat; worker apathy and disillusionment were. The General Tire managers could not overtly destroy the union, but they might still lull it into impotence. Though the specific points of contention at General Tire might seem trivial to visitors from Ashtabula or Sandusky, the stakes were equally high.

By early 1934 Murray began to suspect that Claherty would be of little help to him in this struggle. The organizer's answer to the company union problem was to circulate petitions asking the regional labor board to grant exclusive recognition to the union. If this request did not have the desired result, he planned to ask the board to conduct an election among the rubber workers. Since the board's powers were imprecise and by most interpretations did not include the authority to confer exclusive rights on any group, Claherty had little hope for a legal solution. His real goal was to dramatize the weakness of the company unions and the futility of resisting the AFL. On February 6 Murray and Claherty took the petition with 791 names (or more than 70 percent of the approximately one thousand one hundred em-

[100] See Staughton Lynd, "The Possibility of Radicalism in the Early 1930's: The Case of Steel," *Radical America* 6 (1972), pp. 37–64; James R. Green, *The World of the Worker: Labor in Twentieth Century America* (New York, 1980), pp. 144–48.

ployees) to the Cleveland board.[101] Regional Secretary Lind could do little more than thank them. When they approached Vice-President Jahant at General Tire they received even less satisfaction. He questioned the validity of the signatures and refused to discuss the recognition issue.

In March, Murray and the local officers took their first tentative steps away from Claherty. When Jahant also refused to respond to a contract proposal, they threatened to call a strike vote. The threat had no effect. By April, relations between the union and the company had degenerated into a "running battle," and the union began to explore other options more aggressively. Apparently Murray first suggested the possibility of an extension of the workers' "veto" until every machine had stopped. When he broached the idea to Claherty, he got nowhere. But since he and his colleagues "couldn't find a better method," they decided independently to plan a protest inside the plant, a "sit-down." Murray later recalled that

We started a program of exchanging information with our key people . . . and we run a "school" for a couple of weeks trying to anticipate what actions . . . the company may try to do. . .

For example, if they brought the police in . . . we could give them [the strikers] a signal and they would go to work, and they would work until the police left the plant and then we would shut it down again. . . . We discussed the thing in detail from A to Z. . . .

The stewards were pretty well informed to keep [these plans] . . . under their hat and at the proper, opportune time these people would be given a signal what to do or what not to do. They explained to the rest of the people that a signal was to be given. It wasn't to be done unless the signal was given.[102]

Confrontation became inevitable in mid-June when General Tire cut piece rates in the tire departments. When the tire builders protested, Murray demanded a response within twenty-four hours. The next night, June 19, he gave the superintendent an additional two hours, until 7:00 p.m. When nothing happened, he implemented the sit-down plan.

[The strike] started when I walked through the plant and gave [the workers] the signal to shut it down. That's when it started. And as fast as I could walk from one department to another, throughout the plant, that's when it went down. And one of the plant guards was following me from about the time I got to the second department, telling me I couldn't do it. "You have to stay in your own department." I said, "I'll go back to my department in a little while!" and I just kept walking, one

[101] *SCLN*, Feb. 29, 1934; "Case No. 70," NLRB Papers, RG 25, Box 3, File 70.
[102] Rex Murray interviews. Jack Abshire and W. K. Prather, members of the local bargaining committee, do not recall the "school" (Jack O. Abshire, interview with author, Nov. 2. 1972; W. K. Prather, interview with author, Nov. 4, 1972).

floor to the other. When I gave them the signal they pulled the switches and shut it down.[103]

This action, the first important sit-down strike in American industry, foreshadowed a new era of industrial conflict.[104] It was, most obviously, a grass-roots enterprise. Neither Green, Claherty, nor other Akron area labor leaders, apart from the General Tire local officers, played any role in it. Murray's recollections emphasize his contribution, but the success of the sit-down depended on the unity and discipline of hundreds of rank-and-file workers, who required no "school" to appreciate the significance of their behavior. Equally important was the managers' response. Jahant and the supervisors were taken aback. Was it a strike or not? They decided not to intervene. The next morning Jahant went from department to department "and the people listened to what he had to say and sat tight."[105] But Murray and the other leaders began to worry. They had not counted on a prolonged siege and were unsure of their next step if Jahant closed the factory. For these reasons they responded favorably when Jahant asked to meet the workers in the plant yard at noon on June 20.

The end of the sit-down marked the beginning of the most important strike in the industry since 1913. Amid cries of "Down with the speedup system" and "Give us a raise now," Jahant promised to match the rates of the Big Three and to abolish the company union if 95 percent of the employees voted against it. He finished by calling for an immediate return to work, but Murray interrupted to announce a meeting of union members to vote on the proposals. The crowd moved to a nearby high school auditorium where Claherty, several union leaders, and Garnet L. Patterson, one of the local's attorneys, spoke. When Murray then called for a vote on Jahant's offer, the workers insisted that the company promise in writing to abolish the joint council.[106] Since Murray and the local officers knew that the company would not agree to a written statement, they organized pickets and a commissary to be operated by the strikers' wives. Later they persuaded local retail firms, including several department stores, to donate food, tables, and other necessities and prevailed on other Akron unions to

[103] Murray interviews. In 1937 the U.S. Department of Labor attempted to categorize the sit-down strikes. This paragraph describes one of the five types (see *Monthly Labor Review* 44 (1937): 1233.

[104] I have discussed the origins of the sit-down technique in "The Beginning of the Sit-Down Era: The Reminiscences of Rex Murray," *Labor History* 15 (1974): 89–90. Sit-downs had already occurred in many industries without attracting much attention. See Sidney Fine, *Sit-Down: The General Motors Strike of 1936–37* (Ann Arbor, 1969), pp. 128–31, and Tamara Hareven, *Family Time and Industrial Time* (Cambridge, 1982), pp. 349–51.

[105] Murray interviews.

[106] *ABJ*, June 21, 1934.

contribute money. At Claherty's suggestion, Green sent $1,000, which Murray later returned.[107]

On June 21 the pickets and hundreds of other rubber workers blocked the plant gates and turned away office workers. Jahant, arriving by auto, was incensed when he had to walk in. President William O'Neil issued a statement rejecting all negotiations until the strikers returned to their jobs. That afternoon, he accompanied a group of stenographers when they left the office. As they crossed the picket line, the strikers shouted: "Don't come back. You won't get in." O'Neil turned to the pickets.

O'Neil: "You boys are going about it in the wrong way. You have the wrong man at the head. This man Claherty's a racketeer. . . . It's he, an outsider who is dominating. . . . Don't you know he's getting paid for stirring you fellows up."
William Sweet [a picket]: "The men have chosen their leaders and they are going to stick by them."
O'Neil: "You ought to be solving your own problems."
Sweet: "That's what we hope to do."[108]

O'Neil's suspicions notwithstanding, Claherty played almost no direct role in the strike. The local leaders simply ignored him. His reports reflect a pathetic ignorance of strike activities.[109] During the second week of the dispute he left on an extended trip to the East, his only such sojourn during more than two years in Akron.

Claherty was not the only outsider to incur the strikers' hostility. On June 21 three men identified as Communists appeared at the plant and began distributing literature. The pickets promptly seized their materials and sent them away with warnings not to reappear. A few days later four women arrived and began to sell the *Daily Worker*. The women strikers took care of them in similar fashion. Murray recalled that "some of them got their rear ends kicked pretty hard a couple of times." The Communists did not return.[110]

With Lind's prompting, negotiations between the strikers and O'Neil began almost immediately. After several days of talks O'Neil reaffirmed Jahant's wage offer. He was more reluctant to repudiate the joint council and adamantly refused to sign an agreement. The status of the FLU quickly became the stumbling block to a settlement. For the next two weeks Lind tried without success to find a formula that would satisfy the union without officially recognizing the local or the AFL.

During this period General Tire executives tried to wean halfhearted

---

[107] Jack O. Abshire interview; Murray interviews.
[108] *ABJ*, June 22, 1934.
[109] Claherty to Green, June 25, July 2, 1934, AFL Papers, Local 18323 Correspondence.
[110] Murray interviews; *ABJ*, June 26, 1934.

strikers from the union with the promise of an immediate wage increase. On June 25 the Independent General Workers Union, an anti-AFL group formed under company auspices several months before, announced that it had voted to return to work. Claiming four hundred to six hundred members, it circulated antistrike petitions and distributed postcards, which employees were to mail back indicating their desire to return. Strikers believed that the General Tire public relations department had organized both efforts. The petitions and postcards were signed by "foremen, supervisors and persons known to have been friendly to the employees' representation plan." They were "teacher's pets," "red apple" boys.[111] Thereafter, "red apple" became the most damning epithet of the Akron labor wars.

On July 8, O'Neil publicly attacked the "minority" behind the strike and pledged to meet any group of employees. He reiterated these themes in a radio address the next night.[112] At the same time a local attorney, E. W. Brouse, announced a mass meeting of General Tire employees to take a secret strike vote. Murray and the local officers at first urged strikers to boycott the meeting. However, at a strike rally on the afternoon of July 9, union attorney Stanley Denlinger warned that the meeting "will probably be packed with red apple boys, office workers and strikebreakers."[113] A vote to return to work, even by an unrepresentative group, would harm the union. When he finished, the strikers voted for a confrontation.

The next morning Denlinger, Murray, and Bob Roberts led a crowd of nine hundred strikers to the auditorium where a hundred more union men waited. Supervisors stationed at the doors tried to stop them but the sheriff, a controversial figure involved in a difficult reelection race, appeared at a critical moment and forced them to admit the strikers. Brouse was addressing an audience of several hundred when the strikers burst into the auditorium. Denlinger pushed Brouse aside. "Will you listen to me?" he shouted. The strikers cheered. He asked for a vote on whether to proceed with a secret ballot. The AFL men were unanimously opposed. Brouse and his supporters walked out, while unionists made confetti of their printed ballots. The sheriff then made an impassioned reelection speech and the meeting broke up.[114]

Though O'Neil condemned the incident, he realized that it demonstrated the futility of his policy. On July 17 he summoned Murray and other members of the local's executive committee to his home. He specifically excluded Claherty. During twelve hours of talks, he and Murray devised a mutually satisfactory statement. O'Neil promised to reinstate the strikers,

[111] *ABJ*, June 25, 1934; *SCLN*, June 22, 1934, p. 1.
[112] *ABJ*, July 9, 10, 1934.
[113] *ABJ*, July 10, 1934.
[114] Ibid.

raise wages, end all support for the company union, meet union representatives on request, and consider seniority in making layoffs and recalls. The
document did not mention the union or the AFL and was signed only by
O'Neil. As Denlinger explained, it granted the union recognition and various substantive gains while preserving the company's status as a nonunion
concern.[115] AFL officials in Washington were dismayed that the Federation
was wholly omitted from it.[116] O'Neil subsequently extended the same
concessions to other employees, arguing that it was not necessary to be a
union member.

The ratification meeting, on July 18, was anticlimactic. The strikers, a
reporter noted, wanted to "shout and sing" and "celebrate." The only
tense moment came when Claherty mounted the stage. "Give him five minutes," shouted several workers. Union leaders anxiously awaited his comments and the strikers' reaction. Claherty "came through splendidly" with
a "rousing tribute to the agreement and the committee which recommended
it." When Murray asked for a standing vote on the agreement, "the entire
crowd as one man jumped to its feet with a cheer that could be heard a
block away." For the rest of the evening the strikers celebrated their victory
with impromptu parades and auto caravans. Amid the merrymaking two
comments captured the larger significance of the evening. A truck-tire
builder observed that the strikers had learned "to know one another better
and appreciate our respective problems." A reporter added that "the precedent set may chart the course of future tire labor negotiations."[117]

The General Tire strike was a historic breakthrough for the workers and
the union. The strikers were no more militant than the 1913 strikers, but
better led. Murray and his associates set goals, mobilized the resources of
fellow workers, cultivated a positive public image, and, when necessary,
downplayed their AFL ties. They also benefited from the indirect curbs the
NIRA had imposed on employer behavior. A major manufacturer could not
do what Seiberling and Firestone had done in 1913 or what H. R. Gill,
S. T. Campbell, and other small-town employers did in 1934. This change
substantially favored the unions, at least unions that were prepared to take
advantage of a novel opportunity. Yet by the time the General Tire strikers
returned to their machines, the New Deal recovery program and the busi-
ness-government alliance were in deep trouble. In the future the rubber
workers would be even more dependent on their own resources.

[115] Murray interviews; Jack O. Abshire interview; Agreement, July 17, 1934, FMCS Papers,
RG 280, File 182/524; *ABJ*, July 19, 1934.
[116] Marjorie Black to Green, Aug. 15, 1934, AFL Papers, Local 18319 Correspondence.
[117] *ABJ*, July 19, 1934; *ATP*, July 19, 1934.

CHAPTER SIX

Labor in Transition, 1934–1935

HE WAS "so plodding and earnest and determined that everyone had confidence in him," recalled one acquaintance.[1] He was "honest" and "very, very likeable," observed a second.[2] "I don't know of anyone more honest than Dal," conceded a third.[3] Sherman H. Dalrymple (1889–1962) was homely, inarticulate, and reassuring. His enemies pointed to his fourth-grade education; he admitted that it was less than that. He came to Akron in 1903 to help pay off debts on his family's West Virginia farm. Like other rugged young men, he stayed and prospered. An experienced tire builder by 1917, he joined the Marine Corps, rose from private to lieutenant, and returned a war hero. In the 1920s he found steady work in the B. F. Goodrich tire room and in 1933 helped organize the Goodrich tire builders. Amid the turmoil that followed, Dalrymple stood out as steady, mature, and honest. He won the local union presidency and two years later the presidency of the new United Rubber Workers of America. He was probably the most unpretentious of the union presidents who joined John L. Lewis's Committee for Industrial Organization (CIO). His success was proof that the values of the Akron rubber workers had meaning in a world dominated by men like Lewis and William Green.[4]

THE AFL ON TRIAL

On the eve of the General Tire strike it appeared that Dalrymple and men like him would play only minor roles in the continuing drama of the rubber workers. By the spring of 1934 William Green had done a complete about-face; for the next two years he would devote more attention to the Akron workers than to any other single union group. His interest reflected his sensitivity to his Ohio roots and the industry's potential. It provides an unparalleled opportunity to examine the policies that CIO partisans and liberal historians would later point to as proof of AFL conservatism and incompetence.

[1] James S. Jackson, interview with author, Oct. 5, 1973.

[2] Cyrus Ching, Oral History Memoir, Columbia University, 3: 362.

[3] Harley C. Anthony, interview with author, April 11, 1972.

[4] Sherman H. Dalrymple, interview with Joe Glazer, April 2, 1955; Gary M. Fink, ed., *Biographical Dictionary of American Labor* (Westport, 1984), pp. 70–81.

Green's strategy in 1934–1935 was hardly innovative. As in 1913, he saw his advantage in the employers' temporary weakness. He assigned his organizers to avoid the Scylla of outright rejection and the Charybdis of a strike until federal government assistance made the gains of 1933–1934 permanent. It was a cautious, opportunistic approach, consistent with AFL efforts in the industry since 1900 and Green's preference for political action. Green likewise confronted many of the questions he had faced in 1913. Would the manufacturers regain their self-confidence and independence before he had succeeded? Would Claherty and his staff perform effectively? Most of all, would the government prove more helpful this time?

Already there were warning signs. The aggressive tactics of the General Tire management suggested that some large employers were ready to take the offensive. The growing criticism of Claherty's stewardship was equally disturbing to Green. Most serious of all was the growing disarray in Washington. Defiance of National Labor Board rulings by firms like Eagle Rubber had exposed the hollowness of Section 7a and prompted Senator Robert Wagner to introduce a pro-union labor disputes bill in March 1934. Reacting to the spectacular strike wave of the following months, President Roosevelt proposed a noncontroversial substitute, Public Resolution 44, which reorganized the National Labor Board as the National Labor Relations Board and authorized it to hold employee-representation elections, though the meaning of the elections was not spelled out. Neither Roosevelt nor Congress, which adopted the resolution in late June, took any stand on the critical issue of majority rule and exclusive representation, favored by the AFL and its allies. Green saw winner-take-all elections and legally enforceable grants of exclusive representation as the only peaceful way to compel recognition. He and Wagner continued to work behind the scenes for majority rule and specific enforcement powers.[5]

During the spring and summer of 1934, the labor movement in the rubber industry and particularly in the Akron area expanded to its all-time peak. "The 'outside unions' have quite evidently 'sold' their viewpoint widely," wrote Whiting Williams after a surreptitious visit to several workers' haunts. "Still worse, they appear to have gained wide adoption of their belief that the local employers are so selfish and hard-boiled that employees can hope to gain advantage only through force and warfare."[6] One knowl-

---

[5] William Green to Coleman Claherty, Aug. 22, 1934, American Federation of Labor Papers, Green Files, State Historical Society of Wisconsin, Madison; James A. Gross, *The Making of the National Labor Relations Board, A Study in Economics, Politics, and the Law* (Albany, 1974), pp. 70–73; Irving Bernstein, *Turbulent Years, A History of the American Worker, 1933–1941* (Boston, 1970), pp. 199–215.

[6] Whiting Williams to T. G. Graham, Oct. 14, 1934, Williams Papers, Box 4, Folder 1, Western Reserve Historical Society Library, Cleveland.

edgeable observer estimated that Summit County unions had forty thousand members on January 1 and sixty thousand by the time of the General Tire strike. The number of locals had quintupled to more than 100.[7] The rubber workers claimed approximately twenty five thousand members; the others were divided among manufacturing, the crafts, and services. No one doubted, however, that the two groups were linked, that the rubber workers' presence afforded many truck drivers, streetcar workers, and clerks the luxury of union membership.

By 1934 Akron had become identifiable as a union city. An irrepressible hedonist could have attended a union-sponsored entertainment—a dance, talent show, card party, baseball game, bowling tournament, boxing or wrestling match, picnic or parade—nearly every day of the week. Predictably, several ambitious local union officers cast their hats into the political arena as candidates for city or county offices. They received a sympathetic hearing but few votes. The acquisition of political power would prove far more difficult than any of the union politicians imagined.[8]

In contrast, the exercise of economic power was comparatively easy. During the spring, unprecedented numbers of Akron-area workers struck for wage increases or union recognition. In March and April, match and chemical workers in suburban Barberton brought industry there to a virtual standstill. Local machinists walked out during the same period. The General Tire strike came shortly thereafter. In July, four hundred union members at American Hard Rubber struck for the second time in 1934. Unionists hailed all of these conflicts because they resulted in signed agreements. But except for the General Tire settlement, the union triumphs were costly and sometimes dubious victories. As a local journalist noted, "the A. F. of L. is at a turning point in Akron. It must either show action or its membership is likely to skid downward as rapidly as it climbed upward."[9]

The key to the fate of the Green strategy and AFL prospects was Claherty, who faced formidable challenges during the summer of 1934. Despite successes, including the India Tire contract and the suppression of the Indianapolis rebellion, he was under increasing pressure to show that he could make a difference. His anticompany union petition campaign had underlined the risks inherent in his enterprise. He ran into even greater difficulty when he proposed to negotiate an industry-wide contract. Claherty's scheme—and it was apparently his idea, though Green vaguely approved it—was imaginative and utterly unrealistic. By April he had drafted a document that called for a seventy-five-cent minimum hourly wage (vs. the

[7] *ABJ*, Jan. 1, 1935.

[8] *ABJ*, July 5, July 20, 1934; *SCLN*, Oct. 5, Nov. 2, Nov. 23, 1934.

[9] *ABJ*, May 5, 1934.

forty-cent NIRA minimum), a guaranteed forty-four week year, a thirty-hour week, a thirty-five-cent-per-hour increase for all rubber workers, and seniority rights in layoffs and recalls. Claherty proposed to submit his proposal to the industry trade associations that had drafted the NIRA codes. Whether he really thought it would receive serious consideration is not clear, but from early May, when the locals dutifully approved the agreement, until July, when the Rubber Manufacturers' Association routinely dismissed it, he betrayed no public doubts. Whatever his purpose, the "blanket agreement" fiasco was a major blow to his credibility. His standing, none too high before, declined precipitously.[10]

Claherty did not help his cause by promoting the formation of a United Rubber Workers' Council in the spring of 1934. Councils of federal labor unions were the AFL response to worker demands for international unions in newly organized industries. Green and the executive council saw them as halfway houses for industrial workers until they had reconciled the jurisdictional claims of the established unions. Radio workers unilaterally formed the first council in January 1934. The AFL began to authorize councils in June, when the rubber workers' council was formed. During the next year at least six more appeared. Claherty proposed to combine the thirty-five or more rubber industry FLUs and the eleven or more other unions that represented rubber company employees. No other organizer was bolder in addressing the industrial union issue.[11]

On June 4, 104 delegates representing thirty-three FLU's, eleven Akron craft unions, and two Akron office workers' locals met at the Portage Hotel to form the URWC. The weather was unseasonably warm. Claherty chaired the sessions and served as adviser to the "inexperienced" delegates. When he presented a draft constitution that gave the craft unions a disproportionate voice in the selection of council officers, several delegates, led by Thomas Burns, objected, and the convention voted to defer any action. The next day Claherty was better prepared. He admitted that "some of the delegates feel they cannot sell the plan as submitted to their unions," and offered a concession. "We can say, if necessary, that this is a trial and that after the [blanket] agreement is negotiated the set up can be changed." Still, Burns and his allies persisted. John Dent of the Pennsylvania Rubber local called the plan a "mistake," and a Chicago delegate left in disgust at the presence of the craft unionists. To prevent more serious trouble, the

---

[10] Green to Claherty, May 8, 1934, AFL Papers, Green Files; John D. House, interviews with author, April 15, May 1, 1972; *ABJ*, April 30, 1934.

[11] James O. Morris, *Conflict Within the AFL: A Study of Craft Versus Industrial Unionism, 1901–1938* (Ithaca, 1958), pp. 167, 182–83; Craig Lawrence Phelan, "William Green and the Limits of Christian Idealism: The AFL Years, 1925–1952" (Ph.D. diss., Ohio State University, 1984), pp. 152–58.

craft representatives offered to reserve the council's top positions for rubber workers, providing the crafts were represented on the executive board. Burns, Dent, and the others agreed.[12]

Apart from this setback, Claherty dominated the convention. With the backing of the craft delegates, he defeated Burns for the council presidency by a vote of 81 to 12. Harry Eagle, the fiery president of the Mohawk local, narrowly defeated Burns for the vice-presidency, and Everett White, secretary-treasurer at the Goodyear local, won the treasurer's job. Craft unionists captured six of seven executive board seats. After making minor changes in the blanket agreement, the delegates adjourned, supposedly united and ready for any challenge.

Of the rubber workers who participated in the debates, Burns, Eagle, and Dent had demonstrated impressive political skills. Salvatore Camelio was the "hero of the convention" for his jokes and pranks. Frank Grillo "wasn't in town five minutes until he was acquainted with practically everyone."[13] White of Goodyear and Walter Welsch of the Pharis local were also popular. Among the other Akron delegates only John House and William Carney, also of the Goodyear local, took an active part in the proceedings. Dalrymple served as an election teller. Otherwise he made little impression.

A week later Claherty took Burns, chairman of the council's wage committee, and Stanley Denlinger to Washington to reassure Green that his strategy was succeeding. It was the last time Claherty could honestly report any progress. The General Tire strike and the manufacturers' rejection of the blanket agreement made the issue of Claherty's leadership inescapable. Many rubber workers concluded that the Federation had failed to "show results," and "just quit, gave up."[14] They could not "afford to pay $1 a month just for the privilege of going to a union meeting to hear dull speeches and a discussion of routine business."[15] Soon the Big Three locals were "in a holding position."[16]

Claherty's inability to manage the rubber workers meant that the role of the NLRB loomed ever larger in the Green strategy. Green pointedly suggested at an August meeting that Claherty try to arrange employee elections under NLRB auspices. Even if they did not guarantee recognition, they

---

[12] "Meeting of Delegates to Rubber Workers' Convention in Akron, Ohio, in the Portage Hotel," June 4, 1934, National Labor Relations Board Papers, RG 25, Box 275, National Archives.

[13] *SCLN*, June 8, 1934. A few months later, Dent began a distinguished career in the Pennsylvania legislature and subsequently served with distinction in the U.S. Congress.

[14] Rex Murray, interviews with author, Sept. 19, Oct. 7, 1972.

[15] *ABJ*, May 5, 1934.

[16] John D. House interviews.

would generate interest and enable the unions to invoke "the name of governmental machinery."[17] Claherty returned to Akron with new resolve and suggested that Dalrymple confront T. G. Graham. "In the event he questions us and brings up the issue of the Company Union, we will demand an immediate election."[18]

This plan was harder to implement than Claherty anticipated. Graham's out-of-town travel commitments suddenly increased, and Goodrich laid off one thousand workers with more regard for union membership than seniority. Because of this "runaround," Claherty had little choice but to secure Green's reluctant approval for a strike vote. To his relief two other events intervened before the local could act. The NLRB reaffirmed the principle of majority rule in its Houde decision of August 30, and Graham finally agreed to meet the local committee on August 31. He rejected its demands on September 4, but the delay forced the local to postone the strike vote. Claherty immediately asked Ralph Lind to hold elections in the Goodrich and Firestone plants.[19]

This action seemed to indicate that the period of "laying foundations" had at last ended. The *Summit County Labor News* reported that the Goodrich ballot would occur the following week, and the Firestone election, a week after that. The locals held special meetings "to round up votes for the elections."[20] Claherty had not specifically requested a Goodyear election because of misgivings about the Industrial Assembly, but Goodyear FLU leaders were bolder and asked for an election independently of the other locals. The Industrial Assembly voted to make a similar request on September 8, and launched its own campaign to rally support. When more than ten thousand workers cast ballots in the September 19 assembly primary, Claherty began to worry and Goodyear executives saw the possibility of a coup.[21]

The other executives had no such faith in their employee representation plans. After several weeks of delays and rumors that they would not oppose elections, Goodrich and Firestone executives announced that elections were unnecessary. Lind immediately ordered a hearing at which the company attorneys argued that the regional labor board had no constitutional authority to order employee elections. They also indicated their intention to appeal to the NLRB itself. At the conclusion of the hearing Lind ordered elections but conceded that the companies "will not abide by any majority

[17] Green to Claherty, Aug. 26, 1934, AFL Papers, Green Files.

[18] Claherty to Green, Aug. 20, 1934, AFL Papers, Local 18319 Correspondence.

[19] Claherty to Green, Aug. 28, Sept. 4, 1934, AFL Papers, Local 18319 Correspondence; *ABJ*, Sept. 6, 1934.

[20] *SCLN*, Sept. 14, 1934.

[21] *WCL*, Sept. 12, 1934.

decision.''[22] The NLRB handled the appeal, its most important post-Houde case, slowly and cautiously. In mid-October it ordered new hearings, apparently in an effort to preempt a court challenge. Dalrymple, Kriebel, and Garnet Patterson repeated their demands. The Firestone representative predicted a suit if the NLRB ordered an election. The board took another month to uphold Lind's decision.[23]

When the NLRB finally released its decision, ordering elections at Goodrich and Firestone within three weeks, union leaders were ecstatic. Green issued a special press release and canceled other engagements in order to appear at an Akron Armory rally on November 24. Waving a copy of the NLRB ruling, he made one of his most forceful speeches. "We have won in every court," he told the enthusiastic crowd. "I declare . . . that no corporation is going to deny us the fruits of our victory." Praising the workers' self-discipline, he dismissed the possibility that the manufacturers would appeal the decision.[24]

The union triumph was again short-lived. Presidents J. D. Tew of Goodrich and John Thomas of Firestone promised to defend their company unions and appealed to the federal circuit court on December 4, three days before the scheduled elections. The rash actions of the Goodyear local were no less threatening. Lind decided to go ahead with the Goodyear election because all the parties approved and the power of the NLRB was not an issue. Privately, he confided that he did not know "why the union insists on asking for an election, because I am inclined to think they will be defeated."[25] Slusser was more explicit. He told House that he was "ready for the vote tomorrow because we can lick hell out of you."[26] As the election approached, AFL officials suddenly realized their peril. Though Goodyear union leaders insisted they could win, Claherty insisted that they halt the election. The local officers dutifully demanded that the NLRB rule the Industrial Assembly off the ballot, forcing Lind to call off the election. "The labor board," House told reporters, "will rule the assembly out of the picture." He was more candid in adding that "the manufacturers are trying to put Goodyear out in front in this voting."[27]

While the AFL thus escaped potential disaster, it also compromised its image of law-abiding reasonableness. The manufacturers had resorted to legal loopholes to avoid potentially adverse decisions at Goodrich and Fire-

[22] Lind to NLRB, Oct. 3, 1934, NLRB Papers, RG 25, Box 17; *ABJ*, Sept. 21, 25, 26, 1934.

[23] *ABJ*, Oct. 10, 1934; *SCLN*, Oct. 26, 1934.

[24] *ABJ*, Nov. 26, 1934.

[25] Lind to Paul M. Herzog, Dec. 17, 1934, NLRB Papers, RG 25, Box 16.

[26] Conference with Goodyear Management, Jan. 3, 1935, Local 2 Archives, Local 2 Offices, Akron, Ohio.

[27] Minutes, Dec. 2, 1934, Local 2 Archives; *ABJ*, Dec. 3, 4, 1934.

stone. The Goodyear decision suggested that the AFL was no better. Lind wrote that the unions were "entitled to this maneuvering as much as the . . . companies are."[28] He did not add that the price was the unions' aura of moral superiority, which had accounted for much of their public support. After December, workers and townspeople found it easier to dismiss both sides as cynical and self-serving.

ADDITIONAL SETBACKS

Outside of Akron, the Green strategy faced even sterner tests. Union leaders in New England, Los Angeles, or Ashtabula who assumed that their employers would not oppose them or that the federal government would assist them in a substantial way usually had brief and unhappy careers. Those who were more realistic quickly learned the lesson of the General Tire strike: union success depended on the quality of local leadership and the ability to mobilize friends and neighbors outside the industry.

In the eastern plants there were comparatively few survivors. Thomas Burns negotiated an agreement with the Fisk management in early 1935 that provided modest wage increases and a grievance procedure. It became necessary for a worker to be "in good standing with his union before any grievance of his can receive consideration."[29] Salvatore Camelio won concessions at Boston Woven Hose by foregoing an immediate wage increase. In most eastern plants, however, there was no one of comparable stature. At Armstrong Tire in West Haven, Connecticut, union members refused to stand for local offices after the union president had been laid off, even though he was laid off "according to seniority."[30] At American Hard Rubber in Butler, New Jersey, 80 percent of the employees were union members, but "there is a question of real organization." Workers were "deathly afraid of a strike" and were reluctant even to attend meetings. A local AFL leader explained that "this is about the only place in town to work and if you are let out for any reason, it spells curtains."[31]

Where the employer was determined and resourceful, the union's task was even more formidable. Kelly-Springfield executives professed neutrality but used the company's financial collapse to rid the plant of union activists in late 1934. The local's contentious leaders turned to Claherty, but he proved no more helpful than the government. At best he would dispatch Roberts when their appeals or strike threats became insistent. The local

---

[28] Lind to NLRB, Dec. 11, 1934, NLRB Papers, RG 25, Box. 16.

[29] Thomas F. Burns to Green, Feb. 25, 1935, AFL Papers, Local 19002 Correspondence.

[30] Burns to Green, May 6, 1935, AFL Papers, Local 19002 Correspondence.

[31] John F. Kelly to George B. Roberts, Aug. 25, Oct. 12, 1934, United Rubber Workers Archives, URW offices, Akron, Ohio.

leaders besieged Green with complaints and threats. By October, they were thoroughly exasperated:

The disgusting, vacillating, dilatory and dissimulating policy of Claherty and his associates carried out since last June would make any red blooded, hard working, downtrodden laboring person lose all confidence in any affiliation of workers.

We want a direct reply from you and Claherty as to what you are going to do in this matter, *and we want this in very plain language.* We are pretty sick of *BUNKUM.*[32]

The local also voted to suspend its per capita tax payments. Roberts had the unenviable task of restoring order. In early November he persuaded the remaining members to repudiate their letters to Green; otherwise the AFL could do nothing for them.[33]

After mass layoffs in early April 1935, there was another crisis. Many of the furloughed men wanted an immediate strike; others proposed to "share the work even down to an hour a day."[34] Roberts dissuaded both groups and persuaded the management to rehire half the workers. When he failed to win the reinstatement of some veteran employees, the militants insisted on a strike vote, which failed. Roberts despaired. "Until such time that this company is taken out of its financial difficulties," he reported, "there is nothing much else we could do."[35] It was a measure of the local's condition that Claherty rejoiced when Goodyear announced in July 1935 that it had purchased Kelly-Springfield.

In Ohio, many of the small-town manufacturers felt sufficiently secure to oppose the FLUs openly and to use force, if necessary, to defeat them. The Aetna contract of April 1934 seemed to have no effect on company president S. T. Campbell, who did everything possible "to befuddle the union and break it down."[36] The workers responded with protests, wildcat strikes, and appeals to the AFL and to the NRA. Finally, when Campbell refused to negotiate a new agreement in mid-June 1935, they struck. On the second day of the strike, when approximately fifty nonstrikers reported for work, pickets bombarded their autos with rocks. The nonstrikers replied with pistol fire. Police used tear gas to clear the area and the mayor ordered a crackdown. The police arrested scores of pickets, clubbed others, and escorted nonstrikers to and from their homes. With no prospect of negotiations, no assistance from the AFL, and no relief from police harassment, the strike gradually collapsed. A few months later, when the plant closed,

[32] O'Donnell to Green, Oct. 30, 1934, AFL Papers, Local 19007 Correspondence.

[33] Roberts to Green, Nov. 5, 1934, URW Archives.

[34] Roberts to Green, April 8, 1935, URW Archives.

[35] Roberts to Green, May 4, 1935, URW Archives. Also see *Cumberland Evening Times*, April 23, 1935.

[36] Ralph A. Lind to NLRB, April 22, 1935, NLRB Papers, RG 25, Box 1, Case 6.

union members took grim satisfaction in the knowledge they had lost relatively little.[37]

The Ohio Rubber managers were less erratic if no less hostile. They organized a company union, stockpiled munitions, employed thugs and spies, authorized beatings of organizers, browbeat community groups, and in other ways implemented what would later be known as the "Mohawk Valley Formula." These activities discouraged Green but not Charles Lanning, the FLU president, who shrewdly used them to build the union. In early 1935, when tensions at the plant came to a head, he was ready for a strike.[38]

On February 18 negotiations broke down and Lanning led the men out. Two days of picket-line violence followed, as armed guards and detectives tried to move trucks in and out of the plant and strikers responded with bricks and stones. When the pickets continued to resist, the company's detectives devised a plan to have them arrested. On February 25 several detectives provoked a confrontation with a picket and then summoned guards and sheriff's deputies, who rushed from neighboring houses and bombarded the strikers with tear gas. During the battle that followed, a gas shell exploded in the portable kitchen where the strikers' wives were working. Gradually the fighting subsided and the deputies took the pickets, twenty-three in all, to the county jail. The guards burned the strikers' tents and tried to burn the kitchen.[39] Later that day the county prosecutor demanded that company and union representatives negotiate. After several marathon sessions and threats from the company's customers to find new suppliers, the company agreed to reemploy the strikers, recognize seniority, and stop aiding the company union. The strikers "all felt very happy."[40]

The settlement marked no change in company policy. Supervisors demoted returning union members, continued to favor the company union, and flatly refused to rehire employees who had been arrested. Protests by Ralph Lind were unavailing. Assuming a renewal of the conflict, Lanning recruited pickets from other unions. Alarmed at the prospect of another violent and costly struggle, Green ordered Claherty to intervene. Claherty's response was to request a relief fund for the unemployed workers. Two

[37] Thomas M. Finn to H. L. Kerwin, June 20, Aug. 3, 1935, Federal Mediation and Conciliation Service Papers, RG 280, File 182/526, National Archives; *Ashtabula Star Beacon*, June 20, 24, 25, 1935; Nathan Witt to Charles Fahy, Oct. 12, 1935, NLRB Papers, RG 25, Box 272.

[38] See U.S. Senate, Subcommittee of the Committee on Education and Labor, *Hearings*, 75th Cong., 1st sess. (Washington, 1937), pp. 15300–15343.

[39] R. D. Winstead, "Notes on the Activities and Interviews with Harry A. McGrath," NLRB Papers, RG 25, Box 1, Case 6; *Cleveland Plain Dealer*, Feb. 21, 23, 26, 1935; Charles Lanning to Green, April 22, 1935, AFL Papers, Local 18284 Correspondence.

[40] Claherty to Green, Feb. 25, March 1, 1935, AFL Papers, Local 18284 Correspondence.

hundred dollars, he wrote "would stop a lot of talking."[41] Green reluctantly complied. Lind pressured the company for more concessions, and the unemployed strikers, sustained by AFL funds, drifted away. One man wrote from Michigan that "it does look like I am running away" but ". . . I must have an income . . . in order to make my home life agreeable."[42] The threat of another strike gradually diminished.

In Los Angeles, a combination of company unions, selective discharges, and prolonged legal challenges to the rulings of the labor boards was as threatening to the locals as the heavy-handed methods of the small midwestern companies. The Goodyear organization virtually expired in 1934; the Firestone and Goodrich locals faced increasing opposition. The Goodrich tactic was simply to disregard the union whenever possible. Firestone went a step further and dismissed the local's leaders. The discharged men appealed to the labor board but found that government investigators were powerless. The Firestone local languished.[43]

The problems of the Samson local, the largest and most stable of the Los Angeles FLUs, underlined the limits of union power even under the most favorable circumstances. Samson unionists enjoyed harmonious relations with F. S. Carpenter, the plant manager, and dominated the Factory Council, but made little progress because U.S. Rubber's open shop policy prohibited formal or exclusive recognition, and Carpenter's efforts to encourage a "happy family" attitude made it difficult to rally the workers against a common "enemy."[44] Factory Council discussions gave employees a sense of participation in the operation of the plant that even union members found satisfying. In November 1934, Ching personally assured the workers that the company took them seriously. The local leaders acknowledged that the Samson approach relegated them to a tangential role and asked the regional board to order an election. When Carpenter refused to cooperate, the regional board referred the case to the NLRB, which upheld the regional ruling in March 1935.[45] Carpenter still refused to cooperate, and the NRA collapsed before it could take any action. The FLU continued to command the sympathies of a majority of Samson employees, but its prospects for a larger role in Samson labor policies were no better than they had been in late 1933.

[41] Claherty to Green, May 9, 1935, AFL Papers, Local 18284 Correspondence.

[42] Leonard Duncan to Roberts, July 9, 1935, URW Archives.

[43] Charles C. Humphreys vs. Firestone Tire & Rubber, March 5, 1934, NLRB Papers, RG 25, Box 8; Edward Barnes, interview with author, December 14, 1977.

[44] Minutes, Samson Factory Council, April 12, 1934, NLRB Papers, RG 25, Box 13.

[45] "In the matter of Samson Tire & Rubber and Federal Local Union 19747," May 15, 1935, NLRB Papers, RG 25, Box 9; Harold S. Roberts, *The Rubber Workers: Labor Organization and Collective Bargaining in the Rubber Industry* (New York, 1944), pp. 118–19.

CRISIS IN AKRON

Green's strategy had three bases: employer disarray, union discipline, and government assistance. By the end of 1934 it was apparent that the AFL could not count on immediate or meaningful federal aid, though Green remained hopeful for the future. That setback in turn raised questions about the workers. Green urged "an unusual degree of patience and self-control." He ordered Claherty "to see to it that the workers are not swept off their feet by feeling and passion. Nothing would please the rubber corporations more than . . . a disastrous and losing strike."[46] Even more problematic was employer defensiveness. By the spring of 1935 the integrated companies, like big business generally, enjoyed record sales despite the failure of the NRA and had little taste for new government programs. As evidence of their renewed confidence they announced price increases in late 1934 and adopted a more provocative approach to the AFL. They would test the unions, just as they were testing the market.

While the large firms became more assertive they did not embrace the policy of all-out hostility favored by the small midwestern companies. U.S. Rubber, spurred by Ching, simply reemphasized its policy of biased neutrality. It aided company unions but did not overtly oppose the AFL. Goodrich and Firestone accepted the organization of their workers as a fait accompli but made no pretense of neutrality toward Green, Claherty, or the FLUs. Goodyear policy was similar, except that Goodyear executives had long accepted the principle of organization and were confident that the assembly spoke for most Goodyear employees. There was one other possibility, a General Tire-style *modus vivendi* with the AFL. In late 1934 two other large factories, Seiberling Tire and RCA Rubber, followed O'Neil's example. They were highly organized, vulnerable to strikes, and willing to cooperate. When FLU leaders demanded a contract based on Claherty's "national" agreement, Seiberling production managers agreed to sign an accord with Ralph Lind providing that the union deleted the working rules and wage differentials that the craft organizations had forced Claherty to include in the statement. RCA executives agreed to a similar arrangement several weeks later. Lind saw this technique as a possible answer to the impasse at Goodrich and Firestone, but Goodrich executives would have nothing to do with it.[47]

To show their determination, the labor managers of the large Akron companies began ill-concealed strike preparations in early 1935. Goodrich and

---

[46] Green to Claherty, Jan. 10, 14, 1935, AFL Papers, Local 18321 Correspondence.

[47] V. E. Atkins to Lind, Dec. 31, 1934, Lind to Rubber Workers Council, Dec. 26, 1934, and Lind to Claherty, Dec. 26, 1934, NLRB Papers, Case 452; Transcript of Conversation, Lind, Jett, and Graham, Jan. 1935, NLRB Papers, Box 17, File 376.

Firestone employed Col. Joseph Johnston, a veteran of the Ohio National Guard's many strikebreaking ventures, to train supervisors and loyal workers for guard duty. Goodyear assigned the plant police and Flying Squadron to make similar preparations. The Akron executives also summoned Ching and interrogated him at length. When he insisted that U.S. Rubber would operate independently, "there was a little bit of controversy."[48] Finally, they announced a 5 percent increase in base rates, supposedly as a result of negotiations with the company unions. The raises increased the wage differential between Akron and non-Akron tire plants from 35 to 43 percent and gave the latter a cost advantage for the first time.[49] The manufacturers probably hoped that the 1935 raise would become industry-wide, but they were disappointed. The stakes in the conflict increased.

The employers' actions nevertheless exposed the defects in the Green strategy. When Firestone laid off 380 battery workers in mid-December and refused to transfer them to other departments, the FLU appealed to the regional labor board. The board upheld the firings on January 4, and the local officers insisted on a strike vote, which also failed. Their last recourse was an appeal to the NRA to revoke the company's blue eagle, but even that gesture backfired. On the eve of a hearing before the regional labor board, Claherty abruptly replaced the popular Patterson with Cleveland attorney Joseph Shepler, Green's son-in-law. The FLU leaders were taken aback. Kriebel admitted that "It's got me all mixed up" and performed badly at the hearing.[50] The impartial "public" member of the regional board contrasted the "inadequacy" of the union men, "especially those who are officers," with the "fearlessness" of the company union leaders who were "by far the most impressive and best witnesses."[51] Even the union representative on the board had difficulty supporting the FLU. Lind tried to blunt the board's adverse reaction by asking the NLRB to rehear the case, but this gesture only compounded the workers' frustration. Kriebel, who did not appreciate Lind's diplomacy, complained that "it takes that board an awfully long time to do anything."[52]

The Firestone hearing provided the coup de grâce to the original Green strategy. For more than a year the rubber workers had looked to the government with mounting frustration and impatience. Unlike Green, they had little interest in the legal complexities of the NIRA legislation, the novel

[48] Ching, Oral History Memoir, 1:18.

[49] ABJ, Jan. 24, 1935; John Dean Gaffey, *The Productivity of Labor in the Rubber Tire Manufacturing Industry* (New York, 1940), p. 166.

[50] ABJ, Feb. 7, 1935.

[51] H. F. Affelder to NLRB, Feb. 14, 1935, NLRB Papers, RG 25, Box 17, File 377.

[52] ABJ, Feb. 27, 1935; B. M. Stern to Firestone Tire & Rubber Co., Feb. 23, 1935, NLRB Papers, RG 25, Box 17, File 377.

work of the labor boards, or the political ramifications of their problems. They only knew that reliance on the government meant broken promises and endless delays. By mid-February union activists conceded the necessity of a new approach based on common sense and economic action.

In the following weeks the Akron locals began new drives for support. House told Green that the locals "want to be in a position by April 15 or before to take drastic action."[53] By early March the three locals had agreed to demand recognition, seniority rights, and a thirty-hour week. "We are not going to take no for an answer," House pledged. "We are going to push these negotiations to a conclusion and set up collective bargaining."[54] The Rubber Workers' Council endorsed the locals' actions. Green did not protest.

The Goodyear local officers, Claherty, and Shepler submitted their contract demands to Slusser on March 20. When they returned two days later for his reply, he read a statement praising the assembly and chiding them for sabotaging the NLRB election. When Shepler mentioned the thirty-hour week, Slusser made "caustic" remarks about the India Tire & Rubber Company. Growing more agitated, he turned on Claherty: "Our relations were entirely harmonious until you came to this town, uninvited, and attempted to disturb the condition." He characterized the AFL as "irresponsible" and "antiquated." A brief meeting with Litchfield resulted in more harsh words.[55] Two days later one thousand Goodyear FLU members voted "to force negotiations to a conclusion" and authorized the officers to call a strike vote.[56]

The demands of the other FLUs produced similar responses. On March 25 the Firestone committee presented a draft contract to W. R. Murphy, Firestone's labor manager. Murphy's reply, two days later, was almost identical with Slusser's. He dismissed the union as an organization of six hundred or seven hundred malcontents and accused the officers of fomenting trouble.[57] Afterward the local called for a strike vote on April 7. Dalrymple and Shepler had no more success with Graham. He refused to take any action until the courts had resolved the representation issue and chided them for demanding more. "We've always done what we agree to, haven't we, Dal?" he asked. "I think so," Dalrymple replied, "but it doesn't go far enough."[58] The local then called a strike vote on April 7.

[53] House to Green, Feb. 20, 1935, AFL Papers, Green Files.

[54] *ABJ*, March 11, 1935.

[55] *ABJ*, March 22, 1935; Joseph Shepler to Green, March 25, 1935, AFL Papers, Local 18284 Correspondence.

[56] *ABJ*, March 25, 1935; Minutes of 49th Meeting, March 24, 1935, Local 2 Archives.

[57] Conference with Firestone, March 27, 1935, AFL Papers, Local 18321 Correspondence.

[58] *ABJ*, March 27, 1935; Conference with Goodrich Management, March 27, 1935, Local 5 Archives, Local 5 offices, Akron, Ohio.

"The fight is on," wrote Kriebel on March 29. "There is going to be serious trouble almost any minute."[59] At a series of highly publicized meetings and rallies union leaders emphasized the villainy of the manufacturers, the cowardice and effeminacy of the company unionists, and the undependability of the government. Implied but never stated was their foolishness in subscribing to the Green strategy. They pledged that the "rubber workers are not going to be coerced, influenced or bulldozed . . . any longer." When House reported that government officials hoped to avert a strike, Everett White advised him "to tell them all to go to hell."[60]

The manufacturers seemingly welcomed the prospect of a showdown. They built fences, installed floodlights, stockpiled weapons, recruited employees for paramilitary training, and seized every opportunity to publicize their preparations.[61] They also refused to deny rumors that they would enlist the notorious Berghoff detective agency or call on Governor Martin Davey to keep the plants open. Their actions suggest that they saw the munitions and fences primarily as weapons in a war of nerves, designed to force the workers to choose between themselves and the AFL. Lind, the one outsider who had regular contacts with the companies, did not take their threats seriously.[62] Most workers, however, could not afford a detached assessment. In late March the manufacturers authorized employee referenda on the strike issue. In response to questions like "Do you want to strike?" and "In the event of a strike, do you want to remain at work?" the workers were unambiguous. At Goodyear the vote against a strike was 11,516 to 2,015, and at Firestone, 7,162 to 1,659. FLU leaders attacked the elections but were uncomfortable with the results. "Why, a man would be a fool not to vote 'no,' " White admitted to reporters.[63]

The manufacturers' offensive had brought them other favorable results. In late March anxious townspeople began to organize against a strike. A "citizens committee" and a "Civic Justice Association" pledged to preserve order in the event of trouble, despite AFL charges that they were "chamber of commerce outfits" and "Punch and Judys for the rubber barons."[64] The attitudes of local government officials were no less ominous.

---

[59] Kriebel to Green, March 29, 1935, AFL Papers, Local 18321 Correspondence.

[60] *ATP*, March 30, 1935.

[61] One measure of their effectiveness was an admission by the executive secretary of the local Urban League affiliate that "our Agency assumed the responsiblity for keeping Negro Rubber workers with 'the foot in the middle of the road.' " (George W. Thompson to T. Arnold Hill, Jan. 6, 1936, Urban League Papers, Akron Branch. Courtesy of Prof. Judith Stein.)

[62] Lind to NLRB, March 25, 1935, NLRB Papers, RG 25, Box 17, File 377. Also see Edward Levinson, *I Break Strikes* (New York, 1935), pp. 285–88.

[63] *ABJ*, March 28, April 1, 1935; *ATP*, March 29, April 4, 1935; Dalrymple to Green, March 28, 1935, AFL Papers, Local 18319 Correspondence.

[64] *ABJ*, April 1, 1935. I have been unable to separate fact from fiction in Levinson's enter-

Mayor I. S. Myers ordered the police department to recruit one hundred additional officers and buy extra tear gas. Equally troubling was the attitude of Sheriff James Flower, a popular Republican known for his attacks on gambling. Flower had recently helped break a strike by match workers in Barberton and now enlisted a force of 150 part-time deputies and 850 Goodrich, Firestone, and Goodyear employees "picked by the companies" for strike duty. He asked the unions to select a comparable group but the local leaders refused, charging that the sheriff planned to break the picket line and "start a war."[65]

The manufacturers' ultimate weapon, however, was simple, inexpensive, and effective. Ralph Lind reported that personnel managers advised company union members and other anti-AFL workers "that it might be very smart if they joined the union for the purpose of voting against a strike." The employers' goal was to "control even the A. F. of L. unions."[66] Union leaders suspected such an effort but were powerless to stop it. "You can't tell what these new fellows will do," bemoaned one committeeman. "I don't think they are much of an asset to the union."[67]

The Goodyear strike vote began on March 31 with a large and enthusiastic meeting at the local union hall. More than one thousand workers filled the auditorium and others crowded the sidewalk and nearby shops. Union officers indicated that they would not announce the results until the Firestone and Goodrich workers had voted and Green had approved the result. In fact they never publicly revealed the total vote or the outcome. Claherty informed Green that approximately 90 percent of the Goodyear voters favored the strike, well above the 75 percent the AFL required.[68] House reported "a great majority in favor of a strike."[69] A. A. Wilson, a member of the team that counted the ballots, recalled the outcome differently. According to Wilson the affirmative vote was initially less than 75 percent. "We set there and we counted over three or four times. One fellow get up and get a drink and another fellow get up and get a drink, and by God, we had a majority. . . . I told Claherty . . . use it for a bluff, but don't you dare call the people out or I'll blow the whistle on you."[70]

Despite another week of rallies and parades, the strike votes at Goodrich and Firestone were no more encouraging. After the ballots had been tabu-

---

taining account (Levinson, *I Break Strikes*, pp. 285–88. Also see U.S. Senate, *Hearings*, p. 2971).

[65] *ATP*, March 29, 1935; *ABJ*, April 1, April 3, 1935.

[66] Lind to NLRB, March 25, 1935, NLRB Papers, RG 25, Box 17, File 377.

[67] *ABJ*, April 2, 1935.

[68] Claherty to Green, April 6, 1935, AFL Papers, Local 18282 Correspondence.

[69] House to Green, April 6, 1935, AFL Papers, Local 18282 Correspondence.

[70] A. A. Wilson, interview with author, May 17, 1973.

lated, Claherty left for Washington, supposedly to consult Green. At least as important was his desire to avoid embarrassing inquiries from union members and reporters. In the following weeks he resolutely refused to discuss the outcome, and Akron union leaders did not officially acknowledge that the vote had failed until 1941. They had expected about 90 percent of the total but received only about two-thirds. Whether the blame lay with the manufacturers or the AFL, the debacle gave the employers a tactical and psychological advantage in the following critical days.[71]

By early April the antistrike movement had gathered substantial momentum. At its core were local merchants and professionals, anxious about the effects of a strike on the economy. Regardless of their opinion of unions, workers, or collective bargaining, they strongly opposed any action that would endanger the recovery. The city's newspapers echoed their concern. Together they persuaded Congressman Dow Harter to appeal to Secretary of Labor Frances Perkins on April 9. Joining them was William Green, who viewed the strike preparations as a personal affront and a prelude to disaster. Hesitant to interfere as long as the FLU leaders commanded the workers' support, Green had urged Claherty on April 7 to "advise" the FLU leaders "in a diplomatic and discreet way from time to time that a strike is unthinkable until more than a majority of the rubber workers become affiliated with the unions."[72] When Claherty arrived with news of the failed Goodrich and Firestone strike votes, Green determined to act.

By that time Secretary Perkins had decided that a high-level Washington conference was the only way to prevent a walkout. She conferred with Roosevelt on the evening of April 9, and then invited Tew and Graham of Goodrich, Thomas of Firestone, and Slusser to attend. (Partly to avoid such entanglements, Litchfield had left the week before on an Asian tour.) In meetings with them throughout April 11, she warned that the president would intervene personally if they did not find a way to prevent a strike and suggested three options. She got nowhere with proposals that the manufacturers withdraw their legal challenges to the election orders or agree to elections before the courts had acted. That left only her third proposal, a temporary arrangement of undefined character that would delay the strike.[73]

On April 12 Perkins and Green joined forces. The AFL president conferred with Claherty and the FLU leaders, whom Perkins had also summoned to Washington, and sent them to the Labor Department. By afternoon the manufacturers and union officials were ensconced in separate rooms adjoining Perkins's office. For the rest of the afternoon and evening,

---

[71] *ABJ*, April 11, 1935; Alfred Winslow Jones, *Life, Liberty, and Property: A Story of Conflict and a Measurement of Conflicting Rights* (Philadelphia, 1941), pp. 91–92.

[72] Green to Claherty, April 7, 1935, AFL Papers, Green Files.

[73] *ABJ*, April 12, 1935.

she acted as an intermediary, carrying communications between the offices and badgering both sides for concessions. By late afternoon the manufacturers had agreed to elections, providing they did not involve the NLRB, majority rule, or a postponement of their legal challenges to the board's rulings. Perkins then turned to the unions. Having disavowed government election procedures, Claherty and the FLU presidents were in a quandary. They debated among themselves all evening. At midnight, Perkins permitted the company executives to return to their hotel. Claherty and the FLU presidents remained at the Labor Department until 1:00 A.M., then conferred "far into the morning at their hotel."[74]

On Saturday the impasse continued through most of the day. Finally Perkins appealed to Green, who agreed to speak to Claherty and the FLU presidents. He spared no words. When House proposed that Goodyear workers strike, the Federation president rebuked him.[75] Green then proposed a compromise: the unions would call off the strike, both sides would agree to postpone the elections until the courts had ruled on the Firestone and Goodrich suits, and the manufacturers would negotiate individual grievances and terminate financial support for the company unions until the courts determined their legality. When the meeting ended Perkins invited the exhausted union leaders to her office for sandwiches and coffee served from a tea set she kept near her desk. She sent Green's proposal to the manufacturers, who immediately objected to the company union proviso. Perkins then suggested a substitute. If negotiations deadlocked, either side could appeal to her and she would appoint a fact-finding board to recommend a solution. At about 5:00 P.M. the manufacturers announced that they would take a walk. After twenty minutes on blustery Pennsylvania Avenue, they returned to announce that they would agree to the revised Green plan. Each side then signed a separate document. At no time during the three-day "teacup" conference had there been any direct contact between them.[76]

There remained one obstacle, the three thousand to four thousand union activists who had spearheaded the strike movement. Committed to direct action, they had little faith in Perkins, Green, or Claherty and had become increasingly restive as news reports from Washington suggested the likelihood of a compromise. The workers, Bob Roberts told reporters, "are not going to stand for any more postponements." Everett White warned that "they can do a lot of considering in Washington, but there'll be a lot of considering down here, too." "The workers will settle this trouble in Akron where it exists," echoed Harry Eagle.[77] When reports of the teacup

---

[74] *ABJ*, April 13, 1935; *ATP*, April 13, 1935.

[75] Walter Kriebel, interview with author, Sept. 19, 1972; House interviews.

[76] *ABJ*, April 15, 1935.

[77] *ABJ*, April 13, 1935; *ATP*, April 13, 1935.

agreement arrived on Saturday evening, some men cursed Perkins, Claherty, and their officers. Others vowed to defeat the pact. "This is not settled and those guys in Washington better not think so," shouted White to an indignant crowd at the Goodyear local hall. "It means nothing but stall and delay," added Roberts. A Goodrich worker predicted that his colleagues would turn it down "flatter than a flat tire." When the union leaders arrived on Sunday morning, a small "grim" band of unionists met them at the station. As Kriebel got off the train, E. L. Howard of the Goodyear local approached. "Boy, you have no idea how the rubber workers feel about that business down at Washington. . . . The boys feel as though they've been robbed." "Well," replied Kriebel, "I don't know whether we accomplished anything or not."[78]

At the Goodrich hall, Claherty and Dalrymple faced a perplexed and hostile crowd of more than one thousand. Claherty, unaccustomedly nervous, spoke first. He explained what had happened and denied angry charges of a "runaround." Dalrymple urged the members to "keep cool." He defended the agreement and emphasized Green's role. His comments seemed to reassure many union members. When a critic asked Roberts to speak, Roberts declined. Dalrymple then asked for a show of hands. The count was more than 10 to 1 in favor of the pact. Afterward Roberts explained to a skeptic that "we at least have our foot in the door." "Yes," was the angry retort, "and someone is going to get an ax and chop it off."[79]

The Firestone meeting was similar. "At least we got the names of the manufacturers on the line. That's something," Kriebel explained apologetically. Otherwise he refused to endorse the agreement. Claherty also declined to speak for it. After nearly two hours of heated discussion, Kriebel called for a vote. Again, a large majority supported the agreement.[80]

The Goodyear debate was the most contentious and bitter of all. After House read the agreement, "a veritable outburst of criticism exploded from the floor." There were cries of "sellout" and "traitor." House responded angrily, "If anybody here says I sold out, G—— I'll bust him in the mouth. I'm not here to force this agreement on you. . . . I'm not recommending it. I'm explaining it." Several members came to his defense. After nearly two hours of "rising sentiment for approval," William Carney, a prominent committeeman, came to the front. He seized the agreement and threw it to the floor. "That's what I think of it," he shouted. At that point House interrupted with a report from the Firestone meeting. Carney looked dejected. He conceded: "There is nothing for a good union man to do but

[78] *ATP*, April 14, 15, 1935.
[79] *ABJ*, April 15, 1935.
[80] *ATP*, April 15, 1935.

stick to this agreement. We will use this as a beginning.'' Carney's statement seemed to demoralize the opposition. Some members started to leave.
Claherty arrived and spoke for the agreement. When House called for a
vote almost three hours later, only one dissenter opposed it.[81]

By the evening of April 14 it was clear that the protest movement had
failed, at least temporarily. Green congratulated the Akron workers on their
''sound judgment.''[82] The manufacturers insisted that they had signed an
agreement ''with the secretary of labor and no one else'' and had conceded
nothing new ''except the creation of the fact-finding board.'' Tew was not
worried that the board was ill-defined and potentially powerful. ''I feel that
if we are so stupid that we can't settle things ourselves—well, we are just
stupid.''[83]

FORMATION OF THE INTERNATIONAL

Dalrymple later recalled that he, House, and Kriebel were ''repulsed quite
severely'' for their roles in the teacup agreement.[84] In retrospect, it is apparent that Green and Claherty, not the FLU presidents, were the real losers.
To many rubber workers, including most FLU leaders, the teacup agreement
was the latest in a series of AFL miscalculations and blunders. Like Rex
Murray and the General Tire officers in 1934, they resolved to be more
independent in the future, provided they had another chance.

For several months that prospect seemed increasingly remote, as setback
followed setback. A U.S. circuit court of appeals began to consider the
Firestone and Goodrich cases on April 15, and a Washington court began
to hear the Firestone blue eagle suit the following day. Before the lower
courts could act, however, the Supreme Court struck down the National
Industrial Recovery Act including Section 7a, in its Schechter decision of
May 27. The NLRB immediately dropped the blue eagle suit and the circuit
court voided the board's election orders two weeks later. In Akron, these
actions ''caused hardly a ripple of interest.''[85] The passage of the landmark
Wagner-Connery Labor Relations Act in early July had no greater effect.
The law was also of doubtful constitutionality and had no immediate sig-
nificance.

More threatening were a series of industrial relations debacles. The
Aetna and Ohio Rubber strikes and the sale of Kelly-Springfield to Goodyear jeopardized three formidable locals. Equally serious, because of its

[81] *ABJ*, April 15, 1935.
[82] Green to Claherty, April 29, 1935, AFL Papers, Green Files.
[83] *ABJ*, April 16, 1935.
[84] Sherman H. Dalrymple interview.
[85] *ABJ*, June 8, 1935.

symbolic importance, was the collapse of India Tire. Green's inflated hopes for India Tire had proved to be a pipe dream, and union-management relations declined along with the company's business. On April 26 the company president attacked the workers' "impossible" wage demands and "radicalism," and ordered the plant closed.[86] After recovering from the initial shock, Claherty realized that the company's goal was to jettison the contract. Pressured by Green's frantic calls to "save the situation," Claherty and the FLU leaders had few options. On May 12 the employees voted 141 to 33 against any change in the contract, but a week later, after more promises and threats, voted again, 117 to 43 to delete the union shop clause. Even that concession provided only a brief respite for the failing company.[87]

Within two weeks of the India Tire vote, a dispute at General Tire threatened another important agreement. As part of a citywide reduction in production and employment after April 14, General Tire furloughed several hundred workers without regard to the seniority provisions of the 1934 settlement. When Murray protested, company executives cavalierly replied that the Schechter decision freed them from the agreement. On June 16 the local passed a strike resolution and prepared for a confrontation. At the last moment, however, O'Neil agreed to spell out the company's seniority policy, and the local leaders rescinded the resolution. By the end of the month, O'Neil had "come back to earth again" and was "willing to discuss matters."[88] The General Tire settlement survived.

Coupled with the teacup agreement, these setbacks had a devastating effect on union morale. To many workers the status of the AFL and the FLUS was "a few points above zero."[89] Thousands stopped paying dues. The General Tire local, known for its élan, declined from 934 dues-paying members in March to 344 in May. By the summer the Goodrich local had only 700 paid-up members and the Goodyear local, only 137. By September all of the rubber workers locals could claim only 3,100 paid-up members.[90] The malaise spread to other Akron unions, which typically lost one-third to two-thirds of their members between late 1934 and the end of 1935. Gradually the "labor union culture" of 1933 and 1934 gave way to more traditional activities. In 1935 the Goodyear company picnic drew nearly

[86] *ABJ*, April 26, 1935.

[87] Green to Claherty, May 2, 1935, Claherty to Green, May 6, 1935, and Paul B. Cordier to Green, May 24, 1935, AFL Papers, Local 18346 Correspondence; *ABJ*, May 22, 1935.

[88] Claherty to Green, June 29, 1935, AFL Papers, Local 18323 Correspondence.

[89] W. W. Thompson, "A History of the Labor Movement in Akron, Ohio," Congress of Industrial Organizations Papers, URW file, Catholic University, Washington.

[90] Membership Report, June 17, 1935, AFL Papers, Local 18323 Correspondence; House interviews; Dalrymple interview.

sixty thousand employees and family members; the Goodrich picnic, about forty thousand; and the Firestone affair, about twenty-five thousand. In contrast, when Akron and Canton, Ohio, unionists organized a combined Labor Day picnic, they attracted only fifteen thousand to twenty thousand celebrants. Green once more consented to be the featured speaker. His nationally broadcasted remarks drew a crowd of five thousand.[91]

For Akron unionists the only hopeful sign was the prospect of an international union. As Harley Anthony and Dalrymple explained to Green, the Goodrich local had experienced ''a decided decrease in membership'' with no prospect of an upturn. The union had ''reached a point where some immediate action'' was essential. They believed ''that an Industrial set up is our only solution.''[92] They and most of their fellow activists were pleased when the AFL Executive Council voted to create a rubber workers' union and when Green and Claherty, after polling the locals, set a September date for an organizing convention. Presumably they discussed Claherty's future at the same time. In late August Green appointed the officers of the new United Automobile Workers union over the objections of most of the local leaders. In his Labor Day address, he implied that he would also appoint the Rubber Workers' officers. When reporters asked him if he would name Claherty president, he replied that he ''hadn't thought of that'' but that Claherty ''has done good work.''[93]

Green's plans, or suspicions about his plans, were the principal concern of the forty-nine delegates who gathered in Akron on September 10 and 11 and quickly divided into pro- and anti-Green camps. B. J. Widick, a Trotskyist who reported the convention for the *Akron Beacon Journal* and the *Nation*, portrayed the division as a clash between rival ideologies. He described Green's allies as conservative trade unionists and their opponents as ideologically committed radicals. The radicals' quest for power, he believed, culminated in the convention struggle.[94] If Widick was right, the convention brought to the surface a feature of the workers' experience that had been only dimly evident before. Given the absence of supporting data and Widick's limited knowledge of union activities at the time, it is likely that his interpretation reflected his preoccupations more than the workers'.

[91] Wilmer Tate to John Brophy, Feb. 18, 1936, CIO Papers, URW file; *ABJ*, June 28, July 29, Aug. 7, Sept. 2, 3, 1935.

[92] Harley C. Anthony and Dalrymple to Green, May 23, 1935, AFL Papers, Local 18319 Correspondence.

[93] Morris, *Conflict Within the AFL*, pp. 200–203; Philip Taft, *The A.F. of L. from the Death of Gompers to the Merger* (New York, 1959), pp. 90–91; *ABJ*, July 12, Sept. 7, 12, 1935; Claherty to Green, Aug. 17, 1935, Local 5 Archives; Phelan, ''William Green,'' pp. 174–75.

[94] B. J. Widick, ''Two Defeats for William Green,'' *Nation* 141 (1935): 412; *ABJ*, Sept. 11–21, 1935.

Indeed, the anti-Green "progressive caucus" supplied the most telling critique of the Widick schema. Its leader was Thomas F. Burns, whose controversial associations did not extend to radical politics. Burns's allies included Camelio and Eagle, the "most progressive" of the delegates, but also Frank Grillo, Rex Murray, W. W. Thompson, and Dalrymple, the epitome of the practical-minded, anti-intellectual rubber worker. Most of these men would have been surprised to learn that they were "progressives," or even members of a "caucus."

Ed Heinke, who covered the convention for the *Akron Times Press*, suggested a different basis for the rivalry. Taking his cue from party politics, he saw ambition and self-interest as polarizing forces. Thus, pro-Green "regulars" confronted anti-Green "insurgents."[95] Heinke's categorization explains the alliance of the "progressive" Eagle and the "conservative" Dalrymple, and the shifts of delegates, but it, too, obscures the delegates' overriding desire for unity and a third factor that may have been most important of all. The delegates differed most significantly not in ideology or ambition, but in the extent of their exposure to the AFL. By this measure there were three groups: the Akron representatives (23 with 24 votes) who had had substantial contacts with the Federation and Claherty, the other Ohio delegates (8 with 9 votes) who had had only sporadic contacts, and the non-Ohio delegates (18 with 22 votes) who had had almost no contact with the Federation. The Akron delegates were divided. The officers of the Big Three locals were identified with Claherty and were ambivalent about the AFL's future role. Some of the leaders of the smaller Akron FLUs were "regulars"; others, like the General Tire and Mohawk Tire delegates, were "insurgents." The Ohio group was also divided. Several delegates, like Charles Lanning, had had close relations with the Akron AFL office. Others, like the Pharis delegates, had had only infrequent contacts. The non-Ohio delegates were accustomed to operating independently. Some of them, like the Kelly-Springfield officers, had complained about their isolation; all of them resented their second-class status. At the convention their fear of continued isolation bound them to Burns, the one well-known non-Ohio leader. The non-Ohio locals became the core of the anti-Green group.[96]

Burns arrived early and began to contact other delegates in an effort to thwart Claherty and to win the union presidency for himself. With the support of the Fisk delegation and the other eastern locals, he became the leader of the insurgents. He attracted Akron dissidents like Eagle and won the backing of some members of the Big Three delegations. By the eve of

[95] *ATP*, Sept. 11–21, 1935.
[96] John Marchiando, interview with author, Dec. 22, 1977.

the convention he had persuaded forty delegates to sign a petition demanding the election of the international officers. When he and several of his allies presented the petition to Green, the Federation president was "visibly angry" and demanded "the names of 'the boys' who circulated the petition."[97]

The convention opened on Thursday, September 12, in the ballroom of the Portage Hotel. Claherty assumed the role of presiding officer over scattered protests, and introduced Green, who responded with a mixture of platitudes and warnings. Recalling the rump convention in Indianapolis, he attacked those who were "endeavoring by innuendo and direct charges" to portray the AFL as "some big bad wolf." and promised that the Federation would "never, never desert you." He described the jurisdiction of the new international as including workers "engaged in the mass production of rubber products" but not those who "construct buildings, manufacture or install machinery, or engage in maintenance work." He cautioned the delegates not "to fight over unimportant matters of jurisdiction."[98]

Camelio jumped to his feet. "If we . . . accept this charter, does this give the President the right to appoint its officers?" Claherty rapped the lectern with his gavel but Green waved him off. "It is not for you to decide as to whether or not you will accept the charter," he responded. "It cannot be amended and it cannot be accepted and it cannot be rejected." While the charter gave him the power to appoint the union's officers, he promised "to consider the situation and then arrive at a conclusion."[99]

That evening the conflict shifted to the Resolutions Committee. In a "private meeting" prior to the regular session, Chairman Charles Lanning and committee member John House suggested a compromise to Green. They offered to support a resolution calling for the appointment of Claherty to a single one-year term, the election of the other officers, and AFL financial assistance for an indefinite period. Their plan would unify the convention, keep the rubber workers securely in the AFL camp, and thwart Burns, whom they distrusted for his brashness, ambition, and association with the Indianapolis rebels.[100] In the meantime they would try to persuade the Akron and Ohio delegates to push one of their own leaders for the vice-presidency. Acknowledging the insurgents' influence, Green agreed to the plan. Together, they incorporated it in a resolution that E. L. Gray of the Gadsden local agreed to submit. Lanning and House believed they could count on the support of three of the other five members of the Resolutions Com-

---

[97] *ATP*, Sept. 12, 1935.

[98] *Proceedings of the First Constitutional Convention of the United Rubber Workers of America, Akron, Ohio, Sept. 12–17, 1935* (Akron, 1935), pp. 15–18.

[99] Ibid., pp. 20–21.

[100] House interviews.

mittee (delegates from Firestone, Goodrich, and Pharis versus Camelio and a Fisk delegate). They were surprised when all five men opposed the resolution, suggesting the strength of the insurgent movement. Lanning and House decided to submit a minority report.[101]

When the convention met the following afternoon, Lanning submitted the resolution, with majority and minority reports, prior to the rest of the committee report. House explained that this action was in deference to Green, who wanted to leave that evening. In fact, Lanning, House, and their allies believed that this strategem was the only way to elect Claherty and obtain AFL financial aid, since Green had strongly implied that Claherty was the Federation's price for additional funds.[102]

Lanning's move sparked a heated debate. With Green in the chair, Camelio, Eagle, and Thompson led the attack. Green's reply emphasized the financial link.

Now, if you take it all over today you will have to make funds to finance yourself and where are they? . . . during this interim you will need some help from your daddy. The child will need some help from its father, and in this resolution you ask for that help. . . . Now, you can turn it down if you want . . . but after you have acted upon it I will then be judged with the responsibility of exercising my best judgment in this . . . it is not a question of democracy . . . it is a question of what to do while we are passing through a probation period.

Camelio argued that the union would have to appeal to its "daddy" regardless of who was elected. Green reminded him that the Federation expected "to have the say" when it was "called upon to employ someone." Dalrymple then took the floor for what was to be the decisive speech of the convention. He praised the AFL but insisted that the real issue was membership, not finances. "When we get the membership . . . the finances will be there." He hoped there was enough "red blood" among the workers "that they will immediately come forth in numbers great enough that we will set up this International union and finance it." Green did not answer. The vote on the resolution was anticlimactic, as loud and frequent "noes" rang through the hushed room. The final count was 9⅙ to 45⅝. Only the Goodyear and India Tire delegates, Lanning, Gray, Bob Roberts, and two other Akron men supported it.[103]

Green turned to Burns and asked if he wanted to start an independent union. Burns denied that he had ever been interested in a dual movement. "Didn't you denounce the officials of the American Federation of Labor at meetings of the Goodrich and Mohawk unions?" asked Green, in a refer-

---

[101] *Proceedings*, pp. 80–81.
[102] Ibid., p. 82.
[103] Ibid., pp. 35–36.

ence to early 1934. "I never did," answered Burns, his anger rising. Green then accused him of working with Fred Phillips to form an independent union and asked who had formed the insurgent group. Burns conceded that he had. "That," replied Green, "is what I want to know." Claherty interrupted to charge that "anyone who says Mr. Burns didn't deride the A. F. of L. at the Mohawk union meeting is not telling the truth." Burns could not contain himself. "Those stories are damnable lies and you're a liar for making the statement," he exploded. Dalrymple and Eagle came to Burns's aid, denying that he had attacked the AFL.[104]

Green turned to the other delegates. Many expected him to appoint Claherty to the presidency. "Now you have acted," he began. "I accept your judgment in the matter as final and I respect it because it is so decisive. . . . There's nothing further I can do. . . . You may elect your officers now from top to bottom and you may arrange to finance your convention and your organization work and carry on." He did not rule out financial support or other assistance. He then left for Coshocton, "bitter" at his most recent encounter with the rubber workers.[105]

For the next three days the delegates devoted their attention to the constitution, the remaining resolutions, and the upcoming elections. Their actions on resolutions involving political endorsements emphasized their moderation and New Deal sympathies. However, on Monday evening, as the elections approached, the division between regulars and insurgents reemerged. In a final address, Claherty bitterly attacked the delegates for their treatment of Green. "The only ones who ever conferred with him were those who wanted money," he charged. He then reviewed the events of the preceding spring. He had "no alibis to offer" for his activities. Dalrymple responded: "You have bitterly attacked us . . . and you have no right to give us such a tongue lashing." He denied that there were "bitter feelings between this convention and the A. F. of L." Burns backed him.[106]

Tempers continued to flare during the "stormiest" session of the convention. Burns accused Lanning and House of manipulating the Resolutions Committee. They denied his accusations and called for reconsideration of the compromise resolution. After a long and heated exchange, Burns asked for a recess. Unable to devise a way to request financial assistance without raising the issue of Claherty's appointment, the insurgents moved to table the troublesome resolution.[107]

The convention then turned to the election. The candidates were the leaders of the two factions, Burns and House, and Dalrymple, who was nomi-

[104] *ATP*, Sept. 14, 1935; *Cleveland Plain Dealer*, Sept. 14, 1935.
[105] *Proceedings*, pp. 39–40; *ATP*, Sept. 14, 1935.
[106] *ABJ*, Sept. 14, 17, 1935; *ATP*, Sept. 17, 1935.
[107] *ATP*, Sept. 17, 1935; *Proceedings*, pp. 80–85.

nated by Eagle. If the original division had persisted, Burns would have won by a large margin. With Green and Claherty gone, however, the focus of the convention shifted from the AFL to the relations between the union's center and periphery. Eagle's defection to Dalrymple signaled the change. In the new atmosphere, Dalrymple, a Green critic, an influential local president, and an "honest" man, was the ideal candidate to unite the Akron delegates. He received 29 votes; Burns got 19 and House, 7. Dalrymple's total suggests that he won the votes of nearly all the Akron and Ohio delegates except the Goodyear contingent, leaving Burns with his core followers, the non-Akron delegates. Murray's recollections are apropos. Though Burns "wanted very much to be president," the Akron delegates were "absolutely opposed." Dalrymple, on the other hand, "didn't want it and . . . felt that he wasn't qualified to handle it," but the Akron leaders "knew the honesty and integrity of the individual and there was no one else . . . that we could feel the same way about."[108]

Burns played a decisive role in the other contests. He easily defeated Lanning for the vice-presidency, 41 to 14. He also engineered the election of Grillo as secretary-treasurer over the treasurers of the Akron Goodyear and Goodrich locals. Though Grillo had been unemployed since 1934 and had no accounting experience, his presence enhanced the union's image as a national organization. Burns was equally influential in the selection of the General Executive Board. Camelio, Thompson, Eagle, Marchiando, and Walter Welsch, all outspoken insurgents, won positions. Of the "regulars" only Bob Roberts was elected. The insurgents, Heinke reported, scored "practically a complete victory."[109]

Of the insurgents, the biggest winner clearly was Dalrymple. A politically acceptable alternative to Burns, he was also a symbol of disillusionment with the AFL, the government, and a passive, legalistic approach to the manufacturers. On a deeper level he embodied the rubber workers' distrust of complex strategies and centralized power. He promised to "upbuild" the union and in an oblique reference to Claherty and possibly Burns, to maintain his sense of perspective. His head, he pledged, "will never get larger than the position."[110] Whether militancy and humility would be enough to save the United Rubber Workers from the fate of the Amalgamated Rubber Workers was problematic. The delegates left the Portage Hotel on September 21 with a profound sense of the challenges that lay ahead of them.

[108] Rex Murray, interview with author, Sept. 19, 1972.
[109] *ATP*, Sept. 18, 1935.
[110] *Proceedings*, p. 90.

CHAPTER SEVEN

Union Revival, 1936

THE 1929 ISSUE of *The Coagulator*, the yearbook of the Goodyear Flying Squadron, featured the fifty-five most recent graduates of the elite training program. Their earnest looks and confident smiles betray no doubt about their future or the workers' role in the company. Within a year the Depression would dash most of their hopes and expectations. Yet one of the 1929 graduates did leave an important mark on the company during the 1930s. John D. House (1904–), a Georgia farm youth who had been one-half of his high school class, followed his brother to Akron in 1922 and worked as a tire builder at Goodrich, Firestone, and, finally, Goodyear. Eager to succeed, he enrolled in the Industrial University and applied for a sales position in the Atlanta branch office in 1926. When that venture fell through, he turned to the Flying Squadron, only to suffer another disappointment. After graduation he found little need for his training. Demoted to his old job in 1930, he worked irregularly for three years, avoiding the dole but gaining little.[1] In 1933, he cast his lot with organized labor. As president of the Goodyear local he led the attack on the status quo of the 1920s and joined Dalrymple and others in the search for an alternative to the Green strategy, a search that culminated, unexpectedly, in the months immediately following the constitutional convention.

THE INTERNATIONAL TAKES SHAPE

The most pressing problem for URW leaders in the fall of 1935 was not the Green strategy or their relations with the manufacturers, but the viability of the International union. Except for a few hundred dollars that they borrowed from the locals, the organization was penniless. Dalrymple delayed his resignation from the Local 5 presidency until mid-October to conserve funds, and Grillo, "down and out," lived in a spare room in Dalrymple's house.[2] It was, then, with considerable trepidation that the officers journeyed to Washington to see Green in late September. They found him pleasant and courteous, apparently reconciled to their independent course.

---

[1] *The Coagulator, 1929* (Akron, 1929); John D. House, interviews with author, April 15, May 1, 1972, and John D. House, "Birth of a Union," unpublished MS, Ohio Historical Society, pp. 7–19.

[2] Floyd Gartrell, interview with author, Aug. 15, 1977.

Green gave them $1,000 and authorized Claherty to turn over the treasury of the Rubber Workers Council, which provided an additional $1,856. He also donated the lease on Claherty's offices and later lent the URW funds to start *The United Rubber Worker*, the union's monthly periodical. He apparently said nothing about Claherty's staff—Roberts, Tate, W. H. Wilson, and Agnes O'Conner, who had arrived in mid-1935 to recruit women. The following week, however, Frank Morrison, AFL secretary-treasurer, publicly offered the services of some or all of the AFL organizers in Akron. Tate and Wilson remained on the AFL payroll and worked with the URW. At Dalrymple's request, the AFL reemployed Roberts in January 1936 and assigned him to the URW. He became the union's first full-time organizer.[3]

By early October only one issue remained, and that was important only because of its association with other transcendent events. The charter Green had presented in September distinguished between rubber workers and crafts workers who were employed in rubber factories. At the 1935 AFL convention in Atlantic City, Dalrymple, Harry Eagle, and W. W. Thompson, the URW delegates, sought to remove the distinction. Thompson was presenting the URW plea on October 19 when John L. Lewis confronted William L. Hutcheson of the Carpenters in their famous brawl. If the URW delegates had any sense of the symbolism of that event or of their tangential role in the breakup of the AFL, they did not record their impressions. Nor did they participate in the meeting of Lewis's Committee for Industrial Organization the next day, though they, like the majority of mass production employees, strongly identified with the new CIO.[4]

Having obtained what Dalrymple described as a "very conservative" stake, the International officers turned to the task of union building.[5] On Claherty's advice, Grillo went to Chicago to study the accounting methods of the Brotherhood of Blacksmiths. He was soon absorbed in "setting up the system," which required "a huge amount of effort" and considerable diplomacy because of the skeletons it exposed in the closets of local treasurers. Haphazard bookkeeping and outright defalcation were to plague the union for the rest of the decade.[6]

Grillo himself was not above criticism. He employed four women to do clerical work and spent $400 for office furniture at a time when the union's

[3] General Executive Board, Minutes, Sept. 19, 1935, and Dalrymple and Frank Grillo to George Roberts, Sept. 27, 1935, United Rubber Workers Archives, URW offices, Akron, Ohio; Sherman H. Dalrymple, "Report to the General Executive Board," Sept. 14, 1936, URW Archives; Dalrymple, interview with Joe Glazer, April 2, 1955; *ABJ*, Sept. 30, Oct. 1, 1935.

[4] See William Green to Dalrymple, Nov. 12, 1935, URW Archives.

[5] Dalrymple to John Brophy, Feb. 13, 1936, Congress of Industrial Organizations Papers, URW file, Catholic University, Washington.

[6] Frank Grillo, "Report to the General Executive Board," Jan. 18, 1936, URW Archives.

income consisted largely of charter affiliation fees ($10 per local). In November and December the International ran deficits of more than $300 per month, and by mid-January the URW bank balance was less than $1,000. Roberts, Marchiando, and Thompson, assigned by the executive board to investigate, reported that "it is time to retrench." The board fired two clerks and returned some of the furniture. The officers voluntarily reduced their salaries by $25 per month and ordered that purchases of more than $25 have the approval of the board.[7]

In the meantime Dalrymple and Burns devoted their energies to the locals. By October 28, thirty-three FLU's, with nearly four thousand dues-paying members, had transferred their affiliation to the URW; twelve locals remained outside. In the following months, six more locals affiliated. Dalrymple decided to hire Camelio part time to work with Burns and to employ Roberts to settle a dispute between Local 1 and the Palmer Asbestos and Rubber Company of Chicago. Roberts used a strike threat to win a signed agreement and a modest wage increase. The members were "well satisfied."[8] Dalrymple was more enthusiastic. The settlement was a "historical event . . . since it concerned local union No. 1 . . . the first strike sanction, [and] resulted in the first 100 percent organized plant."[9]

The big Akron locals required more than a part-time organizer. By the fall of 1935 the concensus among Akron unionists was that only John L. Lewis himself could revive the once-formidable organizations. In November Dalrymple and Burns urged Lewis to come to Akron. After Adolph Germer visited on Lewis's behalf in early December, John Brophy, CIO secretary and operating head, presented the URW requests and Germer's report to the CIO Executive Council on December 9. Sidney Hillman then moved to aid the auto and rubber workers with speakers and money. Lewis agreed. "The auto and rubber workers," he concluded, "present the best organizational opportunity . . . the only practical thing as our first thrust." The committee "agreed unanimously" to "go into auto and rubber."[10] Lewis accepted an invitation to speak in Cleveland in mid-January. At first he saw no reason to make a separate appearance in Akron. But Dalrymple was insistent and he finally altered his schedule.[11]

Amid these generally positive developments a series of spy revelations

[7] "Report and Recommendations of the Finance Committee," Jan. 18, 1936, URW Archives.

[8] Roberts to Dalrymple, Dec. 23, 1935, URW Archives.

[9] Dalrymple, "Report to General Executive Board," Sept. 14, 1936, p. 5, URW Archives.

[10] Brophy, "Director's Report," Dec. 9, 1935, and CIO minutes, Dec. 9, 1935, Katherine Ellickson Papers, Box 1, Franklin D. Roosevelt Library, Hyde Park, N.Y.; Melvyn Dubofsky and Warren Van Tine, *John L. Lewis: A Biography* (New York, 1977), pp. 226–27.

[11] Brophy to Dalrymple, Jan. 2, 1936, CIO Papers.

rocked the Akron locals and exposed the underside of the great organizing campaigns of 1933–1934. Though the details are murky, it appears that the Akron Employers' Association, operating through the Corporations Auxiliary Company and other detective agencies, tried to bribe at least one up-and-coming leader in each local. Carl Myers, chairman of the Local 9 (General Tire) executive board, disappeared after union officials accused him of spying. Percy Booth, the leader of the Local 2 (Goodyear) craft workers, admitted his complicity under similar circumstances. Clyde Cassell, an active Local 5 (Goodrich) member, confessed as an angry mob of fellow workers prepared to kill him. There were undoubtedly others who were luckier or more discreet.[12] Their impact is harder to measure. La Follette Committee investigators who later studied the Employers' Association records concluded that the association had spent large sums for inconsequential information. The detectives had exploited the manufacturers' fears of a subversive labor conspiracy.[13] Ironically, the exposures helped give substance to those fears. The spy exposés convinced many rubber workers that they were locked in a desperate struggle with the companies.

By late 1935, then, URW officers had halted the membership decline and created an institutional basis for expansion. With hard work and reasonable luck, they could hope to organize small firms as long as the economy remained healthy and to sustain their foothold in the Big Three until some type of cartel arrangement evolved. Their outlook was no worse than that of the UAW and other unions. What they could not foresee was a series of aggressive moves by the manufacturers that changed the framework of industrial relations in Akron.

THE MANUFACTURERS' COUNTERATTACK

By late 1935 the economic recovery promised new opportunities for the tire manufacturers and their employees. U.S. Rubber, so recently at the brink of failure, entered one of its healthiest periods.[14] Goodrich, also diversified, was less successful largely because its ill-timed expansion of the late 1920s and weak management left it at the mercy of U.S. Rubber and a host of smaller firms. The other integrated companies and most of the smaller tire producers were doing reasonably well. For all of them, however, a

[12] General Executive Board, Minutes, Jan. 18, 1936, URW Archives; Harley C. Anthony, interview with author, April 11, 1972.

[13] U.S. Senate, "Violations of Free Speech and Rights of Labor," *Hearings Before a Subcommittee of the Committee on Education and Labor*, 76th Cong., 1st sess. (Washington, 1939), pp. 2957–70.

[14] Glenn D. Babcock, *History of the United States Rubber Company: A Case Study in Corporate Management* (Bloomington, 1966), pp. 283–322.

major problem remained. Though tire output continued to rise, the bogeyman of the 1920s, price competition, held profits to low, pre-Depression levels. Employment remained steady just below the 1934 peak, but the profit lag hung like a dark cloud over Akron and its labor force.[15]

Contemporary observers agreed that the profit lag was the principal reason for the new round of labor turmoil that began in October. From his editor's desk at the *Akron Beacon Journal*, John N. Knight pointed accusingly at the "senseless selling of tires at and below manufacturing cost" that forced economies until "there is nothing left to slash except the pay of workers."[16] Most of his readers concurred.[17] In retrospect, however, it appears that the demise of the NRA, which the manufacturers associated with government snooping, red tape, and, above all, the wage increase as a union deterrent, must have been a close second. Employers in other industries, such as automobiles and steel, also became bolder in 1935. Profit lag or not, the collapse of the recovery program symbolized for them the end of an abnormal and largely unpleasant experience.

There were disturbances in all of the major plants between October and December. General Tire local leaders protested against layoffs that seemed to violate the new understanding with the company. Goodrich unionists were troubled by persistent rumors of wage cuts and "an increase of hours in a few departments."[18] Firestone tire builders became involved in a far more serious dispute over rate cuts. Their reactions foreshadowed in almost every particular the more sweeping Goodyear protest movement of the following months.

The Firestone conflict began on September 17 with a piece-rate reduction on a popular tire. Firestone managers at first argued that they had changed the job and that the builders' earnings would remain the same. Later they admitted that the "old rate was just too easy. . . . The men had been building tires in much less time than the time allotted . . . [and] were spending too much time in the cafeteria." When the workers protested, "they fell back on the threat to move . . . production to California and lay off men here. . . . It was take the cut or California gets the . . . tires."[19]

Although few of the tire builders were union members, two hundred of them gathered at the local union hall on September 20 to protest. In response, Leland S. Buckmaster, Local 7 vice-president and a tire builder,

[15] *ABJ*, Dec. 19, 1935.

[16] *ABJ*, Oct. 23, 1935.

[17] Dalrymple, "Report to General Executive Board," Sept. 14, 1936, p. 4, URW Archives.

[18] *ABJ*, Oct. 19, 1935. Also see Paul W. Chappell to H. L. Kerwin, Oct. 3, 1935, Federal Mediation and Conciliation Service Papers, RG 280, File 182/524, National Archives.

[19] "Report of Department 16-B Committee on Tire Grievance," Oct. 11, 1935, FMCS Papers, File 176/2196.

arranged a meeting with the management for September 24. At that session the department manager "wanted to talk of nothing but the California rate and the soft job that the . . . builders had here."[20] Finally he agreed to adjust the rate so that the cut was only 10 percent. Buckmaster, still dissatisfied, went to Labor Manager W. R. Murphy. Murphy denied any intention to cut rates and invited union representatives to review the time study data, which they did on October 8. The union men remained dissatisfied.

Concerned that the workers would view their efforts as another defeat, Local 7 leaders invoked the teacup agreement and asked Secretary of Labor Perkins to appoint a fact-finding board. Before responding, Perkins sent their request to the department's solicitor for a legal opinion. He replied on October 17 that the Schecter decision had voided all arrangements based on the NIRA, including the teacup accord. He urged Perkins not to publicize this opinion.[21] Perkins then sent veteran conciliator P. W. Chappell to break the news to Local 7. Chappell's approach was at least vaguely disingenuous. He told the local officers that a fact-finding board was not a good idea, since the company might refuse to cooperate and force the union to "call an ineffective strike in order to save its face." He also urged union officials "not to raise the question of the board at this time for fear the company would throw out the whole agreement and refuse to meet the union representatives." After conferring with Murphy on October 21, he recommended that the tire builders "allow the matter to ride for a few days."[22] The workers reluctantly agreed. The result was a de facto compromise that reduced wages slightly and enhanced the local's position in the plant.

The Goodyear conflict, the most important of the disputes, was an outgrowth of the profit lag, the anti-union tactics of the NRA period, and Litchfield's determination to restore the competitive position of the Akron complex. As he told reporters, the company's "prime objective" in 1936 was "to do business on a basis that it can make money."[23] To eliminate the most immediate obstacle to that end, the inflated piece rates of 1935, he proposed to combine a longer workweek with lower rates. He first called for thirty-six hours per week (versus the 1935 average of thirty-one), average hourly earnings of $.86 (versus $.96) and monthly earnings of $125 (versus $122). Later he raised the averages to $.92 and $133.[24] The cuts were no more severe than the Firestone reductions and probably would

[20] Ibid.

[21] Charles Wyzanski to Kerwin, Oct. 17, 1935, FMCS Papers, RG 280, File 176/2196.

[22] Chappell to Kerwin, Oct. 21, 1935, FMCS Papers, RG 280, File 176/2196.

[23] *ABJ*, Oct. 22, 1935.

[24] Goodyear Tire & Rubber Co., "Statement to Fact Finding Board, Nov. 30, 1935," FMCS Papers, RG 280, File 195/336.

have evoked a similar reaction except for one fatal flaw: to assure higher total earnings it was necessary to end the six-hour day. Litchfield failed to forsee that many workers would instinctively equate longer hours with lay-offs, not higher earnings, despite his assurances that new business would create additional jobs.

The protests came from several quarters. House and Local 2 officials had periodically objected to the eight-hour day in the mechanical goods departments, provoking Slusser to complain about "asinine, impracticable and dangerous" union demands.[25] They redoubled their efforts in September, when some workers in six-hour departments were placed on longer schedules. Their protests became more frequent after October 19, when Goodyear introduced the eight-hour day in Plant 2 tire departments. Secretary-Treasurer Everett White reported that an October 20 rally, the "hottest" since March, attracted more than one hundred new members "including some we never could get before."[26]

More significant was the reaction of the Industrial Assembly, which opposed the Litchfield plan with greater vigor than it had shown since the company union strike of 1926. On October 1, in response to rumors of a return to the eight-hour day, the assembly passed a protest resolution. Citing a "large majority" that favored the six-hour day and the "unrest" caused by the rumors, it asked for a six-hour standard or at least an employee referendum on the change. Slusser was surprised and annoyed. On October 17 he appeared before a joint session of the House and Senate to explain the company's position. Though superficially conciliatory, he left little room for compromise. "The company and the older employees" had been burdened "long enough," and a referendum would be a waste of time "because votes taken in the past have indicated that the men want more time." He chided the assembly for "premature" consideration of the plan.[27]

When he had finished, the House voted for a secret ballot on the eight-hour day. The Senate later concurred. The announcement two days later of eight-hour shifts in Plant 2 and Slusser's veto on October 21 of the assembly's original protest bill created serious divisions in the assembly. When the Senate failed to act immediately to override the veto, House members became agitated. "I, for one, will stand for the rights of this house, even if it breaks up the assembly," fumed Earl Baskey. Another member warned, "We've got to watch out or we'll be just what they sometimes call us, a bunch of —— —— yes-men—that's what we'll be." A third insisted, "We're representatives for collective bargaining and there's no reason we

---

[25] House to Fact Finding Board, Nov. 29, 1935, FMCS Papers, RG 280, File 195/335.

[26] General Executive Board, Minutes, Oct. 25, 1935, URW Archives; *ABJ*, Oct. 15, 1935.

[27] "Findings and Recommendations of the Fact Finding Board," p. 19, FMCS Papers, RG 280, File 182/1010.

shouldn't go ahead.'' Several others called for appeals to the secretary of labor.[28]

The crisis escalated rapidly in the following days. On October 22 Litchfield spoke to a closed assembly session for two hours but refused to commit himself to a referendum. On October 23, he told an assembly committee informally that a vote in the tire departments might be feasible ''but not a factory-wide referendum.'' Afterward Senate president William Cash predicted that the assembly would carry the fight to the board of directors or to the Department of Labor. Other representatives ''expressed disgust at the delay.''[29] Several of them visited Local 2 headquarters to ask if the union would join them in a strike. White told them if ''they would come into the A. F. of L. organization, the A. F. of L. group would call the strike.''[30]

By the following day, the activists could no longer suppress their frustration. ''Do we need any more of a slap in the face?'' asked Ed Wynne, an assembly veteran. Litchfield's stand was a ''dirty trick and a dirty shame,'' added L. B. Holtz. ''We've been playing ball for 17 years. We've been loyal to the company. Now, we must be loyal to ourselves.''[31] Devising a specific plan was more difficult. Both houses demanded an immediate, factory-wide election, and the Senate overrode Slusser's veto of the original six-hour bill. Beyond that there was no consensus, and the moderates, led by J. L. Otterman and Cash, ultimately prevailed. When the assembly adjourned, it was committed to awaiting the response of the Goodyear board of directors, scheduled to meet on October 28.

In the meantime Local 2 leaders watched warily. They suspected a secret deal and predicted that Litchfield would accept the assembly demand for a six-hour day, ''thus demonstrating the possibility of the [assembly] obtaining redress of grievances.''[32] When White mentioned the possibility of a strike, House issued an immediate denial. Dalrymple similarly rejected suggestions that the strike authorization vote of March 1935 was still valid. At a rally of Local 2 members, House attacked both Goodyear and the Industrial Assembly.[33]

On Friday, October 25, House, Dalrymple, and several local officials called on Slusser to present a series of anti-six-hour resolutions. Slusser, who had been drinking heavily, flew into a rage. Responding to his ''opprobrious language'' and ''insulting'' manner, they reminded him of the appeal provision of the teacup agreement. Slusser replied that the April

---

[28] *ABJ*, Oct. 22, 1935.

[29] *ABJ*, Oct. 24, 1935.

[30] Chappell to Kerwin, Oct. 24, 1935, FMCS Papers, RG 280, File 182/1010.

[31] *ABJ*, Oct. 25, 1935.

[32] Chappell to Kerwin, Oct. 24, 1935, FMCS Papers, RG 280, File 182/1010.

[33] *ABJ*, Oct. 23, 1935.

settlement was "all over the dam."[34] Shocked by his statement, they decided to request Perkins's intervention at once. House immediately drafted an appeal, citing the company's intransigence, the prospect of lower wages, and the likelihood of layoffs. He noted Slusser's statement that the teacup agreement was "over the dam" and warned that if Perkins did not act immediately, a "tie up in production . . . may not easily be averted."[35]

Events quickly proved the wisdom of this action. The Friday newspapers reported the assembly deliberations, dispelling any doubt about the authenticity of the revolt. Union leaders suddenly sensed the possibility of a coup. On Friday night they organized a parade of more than a hundred automobiles. A hastily arranged Sunday mass meeting attracted the largest crowd since early 1934. On Monday they received more good news. The Goodyear board of directors listened to Otterman and Cash, praised the assembly, and reaffirmed Litchfield's provocative stand.[36]

On Tuesday afternoon Slusser appeared before the assembly and answered questions for two hours. He emphasized that the length of the day would vary with business conditions and pledged to "put the plant on six hours to avoid layoffs." A. D. Trembly, a veteran senator who had introduced the original six-hour bill, and Otterman announced afterward that they were satisfied. Others were less happy. The assembly voted to renew its demands for a referendum and a return to the six-hour day in the Plant 2 tire departments.[37]

The next day, October 30, was a turning point in the history of the Industrial Assembly. Litchfield told an assembly committee that an "election could not intelligently be held" and refused to order a return to the six-hour day in Plant 2. The committee reported that it was "useless to make any further contacts." In the House the activists, led by Baskey, pushed through a resolution calling for an appeal to the Labor Department. In the Senate, Cash and Trembly attached an amendment requiring an additional conference with Litchfield before turning to Perkins. Even with that change, the final vote was 9 to 9. Cash broke the tie, voting against the motion. He thought that Litchfield and Slusser had learned their lesson. An appeal to the Labor Department was not "called for at this time."[38]

The collapse of the assembly revolt only momentarily blunted the Goodyear protest movement. Local 2 continued to pressure Perkins and hold

[34] House to Fact Finding Board, Nov. 29, 1935, FMCS Papers, RG 280, File 195/335.

[35] House to Frances Perkins, Oct. 25, 1935 in General Executive Board, Minutes, Oct. 26, 1935, URW Archives; *ABJ*, Oct. 25, 1935.

[36] *ABJ*, Oct. 26, Oct. 29, 1935; *ATP*, Oct. 29, 1935.

[37] *ABJ*, Oct. 30, 1935; "Findings and Recommendations," p. 24, FMCS Papers, RG 280, File 182/1010.

[38] "Findings and Recommendations," pp. 25–26, FMCS Papers, RG 280, File 182/1010; *ABJ*, Oct. 30, 1935.

rallies, but it was the tire workers, acting independently, who brought the issue to a head. On Tuesday, November 5, the superintendent of the Plant 2 truck-tire department announced piece-rate reductions of 10 to 15 percent to take effect on Friday. The builders responded by spontaneously turning off their machines and refusing to work until the superintendent agreed to reconsider the cut. Word of the protest, the first sit-down since the General Tire strike, spread quickly. Slusser was surprised and agitated when newspaper reporters appeared at his office.[39] The following day, when Local 2 leaders protested the cut, he denounced the union and denied that the order would be rescinded. "We said that some of the rates were too high and they are," he snapped. "There isn't anything they can do about it."[40] This statement appeared in the local papers on Thursday.

At the 6:00 A.M. shift change on Friday a group of night- and day-shift workers "gathered around the office of the Foreman and would not return to work under the new rates." The foreman notified Slusser, who met a delegation of the strikers and agreed to revise the rates. After discussing the offer, the tire builders voted to resume work, but to continue to demand the original rate and the six-hour day. Some of them also attacked the assembly's failure to intervene. Local 2 scheduled a protest meeting for the next day. Even the assembly condemned the rate cuts and the eight-hour day.[41]

As tensions rose and a confrontation seemed more and more likely, Perkins decided against further delay. After spending much of November 15 studying Chappell's reports, she called Slusser and asked him to cooperate with an impartial board. Apparently they did not discuss the status of the teacup accord or the legality of her proposal. After clearing her plan with Roosevelt later that afternoon, she announced the appointment of a fact-finding board composed of several Labor Department officials and Fred C. Croxton of Ohio State University. Croxton chaired the board and did most of the work.[42]

The board members arrived in Akron on November 22 and conducted a series of closed meetings with URW and Goodyear representatives. They interviewed union and company officers, collected data on the Goodyear labor force, and, after appeals from Otterman and Trembly, listened to the assembly leaders. On December 2 they returned to Washington to present their conclusions to Perkins "as soon as possible."[43]

Croxton's report was a devastating critique of Goodyear policy. It con-

[39] *ABJ*, Nov. 4, 6, 7, 8, 1935; House to Fact Finding Board, Nov. 29, 1935, FMCS Papers, RG 280, File 195/335.

[40] *ATP*, Nov. 7, 1935.

[41] *ABJ*, Nov. 8, 1935.

[42] *ABJ*, Nov. 16, 1935.

[43] *ABJ*, Dec. 3, 1935.

cluded that there was "no justification" for the eight-hour day, reduced wages, or the company's refusal to permit a referendum. Goodyear had been "evasive and confusing," had favored the Industrial Assembly over the URW, and had violated the teacup agreement. Juxtaposing Litchfield's earlier statements on the six-hour day with his current proposals, Croxton implied that the Goodyear president was a liar or a hypocrite. Wage cuts and layoffs, he added, would only reduce the demand for Goodyear products, "and the Goodyear Company can ill-afford to take a backward step at this time." He proposed higher tire prices, rather than lower wages, to alleviate the profit lag.[44]

Perkins and her advisers were shocked at the virulence of the report. H. L. Kerwin, the head of the Mediation and Conciliation Service, told Perkins that it would embarrass her and cause additional discord in the industry. He blamed the company's initiatives on pressures from its bankers and stockholders. "If some of the pressure from the financial interests could be allayed, management would work out some amicable adjustment with its employees." But the strong, partisan language of the fact-finding board report would force Litchfield to refuse any "amicable adjustment."[45] They decided to try to minimize its effect. Though Croxton announced on December 18 that the report was complete, Labor Department officials refused even to acknowledge its existence three days later.[46] Perkins also arranged to meet Litchfield privately in New York on December 20. There is no report of their conversation but it is likely that she summarized the report and offered to delay its release as long as possible if Goodyear would not attack it or the Labor Department publicly. When she finally released the document on January 6, and Goodyear officials refused to make any statement, its news value quickly died. The incident nevertheless left a residue of ill will. Goodyear executives became even more convinced that the government was biased and irresponsible. Union leaders were almost as dissatisfied; for them, the investigation was more evidence of the futility of the Green strategy. The Labor Department, it appeared, was no more helpful than the NLRB.

THE SIT-DOWN MOVEMENT SPREADS

Other developments in December and January seemed to support Croxton's conclusions. The rubber companies' year-end financial statements reported substantial sales and profit increases and optimistic projections for 1936. In

---

[44] "Findings and Recommendations," pp. 1–5, FMCS Papers, RG 280, File 182/1010; *ABJ*, Dec. 17, 1935.

[45] Kerwin to Perkins, Dec. 18, 1935, FMCS Papers, RG 280, File 182/1010.

[46] Kerwin to House, Dec. 21, 1935, FMCS Papers, RG 280, File 182/1010.

late December the major firms called back hundreds of laid-off employees, and on January 3 Litchfield publicly announced his commitment to price stability. A few days later the Federal Trade Commission, at the instigation of the independent tire retailers, announced a conference of tire manufacturers to consider additional antidiscounting measures. In short, the economic outlook suggested the likelihood of more jobs and higher pay, not cutbacks and sacrifices. Litchfield might be sensitive to the stockholders' impatience, but the workers were more impressed with the possibilities of the new year.[47]

URW leaders also appreciated the opportunities of the moment. At a mass meeting on January 12, 1936, they criticized the manufacturers and praised the fact-finding board. The workers responded enthusiastically. On January 19, John L. Lewis addressed the largest local labor meeting in nearly six months. In characteristic style, he attacked the rubber companies, the Supreme Court, and the AFL, and offered to assist the URW. "Your destiny is in your own hands," he told the cheering crowd of two thousand. "I hope you'll do something for yourselves." Thomas Burns followed with selections from the fact-finding board report. Judging from the recollections of men who attended, the rally was an immense success. Union morale revived miraculously.[48]

Three days after the Lewis rally, Firestone managers cut piece rates in the Plant 1 truck-tire department, a union stronghold. The tire builders soon complained that "they were unable to make their average day's pay" under the new schedule. They were even less happy when the department manager brought in Hugh Godfrey, a nonunion tire builder from another department whom they viewed as a "pacemaker." Clay Dicks, the Local 7 committeeman, exchanged angry words with Godfrey. When they met again accidentally after work, Godfrey supposedly taunted Dicks: "You won't fight unless you've got a gang." Dicks replied that he "had no gang" then and knocked Godfrey unconscious.[49] On Monday, January 27, Labor Manager Murphy ordered Dicks suspended without pay for the rest of the week, and the tension in the truck-tire department became palpable. The following afternoon, while Local 7 officials were waiting to see Murphy about Dicks's suspension, the truck-tire builders stopped their machines and refused to work until Dicks had been reinstated. When Murphy refused to change his order, they remained at their machines. For fifty-five hours, a "carnival spirit" prevailed. Strikers talked or played cards or lounged in the cafeteria. Wednesday night many of them went home to "rest up a bit."

[47] *ABJ*, Jan. 3, 11, 1936.
[48] *ABJ*, Jan. 20, 1936; John D. House interviews; Harley C. Anthony interview.
[49] *ATP*, Jan. 29, 30, 1936.

A Local 7 committeeman assured reporters that they would return and "stick it out until the grievance with the management is settled."[50] Union leaders described their action as a "sit-down," not a strike. The term, which had been used casually before, officially entered the lexicon of industrial protest on January 29.

Amid rumors of sit-downs in other departments, the local officers, aided by Dalrymple, conferred with Murphy on Wednesday and Thursday. They accepted the latter's offer to pay the tire builders half their usual base rate for the time they had not worked, but insisted that he also pay Dicks, at least until they investigated the Godfrey incident. On Thursday evening Murphy reluctantly agreed. When Dalrymple announced that Dicks would receive half pay during his suspension, the workers greeted his statement with a "whoop of satisfaction." Dicks called it "the finest thing in the world." The workers filed out of the plant. At an impromptu rally later that evening, Dalrymple attempted to put the best face on the incident. It "will teach the company not to be too hasty . . . and it will teach the men what an organization can do to settle their grievances," he told his cheering audience.[51] At no time had he or the other union negotiators discussed the rate cuts, which remained in effect.

News of the Firestone "victory" ignited protests in the other plants. On January 31, one hundred Goodyear Plant 1 pit workers, all nonunion, sat down to protest a 10-percent rate cut. They left six hours later when personnel manager Fred Climer promised to consider their complaints, but resumed their protest on February 3, when he refused to change the rate. This action prompted three important meetings on February 4. At the first, representatives from the pit met Climer to discuss the rate cuts and sit-downs. After more than three hours of discussion, Litchfield appeared. Expressing "keen disappointment that the long era of mutual confidence . . . has been marred by sitting-down tactics," he insisted the rate had been "intelligently and fairly determined" and employees "cannot fairly challenge the rate." He told them to accept the rate or find other employment.[52] Later that day, at House's invitation, one hundred fifty pit workers gathered at the Local 2 hall and voted to ask the union to negotiate for them. White told reporters that so many of them had joined the local since the sit-down that the union represented a majority of the protesters. The Industrial Assembly, on the other hand, met and adopted a "hands off attitude."[53] Trembly, who had succeeded Cash as Senate president, explained that the issue involved only one department. Whether this or the recollection of the

[50] Ibid.

[51] *ABJ*, Jan. 31, 1936; *ATP*, Jan. 31, 1936.

[52] *ABJ*, Feb. 5, 1936. Also see *ATP*, Feb. 1, 4, 1935.

[53] *ABJ*, Feb. 5, 1936.

long and costly fight for the six-hour day was the reason for the assembly's inaction, the appearance of timidity at this juncture left Local 2 as the only resolute opponent of the company.

On the following Friday, February 7, 150 Goodrich third-shift tire builders sat down to protest a loss of pay when they changed machines. At midnight, night-shift tire builders joined the protest. By 2:00 A.M. Graham and L. L. Callahan, the new Local 5 president, announced that the company would pay the men for lost time when they switched machines. Union representatives hailed the settlement as a victory; Graham had "given more than had been asked for." Yet at 3:00 A.M. the tire builders sat down again when they learned that they would not be paid for the time they had been idle. After more negotiations, an exasperated Graham ordered the plant closed for the weekend. He charged that workers had brought liquor into the plant and had threatened other employees.[54] Several hundred tire builders, perhaps half of the strikers, nevertheless refused to leave until they received assurance of compensation. Together with a few others, they remained in the plant until 7:00 P.M. Graham made no effort to expel them.

Union leaders were angry and embarrassed. At a Saturday morning meeting of the Local 5 executive board, Callahan strongly opposed the strikers' demand because it obscured the more fundamental problem of wage cuts. Dalrymple, who had spent the night at the local hall, argued that a Firestone-type settlement would "induce workers to sitdown" and that to ask for compensation "was equivalent to demanding that the company furnish 'strike defense funds.' "[55] He assured the strikers that there would be no reprisals. A large majority then agreed to drop their demand and go home. Callahan praised them for accepting the "more sane leadership" of the union.[56]

Fourth-shift tire builders at Goodyear were less impressed. As likely candidates for layoff when the plant went to a permanent eight-hour schedule, they were more attracted to the tactics of the militants than to "sane leadership." When the tire room foreman began to pass out layoff notices at midnight on February 14, they stopped their work and protested. The foreman urged them to select a committee to talk to the shift foreman. The six men they chose, none of whom were union members, included C. D. "Chuck" Lesley, a former anti-union militant who "spoke well"; George Boyer, a spare Ohioan who had just returned from his hardscrabble farm; and James W. "Jimmy" Jones, a "dapper," fiery Georgian. After several hours of arguments, they returned about 5:00 A.M. to report that they had

[54] *ATP*, Feb. 8, 1936.
[55] *ABJ*, Feb. 8, 10, 1936.
[56] *ATP*, Feb. 9, 1936.

been unsuccessful. A few minutes later, when the superintendent asked them to leave, Lesley challenged his co-workers: "What are we, mice or men? If we're going to be men, let's stick with it." The workers responded: "We're going to be men."[57] They sat down for the rest of their shift and half of the morning shift. When they left at 9:00 A.M., after Climer and the Plant 2 superintendent promised another meeting, House was waiting at the gate. He offered the local's help and suggested a meeting of tire builders at the union hall. They accepted. From that point the fate of the union would be inextricably associated with the sit-down movement.

The conflict escalated rapidly. At noon, the second-shift tire builders sat down to protest the fourth-shift layoffs until Climer promised to meet them, too. At 6:00 P.M. the third-shift tire builders staged their own sit-down to protest the layoffs. At 8:30, after the "doors had been locked and elevator operators instructed not to stop at the third floor," Climer appeared. He pulled out a pocket watch and gave them thirty minutes to resume work or face discharge. Three men, Flying Squadron members, went to their machines; the other 137 remained idle. At 9:30 the foremen distributed "pass-out" checks, marked "Quit, no notice."[58] Still the men refused to leave. After 11:00 P.M., they gradually went back to their machines and built at least one tire. In the meantime, supervisors had sent home hundreds of other workers and had canceled the fourth shift. Since no work was scheduled for Saturday or Monday, the plant would not reopen until Tuesday, February 18.

The firing of the third-shift tire builders, veteran employees who had not been involved in earlier protests, brought the tensions of the preceding months to a head. House and Trembly both demanded that the men be reinstated and called special meetings. After extended deliberations, an assembly committee met Climer on Saturday evening and won a promise to rehire the 137 men on Monday, providing they applied at the employment office. On Monday, after a second conference, Climer announced that the layoff would be "suspended" pending a reexamination of the production schedule.[59] Meanwhile, the union militants became more vocal as it became apparent that the company would cooperate with the assembly. At a Local 2 rally on Sunday, an angry crowd of fifteen hundred heard Wilmer Tate, William Carney, "Red" Bessemer, and House attack the company and the Industrial Assembly. Tate told the workers that Litchfield was "sending up trial balloons. . . . The first balloon . . . reducing wages . . . seems to be getting along all right. But the second one, laying off men, just

[57] George Boyer, interview with author, July 1, 1976.
[58] *ATP*, Feb. 15, 1936; *ABJ*, Feb. 15, 1936.
[59] *ABJ*, Feb. 15, 17, 1936; *ATP*, Feb. 16, 1936.

went pop!'' Carney added that if the company refused to reinstate the tire builders, ''the thing for us to do . . . is to go over to Plant 2 and shut down the whole works.''[60]

On Monday tensions increased. The Plant 2 tire builders met at the local hall and heard Lesley report that Climer had refused to discuss future lay-offs. That evening approximately one thousand rubber workers attended another rally at the Local 2 hall. The tire builders voted not to work and other workers pledged to join them. Amid the uproar House's calls for more negotiations were almost drowned out. Finally, C. M. ''Skip'' O'Harrah, a small, fiery tire builder, shouted above the din: ''There's talk that we'll have a picket line at 5 in the morning. I have the captains picked. I want to know if you'll join them at Plant 2.'' The crowd roared its approval. O'Harrah seized the local's flag and led an impromptu parade toward Plant 2. By 11 P.M. five hundred men and a few women were marching ''in chainlike fashion'' outside the gate. Periodically pickets would drop out of line to seek shelter from the subzero temperatures and bone-chilling winds. Some went to other Goodyear gates. A few managed to sing. At midnight they turned away several hundred fourth-shift employees.[61] A few hours later, five hundred Plant 1 tire builders and pit workers sat down in support of the strike, gradually paralyzing that plant too. By late Tuesday operations at Goodyear had come to a virtual halt. The great Goodyear strike, the rubber workers' final answer to Litchfield's wage cuts, had begun.

Goodyear Strike: February 18–March 2

The issues that had ignited the protests were settled almost immediately. On February 19 Litchfield appeared before an informal joint session of the Industrial Assembly and pledged to continue the six-hour day and to maintain existing base rates—in effect, to defer his plan to revitalize the Akron plants.[62] But if the provocative Litchfield plan was not an issue after February 19, the strike soon raised a more fundamental question: What type of organization would represent Goodyear employees? Litchfield was unequivocal. For two years he had deferred to the New Dealers and had suffered a succession of indignities culminating in the sit-downs, the fact-finding board report, and the most serious strike in the company's history. Now he would deal with the strikers in his own way. He began a series of efforts to break their morale and induce a back-to-work movement. The success of any of these probably would have sealed the fate of the URW for the foreseeable future. As one observer wrote, ''It is either utter defeat, or

[60] *ABJ*, Feb. 17, 1936.
[61] *ABJ*, Feb. 18, 1936.
[62] *ABJ*, Feb. 25, 1936.

partial victory for the unions."[63] Yet the contest was not wholly one-sided. If Litchfield failed, the union might become stronger rather than weaker. A "partial victory" might be as much as House, White, and the International needed.

Litchfield personally directed the company during the early phases of the strike, partly because of the seriousness of the situation and partly because of Slusser's absence. During the tumultuous months that preceded February 18, Slusser had been drunk more and more often, and by early 1936 he was unable to function. Litchfield finally persuaded him to enter a Connecticut sanitarium and called back thirty-four-year-old Edwin J. Thomas from the English subsidiary to take over many of Slusser's duties. In the meantime Litchfield faced a greatly increased burden and, as the strikers directed more and more criticism at the special privileges of the Flying Squadron and the Industrial Assembly, a personal crisis of his own.

From the beginning Litchfield adopted a "hard boiled attitude" toward the strike and the URW, which he believed had fomented the incident.[64] At 5:30 A.M. on February 19, he stationed himself at the Plant 1 gates and demanded that police help first-shift workers cross the picket line. When that tactic failed, he retired to his office; he remained in the plant for the next twelve days, together with several hundred other executives and employees. When P. W. Chappell interviewed him on February 20, he was exceedingly bitter toward the six hundred "malcontents" he blamed for the sit-downs and the Local 2 officers, whom he "would not deal with . . . even if the plants had to remain closed indefinitely." Nor did he desire government assistance, except for an injunction to restrain the pickets. Essentially, he planned to "sit tight" while loyal employees pressured the mayor and the sheriff to reopen the plants.[65]

The last assembly meeting of the strike period, on February 19, coincided with the first meeting of the "nonstrikers," the informal organization of anti-URW employees. Local 2 officials dismissed the nonstrikers as "foremen and supervisors," but Lyle Carruthers, the group's leader, insisted that they were "not connected with the company in any way. Piece workers . . . are running this entirely."[66] Regardless of the original initiative, it is clear that most of the prominent nonstrikers, like Carruthers, were long-service men associated with the old elite. Veterans of the Industrial Assembly and the Ku Klux Klan, they boasted of their superior experience,

[63] Chappell to Kerwin, Feb. 24, 1936, FMCS Papers, RG 280, File 182/1010.
[64] Cyrus Ching, Oral History Memoir, Columbia University, 1: 14–15.
[65] Chappell to Kerwin, March 21, 1936, FMCS Papers, RG 280, File 182/1010.
[66] ATP, Feb. 22, 1936.

dedication, and loyalty. For the first two weeks of the strike, they, not the union militants, posed the greatest threat of violence.[67]

The nonstrikers quickly made their presence felt. On February 19 several hundred men jammed city hall, demanding police protection and booing Mayor Lee D. Schroy and Police Chief Frank Boss when they urged patience. Many volunteered to serve as special deputies. On February 20, three thousand or more angry nonstrikers met at a high school auditorium. As the crowd grew, Carruthers and other nonstriker leaders decided to move the meeting to the armory, a larger facility. When National Guard officials refused to open the armory, Carruthers lost control.

"Let's take it," the workers shouted, and a general rush began for the doors. A cheering section of nearly 200 shouted derision at Mayor . . . Schroy and Sheriff Jim Flower.

Leaders brandished placards bearing such sentiments as "it's up to you to protect us, Mr. Mayor." "We have the right to work." "Down with mob rule" and "We work, you strike."

A petition . . . demanding protection for the company and the non-strikers was circulated in the crowd as it swept down Mill Street.[68]

After breaking into the building, they summoned the mayor and sheriff for interrogation. Threats against the strikers were "wildly applauded." The mayor and the sheriff refused to deputize the militants.

For the next four days the nonstrikers reassembled daily at the armory to devise strategy and intimidate public officials. On February 21 Carruthers selected fifty men, who "will be ready to go help Sheriff Flower or city police . . . and will round up non-strikers when any unexpected meeting is called." Later he appointed committees to organize the nonstrikers into "mobile units." At the end of the session the crowd joined in loud choruses of "Let Me Call You Sweetheart," "I Want a Girl," and other songs.[69] During the February 22 meeting, the nonstrikers received news of the injunction Litchfield had demanded. The men adjourned in high spirits, believing that local officials would have to aid them. On February 24, the day before the sheriff was to enforce the injunction, Carruthers announced that the mass meetings would end. The men left the armory with every expectation of returning to their jobs the next day.

Barring a direct assault on the picket line, the nonstrikers' hopes depended on Sheriff Flower and Mayor Schroy. Flower, who had no jurisdiction in the city until the judges issued the injunction, was, in Chappell's

[67] Daniel Nelson, "The Leadership of the United Rubber Workers," *Detroit in Perspective* 5 (1981): 25; *ABJ*, Feb. 24, 1936; *ATP*, Feb. 28, 1936.

[68] *ATP*, Feb. 21, 1936.

[69] *ABJ*, Feb. 22, 1936.

words, "on one side one minute and then on the other."[70] Schroy, on the other hand, was the epitome of blandness and reliability. A merchant active in civic affairs, he had campaigned successfully in 1935 as a nonpartisan administrator who would bring business skills to municipal government. Although this image was partly a political tactic, no one doubted that the mayor reflected the views and values of the city's middle class. Like most of his west-side neighbors, he was ambivalent about the rubber companies. Their competitive tactics created needless uncertainties for the shopkeepers, lawyers, and local industrialists who preferred slow, steady growth. Schroy was also apparently miffed at the rubber company executives for their failure to support his campaign.[71] His ties to organized labor were no stronger, though he recognized the importance of working-class support for any mayoral candidate. Basically, he applied a simple test to his duties. If an action was likely to advance the city's recovery and future economic growth, he favored it; if it was not, he opposed it. This perspective dictated a posture that was neither inherently prolabor nor promanagement but that might strongly favor either side at a given time.

During the first week of the strike, Schroy strongly resisted the entreaties of Litchfield and the nonstrikers. He supported negotiations, opposed an appeal for the National Guard, and assured worried citizens that he would not tolerate violence. By February 21, he was trading barbs with Litchfield over the latter's criticism of his evenhanded approach. These actions surprised union officials who had not expected assistance from city hall.[72]

At that point Local 2 leaders welcomed help from any source. Despite House's role in the events of February 14–17, they were ill-prepared for a full-scale confrontation and had to create a strike organization from scratch. House and the other officers worked around the clock for more than two days; White told reporters he had slept only four of the first hundred hours of the strike. One of their first decisions was to delegate responsibility for the pickets to the popular, diminutive O'Harrah, who adopted the title "field marshal" and carried an oversized pistol appropriate to his rank. Within twenty-four hours he had provided each picket outpost with a steel drum stove. The men themselves erected makeshift huts for further protection. The post office authorized mail delivery to "Camp Roosevelt," "John L. Lewis Post," and the other shacks.[73]

---

[70] Chappell to Kerwin, Feb. 21, 1936, FMCS Papers, RG 280, File 182/1010.

[71] Alfred Winslow Jones, *Life, Liberty, and Property: A Story of Conflict and a Measurement of Conflicting Rights* (Philadelphia, 1941), p. 107.

[72] *ATP*, March 1, 1936.

[73] John Kumpel, interview with author, Oct. 25, 1972; Rose Pesotta, *Bread Upon the Waters* (New York, 1944), p. 198; John Brophy, *A Miner's Life* (Madison, 1964), p. 264; *ABJ*, Feb. 29, 1936.

The strike headquarters was the Local 2 hall, across from the Goodyear main gate. House and White lived there, and their presence, together with a constant stream of rubber workers, reporters, and curious onlookers, gave the building an atmosphere of excitement and upheaval. A. A. Wilson managed the hall during the day and John Kumpel took his place at night. They installed a public address system to make themselves heard over the constant din. The basement housed a commissary where off-duty pickets and other strikers gathered at all hours of the day and night. Members of the Union Buyers Club and strikers' wives did the cooking. Besides hamburgers, soups, stews, and coffee, they provided visible proof that in many south and east Akron homes the strike was a family enterprise.

From the beginning, other Akron unionists recognized that their future and the future of the local labor movement were ineluctably tied to the fate of the local. Dalrymple insisted that other URW members continue to work, but many off-duty Goodrich, Firestone, and General Tire employees served as pickets or as picket-line reinforcements. Harley Anthony was a "call boy" in his neighborhood. When pickets reported possible trouble at night, he would dress, arm himself with a shotgun and revolver, and "set out through the fields knocking on doors, telling them to get to the Goodyear, and the last one I woke up I'd ride with."[74] The locals provided immediate financial aid until the International Executive Board could meet and vote to raise funds and coordinate contacts with the Central Labor Union, the AFL, the CIO, and the press.[75] Thereafter, Dalrymple, Burns, and a variety of outsiders played major roles in the strike effort.

Of special importance was the new CIO. Lewis and Brophy, already alert to the potential of the Goodyear turmoil, perceived the conflict as an opportunity to establish their credibility with employees in other industries. Following visits by Adolph Germer on February 22–23 and Brophy on February 23, the CIO threw all its resources into the Goodyear cause. Germer returned on February 24 and worked behind the scenes with the strike leaders. Powers Hapgood and Rose Pesotta arrived on February 26 and managed the strikers' public relations. Brophy made three short visits; Leo Krzycki of the Amalgamated Clothing Workers and Ben Schafer of the Oil Workers remained for longer periods; and envoys from the Clothing Workers, Mine Workers, and Auto Workers spoke at rallies and meetings. The CIO also contributed $3,000 to the strike fund. In contrast, the AFL role was negligible. Apart from Akron-area functionaries who provided assistance through the CLU, the only AFL organizer to appear was Coleman Claherty,

---

[74] Anthony interview.

[75] General Executive Board, Minutes, Feb. 24, 1936. Also see Joint Meeting, Executive Board and Defense Committee of the Central Labor Union, Feb. 25, 1936 in General Executive Board, Minutes, Feb. 24, 1936; *URW* 1 (April 1936): 16.

11. *February 25, 1936. Pickets gather on Market Street outside Goodyear in anticipation of an effort to reopen the plant. United Rubber Workers Archives.*

who toured the picket line one Sunday afternoon. No strike leader greeted him.[76]

The first important test of the strike organization came as a result of the injunction, issued by the the county's common pleas judges on February 22. The injunction permitted only ten pickets per gate and barred acts of intimidation against Goodyear employees. Flower, who had only twenty-three regular deputies and nine special deputies, made no effort to enforce it until Monday, February 24, when he announced that he would go to the Local 2 hall. As word of his plan spread, thousands of pickets crowded the area around the hall. House met him at the door and escorted him to the microphone. Flower pledged not to deputize nonstrikers and to "keep the human angles foremost in my mind." A striker interrupted: "Are you going to let them in?" The crowd roared a collective "No!" House then accompanied Flower across the street to the main gate. As they emerged

[76] Brophy, *A Miner's Life*, p. 263; *URW* 1 (April 1936): 16; Lorin Lee Cary, "Institutionalized Conservatism in the Early CIO: Adolph Germer, A Case Study," *Labor History* 13 (1972): 488–91.

from the hall a huge crowd of pickets and onlookers converged on the hall, blocking traffic in every direction. House, hoisted to the shoulders of several strikers, appealed for silence. Several men raised Flower so he could be seen and he repeated his speech. When he had finished, another voice rose from the crowd. "Are we going to let 'em in?" Again the answer was a resounding "No." Flower proceeded to Plant 2, where another crowd waited and where he received a similar response. Meekly, he retired to city hall. At Goodyear the pickets moved in an endless chain up and down the sidewalk. "Keep on going, boys, don't stop," their leader ordered.[77]

For the rest of the afternoon and evening Flower pondered his next step. According to Chief Boss, "he changed his mind . . . three or four times." At midnight he was still uncertain. He promised Schroy and Boss to have a complete plan by the morning. After talking to Goodyear executives and Col. Joe Johnston, who now worked for Goodyear, he decided to confront the strikers directly. He ordered all available deputies and city police officers to assemble near the plant, march to the main gate in a "flying wedge," and arrest pickets who continued to violate the injunction. To prepare for the assault he asked city police to block traffic in the area. By 9:00 A.M. Flower had approximately 130 police and 18 deputies at the intersection of Exchange and East Market streets, a block from Plant 1. He ordered them to move out at 9:45.[78]

URW officials were prepared. They had alerted the pickets and other union members and by 9:00 A.M. thousands of sympathizers had assembled on Market Street, ready for battle. Many carried guns or other weapons:

There were ten pins from bowling alleys, sawed off billiard cues, short but stout clubs of rough wood with hand holds whittled at one end. A woman in a fur coat brandished a club on the sidewalk. A boy of seven or eight carried a short club and . . . a pair of handcuffs.

There were scores of football helmets. . . . Others had caps stuffed with padding. Several men turned out with hunting costumes, [and] aviation helmets.[79]

Four men, carrying a flag and strike banners marched up and down the street until it became too crowded. By 9:30 A.M. a human sea of five thousand men, women, and children blocked the street from the edge of Plant 1 to the main gate a hundred yards to the southeast.

When Schroy and Boss learned of Flower's plan they were aghast. "I knew it was suicide," recalled Boss.[80] After conferences with the police,

[77] *ATP*, Feb. 24, 1936; *ABJ*, Feb. 24, 1936.
[78] *ATP*, Feb. 25, 1936.
[79] Ibid.
[80] *ATP*, Feb. 26, 1936.

Schroy concluded that "it would not be good police tactics" to follow Flower's plan. At 9:25 A.M. he called Flower, told him of his misgivings, and asked the sheriff to make a personal appeal to the strikers. Flower was indefinite. As 9:45 approached, Boss decided to act. He called Flower, revoked his authority to command the police, and rushed to the strike scene. He intercepted the officers, called them aside, and then led them single file up the hill to their usual posts. When it became apparent that the police would not attack, the mood of the crowd changed. A striker asked one of the officers if he needed another night stick. "I don't expect to use the one I've got," he replied. The crowd roared.[81]

This dramatic event prompted county prosecutor Herman Werner to enter the Goodyear offices and ask Litchfield to negotiate. Litchfield refused and asked why the sheriff did not enlist special deputies. Werner replied that Flower had been unsuccessful. When the prosecutor emerged to face the strikers, he explained what he had done and said that Litchfield "didn't say yes or no, but he will make a decision this afternoon."[82] Werner continued: "There will be no attempts to enter the plant or to break the picket line until this thing is settled." He may have added that he would stop any strike-breakers, if necessary with a gun.[83]

The crowd roared its approval. Strikers hoisted Werner to their shoulders and cheered. Others raised House, O'Harrah, and two policemen and carried them through the crowd. From his perch, House signaled for quiet.

Fellows, I'm so full of feeling I can hardly talk. . . . There is nothing that can stop us. We are in this fight to win and we are going to win in spite of hell and high water. . . . We are going to continue until we have reached a satisfactory agreement with the management.

The strikers cheered themselves hoarse. O'Harrah went to each picket post, asking everyone except the designated pickets to go home. By noon, the crowd had dispersed. House told supporters that "we've got this thing licked."[84]

Flower, however, was not finished. He called Governor Martin Davey to ask for National Guard troops. "This crowd includes union sympathizers from other factories, miners from West Virginia and Pennsylvania, Communists, and hoodlums from everywhere," he explained. In response to Davey's questions, he admitted that he had arrested no one and that there had been no violence. To arrest a striker, he added, "would be like sticking a match in a keg of powder." Davey, who was at that moment meeting

---

[81] *ATP*, Feb. 25, 1936.
[82] Ibid.
[83] *ABJ*, Feb. 25, 1936.
[84] *ATP*, Feb. 25, 1936.

leaders of the Akron CLU and the State Federation of Labor, dismissed the request later that day. Flower subsequently denied that he had asked for troops. "I guess I didn't say what I wanted to say," he explained.[85]

Thus the first and most significant of Litchfield's efforts to break the strike backfired. Rather than destroying the union, it isolated the nonstrikers, encouraged many uncommitted Goodyear workers to turn to Local 2, and created a heroic image for the local. Mayor Schroy also gained in stature, while Flower suffered. Most of all, the Goodyear initiative enhanced the standing of the union militants. Whether this would help or harm the URW was unclear on February 25, but it was apparent that the strikers, having turned back the sheriff, were more self-confident and "cocky"—in Chappell's language—than before.[86]

During the following week, these effects became clearer. The nonstrikers began to fall under the sway of Litchfield and the executives—victims, it seemed, of the passions that polarized Akron workers. Schroy resumed his former role and Flower sulked in isolation. Werner also suffered. His misleading description of his conversation with Litchfield and his promise to use "a gun" sparked criticism from both sides. Litchfield remained unyielding, and the URW, with CIO help, was sufficiently confident to launch a sustained campaign of newspaper ads and radio broadcasts.

The most important event of the following days, however, grew out of Schroy's peace efforts. Fearful of a new confrontation, the mayor persuaded Secretary Perkins to send Undersecretary Edward F. McGrady to make a personal appeal for negotiations. McGrady arrived on February 26 and proposed an immediate end to the strike, reinstatement of the strikers, and arbitration of differences between the company and the union. Despite misgivings, the union negotiators felt compelled to accept the plan. At an impromptu meeting at the Local 2 hall that night, Dalrymple announced their decision and called for a membership vote. As he explained the arbitration proposal, there were shouts of "No! No! No!" He continued, only to be interrupted again.

A storm of dissension rose powerfully from every corner of the hall. . . . A big man shoved forward and the crowd surged after him.

"I'd like to know what the hell we walked out that night to freeze for?" he demanded. A great shout shook the hall.

William Carney, who had emerged as a representative of the militants, stepped forward to shouts of "Take the microphone, Bill!" Carney opposed the McGrady plan and called for a postponement of the vote. When Burns tried to defend the committee's action, he was interrupted. Another

---

[85] Ibid.; *ABJ*, Feb. 25, 1936.
[86] Chappell to Kerwin, March 21, 1936, FMCS Papers, RG 280, File 182/1010.

union officer asked Powers Hapgood to speak for the committee, but the crowd shouted him down and called for Carney. Before Carney could come forward, Dalrymple called off the vote and adjourned the meeting.[87]

GOODYEAR STRIKE: MARCH 2–21

At noon on March 2 Litchfield emerged from the plant, drove to the Mayflower Hotel, and met reporters for the first time since the strike began. Bristling with defiance, he attacked McGrady, urged Flower to "carry out the order of the court," and vowed to "stand by" the Industrial Assembly. "Under no circumstances" would he enter into an agreement with the URW.[88] His words, however, were hollow and unconvincing. By abandoning his vigil, he acknowledged, in effect, that a 1913-style victory was unlikely, and that his actions had strengthened, not weakened, Local 2. Vice-President Thomas was even more certain. He had consistently advocated a more conciliatory approach, sparking rumors of a conflict and even a "coup" that would put him on top.[89] In fact the two executives saw eye to eye on fundamentals. Thomas was prepared to live with the union but did not favor additional concessions. By late February he and Climer had persuaded Litchfield to consider a settlement based on the prestrike status quo, plus the concessions he had made to the Industrial Assembly on February 19 and an offer Climer had made on February 19 to terminate the special seniority rights of Flying Squadron members.[90]

On February 29 Thomas and Climer made the first effort to break the deadlock. They employed a local attorney, Lisle M. Buckingham, to propose a truce, negotiations, a reduction in the number of pickets, and the resumption of tire shipments. URW leaders submitted a counteroffer. They called for a signed truce and no shipping or production during the negotiations. They also asked that Goodyear abandon the injunction. To outsiders it appeared that "little of real importance" separated the two sides. Yet Goodyear officials rejected the counteroffer as well as a union request for additional time, prompting union leaders to dismiss the company offer as a trick. Prodded by government mediators and McGrady, Burns then proposed secret face-to-face meetings without a set agenda. Thomas and Cli-

[87] *ABJ*, Feb. 29, 1936.

[88] *ABJ*, March 3, 1936.

[89] Chappell to Kerwin, March 1, 1936, FMCS Papers, RG 280, File 182/1010; Adolph Germer Diary, March 3, 1936, Adolph Germer Papers, State Historical Society of Wisconsin, Madison.

[90] Edwin J. Thomas, interview with author, Aug. 6, 1982.

mer agreed. Negotiations began on March 5 and lasted intermittently until the end of the strike.[91]

By that time the URW and CIO had created a formidable strike organization. URW leaders ran the strike, raised funds, and conducted negotiations. The CIO advisers managed the strikers' public relations. In the hectic early days of the strike, Germer personally wrote all the strikers' press releases, met with reporters, and coordinated the publicity work of the other CIO representatives. Presumably it was he who decided that the strikers should rely on the radio to communicate with sympathizers and potential allies. Dalrymple, Burns, Grillo, and the Local 2 officers made frequent broadcasts; their statements, with only two exceptions between February 26 and March 10, were products of Germer's facile pen. Thereafter, McAllister Coleman, a labor journalist Germer brought from New York to relieve the burden, composed both press releases and broadcast scripts. His work, like Germer's, was of high quality and undoubtedly helped minimize the erosion of public support as the strike dragged on and the drumbeat of Goodyear propaganda intensified. Even union critics agreed that the strikers won the battle of the airwaves.[92]

CIO representatives were equally effective in their public appearances. Germer, Hapgood, and Pesotta made daily inspection tours of the picket lines, often pausing for impromptu rallies. They also participated in countless meetings at the union hall and in a series of mass rallies at the armory. Beginning on March 3, the union sponsored daily programs at a theater near the Goodyear plant. Pesotta recruited amateur theatrical groups and led the strikers in labor songs. Hapgood specialized in inspirational talks. His dapper appearance and enthusiasm attracted large audiences. Goodyear executives seemed to despise him more than the other CIO representatives.

Despite a generally harmonious partnership at the top and a widespread sense that the union had the upper hand after the beginning of negotiations, the strikers still faced dangers. Litchfield had only suspended his original strategy, and the nonstrikers, with or without direct company encouragement, remained a threat. The strike militants were another question mark. Their responses to the McGrady plan and their role in another, more important incident on March 7, were potentially as menacing as the intrigues of the nonstrikers.

After the injunction fiasco, the nonstrikers shifted their focus and demanded the removal of the pickets' shelters. The mayor could hardly deny this request; the huts violated city ordinances and were visible reminders of

[91] Chappell to Kerwin, Feb. 12, March 21, 1936, FMCS Papers, RG 280, File 182/1010; *ABJ*, March 4, 1936.

[92] Germer Diary, Feb. 26–March 10, 1936; *ABJ*, March 23, 1936; Pesotta, *Bread Upon the Waters*, pp. 221–22; *URW* 1 (April 1936): 2.

the strikers' defiance of authority. Schroy conferred with House and O'Harrah several times during the week of March 2–6 and elicited pledges to remove the shelters "as soon as possible." In fact they did nothing. O'Harrah probably did not even inform the pickets of his promise to remove the huts.[93] By March 6, Schroy's impatience was exhausted. Believing his political future was at stake, he ordered sanitation workers to remove the huts on March 7. At 7:00 A.M. five trucks and fifty-six workers accompanied by seventy-five policemen arrived at the Goodyear gate. They destroyed four of the shanties before the surprised and sleepy pickets realized what was happening and sounded the alarm.

Ed Heinke described the response:

Pickets poured out of the nearby union headquarters. Hurry calls were sent out for reinforcements. . . .

A moment later, at the General [Tire] Plant . . . the word went down the production line that trouble had developed at Goodyear.

The men dropped their tools, shut the presses and rushed from the building. . . .

Union men in the Goodrich plant were told to stand by. Men in the union headquarters at Firestone rushed to the scene. . . .

Down over Newton Street hill machine loads of strike sympathizers, with hatless, coatless men hanging to the running boards, raced toward the strike scene. Picket reinforcements filled the streets.[94]

Within minutes two to three thousand men jammed the street, forcing the police and sanitation men away from the huts. In the scuffles that ensued, two officers were injured. Outraged, Mayor Schroy ordered a renewed assault, then hesitated when the police warned that they would "have to go back shooting."[95] Several hours later he met House and O'Harrah and agreed to postpone any action if the union removed the huts from major thoroughfares. After March 7 pickets sat in cars near the gates and city officials made no effort to interfere. The crisis had passed.

The incident nevertheless troubled union leaders. It was hardly surprising that Germer, who characterized himself as a "servant" or "first mate" to "Captain Dalrymple" but whose real job was to see that the strike did not fail, began to pressure URW leaders for an agreement—virtually any agreement that would preserve the union foothold at Goodyear.[96] Given the company's position, Dalrymple and House could expect few immediate

[93] Germer Diary, March 6, 1936.

[94] *ATP*, March 7, 1936.

[95] Ibid. Brophy recalled a striker showing him a gun and confiding, "We've passed the word to the police that we'll give them as good as they send" (Brophy, *A Miner's Life*, p. 264).

[96] *ABJ*, Feb. 28, 1936.

concessions. At best they might wring enough to win rank-and-file approval before another incident led to disaster.

By March 7 their private meetings had produced understandings on a number of issues. Thomas and Climer agreed to reinstate all employees, give Local 2 "equal representation" with the assembly, notify union leaders of layoffs and rate changes, reconsider recent rate cuts, reduce the number of Flying Squadron members, and maintain the six-hour day. Union leaders intended to report these results to the strikers at a meeting on Sunday, March 8, and ask for their approval. However, when Ed Heinke learned of their plan and announced it in the *Times Press* on Sunday morning, Goodyear officials objected and House confined his report to a summary of the negotiations. If he had asked for a vote, he probably would have encountered substantial opposition.[97]

The Heinke story had other repercussions. Litchfield had second thoughts about the Thomas-Climer offer and decided on a different, less generous plan. On March 9, he broadcast a new proposal: Goodyear would reinstate all employees, consult representatives of all groups, give prior notice of rate changes, keep the thirty-six-hour week and six-hour day in the tire departments, and post layoff notices before they became effective. He said nothing about hours in nontire departments, the February wage cuts, Flying Squadron members, or the union role in grievance discussions. He categorically stated that the assembly would "continue to function as it has successfully functioned for the past seventeen years." Union leaders believed they had been "double-crossed."[98] Germer wrote a reply, which House broadcast the following night. It forcefully spelled out the differences between the two company positions and the reasons for the workers' unhappiness with Litchfield's address. The International officers pondered ways to pressure Litchfield, including strikes at Cumberland and Gadsden.[99]

With the encouragement of federal mediators the negotiators resumed their talks on Wednesday, March 11. Thomas and Climer assured the union representatives that they had not reneged on their earlier concessions but that "they could not publicly express [them] in language other than . . . Litchfield's proposal." The company would "abide by the agreements of the previous week in spite of Mr. Litchfield's later statements." Thomas insisted that they could offer no more and demanded a ratification vote on

[97] Chappell to Kerwin, March 12, 21, 1936, FMCS Papers, RG 280, File 182/1010; *ABJ*, March 9, 1936; *ATP*, March 8, 9, 1936.

[98] Chappell to Kerwin, March 21, 1936, FMCS Papers, File 182/1010; *ATP*, March 10, 1936.

[99] *ATP*, March 11, 1936; *ABJ*, March 11, 1936; Germer Diary, March 10, 1936.

the Litchfield proposal.[100] The union negotiators reluctantly agreed. They scheduled a vote for the following Saturday afternoon at the armory.

For several days it appeared that the vote might succeed. Both city newspapers called for ratification, and Goodyear executives expressed confidence that the strikers would accept. Germer "hoped the men would accept the company's proposition and then build up their union."[101] Many strikers, however, grumbled in private about Thomas and Climer's verbal assurances. A Friday night strike meeting effectively settled the issue. Before eight hundred to one thousand strikers, Carney blasted the newspaper endorsements of the agreement and vowed that "No power on earth" could make him vote for the pact. Other speakers echoed these statements. The audience responded enthusiastically. Afterward, Germer questioned whether the agreement "will get any support."[102]

On Saturday morning the strike leaders and Germer met to plan the afternoon meeting. They decided that House would call on George Hull, a member of the negotiating committee, to read the Goodyear proposal, ask Dalrymple to explain the procedure for amending the company plan, and then open the meeting to discussion. Afterward, they would vote by secret ballot. At that point W. H. Ricketts, a Local 2 activist, appeared. Ricketts claimed to represent a group of pickets and announced a plan to amend the agreement. His plan was the work of James Keller, the local Communist party organizer. Keller's proposals called for the strikers to accept most of the company offer, demand restatements of several provisions, and press for plantwide seniority and an end to the Industrial Assembly. He hoped that these changes would encourage the union negotiators to resign so that more assertive and malleable men could take charge.[103] In substance, though, the Keller-Ricketts amendments were little more than the earlier union demands. Their only effect was to commit the union negotiators to specific modifications of the proposed agreement. House and other URW leaders did not find them objectionable. Germer was apparently the only dissenter.[104]

By 2:00 P.M. the armory overflowed with four thousand or more strikers, many of whom made little effort to disguise their dissatisfaction. A reporter

[100] Chappell to Kerwin, March 11, 12, 21, 1936, FMCS Papers, RG 280, File 182/1010.

[101] Chappell to Kerwin, March 12, 1936, FMCS Papers, RG 280, File 182/1010; Germer Diary, March 13, 1936.

[102] Germer Diary, March 13, 1936; *ABJ*, March 14, 1936.

[103] Ruth McKenny, *Industrial Valley* (New York, 1939), pp. 354–55. Also see *URW* 4 (March 1939): 7 and the handbill in FMCS Papers, RG 280, File 182/1010; Richard Shrake, II, "Working Class Politics in Akron, Ohio, 1936: The United Rubber Workers and the Failure of the Farmer Labor Party" (M.A. thesis, University of Akron, 1974), p. 20; *Daily Worker*, March 23, 1936. John Williamson, "Akron, A New Chapter in American Labor History," *Communist* 15 (1936): 416, 424–25.

[104] Germer Diary, March 14, 1936.

who eluded the union guards noted that it was "pretty plain from the start that the crowd wasn't going to accept the company's peace plan." When a malfunction of the public address system delayed the start of the meeting, House led the group in singing. On cue a handful of Communists began to chant "No, No, a Thousand Times No," a refrain the pickets had often used. The crowd joined in the chant. When House finally stepped to the microphone to begin the meeting, he was greeted by cries of "No! No! No!" After a brief introductory statement, House turned to Hull, who discussed the negotiations rather than the agreement. Before Dalrymple had spoken, Ricketts jumped up and read his proposal. Afterward, Germer reported, House "called Burns and Dalrymple into a huddle at the table and had Burns say 'the negotiating committee accepts the resolution as part of its report.' " Carney proposed several minor amendments, which the strikers also adopted. When House gestured toward the ballot box, he was loudly booed. He then called for a show of hands and the strikers adopted the amended report. Skip O'Harrah again had the last word: "I'm telling you right now," he shouted, "this strike has just started. We're going out to hold that picket line."[105]

The strikers' action gave Litchfield a final chance to settle the strike on his terms. As soon as he heard of the vote, he issued a statement attacking it and promising to reopen the plant. Later he withdrew his offer to reinstate the strikers because "Akron's reputation for lawlessness . . . is becoming so generally known."[106] His statements coincided with an announcement by former mayor C. Nelson Sparks of the formation of a Law and Order League that would "gang up on the out of town radicals and communist leaders" who threatened "a reign of terror." Sparks maintained that the nonstrikers had asked him to organize the group the day before. The actual catalyst had been the February 25 break between Flower and Schroy. Isolated and embarrassed, the sheriff had rallied various antistrike groups and recruited Sparks. Litchfield provided $15,000 in cash and paid for the group's headquarters at the Mayflower Hotel. Colonel Johnston served as liaison between the sheriff and Sparks. On March 10, Sparks met Governor Davey at a Columbus, Ohio, hotel to discuss the use of National Guard troops in Akron. At the same time, he began to solicit Akron businesses for support. By Friday night, when Carruthers and other nonstrikers supposedly approached him, Sparks was ready to act. On Saturday "the downtown area became a hive of strike and counter-strike activity."[107]

Sparks's objective was to unite various nonunion groups into an anti-

[105] *ATP*, March 14, 15, 1936; Germer Diary, March 14, 1936.

[106] Paul W. Litchfield to Chappell and Edward McDonald, March 16, 1936, FMCS Papers, RG 280, File 182/1010.

[107] U.S. Senate, "Violations of Free Speech and Rights of Labor," p. 2951; *ABJ*, March 15, Oct. 28, 1936.

strike majority. In inflammatory radio broadcasts at noon and 9:15 P.M. on Sunday, he stressed the economic growth issue. His target, ironically, was not the local militants but the CIO representatives, the "outside agitators" who had worked for a moderate settlement. Germer, Hapgood, and the others, Sparks told his audiences, "have come into our community with the sole intent to either make Akron's rubber industry 100 percent unionized, or wreck the industry. And wreck the city in the effort."[108] What precisely he planned to do is unclear. While claiming to have "5,200 organized vigilantes under 168 captains" (presumably the nonstrikers and some veterans groups), his immediate goal was to persuade ordinary citizens to enlist in the Law and Order League. Sparks later insisted that his aim was merely to "crystallize public opinion." In another statement he indicated that he sought to enlist "every civic, fraternal, social, business and religious organization."[109] Perhaps he saw his group as the equivalent of the Citizens Welfare League of 1913. He probably hoped to intimidate the strikers, force Schroy to adopt a more partisan stance, and, if necessary, create a pretext for the entry of the National Guard.

By Sunday night the "town's excitement was bordering on panic."[110] After Sparks's Sunday evening speech, Wilmer Tate broadcast a vigorous counterattack, characterizing the former mayor as the "Mussolini of Akron." URW leaders pledged to resist any attack on the picket line. Hundreds of union members gathered at strike headquarters and thousands more planned to be on East Market Street on Monday morning. Rumors were rife, but two critical questions remained unanswered. What would Schroy do and when would Goodyear reopen the plant?

The mayor's actions Sunday night and Monday probably persuaded Goodyear officials not to open the plant Monday or Tuesday. After consulting the police, the mayor concluded that any attempt to reopen the plant would lead to violence. In a meeting with the sheriff and police officers early Monday he was "firm" in rejecting assistance to the antistrike forces. " 'The officers will be [at Goodyear] only to preserve peace,' he declared. 'They will not take sides with either group.' "[111] To Sheriff Flower's pleas that more officers were necessary (he had sworn in Sparks as a special deputy a few minutes earlier), Schroy turned a deaf ear. Later that day, when Flower proposed that they ask Governor Davey for troops, Schroy again demurred. Without the mayor's support Flower and Sparks were at least temporarily stifled.

By Monday afternoon the antistrike leaders had lost the initiative. Both

[108] *ABJ*, March 16, 1936.
[109] *ATP*, March 17, 1936.
[110] Chappell to Kerwin, March 21, 1936, FMCS Papers, RG 280, File 182/1010.
[111] *ABJ*, March 16, 1936.

Akron newspapers attacked Sparks and the league in outspoken editorials. "A pitched battle will give a black name to the community, without a single benefit accruing," wrote Knight, a close friend and political ally of Sparks.[112] Sparks was taken aback; league operations virtually came to a halt. Later that afternoon Davey refused to intercede, and Secretary Perkins sent telegrams to House and Litchfield calling for renewed negotiations.[113] By Monday evening the antistrike movement was in disarray.

Union leaders mounted the last of their innovative public relations offensives that night. At eleven o'clock, when a local radio station ended its broadcast day, Grillo and Coleman began an impromptu all-night program, ostensibly to warn the strikers if the Sparks group attacked the picket line. For nine and a half hours they read prounion statements, newspaper editorials, and parodies of popular songs and poems. At times they played records. For several hours a band from a local theater provided live music. One listener requested "I'll Be Glad When You're Dead, You Rascal You," dedicated to Sparks.[114] Through the night, radios blared in union halls, in workers' homes, and in cars parked along East Market Street. Like other union publicity coups, the broadcast symbolized the strikers' determination and imagination.

By Tuesday Litchfield apparently had concluded that the Law and Order League was a failure. When Perkins called, he was conciliatory. On Tuesday evening, Buckingham and union attorney E. E. Zesiger arranged new talks for the following day. On Wednesday Thomas and Climer agreed to a thirty- to forty-hour workweek in nontire departments and employee referendums before the workweek was increased in both tire and nontire departments. They also made more explicit verbal assurances, which became an addendum to the agreement, signed by Buckingham. They refused to consider any change in the status of the Industrial Assembly. Union negotiators in return abandoned their demands for piece-rate adjustments, an end to the assembly, and a signed contract. The Ricketts resolution had no effect on their actions. By Friday they concluded that they could gain no more and called another armory meeting for Saturday, March 21.[115]

The second ratification meeting was anticlimactic. The strikers' mood was buoyant, and no opposition emerged, save for a last-minute effort by a small Trotskyist group. After minimal discussion Local 2 members voted almost unanimously to accept the agreement and return to work. The unsigned statement was similar to the General Tire agreement of 1934, except for its omission of any curbs on the Industrial Assembly. "At first glance,"

[112] Ibid.

[113] Frances Perkins to Litchfield, March 16, 1936, FMCS Papers, RG 280, File 182/1010.

[114] *ABJ*, March 17, 1936.

[115] Chappell to Kerwin, March 21, 1936, FMCS Papers, RG 280, File 182/1010.

Chappell wrote, "it appeared that the union gained relatively little." However, on reconsideration, "it will be seen that not only were the main objectives of the strike obtained but that the workers secured additional benefits as well."[116]

The "benefits" took several forms. The strike stalled Litchfield's immediate plans and raised doubts about his vision of the ideal factory. During the following months Goodyear executives would suffer a crisis of confidence at least as severe as the trauma that they had experienced during the worst days of the Depression. The conflict had even more devastating effects on the Industrial Assembly. By late March it had become what its opponents charged—a band of company loyalists dedicated to defending its special privileges. It never recovered and ceased to be an influence in the Goodyear plants long before its official demise in April 1937. The strike had the opposite effect on the URW, which now had a history of successful combat and a new claim to legitimacy. Many participants, and undoubtedly many observers, became as firmly committed to the URW as the assembly partisans had been to their organization.

The strike also helped preserve the union's original character. Germer frequently inveighed against the "chaotic" operations of the URW, and continually urged Burns, whom he regarded as the only sophisticated URW leader, to "have a showdown with John House as to proper authority in this strike."[117] But Burns did nothing. He knew that Dalrymple would not favor such a move; and he, too, had absorbed some of the values of the midwestern workers. Despite the many crises of February and March 1936, the URW continued to be decentralized and "chaotic."

The strike had other important effects. First, it confused the economic growth issue. Were the policies of Goodyear executives conducive to local prosperity? In the 1920s most Akron residents would have answered in the affirmative; in the early 1930s a somewhat smaller majority would have agreed. The price wars of 1933–1936 reduced the margin still further, and by the second week of the strike, a majority probably would have answered "no." Mayor Schroy reflected this shift. A friend of business, he nevertheless realized that the plant could not be opened peacefully and that violence would be detrimental to the city's reputation and future prosperity. The economic growth issue now favored the union. This shift explained the irony of a businessman, heading a self-proclaimed "business" administration, acting to save the "first CIO strike." Second, the conflict over the Litchfield plan had rallied workers to the six-hour day and created a union goal that would influence the industry for decades. Finally, the hours dis-

---

[116] Ibid.; Pesotta, *Bread Upon the Waters*, p. 224.
[117] Germer Diary, March 18, 1936.

pute and the strike provided a major stimulus to worker militancy. At various times, small groups of recalcitrant workers had wielded substantial power. The sit-downs, the strikers' reaction to the McGrady plan, the rank-and-file response to Schroy's effort to remove the shacks, and the ratification vote of March 14—all seemed to show that militancy was effective. Few strikers were oblivious to that fact when they reported for work on March 24.

CHAPTER EIGHT

Labor on the March, 1936–1937

TALL, HEAVYSET, and loud, he impressed most of his contemporaries as a bully rather than a union zealot. In other ways C. D. "Chuck" Lesley (1909–1942) seemed even less suited for his role in the mid-1930s. Born in southern Ohio, he had come to Akron in the mid-1920s, gotten a job in the Goodyear tire room, and joined the notoriously anti-union Ohio National Guard. During the strike scare of 1935, he instructed supervisors, Flying Squadron members, and other employees in the use of tear gas and antiriot techniques.[1] A few months later he changed sides and began a new and more visible career as a union militant. For the next six months no one in American industry would do more to demonstrate the latent power of the semiskilled worker. Lesley's motives were and are uncertain; the effects of his actions are clearer. He personally became more influential; union members became more confident and assertive; and Dalrymple, House, and other leaders began to worry that their new approach to the manufacturers, based on the workers' power, would prove no more successful than the Green strategy. As late as March 23, 1936, the URW commanded broad public support. By the end of 1937 it was isolated and increasingly cast as an obstacle to progress. Lesley and his fellow militants had helped define the limits of union power.

THE SIT-DOWN ERA

In July 1936, at the height of the sit-down movement, E. S. Cowdrick, secretary of the elite Special Conference Committee, visited Akron to observe the new phenomenon. He blamed the sit-downs on the Roosevelt administration; the CIO; the workers, who were "more than unusually independent"; and local public opinion, which was "not very friendly toward the manufacturers."[2] Surprisingly, he did not mention the most obvious stimulus, the Goodyear strike. Having discovered that they could shape their destiny, the workers became more confident; URW membership boomed, union leaders bargained more aggressively, and the locals began

---

[1] U.S. Senate, "Violations of Free Speech and Rights of Labor," *Hearings Before a Subcommittee of the Committee on Education and Labor*, 75th Cong., 1st sess. (Washington, 1937), pp. 2993–97.

[2] Ibid., pp. 17070–71.

to reassert themselves in civic affairs. The strike created other possibilities on the shop floor. Just as the NIRA had given union leaders temporary immunity from discharge, the Goodyear turmoil gave union militants temporary immunity from shop discipline. In this atmosphere, men like Lesley enjoyed unprecedented influence.

For six weeks after the resumption of production on March 24 there were hints of the conflicts that would follow. The company reported five sitdowns, four beatings of nonunion workers, five murder threats, seven other acts of intimidation, and one bombing. The most serious incidents involved fourth-shift tire builders and revolved around two issues that the militants appropriated: the presence of nonunion workers and the enforcement of the informal production limits that had long been the workers' defense against rate cuts. On April 7, for example, Lesley pulled the electrical switches in the tire department and demanded that the foreman remove a nonunion worker. When the foreman agreed, Lesley and several dozen union men surrounded other nonunion workers and threatened to kill them if they did not hold down production. One of the men subsequently went to the police and swore out a warrant for the arrest of two union members. Later the same day, fifteen to twenty cars appeared at his home "with occupants booing, jeering, etc." A week afterward, twenty-five union men gathered around his machine and taunted him; they refused to leave until Lesley gave them a signal. When they used similar tactics to intimidate other nonunion workers, "the management agreed to have employees stay within [the] limit . . . to avoid trouble." The tire room was comparatively peaceful until April 25, when the fourth-shift committeeman ordered a sit-down to protest the removal of a conveyor repairman. The sit-down spread through Plant 2 as other union committeemen ordered union members to stop work. Some militants blockaded the doors to prevent nonunion workers from leaving. The sit-down continued until 5:30 A.M., when supervisors agreed to study the conveyor problem.[3]

The Goodyear incidents aggravated an already tense environment. Although the Industrial Assembly was now moribund, the nonstrikers continued to meet and to proclaim the likelihood of new battles. Litchfield roiled the waters further by publicly repudiating the oral agreement that supplemented the strike settlement and announcing a large increase in tire production in Gadsden. Goodrich, Firestone, and General Tire contributed to public anxiety by announcing that they had acquired new plants in Oaks, Pennsylvania; Memphis, Tennessee; and Wabash, Indiana, respectively.[4]

[3] Goodyear Tire & Rubber Co., "Resume of Sit-downs, Intimidations, and Violence at the Akron Plants," Box 59, pp. 2–3, Archive Organization File, Labor-Management Documentation Center, Cornell University.

[4] See *ABJ*, March 25, 26, April 3, 5, 7, 8, 1936; *WCL*, March 26, 1936.

The last hopes for peace disappeared on the evening of May 6, when third-shift tire builders at Goodyear and Firestone sat down to protest excessive production by nonunion workers. The Firestone tire builders charged that the nonunion men were "pace-setters" who would "spoil the job" and demanded limits on production and earnings. When they still refused to work or leave the following afternoon, Firestone labor manager W. R. Murphy closed the department for the rest of the week. At Goodyear the sit-down in the Plant 2 tire room quickly spread to the Plant 2 heel department, the Plant 1 pit, and other departments. Outside, three hundred workers gathered at the Plant 2 gate. When several union members tried to prevent nonunion men from distributing an anti-union pamphlet, the nonunion men drew revolvers; one, shouting "I'll fill every one of you full of lead," fired into the pavement, injuring several bystanders before police could disarm him. When rumors of the shooting spread through the plant, fourth-shift tire builders led by Lesley, Jimmy Jones, and other activists, sat down. When they refused to resume their work, Slusser closed the department for the rest of the week.[5]

URW officials moved quickly to end the sit-downs. Local 7 officials obtained Murphy's promise to make a "close checkup" when workers exceeded 110 percent of the base rate and insisted that the men go back to work. "Unsanctioned stoppages of work must end," they declared. Dalrymple added that "violators may be dismissed from membership."[6] However, it was too late to avoid widespread criticism of the workers and the union. The Akron newspapers printed identical editorials entitled "Killing the Golden Goose."

On the night of May 19–20, another round of sit-downs at Goodrich and Goodyear raised new questions about union authority and discipline. At Goodrich, workers in three mechanical goods departments sat down in response to the layoff of several veteran employees. Local 5 president L. L. Callahan threatened a larger strike if the men were not rehired. After a brief conference, T. G. Graham rehired the men.[7] At Goodyear, committeemen in the Plant 2 pit protested the appointment of a nonunion man to head a crew. Their complaints triggered a sit-down that spread throughout the plant and precipitated one of the most famous incidents of the sit-down era. Tire room workers soon voted to join the protest and Jimmy Jones took over the supervisor's desk. Brandishing clubs and knifelike tools called "tomahawks," Jones and other strikers ordered foremen and nonunion workers into a crude "bull-pen," fashioned from stock tables and racks.

[5] *ABJ*, May 7, 1936.

[6] *ATP*, May 9, 1936.

[7] *ATP*, May 20, 1936; *ABJ*, May 20, 1936.

"You'd better go down or we'll take you down," Jones told one supervisor. Guards with tomahawks and clubs watched them throughout the night and strikers hung a sign, "red apple orchard," on one of the racks. Jones issued passes when they wanted to go to the bathroom or cafeteria. A pit worker who had been beaten was forced to stand for ten minutes before he was permitted to go to the hospital. The strikers kept the supervisors in the bullpen until noon, when Lesley informed them that the management had agreed to cancel the appointment of the pit worker. When some of the strikers objected that "there are men we don't want to work with," Lesley assured them that "we'll take care of that in time."[8]

The end of the sit-down was not the end of the controversy over the bullpen. Goodyear attorneys interrogated the hostages and took their reports to the county prosecutor, who charged thirty-one union men, including Jones, Lesley, and Boyer, with riot.[9] The prosecutor tried Jones first, portraying him as the instigator of a reign of terror. Jones and Stanley Denlinger, the URW attorney, vehemently rejected the charges. They received unexpected help from several bullpen victims, who told of banter and card games as well as threats, curses and tomahawks. The jury deadlocked and Jones and the other men, in effect, went free.

What, then, was the meaning of the bullpen incident? Was it "guerrilla war," as the *Akron Beacon Journal* charged, or something more conspiratorial? Jones's trial provided only limited and partial answers. The jury found the guerrilla war analogy unconvincing, and Goodyear attorneys, despite an intensive investigation, were never able to find any evidence of a larger plan. At his trial Jones variously described the bullpen as a way to protect supervisors from marauding workers and as a lark. The school bullies, he seemed to suggest, had briefly taken over the playground.[10] In fact, his analysis probably came closest to the truth. The sit-downs were a logical extension of the workers' longstanding efforts to regulate the pace of work; the takeover of the department added nothing, apart from a night in jail.

---

[8] *ABJ*, May 25, 1936, June 25, 1936.

[9] The thirty-one militants were comparatively short-term workers, at the opposite end of the social spectrum from the assembly loyalists and nonstrikers. The following figures, taken from city directories, trace their residential and employment history in the 1930's. No more than six of them were homeowners in 1936.

	Listed	Employed at Goodyear
1930	16	13
1934–35	21	20
1938–39	18	7

[10] *ABJ*, June 30, 1936. For the goals of other CIO militants see David Brody, "Radical Labor History and Rank and File Militancy," *Labor History* 16 (1975): 123.

Jones's act was notable only because it suggested a willingness to exercise the workers' veto frequently and flagrantly.

In the uproar over the bullpen no one bothered to ask the more important question of why, in a plant known for aggressive, even overbearing, management, there was so little effort to restore order. No supervisor ventured into the department after the beginning of the sit-down. No Goodyear policeman interfered when guards escorted men to the cafeteria. The executives fumed in private but made no effort to discipline Jones, Lesley, and the others. Instead they turned to the county prosecutor. Litchfield attempted to explain: "The strike showed the futility of attempting to act . . . while the forces of disorder are in the ascendancy. Goodyear lost five weeks of production. . . . The policy of the management, therefore, has been to avoid any further serious interruptions during this period."[11] He implied that the company would not interfere as long as some tires were produced and the union remained in turmoil. In private, Goodyear executives indicated that they did not expect to regain the initiative until a business decline necessitated layoffs, the union blundered into a second strike, or the 1936 elections signaled a change in the political climate.[12] In the meantime they would let the union destroy itself.

On Thursday morning, May 22, at the end of the first night shift after the bullpen incident, another incident underlined the union's vulnerability. As a group of Local 2 members left the Plant 2 tire room they accidentally confronted Lyle Carruthers. Someone shouted, "Let's get him," and approximately twenty-five men chased Carruthers through the tire room, hitting him with fists and tomahawks. When Russell Moats, another nonstriker, tried to help Carruthers, he was attacked too. Both victims required hospitalization. Goodyear added to the controversy by again instigating legal action against the attackers. The prosecutor charged three of the tire builders, all veterans of the bullpen episode, with assault with intent to kill. John House called the charges "trumped up," and they were later dropped.[13]

The events of May 19–22 illustrated the dilemma of URW leaders in 1936. If they acted against Lesley, Jones, and the others, they risked alienating the militants. If they did not act they risked losing the public good will they had gained from the strike. Dalrymple inadvertently summarized his problem to CIO secretary John Brophy several months later. After a

[11] *ABJ*, June 3, 1936.

[12] E. S. Cowdrick, Memorandum, July 21, 1936, in U.S. Senate, "Violations of Free Speech and Rights of Labor," p. 17073. Labor unrest was "in large measure" responsible for "the failure of productivity to advance in 1936" (John Dean Gaffey, *The Productivity of Labor in the Rubber Tire Manufacturing Industry* [New York, 1940], p. 116).

[13] *ABJ*, May 25, 1936.

recent "unjust sit-down," which ended when "the members admitted their wrong" and resumed work, the local added "hundreds of new members . . . within the next few days."[14] Although sit-downs might hurt the union's and the community's long-term prospects, they were unmistakable evidence of the workers' collective power. The employees responded by swelling the union's ranks. No union official could be oblivious to the connection. Trying to maintain a delicate balance, union leaders attempted to stop the sit-downs without antagonizing the participants or the many workers who took vicarious pleasure in the behavior of Lesley, Jones, and others. Their approach was at best a mixed success. Between March 22 and the Carruthers beating, there were twenty-three Akron sit-downs. Between late May and December, when the General Motors strike made the sit-down movement a national phenomenon, there were at least twenty-nine more.

Labor-management tension, particularly at Goodyear, was the single most important stimulus to the sit-down movement. In early June, when Dalrymple was nearly killed by a Gadsden mob, the workers, "highly agitated," responded with a twenty-four-hour sit-down at Goodyear and a shorter sit-down at Goodrich.[15] Controversies over piece rates, production standards, and related issues precipitated eleven other sit-downs, seven at Goodyear. Most of them lasted only a few hours, usually until a supervisor agreed to consider the workers' complaints, but they were a measure of the poststrike atmosphere in the Akron plants. Workers no longer felt compelled to exercise their veto furtively or take complaints to first-line supervisors or union committeemen. The results may not have been different, but the process ensured that shop floor issues received as much consideration as other problems.

The second major stimulus was the Goodyear anti-union group. By March 24, the nonstrikers were an identifiable minority, subjected to harassment and reprisals. They could either defer to the majority or create a successor organization to the Industrial Assembly. On June 10 several hundred of them met at a Goodyear Heights park to inaugurate the Stahl-Mate Club. The name was supposedly taken from a chess term meaning "to pause for reflection," but the use of the German "stahl" (steel), rather than the English "stall," gave it an ominous connotation. Stahl-Mate Club leaders explicitly disavowed any tie to the Law and Order League or to the Black Legion, a contemporary fascistic organization with roots in the Ohio Ku Klux Klan, but there was little doubt about their militancy. Garnet Pat-

---

[14] Sherman H. Dalrymple to John Brophy, Oct. 7, 1936, Congress of Industrial Organizations Papers, URW file, Catholic University, Washington.

[15] "Report of General Secretary Treasurer Frank Grillo," in *Report of Executive Officers and Research Director to the First Convention, United Rubber Workers of America, Sept. 14, 1936* (Akron, 1936), p. 10.

terson, now an NLRB official, described the club as "militaristic."[16] Its most important antecedent was probably the Akron Ku Klux Klan of the 1920s. Club members emphasized respectability, law and order, and the intimidation of public officials. They were generally older and more likely to be familiar with Klan methods than the majority of rubber workers. Whether they plotted violence or simply shielded a small terrorist wing is uncertain. In either case their goal was to prevent URW and Local 2 leaders from consolidating their gains.

Two incidents in early June illustrated their approach. On June 2, a car with several unknown men followed Lesley and two union colleagues as they left his house for work. After a chase through south Akron, the pursuers fired a small tear-gas shell into the unionists' vehicle, temporarily blinding the driver. At the same time several armed men abducted William Boyle, a sit-down leader in the pit, and drove him to an Akron suburb, robbed him, and threw him out of the car. When he did not appear at the plant, Lesley and the tire builders voted to sit down until he reappeared. A week and a half later, as fourth-shift Goodyear employees arrived for work, three large crosses near the Plant 2 gate burst into flames and firecrackers exploded. Angered by this display, pit workers refused to work until the company removed all nonunion employees from the curing department. Lesley simultaneously led tire builders in a short "sympathy" sit-down. When the shift ended, he and other tire builders confronted L. M. Groves, a veteran first-shift worker and Stahl-Mate member. Only a supervisor's hasty intervention saved Groves from the fate of Carruthers and Moats.[17]

The friction between pro- and anti-union Goodyear employees culminated on July 13 when fourth-shift workers in the Plant 2 mill, calender, and tire rooms sat down for five hours to protest the presence of nonunion men whom they accused of "agitating trouble." Day-shift workers staged several brief sit-downs on the thirteenth and fourth-shift mill room workers sat down again on July 14. The protest spread to the pit and tire rooms "and within a few minutes the entire plant was down." Lesley and about fifty colleagues went from department to department ordering nonunion employees to leave. Altogether they expelled seventy-five Plant 2 workers, in many cases with "kicks" and "rough treatment."[18] When the mayor learned of the incident, he ordered the police to prevent further expulsions and guard nonunion workers. Schroy pledged "to keep the factories run-

---

[16] *ABJ*, June 12, 1936; Morris Janowitz, "Black Legions on the March," in Daniel Aaron, ed., *America in Crisis* (New York, 1952), pp. 305–308; Press Release, July 11, 1936, National Labor Relations Board Papers, RG 25, Case 8-C-33, National Archives.

[17] *ABJ*, June 2, 1936; *ATP*, June 2, 1936.

[18] Paul W. Chappell to H. L. Kerwin, July 15, 1936, Federal Mediation and Conciliation Service Papers, RG 280, File 182/1010, National Archives.

12. Harry Eagle, Skip O'Harrah, John House and Everett White prepare to lead a union parade at the height of the sit-down era, 1936. American History Research Center.

ning at all costs. The city," he added, "is absolutely through with sit-downs."[19]

Sensing the seriousness of the situation, Local 2 leaders pledged to stop the sit-downs. Everett White told reporters that they were "going to cut out this wildcatting and these little sit-downs."[20] At a membership meeting on July 19 more than three thousand Goodyear union members adopted a resolution promising "summary" action for those who violated the union constitution. "Those who feel they cannot abide by the resolution should get out before they get kicked out," one official declared.[21]

This statement reflected a growing conviction that the sit-downs were in part the work of provocateurs. House claimed to have "direct evidence" that Goodyear was promoting sit-downs to wean the city administration from its neutral course. He did not reveal his "evidence," but union offi-

[19] *ABJ*, July 14, 1936.
[20] *ATP*, July 15, 1936; *ABJ*, July 14, 15, 1936.
[21] *ATP*, July 20, 1936.

cials suspected several fourth-shift workers of being company agents or aspiring union office seekers. Their suspicions centered on Lesley and Boyle.[22] Ironically, Goodyear executives also subscribed to the conspiracy theory. They believed that the "radical group," led by Lesley, Jones, and Boyle, was "being instructed and possibly financed by some outside group" eager "to cash in on any interruptions of production." At first they blamed "a bunch of labor racketeers" from Cleveland but later acquired information that implicated "a well-known detective organization" that intended "to step in at the opportune time and for a large fee break up this group."[23] Given the many cases of betrayal, it is possible that these suspicions had substance. It is equally possible that one or more of the tire builders took money for doing what he would have done anyway.

The July 19 statement also reflected union fears that an unchecked sitdown movement would compromise or even destroy the URW. The decentralization reports, the increasingly hostile tone of the city's newspapers, and the formation, on July 17, of the Greater Akron Association, an organization of merchants and professionals to solicit new industry and make decentralization "unnecessary," were all unmistakable warning signs. With growing anxiety, URW leaders concluded that they needed assistance. On July 2, the URW formally cast its lot with the CIO. In return John L. Lewis agreed to assign a special adviser to the union and to employ several URW organizers. Dalrymple's statements leave little doubt that this quid pro quo was the decisive factor in the timing of the URW decision.[24]

Lewis supplied Allan S. Haywood, the shrewdest of the many outsiders who sought to influence the rubber workers. An English immigrant miner and veteran of the United Mine Workers bureaucracy, Haywood was outwardly reasonable and accommodating. Yet he minced no words. His "present task," he told reporters on his arrival, was "to iron out chaos." Union members "must have a united policy . . . and they must move with the union."[25] For nearly ten months he worked closely with House and Local 2. He also used his patronage power effectively. He hired William Carney of Goodyear and Charles Lanning of Ohio Rubber for CIO posts in Detroit and northern Indiana, respectively. By September he had persuaded

---

[22] See G. L. Patterson to Charles Fahy, July 20, 1936, NLRB Papers, RG 25, Case 8-C-33; *ABJ*, May 22, 1936; *ATP*, May 22, 1936; telephone call, House to FMCS, n.d., FMCS Papers, RG 280, File 182/1010.

[23] L. A. Hurley to E. S. Cowdrick, July 20, 1936, in U.S. Senate, "Violations of Free Speech and Labor Rights," p. 3212.

[24] CIO Minutes, July 2, 1936, Katherine Ellickson Papers, Box 1, Franklin D. Roosevelt Library, Hyde Park, N.Y.; *ATP*, July 3, 1936; Melvyn Dubofsky and Warren Van Tine, *John L. Lewis: A Biography* (New York, 1977), pp. 239–41. See Dalrymple's statements in *ABJ*, July 9, Aug. 8, 1936.

[25] *ATP*, July 22, 1936. Also Ray T. Sutliff, interview with author, April 18, 1979.

Dalrymple to create a similar job for Lesley. None of these men had figured in the union's plans, and Lesley's only prior organizing experience, in Gadsden, had raised new suspicions about his loyalty. It is possible Haywood detected qualities in them that URW leaders had overlooked, but his immediate goal, at least in the cases of Carney and Lesley, was to remove them from the "chaos" that he intended to "iron out."

By that time the possibilities of the sit-down were apparent to a wide spectrum of industrial employees. Sit-downs at the Columbia Chemical Company in Barberton on February 18, after the start of the Goodyear strike, and at the Colonial Salt Company in south Akron on May 10, demonstrated this appeal. A sit-down of Goodrich mechanical goods employees on May 20 was the first rubber industry sit-down that did not involve tire workers, and a sit-down of two hundred Firestone mechanical goods employees on August 18 was the first to involve large numbers of women workers. Between August and December Goodyear Plant 2 remained the center of the sit-down movement, but employees in final inspection, tire balancing, and mechanical goods joined the tire builders and pit workers. There were two sit-downs in the Plant 1 tire room, one in the Plant 1 pit, and one in the Goodyear reclaiming plant. At Goodrich, there were sit-downs in the mill room and in a mechanical goods department. A sit-down of two hundred Goodrich braided hose workers on September 21 precipitated the most serious dispute of the fall. The protest spread to the tire department, the pit, and other mechanical goods departments. When the strikers ignored the appeals of local union officials, Graham closed the entire plant and Dalrymple backed him; this tactic became the standard Goodrich response to sit-downs.[26] At Firestone the only sit-downs after August 18 involved tire builders and pit workers. The single General Tire sit-down of this period started in the tire room.

The sit-downs soon blended into a larger mosaic of conflict that made Akron second only to New York City in number of strikers during 1936.[27] The rubber industry turmoil, reported in detail in local newspapers, created an aura of unrest that spread irresistibly. Pressured by union leaders, workers in other industries generally favored conventional strikes. Their employers also responded with conventional antistrike techniques. The result was a series of clashes, including a nightlong gun battle between strikers and strikebreakers at the Black & Decker Co. plant in nearby Kent, in June, and a confrontation at the L. E. Shunk Latex Products Company in August. URW members at the Shunk Co., mostly women, struck on August 20 after the company laid off thirty-eight veteran workers because of a new con-

[26] ABJ, Sept. 23, 1936.
[27] "Review of Strikes in 1936," Monthly Labor Review 44 (1937): 1227.

veyor. When Shunk executives announced that they would hire new employees, the striking women, "armed with small clubs," took "a militant stand at the gates." The company soon agreed to reduce hours rather than carry out the layoffs.[28]

By far the most important of the conflicts was an August 5 strike by municipal employees against the layoff of a group of workers. When the strikers and hundreds of Local 2 members formed a picket line at the Johnston Street municipal yards on August 6 to prevent trucks from leaving, the mayor ordered police officers to intervene. The pickets responded with a shower of bricks that forced the police to turn back. Furious, Schroy at first ordered the police and fire department to use force but relented when the officers in charge warned that his order would mean bloodshed. Calmer heads ultimately prevailed and the strikers voted to return to work the next day. But neither the mayor nor the unions ever forgot the Johnston Street "riot."

Advances in Collective Bargaining

Though labor unrest continued to paralyze the Akron plants in 1937, the mood of the city gradually improved. The spread of the sit-down movement to other communities and the excesses of the more notable auto and textile industry sit-downs put the Akron experiences in a new perspective and made even Lesley and the fourth-shift militants appear reasonable.[29] Several peaceful sit-downs in early 1937 inspired confidence that the worst had passed. The first, at Goodrich on January 29, became known as the "friendliest" sit-down in the city's history when the negotiations forced T. G. Graham to miss his birthday party and the strikers sang "Happy Birthday" to him.[30] The other five sit-downs of January and February were equally benign. Managers, workers, and local residents became more relaxed. Strikes no longer "particularly perturbed them."[31]

By far the most hopeful signs came from Goodyear. The conflict between Local 2 and the Stahl-Mate Club reached a climax on February 2, when third-shift Plant 2 tire builders sat down to protest the presence of a nonunion man and refused to talk with the plant superintendent. "You may

[28] *ATP*, Aug. 21, 1936; *ABJ*, Aug. 24, 1936.

[29] For the larger sit-down movement see Sidney Fine, *Sit-Down: The General Motors Strike of 1936–37* (Ann Arbor, 1969); Sidney Fine, *Frank Murphy: The New Deal Years* (Chicago, 1979), pp. 326–52; Carlos A. Schwantes, " 'We've Got'em on the Run, Brothers': The 1937 Non-Automotive Sit-Down Strikes in Detroit," *Michigan History* 56 (1972): 179–99.

[30] *ABJ*, Jan. 29, 30, 1937.

[31] *Cleveland Plain Dealer*, April 25, 1937.

manage this plant, but you don't control it," they shouted defiantly.[32] Slusser immediately closed the plant and union members prepared to strike. After three days of talks, House, Dalrymple, and Haywood persuaded Slusser to reinstate the strikers and repudiate the Stahl-Mate Club. Seeing an opening, they also asked him to negotiate "on the issue of the union being the sole collective bargaining agency" and on a way of "adjudicating disputes."[33] Slusser agreed to find a way to resolve conflicts. On February 7 more than five thousand Local 2 members ratified the understanding.

Local 2 leaders dropped their request for exclusive representation because the agreement offered unprecedented concessions. Slusser's promise not to aid the Stahl-Mate Club broke the last tenuous tie between Goodyear and company unionism and left Local 2 in a commanding position. His promise to work with the union to stop sit-downs and other disputes was also important. It led to the formation, in late February, of an informal "supreme court" (as the workers called it) that supplemented the work of the union committeemen. The "court" had "quite a few trials."[34] It considered the cases of Stahl-Mate Club members who were attacked during the February sit-down and later judged the appeals of men penalized for inciting sit-downs. Yet it was not as successful as union leaders originally hoped because of "a lack of cooperation on the part of the witnesses," especially union men.[35] Its most important function was to remind Goodyear workers of the union's enhanced stature.

The new climate of restraint was also evident at Firestone, where Local 7, facing only nominal opposition from the Employees' Conference, regained much of its earlier strength. In late 1935 president Walter Kriebel retired in favor of his vice-president, Leland S. Buckmaster, a tall, gangling Ohioan who strongly opposed the ad hoc activism associated with Lesley and the militants. Due largely to his influence, Firestone experienced only two sit-downs in the summer and fall of 1936. As the Akron climate changed, he became more insistent. On January 19, for example, when two crane operators in the steel products plant refused to work and other workers began "a sympathetic sit-down," he refused to take their complaints to the management until they followed "the sensible course" and returned to work. Local observers hailed this "crackdown" on the workers.[36]

However, even Buckmaster's firm hand could not prevent a major con-

---

[32] *ATP*, Feb. 3, 1937.

[33] Local 2 Committee to Clifton Slusser, Feb. 4, 1937, NLRB Papers, RG 25, Box 350, Folder 8, Case 8-C-378.

[34] C. L. Skinner, interview with author, April 23, 1976.

[35] Minutes, June 15, 1937, NLRB Papers, RG 25, Box 350, Folder 8, Case 8-C-378.

[36] *ABJ*, Jan. 20, 22, 1937.

frontation in early 1937. On March 2, a dispute between union and nonunion employees on the third shift sparked a sit-down that continued through the night. When a number of first-shift employees also refused to work, the superintendent closed Plant 2 for the rest of the week. Union committeemen protested bitterly. That night, workers gathered on the street outside Plant 1, blocking the entrance and complaining about the "lockout" of Plant 2 workers. The next morning impromptu pickets, including some Goodyear workers, turned away the first shift at 6:00 A.M. When automobiles approached the gate, they shouted, "Nobody's going in today! Nobody's going in today!" At noon they turned away the second shift and closed the steel products plant. By the afternoon ten thousand Firestone employees were idle.[37]

Negotiations between Local 7 leaders and Labor Manager W. R. Murphy began on March 4. In response to union demands for the abolition of the Employees' Conference Plan, Murphy agreed to stop paying conference plan representatives, which he argued would have the same effect. Union representatives also insisted on a formal statement of exclusive representation. They had followed the General Motors strike and were aware of "outspoken sentiment . . . among a section of the rank and file" in favor of formal recognition.[38] They also had Haywood's assurances that exclusive representation would make Firestone "the spearhead of the [CIO] . . . drive to win exclusive bargaining rights from a major corporation."[39] When Murphy flatly refused to consider their demand, the meeting ended. The following afternoon Buckmaster won rank-and-file approval for a continuation of the work stoppage and three demands: abolition of the company union, recognition of Local 7 as exclusive bargaining agent, and immediate negotiations for a signed contract. Henceforth the dispute would revolve around the issue of exclusivity.[40]

On Sunday, March 7, when negotiations resumed, Murphy insisted that the local represent union members only, as the UAW did under the GM contract. In return, he offered to abolish the conference plan outright. His proposal reflected the knowledge that Chrysler Corporation executives in Detroit had refused to concede more than GM, even at the cost of a strike, which began on March 8.[41] Even though the Local 7 negotiators rewrote their demands to make them more palatable, Murphy refused to consider

---

[37] Memo for Strike File, March 17, 1937, Firestone Archives, Firestone Tire & Rubber Co., Akron, Ohio; *ABJ*, March 3, 4, 5, 1936.

[38] *ABJ*, March 8, 1937.

[39] Ibid.

[40] Ibid.

[41] Memo, March 17, 1937, Firestone Archives. Also see Alfred Lief, *Harvey Firestone: Free Man of Enterprise* (New York, 1951), p. 293.

exclusive representation in any form. By Tuesday the talks were dead-locked.

Having committed themselves to exclusive representation, union leaders now faced the necessity of preparing for a major strike. On Monday Buck-master asked state officials to stop liquor sales near the plant and appointed picket captains. On Wednesday, the strikers built "canvas, wood or metal shacks" at most of the gates in anticipation of "a long siege," and the union took over two restaurants near the plant to provide meals.[42] On Thursday the strikers voted overwhelmingly to make the strike official.

Anticipating these actions, Firestone executives also prepared carefully. Between Sunday and Tuesday they set up offices in downtown buildings for the executives and sales staff. On Tuesday night, two hundred to two hundred fifty other managers remained in the plant in a reverse sit-down. Their goal was to avoid picket-line confrontations reminiscent of the early days of the Goodyear strike. One prominent executive observed that "for an employer to succeed in a labor controversy such as this, he must not only (1) stand upon an issue which is fair and reasonable, but (2) handle himself as to *procedure* according to the standards which the public will regard as also fair and reasonable." Correct procedure included a willing-ness to meet union representatives whenever they requested a conference. Accordingly, when Buckmaster called on March 12, Murphy agreed to meet, but at the downtown offices. Firestone executives "did not want to give the union a chance to take pictures of their committee or Messrs. Mur-phy [and the other management representatives] . . . going through a mass of pickets at the main gate . . . [or] to risk any excitement that might be provoked." They resolved "to avoid anything spectacular or exciting."[43]

Once the session began Murphy took the initiative. He announced that "all previous proposals . . . are withdrawn" and "we start from scratch." "You created this exclusive representation issue. . . . *The situation is your responsibility.*" He would not accept exclusive representation "for any pe-riod (no matter how short)" and refused to consider union requests that his superiors, Firestone or President John W. Thomas, closeted at Firestone's Florida home, participate in the discussions.[44] When Buckmaster and Hay-wood indicated that they might accept a compromise like the GM agree-ment, which gave the union six months to recruit members without man-agement interference, Murphy emphatically refused. The meeting ended without an agreement to meet again.

For the next three weeks the strike was uneventful. Company executives

[42] *ABJ*, March 11, 1937.

[43] Mr. X to Mr. Y, March 16, 1937, Firestone Archives (names withheld at request of Firestone Archives).

[44] "Essentials to Keep in Mind," ca. March 1937, Firestone Archives.

refused to talk to reporters or make additional concessions. Buckmaster and the local leaders were hardly more demonstrative. They hoped the Chrysler negotiations in Detroit would resolve the representation issue and were hesitant to accept any agreement that might in retrospect look less favorable. Both considerations dictated patience and delay, as did the prospect of a Supreme Court decision on the Wagner Act. Increasingly, the Firestone strike became captive to outside events.

The first break in the dispute came on April 6, when the Chrysler agreement was announced. The automaker agreed to bargain with the union for union members and to suspend all support for other groups; in return, the UAW agreed to prohibit sit-downs. Firestone executives immediately sent a copy of the contract to Firestone and Thomas in Florida with a notation that the Firestone strike "could be settled on Chrysler basis." They also enclosed a message from a representative in Detroit indicating that Chrysler "gave as little as anyone could give away."[45] On April 9, Firestone and Thomas approved an agreement based on the Chrysler settlement.

In the meantime, the negotiations had resumed on April 6, and on April 8 one of the union men referred to the Chrysler pact. Murphy "was not at liberty to pick up the suggestion" until he had the approval of his superiors. Later that day URW negotiators met and decided to hold out for an unambiguous statement of exclusive representation. They insisted that a Firestone settlement would not "follow closely" the Chrysler agreement.[46] Whether they might have been tempted to settle immediately if Murphy had responded to the initial reference is unclear, but after April 8 they refused to back down for nearly three weeks. On April 9, after hearing from Firestone and Thomas, Murphy offered to accept the language of the Chrysler agreement. He was surprised when this move did not break the impasse.[47] Union negotiators did agree to form a subcommittee to work on wages, hours, and working conditions. By mid-April the negotiators had completed their work except for the representation clause.

The Supreme Court's Jones & Laughlin decision of April 12, upholding the Wagner Act, had little immediate effect on the deadlock. Firestone executives insisted they were in compliance with the statute, and union representatives continued to demand exclusive representation. Buckmaster nevertheless found the decision useful. By arguing that Firestone was violating the law, he was able to justify his uncompromising stand to restless strikers. P. W. Chappell speculated that without the Supreme Court decision "there might have been a [rank-and-file] reaction against their lead-

[45] Memo, April 10, 1937, Firestone Archives.

[46] SCLN, April 9, 1937; ABJ, April 8, 1937.

[47] Memo, April 16, 1937, Firestone Archives.

ers.'' He believed that Local 7 leaders planned to draft Goodrich and Good-year workers for picket duty if ''the Firestone strikers decided to rebel.''[48]

The immediate cause of the strikers' unhappiness was not the union, however, but the Firestone employees who remained in the plant. When negotiations collapsed again on Saturday, April 17, ''men with clubs in their hands'' went ''from one picket post to another'' urging their expulsion in ''heated language.'' Until early Sunday morning an attack seemed imminent.[49] Two days later, after a local liquor store sale, there were renewed threats. On April 21 pickets seized several Firestone guards who opened the gates for mail trucks. As the police mobilized for battle, Firestone officials announced that the employees inside would leave voluntarily. Buckmaster ordered the strikers ''not to touch them or follow them,'' and the strikers confined themselves to boos and catcalls. When Lou Hannah, the notorious employment office boss, emerged, one exuberant striker could not contain himself. ''You're fired, you bald headed son of a bitch,'' he shouted, to the delight of his comrades.[50] The following night another crowd gathered outside the Firestone gates to demand that the plant guards leave. As police reinforcements arrived, Buckmaster ordered the union's microphone and loudspeakers moved outside and urged union members to ''clear the streets.'' When his appeal failed he persuaded the police to rope off an area in front of the plant. Union leaders recruited a ''hillbilly'' orchestra and a caller ''and within a few minutes scores of couples were dancing on the streets, the threat of 'trouble' forgotten.''[51]

The incident nevertheless was an effective warning to Buckmaster and the officers. On April 27, they used a routine meeting with Murphy to reopen negotiations and on April 28 agreed to the first formal contract between a major tire manufacturer and a union in the history of the industry. On the all-important issue, they accepted a statement that Local 7 would represent union workers and others ''who desire their services.'' Like Chrysler, Firestone agreed to suspend support for the company union, and the local pledged not to intimidate nonunion employees or ''cause or tolerate'' sit-downs. The agreement retained the six-hour day and the thirty-six-hour week, overtime pay, existing piece rates, vacation and insurance policies, and a seniority system. The company agreed to lay off workers only after the average workweek had fallen to twenty-four hours for eight weeks.[52]

As news of the agreement spread, thousands of rubber workers and their

[48] Paul W. Chappell to Kerwin, April 14, 1937, FMCS Papers, RG 280, File 182/2448.

[49] *ABJ*, April 19, 1937.

[50] *URW* 2 (May 1937): 1; *ABJ*, April 23, 1937.

[51] *ABJ*, April 24, 1937.

[52] *ABJ*, April 29, 1937.

neighbors and friends gathered along South Main Street. A large crowd filled the union hall, drowning out an orchestra. Others remained outside, where police cars blocked part of the street and a loudspeaker provided music for square-dancing. At the plant gates, pickets and Firestone police shared cigarettes. In nearby bars "bottles clinked against whiskey glasses" as smiling proprietors became reacquainted with their customers. One man with a "rich Southern drawl" summarized the prevailing mood: "If it's as good as what Buck says it is, I'm certainly agoin' to vote for it."[53]

On Friday morning Firestone workers filled the armory and an overflow crowd of several hundred met at the Goodrich union hall. Thomas Owens of the strike committee read the contract. A lengthy discussion followed. Several strikers complained that the contract did not provide for exclusive representation. Haywood replied that it provided de facto exclusive representation. The vote, by show of hands, was 4,300 to 200, and at the Goodrich hall, 250 to 0.[54] The local seemed to have found a middle way between managerial authoritarianism and the sit-downs that cost little, enhanced the power of the local officers, and satisfied most workers. Buckmaster and Haywood were pleased.

Shortly afterward Callahan and House asked Goodrich and Goodyear executives to discuss similar agreements. By late May they had "almost completely worked out" agreements on wages and layoff procedures. Haywood, confident the "bitterness had disappeared," prepared to leave.[55] To resolve the most important remaining issue, recognition, the local leaders turned to the NLRB. Goodrich and Goodyear executives resigned themselves to this step and "agreed to abide by the decision of the labor board."[56] After an investigation and hearing, the NLRB ordered employee elections on August 24. The balloting proceeded smoothly despite the appearance of a new anti-union group, the Goodyear Employees Association. The results, which provided the first actual measure of union support, confirmed the impressions of most observers. At Goodyear 89 percent of the eligible voters gave Local 2 an 8,464 to 3,193 victory. At Goodrich 75 percent of eligible employees favored Local 5 by a margin of 8,212 to 834.[57] The issues of union strength and exclusive representation, the most serious barriers to a new and presumably stable relationship between the integrated companies and the maturing Akron locals, seemingly had disappeared.

[53] Ibid.

[54] *ABJ*, May 1, 1937.

[55] *ABJ*, May 22, 1937; *SCLN*, May 14, 1937.

[56] Ralph A. Lind to NLRB, June 3, 1937, NLRB Papers, RG 25, Case VIII-R-29, VIII-R-30; *ABJ*, May 29, 1937.

[57] *ABJ*, Aug. 25, 27, 1937.

LABOR UNION CULTURE, 1936–1937

The Goodyear strike, the sit-downs, the Firestone contract, and an intangible sense of "labor on the march" revived the aura of Akron as one of the capitals of organized labor. By late 1936, the URW had twenty-five thousand members in Summit County; by late 1937, it had approximately thirty-five thousand.[58] Its success revived other CIO and AFL unions and the "labor movement culture" that had languished in 1935 and created interest in the services that Popular Front activists now eagerly provided.[59] In 1933 rubber workers had listened to Jacob S. Coxey or "Red" Bessemer; in 1937 they heard Norman Thomas, Earl Browder, or A. J. Muste and watched the Brookwood Labor College Players, whose repertoire ranged from skits on the virtues of the Farmer-Labor party to an "anti-Fascist Mass Recitation." Devotees of proletarian drama could attend the Akron Labor Theatre, which performed an antiwar play, a musical comedy exposé of the Supreme Court, and "Virtue Rewarded, Or Company Union Gets the Gate."[60] Readers of the *Summit County Labor News*, the most influential local labor publication, became familiar with the fortunes of the Spanish Republicans.

There is much less evidence that the radicals had any impact. The most prominent political groups, the Socialists, Communists, and Trotskyists, could collectively claim less than a thousand local members, and most of them had been active since the 1920s.[61] How many other people were influenced by what they saw and heard is more difficult to determine, but the contrast between the level of activity and the small number of radical activists suggests that many workers thought of the speeches and "recitations" as cheap entertainment or as opportunities to reinforce biases against employers and symbols—"Wall Street"—that they associated with employers. The clichés of the radicals were not very different from the clichés of the labor movement. The December 1936 issue of the *United Rubber Worker* is suggestive. Next to a long article on a new union bowling league is a diatribe by L. L. Callahan, an uncompromising anti-Communist, entitled "Smash Fascism."[62]

Radicals survived in the URW hierarchy only as long as their trade union credentials remained unblemished. No one questioned the contributions of

[58] "Report of General Secretary Treasurer," 1936, p. 45.

[59] For the origins of the Popular Front, the loose association of Communists and other leftists, see Harvey Klehr, *The Heyday of American Communism: The Depression Decade* (New York, 1984), pp. 171–85.

[60] *SCLN*, April 16, 1937.

[61] Alfred Winslow Jones, *Life, Liberty, and Property: A Story of Conflict and a Measurement of Conflicting Rights* (Philadelphia, 1941), p. 302.

[62] *URW* 1 (Dec. 1936): 1.

Harry Eagle, H. R. "Whitey" Lloyd, or Salvatore Camelio, all of whom were or were suspected of being Communists. But Eagle, Lloyd, and Camelio were rubber workers and in other respects indistinguishable from anti-Communist leaders. This was not true of B. J. Widick, the Trotskyist whom the International hired in the spring of 1936 to edit the *United Rubber Worker*. A former student activist at the University of Akron and a one-time *Akron Beacon Journal* reporter who had lost his job because of his politics, Widick brought energy and idealism to his new position. He found the workload heavy and the atmosphere stifling. During the General Motors strike he spent much of his time in Flint and Anderson, Indiana, supposedly as a liaison between the UAW and URW. By the spring of 1937 he had exhausted the patience of the International officers, who fired him. Widick later blamed his discharge on the machinations of Eagle and Camelio, but the executive board committee that investigated him consisted wholly of conservatives. His successor, Robert L. Cruden, a Communist who had worked for the Locomotive Engineers, supposedly begged Widick not to expose him. By quietly and competently attending to his duties he escaped detection and discharge until the 1940s.[63]

In general, however, the rubber workers welcomed new ideas and innovative uses of their power. In July 1936 union activists led by Ray A. Sullivan of General Tire organized the Akron Consumers Cooperative. Their concern was the "burden. . . forced upon those who toil" by the "economic waste of our present system."[64] By mid-1937 the cooperative had seven hundred members and two east Akron gas stations, a dry cleaning shop, a coal yard, and a grocery.[65] Several locals organized educational programs that offered courses in public speaking, English, labor journalism, "political systems," and "labor problems."[66] During the summer of 1937 the URW employed an industrial engineering firm to train union men in time-study techniques. P. W. Chappell reported that the union experts "have not only received the cooperation of several of the managements . . . but have converted many union members to the benefits of the heretofore much hated system."[67] A CLU committee headed by Jimmy Jones planned a coordinated rent strike during the summer of 1937, using a UAW project in Pontiac, Michigan, as a model. Fears of legal reprisals led CLU leaders to have second thoughts and ultimately to veto the proposal.[68]

---

[63] B. J. Widick, interview with author, Oct. 23, 1976; General Executive Board, Minutes, April 28, 1937; *SCLN*, May 7, 1937; *ABJ*, May 14, 1937.

[64] *URW* 2 (Oct. 1936): 3.

[65] "The Akron Consumers Cooperative, Inc." (Akron, 1937); Ray A. Sullivan, interview with author, July 21, 1982.

[66] *Local 2 News*, March 12, 1937.

[67] Chappell to J. R. Steelman, Sept. 7, 1937, FMCS Papers, RG 280, File 182/1010.

[68] *ABJ*, July 13, 1937.

By far the most common activities were events that promoted fellowship among union members and their families. The 1937 URW convention authorized women's auxiliaries, and the Mohawk local took an additional step with a Junior Unionist League to "educate youth in the union movement."[69] All locals sponsored athletic teams. Dances were even more popular. The rubber workers' seeming obsession with ballroom dancing was partly a reflection of a broader cultural development; the same music and steps were being performed at the Portage Country Club. But dances also helped interest wives (and some husbands) in the labor movement, offered a respite from the often pinched and dreary routine of working-class life, and helped satisfy the desires of union families for middle-class status.

The summers of 1936 and 1937 featured a series of mammoth picnics that attested to the unions' power. In 1936 the Goodyear, Goodrich, and Firestone company picnics, organized with the sufferance of URW locals, attracted sixty thousand, sixty thousand, and forty thousand, respectively. In September, the URW Labor Day picnic at Geauga Lake Park drew seventy-five thousand. Regardless of the sponsorship, baseball games, bathing beauty contests, and dancing were the order of the day. The highlight of the 1937 Firestone picnic, for example, was the selection of "Miss Firestone of 1937." Judges also chose a juvenile "Miss Firestone" who received fifteen dollars, a doll, and a bathing suit. The winner of a separate contest for blacks received ten dollars, a doll, and a bathing suit.[70]

LABOR AND POLITICS

For many union members, a larger role in local politics was the logical capstone to the revival of 1936. South and east Akron had had no demonstrable political impact since the quixotic Klan campaigns of the 1920s, and Ray T. Sutliff summarized the prevailing view when he observed that "no elections have ever been won or lost because of a labor vote."[71] The union resurgence brought new opportunities. The approach of the presidential election, the intense national debate over the future of the New Deal, and the turmoil in the AFL created interest among union members. Locally, two factors heightened that interest. The Goodyear strike reminded unionists of the link between local government and union success, and the victory of Wilmer Tate over Frank Patino in the CLU presidential election of February 1936 provided new, militant leadership. By the spring of 1936, as Sutliff recalled, "the boys . . . wanted some action on the political front."[72]

[69] *ABJ*, Oct. 23, 1937.
[70] *ABJ*, July 17, Aug. 10, 17, Sept. 8, 1936.
[71] *ATP*, April 25, 1936.
[72] Ray T. Sutliff, interview with author, April 18, 1979.

During the spring of 1936 Tate tried to rally activists of all types to the independent Farmer-Labor party, which operated in several midwestern states.[73] He welcomed James Keller, the local Communist organizer, as well as H. B. Blankenship, an AFL veteran and political conservative. In late March he persuaded the CLU to endorse an Ohio party and sponsor a June organizing convention in Akron. Tate denied rumors of Communist infiltration. "There will be many trying to grab the tail of our kite but this is strictly a Farmer-Labor setup," he insisted. He took "considerable pains" to reject any "red" ties.[74] Keller publicly accepted his disclaimers.

The June 6 Akron convention seemed to confirm Tate's denials. Five hundred delegates listened to the attorney general of Minnesota, appointed a committee to organize a statewide campaign, and named Tate their local chairman and candidate for Congress. The party platform called for the thirty-hour workweek, child labor legislation, crop insurance, extended unemployment compensation, and repeal of the sales tax. Keller and a handful of Communists were unexpectedly cooperative. They did not "make a move that was any further left than the mass of delegates wanted."[75] Many union representatives seemed more radical.

Thereafter the Akron group, like the Farmer-Labor party elsewhere, became more closely identified with the Communists. On July 4 Earl Browder opened his campaign for the presidency on the Communist party ticket in Akron, supposedly because of the Goodyear strike and the Farmer-Labor party. Tate joined him on the platform. A week later the Farmer-Laborites held a second meeting to pick the rest of the local ticket. The 125 delegates who attended chose May Probst, president of the Union Buyers Club, and Redmond Greer of Local 5, both Communists, as candidates for the state legislature, along with several non-Communists. The Communist role evoked a storm of criticism from the building trades unions, which were Tate's customary enemies, and from other, usually friendlier organizations; the non-Communists all subsequently resigned from the ticket. On July 9, the CLU voted to withdraw its endorsement. Tate felt betrayed.[76]

No less serious was the hostility of the URW. In January 1936, the International Executive Board rejected a move by Camelio and Eagle to endorse

[73] See Donald R. McCoy, *Angry Voices: Left of Center Politics in the New Deal Era* (Port Washington, 1958), pp. 38–107; Hugh T. Lovin, "The Persistence of Third Party Dreams in the American Labor Movement, 1930–1938," *Mid-America* 58 (1976): 142–43; Hugh T. Lovin, "The Ohio 'Farmer-Labor' Movement in the 1930's," *Ohio History* 87 (1978): 419–37.

[74] *ABJ*, May 22, 23, 1936. Also see Richard W. Shrake, II, "Working Class Politics in Akron, Ohio, 1936: The United Rubber Workers and the Failure of the Farmer-Labor Party" (M.A. thesis, University of Akron, 1974), p. 35.

[75] *ATP*, June 7, 14, 1936.

[76] *ABJ*, July 2, 4, 10, 13, 20, Aug. 22, 1936.

some form of labor party.[77] In the following months, as the URW became more closely identified with the CIO, the International officers became increasingly wary of the dissidents. At the URW convention in September 1936, they led the opposition to a resolution, promoted by a combination of leftists (Camelio, Eagle) and militants (Callahan, Carney), to endorse the Farmer-Labor party. They persuaded the delegates to hear a speech by John Owens, the state head of Labor's Non-Partisan League (LNPL), the CIO-sponsored group that sought to rally industrial unionists to Roosevelt. Before the vote on the resolution, Dalrymple stepped down from the presiding officer's chair to attack the Farmer-Labor party as impractical and naive, a move toward "heaven on earth." The roll call vote was 61 to 39 against the resolution.[78]

In Akron, as in many other industrial communities, the LNPL succeeded where local militants, reformers, and Communists failed. Focusing on the presidential race and abjuring long-term goals, it offered militants the hope of eventual third-party action, conservatives the prospect of a union effort free from extremist ties, Republican workers a convenient way to support Roosevelt, and unionists of all perspectives an opportunity to operate as an identifiable interest group. In Ohio, as in Pennsylvania and West Virginia, the LNPL was usually an adjunct of the United Mine Workers; in Summit County it reflected the more diverse character of the labor movement. M. R. Crouch, president of the Painters and Decorators local, agreed to become the county head, ensuring that AFL-CIO tensions did not interfere. Many militants, including Tate, threw their support to the LNPL after the collapse of the Farmer-Labor party. Only Keller and the Communists were not welcome under the LNPL umbrella.[79]

Roosevelt's landslide victory over Alfred Landon seemed to confirm the wisdom of the LNPL approach and the political potential of the rubber workers. In Summit County, Democrats scored their greatest victory of the century, even defeating popular local Republicans like Sheriff Flower and Prosecutor Herman Werner. The outcome convinced them they could do as well on the municipal level if they could find a mayoral candidate for 1937 with "a liberal record that will pass with organized labor."[80] Two days

[77] General Executive Board, Minutes, Jan. 20, 1936, URW Archives.

[78] *ABJ*, Sept. 21, 1936 (also see Sept. 17, 18, 1936); *Proceedings of the First Convention of the United Rubber Workers of America, September 13–21, 1936* (Akron, 1936), pp. 354–55. County and state election officials eventually ruled the Farmer-Labor party off the ballot.

[79] Thomas T. Spencer, "Auxiliary and Non-Party Politics in the 1936 Democratic Presidential Campaign in Ohio," *Ohio History* 90 (1981), 117–18; Dubofsky and Van Tine, *Lewis*, 249–52; Lovin, "Ohio 'Farmer-Labor' Movement," 435–36. For AFL policy toward the LNPL see James O. Morris, *Conflict Within the AFL: A Study of Craft Versus Industrial Unionism, 1901–1938* (Ithaca, 1958), p. 274.

[80] *ATP*, Oct. 18, 1936.

after the election, J. Earl Cox, Democratic county chairman, Crouch, and other labor leaders began the search for a mutually acceptable candidate.

On January 1, Democratic Governor Martin L. Davey appointed Garnet L. Patterson to a vacant Akron municipal judgeship, apparently without consulting Cox. Davey called it a personal choice; in fact, "when [the vacancy] occurred . . . Labor's Nonpartisan League . . . made an immediate demand upon Governor Davey for Patterson's appointment."[81] Since his break with Claherty in 1935, Patterson had become one of the National Labor Relations Board's most promising attorneys.[82] However, he retained his Akron residency and his ties to the local labor movement. Whether he had the mayoral race in mind is not clear, but he could not have been oblivious to the political awakening of Akron's workers.

Patterson quickly emerged as a force in local politics. Known for a "hatred of pettifogging," he performed his judicial duties with unusual efficiency. His impartial, forceful treatment of traffic law violators amazed local observers. Proclaiming himself "a bitter enemy of the fix," he had his home telephone removed to avoid "calls at odd hours."[83] Police officers begged him to stay when his term as traffic court judge ended. By the spring of 1937 he had become one of the city's best-known officeholders.

In the meantime LNPL leaders made plans to use their new power. On February 24 the officers and executive board voted unanimously to "put the League right into the coming municipal election," and later voted to continue their alliance with the Democrats. Their decision was small comfort to Cox and the Democrats since they made no secret of their determination to be the dominant partner in the alliance. The issue, as Crouch explained, was "how far the [Democratic] organization is willing to go with labor." Once the unions had elected a mayor, he foresaw either of two possibilities: the takeover of the local party organization or the creation of a new party. Like many of his colleagues he viewed the league as a catalyst for "a fusion of progressives and liberals from both of the old parties."[84]

At a series of meetings in May 1937, the LNPL Executive Board endorsed Patterson for mayor and union members or sympathizers for council seats in the Democratic primary. When Tate declined to run, league officials selected Tom Owens of Local 7 and lesser known Local 5 and Local 9 officers for the at-large races. For the Fifth Ward, the heart of south Akron, they chose Ben Graves, a longtime Typographical Union officer and "rip-snorting orator." For the Sixth Ward, Goodyear Heights, the unionists selected Local 2 vice-president Ralph Turner. For the Seventh Ward, Fire-

[81] *ABJ*, Aug. 11, 1937.
[82] Peter H. Irons, *The New Deal Lawyers* (Princeton, 1982), pp. 240, 256–58.
[83] *ABJ*, May 15, 1937.
[84] *Cleveland Plain Dealer*, May 8, 1937.

stone Park, they endorsed William B. Ridgeway, the incumbent and a Local 7 member; for the Ninth, a working-class area on the city's southwest corner, a Local 2 member; and for the Tenth, a Goodyear stronghold adjacent to Ward Six, Local 2 secretary Virginia Etheridge. A University of Alabama graduate who had taught school before coming to Goodyear in the mid-1920s, Etheridge described herself as "a housewife [and] a businesswoman." She became the first serious woman candidate in the city's history.[85]

The LNPL platform called for a "new deal" in local government. It advocated parks, playgrounds, and summer camps for the poor; free clinics and public health facilities; public housing, slum clearance, and street paving; the appointment of "common people" to the board of trustees of the University of Akron; the right of all workers to organize, bargain, strike, and picket; and public works for the unemployed. It supported a child labor amendment, greater protection for women and children in industry, equal pay for equal work, and an end to racial discrimination. It promised "to shift the tax burden where it belongs."[86]

Long-suffering Democrats, having tasted victory for the first time in a decade, found themselves reduced to the role of observers. Some blamed Cox; others tried to pressure Patterson to run for a judgeship. Cox and other regulars supposedly concluded that it was "essential" for some prominent Democrat to oppose Patterson in the primary. At an unprecedented meeting of all the city's precinct committeemen, many veteran politicians expressed similar sentiments.[87] Henry Bixler, a county commissioner and ally of Cox, announced his candidacy on May 21.

In the "biggest primary fanfare" since the 1910s, Patterson emphasized his determination to put "New Deal democracy in city hall." Employing a speaking style that mimicked Roosevelt, he devoted special attention to housing and slum clearance. To underline his concern, he took reporters on an inspection tour of a squalid apartment house on Crosier Street where thirty-six families lived in the most desperate circumstances. To attract women voters, he attacked the paucity of playgrounds and libraries. To interest black Democrats, he stressed Bixler's failure to embrace the New Deal. To win Italian votes, he attacked his opponent's unwillingness to "climb on the New Deal bandwagon."[88] On August 8 he defeated Bixler, 17,600 votes to 6,500; his total was the highest of any primary candidate

---

[85] SCLN, Aug. 24, 27, 1937. Etheridge, however, was no Marguerite Prevey. There is no evidence that she or the handful of other women who occasionally appear in leadership roles ever acted as leaders of the women employees.

[86] ABJ, May 17, 1937.

[87] ABJ, May 20, 1937.

[88] ABJ, June 5, 29, 1937; SCLN, July 23, 1937.

in the city's history. The LNPL council candidates also defeated their opponents, including the Fifth and Tenth Ward incumbents and a prominent
Democratic regular running for an at-large seat.[89] Local gamblers made
Patterson and the council candidates heavy favorites to win the general
election.

Patterson and his advisers were less sanguine. To defeat Schroy they
estimated they would need at least 17,000 more votes. One possibility was
to rely exclusively on south and east Akron, become more dependent on
the URW, and work for a large turnout in working-class neighborhoods. The
other was to combine labor voters with Democrats and independents who
could be swayed by party loyalty or the candidate's eloquence, as Roosevelt had done. Patterson personally favored this approach. He was more
pro-New Deal than pro-union and may have worried about governing if his
only supporters were union activists and sit-down strikers. He opted for an
appeal "aimed at building up confidence among substantial citizens of liberal leanings."[90]

To make himself more acceptable and to blunt Republican efforts to link
him to the Lesleys and "Communistic" elements, Patterson changed the
focus of his campaign. He met Cox frequently and hosted several "harmony" sessions for Democratic ward and precinct workers. Rather than
visiting Crosier Street, he devoted his speeches to the achievements of the
New Deal. He attacked the mayor's "closed," "undemocratic," and big-
business-controlled administration but avoided labor issues, never men-
tioning, for example, the Johnston Street riot, which unionists considered
Schroy's one unforgivable sin. Observers complained that there was little
in his speeches to which "any zealot for good government could take exception."[91]

By mid-October it was clear that these tactics had failed. A substantial
group of regular Democrats refused to be placated and there were few signs
that the city's "liberals" were impressed. Bixler, and an influential minority of well-known Democrats (including E. E. Zesiger and the local friends
of Governor Davey), endorsed Schroy. In north and west Akron wards,
rank-and-file Democrats-for-Schroy clubs appeared. Unionists found "the
going rough when they sought to line up the committeemen for ward and
precinct meetings."[92] Patterson's new blandness annoyed rather than attracted other voters.

Nor did his approach deter the Republicans, who seized every opportunity to make him and his supporters the central issue of the campaign. After

[89] *ABJ*, Aug. 11, 1937; *SCLN*, March 6, 1937.
[90] *ATP*, Oct. 10, 1937.
[91] *ABJ*, Oct. 5, 9, 1937.
[92] *ABJ*, Oct. 9, 1937.

the primary, the mayor's advisers decided to wage an aggressive campaign aimed at Patterson's union connection. The architects of this effort were L. L. Poe, a public relations expert with close ties to Governor Davey, and Ray C. Bliss, a young political activist whose successes would make him a fixture in state and national Republican affairs for nearly half a century. In early September Poe arranged a secret meeting between Davey and Bliss at the state house in Columbus. The governor, who had broken the Little Steel strike and was trying to build a national constituency as an anti-New Deal, anti-CIO Democrat, offered to throw the resources of his administration behind the Republican effort. Bliss eagerly accepted.[93] Henceforth state employees and Davey allies worked directly or indirectly for the Republicans. In late September, the governor himself appeared before an Akron business group. His address was officially nonpolitical but his attacks on John L. Lewis and the CIO were tantamount to a Schroy endorsement.[94]

Poe and Bliss devised other ways to focus attention on the unions. The mayor's speeches, written by Poe, emphasized the sinister character of the opposition. "The principles of the Nonpartisan League," he declared, "are the same as those of the Communist party." Union victory would be synonymous with a "radical" takeover. Business would flee the city.[95] When Bliss learned that Earl Browder would endorse the Patterson effort in an Akron speech, he arranged to have Browder's remarks broadcast over a local radio station. Later, when union zealots defaced Schroy billboards, Bliss left them as visible symbols of the unions' destructive potential. By the end of October, local observers predicted a closer race than had seemed possible in August.[96]

Frustrated that his strategy was not working, Patterson turned increasingly to the workers. He spoke to more south Akron audiences and often shared the platform with Tate, Dalrymple, or Frank Grillo. To shouts of "Attaboy judge" and "Lay it into 'em," he attacked Schroy and Bixler and predicted a return to the eight-hour day if Schroy were reelected. His success, Patterson acknowledged, depended on mobilizing every possible union voter.[97]

But here, too, there were problems. The sit-downs and CIO strikes had antagonized many residents, including conservative union members. Even more threatening was the worsening AFL-CIO split. In late June, when William Green demanded the expulsion of CIO unions from CLUs, the Akron

[93] Ray C. Bliss, interview with author, June 16, 1981.

[94] *ABJ*, Sept. 24, 1937.

[95] *ABJ*, Oct. 22, 1937.

[96] Ray C. Bliss interview; *ATP*, Oct. 31, 1937; Robert Morehead, "The Test Tube City Rejects the Union," *Nation's Business* 26 (1938): 55–56.

[97] *ABJ*, Oct. 13, 1937.

CLU simply filed his order. In August, under growing pressure, it arranged a "friendly" purge. CIO unions formally withdrew from the organization but agreed to meet AFL representatives regularly in a new unofficial council. However, in September, Tate spoke to the URW International convention and attacked Green and the AFL hierarchy. He had made similar declarations before, but the convention speech produced a strong reaction. H. A. Bradley, a shadowy figure who was an officer of the Gas Station Attendants and a Federation organizer, publicly rebuked him. Several days later, Bradley announced that the AFL had ordered Tate's removal as CLU president. Tate vowed to fight the order.[98]

As a result the CLU meeting on September 23 was "one of the most hectic" ever. With rubber workers and other CIO members huddled outside the open windows, Bradley and the building trades leaders confronted Tate. Bradley took over the platform and arbitrarily seated several new delegates from his own local. When other delegates moved to reject the charges against Tate, Bradley ruled them out of order. After numerous protests, Bradley finally accepted a motion to table the charges. It carried, with the building trades group united in opposition. Bradley refused to accept the decision. "I'm not going to fool around any longer," he declared. "Unless this body is ready to proceed in an orderly way, it will be necessary for me . . . to put out this charter. If that is done a new charter will be here in the morning for a new central body of unions that are loyal to the A. F. of L." He formally suspended Tate until an investigation could be completed. On September 27 he announced that the AFL had withdrawn the CLU charter and authorized a new organization, the Summit County Trades and Labor Assembly. Five of the nine CLU board members charged him with "brazen and dictatorial" actions and vowed to fight.[99]

The breakup of the CLU and the creation of rival AFL camps reflected local conditions as well as the larger AFL-CIO conflict. With the LNPL seemingly on the verge of capturing the city government, Bradley, Patino, and the building trades leaders worried about losing influence in local politics. One reason for the timing of their anti-CIO offensive was "a desperate desire to channel a small minority of the labor vote into the Lee D. Schroy camp."[100] When the delegates arrived for the fateful September 23 confrontation, for example, they found Republican campaign leaflets on their seats.

The uproar over Tate and the CLU continued through the campaign. Tate

[98] *ABJ*, July 23, Aug. 19, Sept. 14, 1937; *SCLN*, Sept. 3, 1937; *Proceedings of the Second Convention of the United Rubber Workers of America, September 12 to 20, 1937* (Akron, 1937), pp. 27–28.

[99] *ABJ*, Sept. 24, 28, 1937.

[100] *ABJ*, Sept. 28, 1937; *SCLN*, Oct. 1, 1937.

rallied about two-thirds of the AFL organizations to his side and appealed to the AFL convention. Characteristically, he minced no words in attacking his enemies. Their action, he declared,

is without any question part of the program which the sniveling political connivers of the political gutter have set up to keep New Deal Democracy out of Akron's City Hall. . . . I know of trade unionists who have spurned offers of shady political figures to accept bribes in return for sabotaging support of Labor's Nonpartisan League.[101]

Tate's allies at first argued that the Patino group controlled no more than 5 percent of union voters. But when the AFL rejected the appeals and the Machinists expelled Tate, they became more apprehensive. By the end of October, informal polls showed Schroy with a slight edge.[102]

On November 2, a record number of voters gave Schroy a victory of 44,212 to 36,100. Patterson won by narrow to moderate margins in the south and east Akron wards; Schroy took the rest by large majorities. The three Republican at-large candidates also received more votes than Patterson and easily defeated their union opponents. In the ward races, Graves, Turner, Ridgeway, and Etheridge were successful, although Turner edged his opponent in Goodyear Heights by only fifteen votes. Considering the city's large union membership and Patterson's appeal, it was a humiliating setback. Contemporary analysts blamed the breakdown of the labor-Democratic coalition. Nonunion Democrats, troubled by union excesses during the previous year and the Poe-Bliss strategy, supposedly rejected Patterson for the less attractive but safer Schroy.[103]

Election statistics document the shift in voter sentiment between 1936 and 1937. Alfred Landon had received only 29 percent of the votes; Schroy won 55 percent. In 73 percent of the precincts Schroy won more votes than a Republican could reasonably expect.[104] In addition to virtually all the Landon supporters, the mayor apparently attracted one quarter of the Roosevelt partisans and persuaded another quarter not to vote at all.[105] The defectors included professionals and executives but also small-business proprietors, clerks, and service workers whose incomes were no higher than those of the rubber workers but who subscribed to the Republican argument that a Patterson victory would be bad for business. Like most American white-collar workers, they flirted with organized labor when it

[101] *SCLN*, Oct. 1, 1937.

[102] Ibid.; *ABJ*, Nov. 1, 1937.

[103] *ABJ*, Nov. 2, 3, 1937; *ATP*, Nov. 3, 1937.

[104] See Daniel Nelson, "The CIO at Bay: Labor Militancy and Politics in Akron, 1936–1938," *Journal of American History* 7 (1984): 578–84.

[105] Ibid., p. 578.

promised to enhance their prospects and rejected it when, as in 1937, it seemed to endanger those prospects.[106]

But was Schroy's success due simply to a large turnout of nonunion and anti-union voters? A closer examination of the blue-collar vote suggests a more fundamental problem. Despite the imagery of the campaign, the workers were far less united than their neighbors. Three trends stand out.[107] Nonunion rubber workers opposed Patterson, craft workers were only mildly supportive, and the poor and unemployed were overwhelmingly favorable. The behavior of the nonunion and craft employees reflected the influence of the company union loyalists and the work of the Patino-Bradley group. Several factors probably accounted for the enthusiasm of the poor, including a tradition of Democratic voting and Schroy's opposition to local spending for public works or relief. One of the mayor's more accurate claims was that he had alleviated the city's financial plight by carefully husbanding public funds. In 1937 his frugality precipitated a series of public relief crises that severely restricted payments to individuals who did not qualify for federal aid.[108] It is hardly surprising that Patterson's early calls for expanded public services, slum clearance, and housing relief struck a responsive chord among them.

The rubber workers apparently fell somewhere between the nonunion workers and the poor. Goodrich and Firestone workers appear to have supported Patterson as strongly as the unemployed, while Goodyear workers were only marginally more united than the craft employees.[109] The legacy of Goodyear personnel work and the Depression-era decline in labor mobility partly explain this disparity, as do the Goodyear upheavals of 1936 and 1937. Viewed by outsiders as indicators of worker militancy, of "labor on the march," the Goodyear turmoil was a sign of dissension and weakness. In the Akron plants militancy and union power were inversely correlated. Local 7's "conservatism," which troubled the militants, was in reality a sign of union solidarity.

---

[106] See Jones, *Life, Liberty, and Property*, chaps. 13, 16. Also see Jurgen Kocka, *White Collar Workers in America, 1890–1940* (London and Beverly Hills, 1980), chap. 4.

[107] Nelson, "The CIO at Bay," pp. 580–82.

[108] See U.S. Department of Commerce, Bureau of the Census, *Financial Statistics of Cities Having a Population of Over 100,000, 1936* (Washington, 1938), pp. 52, 72, 172.

[109] Ecological regression estimates, based on the fifteen precincts with the highest concentrations of Goodyear and Firestone workers, suggest that 41 percent of Goodyear workers and 95 percent of Firestone workers voted for Patterson. Compared with local Democratic candidates in 1934 and 1936, Patterson received 81 percent of the "normal" Democratic vote in the Goodyear precincts but 164 percent of the Democratic vote in the Firestone precincts. The anti-CIO Goodyear Heights militants helped account for the unusually low Goodyear estimates. Goodrich workers and other CIO members were much more widely dispersed, making direct estimates of their voting behavior less reliable.

The workers' desire "for action on the political front" thus exposed their vulnerability to outside attack and internal divisions. Even at the height of union power and expectations, the rubber workers were unable to play the role in civic affairs that they and others anticipated. Like the sit-down movement of 1936, the Patterson debacle underlined their ability to discard failed policies, seize the initiative, and yet allow opportunity to slip between their fingers. By late 1937 only the collective bargaining triumphs of the preceding eighteen months seemed immune to this process. And within a few weeks even they came under attack.

CHAPTER NINE

Labor on the March: Outlying Cities, 1936–1937

HE WAS BURLY, good-natured, and personable. He was also an ex-convict with "a bad reputation for veracity."[1] The two sides of Lucius Grady Cleere (1910–1938) account for his role in the Rubber Workers most challenging organizing campaign, his rise to prominence, and his ambiguous legacy. Like Lesley, Cleere was at first a member of the anti-union contingent at Goodyear, but in Gadsden, which made a critical difference. Whereas Lesley instructed workers in paramilitary techniques, Cleere became involved in a violent struggle that had many earmarks of the small-firm, small-town battles of 1933–1935. Disillusioned by mid-1936, Cleere switched sides and became one of the era's most celebrated informants. Yet at that point his career diverged from Lesley's, and he became the one possible fatality of the Akron labor wars. Was he a victim of Goodyear vengeance or a petty criminal who tempted fate once too often? Whatever the correct answer, it should not obscure the more important fact: Cleere's brief, troubled life symbolized the hazards of operating on the organizational frontier of the 1930s.

GADSDEN, ALABAMA

Until 1935 Goodyear's Gadsden operation was simply one of many small, outlying tire factories. The Depression and the Federal Trade Commission attack on the Sears contract in the mid-1930s prevented it from living up to Litchfield's expectations or its local promoters' hopes. Similarly, Gadsden Local 12 was one of many marginal URW organizations. With four hundred members out of eight hundred to nine hundred employees, it was too weak to win recognition or a contract. Like the Gadsden plant, its future depended on circumstances beyond its control.

A surging economy and the upheavals in Akron altered the prospects of both organizations and inaugurated one of the classic labor conflicts of the decade. In early April 1936, Litchfield announced the expansion of the Gadsden plant, a step that Akron observers attributed to the Goodyear strike. Fred Climer confirmed the link in October 1936, when he wrote that "attitudes in the community" explained "why we failed so miserably in

[1] National Labor Relations Board, *Decisions and Orders of the NLRB* 21 (1940): 324.

our difficulties here in Akron and why Gadsden has been so wonderful."[2] For Goodyear executives, Gadsden was a placid isle in a tumultuous sea. URW leaders preferred a different metaphor: Gadsden was a safety valve that would keep the union in check.

Community "attitudes," the key to Gadsden's allure, only partly reflected the city's location and culture. Public attitudes toward unions were no different in Gadsden than in hundreds of northern towns where low wages and underemployed workers were a problem and a resource. What made Gadsden attractive to Goodyear was not its southernness but its leaders' sense of insecurity. As the *Akron Times Press* noted, Gadsden residents were far more worried about plant closings than anyone in Akron.[3] Gadsden's leading employers, Dwight Manufacturing, Gulf States (Republic) Steel, and Goodyear, all northern companies, exploited this anxiety to win financial and legal favors and to operate virtually with a free hand against organized labor. As the NRA faded, they took the offensive. Led by Gulf States, they recruited gangs of toughs and pressured AFL members to quit the union or their jobs. As late as 1934, all three plants had had flourishing federal labor unions; by 1936, union workers were "in a very small minority."[4]

Grady Cleere was one of the men employed for anti-union duty. A strapping ex-high school football star who had worked briefly at the Firestone plant in Akron and had served a short prison term, he came to the attention of Mike Self, the chief "watchman" at Gulf States. In 1934 Self hired him as a chauffeur and labor spy. Cleere understood his assignment but later insisted that he never intended to harm anyone. In early 1936, Self sent him to T. L. Bottoms, a "spotter" for Goodyear who recruited men "who wouldn't join the union." Bottoms in turn introduced him to L. E. Miller, the head of the Flying Squadron. Miller assigned him to tire building and asked him to report on the activities of union members. Cleere found that union members avoided him. Miller and Bottoms were probably not concerned; they valued him more for his brawn than his information. With perhaps fifty others, including squadron members and some low-level supervisors, he was available for strong-arm duty. On one occasion Bot-

[2] U.S. Senate, "Violations of Free Speech and Rights of Labor," *Hearings Before a Subcommittee of the Committee on Education and Labor*, 75th Cong., 1st sess. (Washington, 1937), p. 2979.

[3] *ATP*, June 26, 1936.

[4] William F. White to H. L. Kerwin, June 14, 1936, Federal Mediation and Conciliation Service Papers, RG 280, File 182/1515, National Archives; Charles H. Martin, "Southern Labor Relations in Transition: Gadsden, Alabama, 1930–1943," *Journal of Southern History* 47 (1981): 545–68.

toms asked Cleere to help him follow two suspected union organizers until they left town.[5]

As the anti-union campaign became more vigorous, Local 12 declined. On February 16, 1936, local secretary Zella Morgan reported to Dalrymple that the union was in a "critical condition." The company was moving in tire machines from Akron but "we are not strong enough to resist . . . we can't help ourselves. . . . What we need now, and need bad," she added "is a man from the Goodyear local to organize us." She specifically requested House.[6] The Goodyear strike and Litchfield's announcement of the Gadsden expansion in April gave her plea new urgency. When URW leaders learned in late May that Local 12 president E. L. Gray had been discharged, they decided to act. Since House was preoccupied with the sit-downs, Dalrymple decided to go himself. He asked Local 12 officers to arrange a meeting with plant manager A. C. Michaels and a large rally of Gadsden workers. Leaving the International office in Grillo's hands, he and his wife drove to Gadsden. They arrived on June 4.

Dalrymple found more trouble than he had anticipated. Soon after his arrival, he learned that Gray had been arrested for passing out the *United Rubber Worker*. The police chief acknowledged that Gray had violated no law; the arrest was a warning against "creating a disturbance in Gadsden." When Dalrymple asked Michaels to reinstate Gray, he refused and insisted that Gray and another fired union member were "radicals" and "communists." When Dalrymple invited him to attend the public meeting planned for the following evening, Michaels demurred. Dalrymple was personally "all right," he added, "but we are not in accord with your union meetings."[7]

The atmosphere in Gadsden became more tense as both sides prepared for the public meeting. Dave Greene, the CLU president, urged union men to "pack the Court House Saturday night."[8] Goodyear managers likewise "advised [a]ssemblymen, squadron and key men . . . of the agitation in the Akron strike, and its effect on employees, lost wages, etc."[9] On June 6 the situation became more ominous. M. G. "Pete" Dunn, a squadron member, proposed to "go over there and beat hell out of him and run him out." When asked about the police, Dunn replied: "We done called up over

[5] U.S. Senate, "Violations of Free Speech," pp. 3044–45.

[6] Zella Morgan to Sherman H. Dalrymple, Feb. 16, 1936, Local 12 File, United Rubber Workers Archives, URW offices, Akron, Ohio.

[7] U.S. Senate, "Violations of Free Speech," pp. 3003–3004; NLRB, *Decisions and Orders*, p. 326.

[8] Dave Greene Statement, June 12, 1936, FMCS Papers, RG 280, File 182/1515.

[9] "Memo on Gadsden Situation," June 10, 1936, in U.S. Senate, "Violations of Free Speech," pp. 2982, 3208.

13. *Grady and Mildred Cleere,*
probably on their wedding day,
1935. Courtesy of Mildred
Cleere Neill.

there, Mr. Miller has, and made arrangements that nobody won't get arrested over there.'' Ralph Chalfant, a foreman, explained that ''you haven't got a damn thing to worry about. . . . We done got that fixed with [Sheriff] Bob Leath and the city commission.''[10]

That night several hundred union men, with their wives and children, and a large group of squadron members and allies gathered in the courthouse auditorium. As Greene introduced Dalrymple several squadron men and a supervisor distributed bags of eggs. When Dalrymple began his talk, someone shouted: ''Who in hell sent for you?'' The squadron men booed and started to throw eggs. After several minutes of disorder, Sheriff Leath and a number of police officers entered and began to search the union men for weapons. At that point a group of men ''began to rush toward the speakers' platform.'' R. Clyde Turner, a Goodyear employee, called Dalrymple a ''God damned son of a bitch,'' and hit him in the face. A police officer standing next to Dalrymple did nothing. As the meeting broke up, Leath

[10] NLRB, *Decisions and Orders,* pp. 326–27.

14. John House, URW president Sherman H. Dalrymple, and URW secretary-treasurer Frank Grillo after Dalrymple returned from Gadsden, Alabama, June 1936. United Rubber Workers Archives.

offered to escort Dalrymple back to his hotel. He waited until the crowd had gathered at the back of the building and then guided Dalrymple out the rear door. "Sheriff," Dalrymple exclaimed, "you are leading me out here into a mob." "Never mind," Leath replied, "I'll take care of you."[11]

Dalrymple ran a gauntlet between the courthouse and his hotel. Some of the attackers pulled his hair; others punched him or kicked him. Bottoms later bragged that "I hit him every chance I got." There were shouts of "Hit him a lick for Carruthers" and "Hit him once for Carruthers." Leath did not intervene. When Dalrymple reached the hotel door several men pulled him back with such force that he tore off the screen. Conscious but nearly blind, he pleaded for medical attention. Leath refused. Finally, several of the attackers turned to Grace Dalrymple: "Now, God Damn you, if you want him now, you had better take him out of here." She hurriedly gathered their possessions while police officers broke into their car.[12]

Grace Dalrymple described the journey back to Akron:

[11] U.S. Senate, "Violations of Free Speech," p. 3006.
[12] "Statement of Tom Davis," n.d., and "Statement of Sheriff Robert Leath," FMCS Papers, RG 280, File 182/1515; *Gadsden Times*, June 9, 1936; "Statement of Mrs. S. H. Dalrymple, June 15, 1936," Local 12 File, URW Archives.

I drove about thirty miles to Collinsville, Alabama and I stopped at a tourist camp there and . . . got the Doctor out of bed. . . . He said, "This man has lost enough blood to kill him let alone the injuries he has" and he begged Sherman to let him . . . take care of him, but Sherman said, "No" that he had to get to Akron. The Doctor . . . put some shots in his nose, eyes and mouth to clot the blood . . . and fixed me some ice bags to put on his head when we stopped.

I drove then about one hundred and thirty miles before I stopped that night and I got him into a tourist camp and put the ice on him, but he didn't rest any. We had only been in bed a couple of hours, when he turned over and laid his arm on me and said, "Oh mom, please let's go to Akron." So I got him dressed at once and I drove four hundred and eighty miles to my sister's place at Blanchester, Ohio, . . . and my sister insisted upon him having her Doctor there.[13]

Dalrymple spent the next week in a hospital recovering from a concussion, shock, and bruises. He had earned the painful distinction of being the highest-ranking union casualty of labor violence in the 1930s.

After the beating, Dunn, Turner, and others, possibly in consultation with Miller, decided to drive the union men out of the plant. On Monday, June 8, they attacked three union members, kicking and shoving them until they "escaped and ran out of the plant." They escorted others to the gate. As the men were leaving, Michaels drove up and asked one of the squadron men what was happening. "You know what is going on," he replied. Michaels supposedly smiled and drove away. When personnel manager H. S. Craigmile appeared, squadron members told him that loyal employees were "running these agitators out of the plant." He ordered the attackers back to work.[14] Later Bottoms and Turner presented a list of twenty unacceptable employees to Craigmile, who told them that he wanted to do "whatever you fellows think is right," but suggested that they reconsider eight of the union members.[15] After questioning the eight and exacting promises of good behavior, they agreed to let them remain.

The initial URW reaction to the beating and expulsions was to enlist the aid of the federal government. After listening to Dalrymple's account, Grillo and other URW leaders sent House, Rex Murray, and Thomas Owens to Washington, where they obtained promises of investigations from Labor Secretary Perkins, NLRB Chairman J. Warren Madden, and Senator Robert M. La Follette, Jr. Another delegation went to William Green, who prevailed on Alabama governor Bibb Graves to send representatives from the

---

[13] "Statement of Mrs. S. H. Dalrymple." Also see James S. Jackson, interview with author, Oct. 5, 1973.

[14] "Evidence in Regard to Dispute," June 11, 1936, FMCS Papers, RG 280, File 182/1515; NLRB, *Decisions and Orders*, pp. 334–35.

[15] NLRB, *Decisions and Orders*, pp. 334–35.

state labor department and the highway patrol to Gadsden. The city was quickly deluged with government officials.[16]

The URW's next steps were more difficult. Burns and the Executive board members did not want to encourage additional violence or sit-downs and their other options were all undesirable. Essentially, they could try to re-establish the Gadsden local in the face of intense opposition or wait for the government to act. In spite of the dangers, "it was thought best . . . to answer these attacks with a militant campaign of organization."[17] They brought Gray and three other Local 12 men to Akron to tell their stories, announced a $100,000 fund-raising effort to finance a southern organizing campaign, and recruited activists from the Akron locals to spearhead the campaign in Gadsden.

By June 15 the preliminaries were complete. The financial appeal had raised enough money to sustain the campaign for two or three months, and Burns had received the governor's promise of state police protection for a large Gadsden rally on June 20. An "advance guard" of the four Gadsden men; Bob Roberts; Chuck Lesley and William Boyle, who were to guard Roberts; and Jerome Foreman, a Mohawk worker and Gadsden native, left for Alabama. A second contingent, led by House and W. W. Thompson, was to join them at the end of the week. Burns and B. J. Widick were to go for the Saturday rally. Burns predicted that they would have "at least 40 percent of the union workers back in the fold" within three weeks.[18]

Gadsden officials followed these preparations with keen interest and ill-concealed hostility. The city commissioners promised not to permit the "molestation of any firm, individual or corporation" and adopted a series of ordinances giving police sweeping powers to harass labor organizers.[19] The police chief recruited an auxiliary force of one hundred and fifty men from Goodyear, Gulf States, and Dwight. For the Goodyear men he turned to Miller, who selected "dependable, reliable boys who were broad minded." Miller's list was virtually a list of the men who had beaten Dalrymple. On June 18 Bottoms called a meeting of the deputies and urged them not "to let these damned Yankees come down here and take our jobs. . . . The company and the law is behind you." Cleere, one of the deputies, reported that the men were told informally that the Saturday rally "was going to be broke up."[20]

[16] J. D. House, T. Owens, R. Murray to URW, June 16, 1936, Local 12 File, URW Archives; John Brophy to Frank Grillo, June 10, 1936, Congress of Industrial Organizations Papers, URW file, Catholic University, Washington.

[17] U.S. Senate, "Violations of Free Speech," p. 3000.

[18] ABJ, June 17, 1936.

[19] ABJ, June 16, 1936.

[20] U.S. Senate, "Violations of Free Speech," pp. 3046–47. Also see Gadsden Times, June 18, 1936.

URW organizers were as conciliatory as possible. When Roberts and Yelverton Cowherd, a Birmingham labor lawyer, applied for a meeting permit on June 19, they assured city commissioners of their peaceful intent. Cowherd confirmed that he had rejected offers of assistance from the American Civil Liberties Union and the Communist party. His assurances, plus the presence of highway patrol officers and out-of-town newspaper reporters, had the desired effect. More than two thousand people listened to speakers from the Textile Workers, Steel Workers Organizing Committee, and URW. Hecklers interrupted several times, and someone cut the wires to the microphone, but there were no serious incidents. With sufficient strength, organized labor could operate peacefully in Gadsden.[21]

For the next week URW organizers tried to contact former union members amid growing intimations of the violence they had been warned against. On Sunday night, Foreman was called to the lobby of his hotel. Several men tried to provoke a fight and warned him to leave before morning.[22] On Tuesday, Craigmile sat in his car across the street from the organizers' Tolson Building office, conferring with men who emerged from a nearby poolroom. On Tuesday night, Foreman's sister and Cleere reported that Craigmile and Bottoms had ordered the squadron men and others to attack the union office the next day. The organizers decided to avoid a confrontation by meeting in their hotel rooms on Wednesday.[23] On Thursday morning, June 25, the organizers received more reports of mob action. Roberts and Lesley went to the police department and received assurances of protection. They and the others then gathered at the Tolson Building to wait.

At noon, Bottoms and other Goodyear supervisors began to recruit workers in the plant. Bottoms assured them that "the law ain't going to bother you." Some foremen encouraged workers to join the mob; others merely gave them permission to leave. In all, two to three hundred men left the plant. Michaels, supposedly surprised, ordered the foremen to stop the exodus and "gave strict orders for everybody to be docked every minute they spent away from the plant that day."[24] Neither order was carried out, probably because most supervisory workers had already joined the mob. Cleere, who had left town the day before on a ruse to avoid involvement, was in a downtown restaurant when the Goodyear workers began to gather near the

[21] *Industrial Unionist*, June 16, 1936; *Gadsden Times*, June 19, 20, 22, 1936; "Statement of W. W. Thompson," June 27, 1936, NLRB Papers, RG 25, Box 214, Case 149, National Archives. The Yelverton Cowherd Scrapbook includes flyers distributed in adjoining counties (scrapbook in possession of Mrs. Cowherd).

[22] "Statement of J. E. Foreman," June 27, 1936, NLRB Papers, RG 25, Box 214, Case 149.

[23] J. D. House, "Experiences in Gadsden, Alabama, June 22 to June 25," FMCS Papers, RG 280, File 182/1515; "Statement of J. E. Foreman."

[24] NLRB, *Decisions and Orders*, p. 347; U.S. Senate, "Violations of Free Speech," p. 3029.

Tolson Building. He joined the crowd of spectators. Three Local 12 men, returning to the Tolson Building after lunch, also understood what was happening. "Boys," one of them exclaimed, "it [is] no bluff this time. Drive on."[25]

In the union office, Roberts directed the defense. He called the police again and asked Foreman, who had remained at the hotel, to go to the police station to demand assistance. Neither effort produced any action. Roberts and House then tried to address the crowd. Leaning out the second-story window, they emphasized their peaceful intentions; House noted his own southern origins and squadron service. When that effort also failed, they tried to barricade the office. House, Gray, and Cecil S. Holmes, another Local 12 officer, pushed a heavy table against the door. Gray armed himself with a hammer and Lesley and others picked up tools that an electrician had left in the office. Another organizer had a handful of pepper.[26]

At a signal the crowd rushed the building. The leaders ran up the stairs, shouting "Open up," "Open the door." One of them smashed the window in the door with a pistol. Clarence Lumpkin, a tire builder, warned that if they resisted, "We will kill the last one of you." As Lumpkin and others smashed the door, Gray raised his hammer. One of the attackers pointed a pistol at him and Gray dropped the hammer. A half-dozen men seized him and House. "Here is the damn son-of-a-bitch that I want," one said.[27] They beat House and Gray with blackjacks and brass knuckles. House recalled:

A million clubs seemed to rain upon my head and shoulders and over my kidneys. Someone struck me in the other eye and another lick caught me on the nose. It seemed ages before, half conscious, I made my way to the door. . . . There two others grabbed me and kicked me down the first flight of stairs leading to the street. I broke loose and half ran down the other flight of steps and was caught near the bottom again and beaten over the head and shoulders with fists and blackjacks. As I pushed through the door and up the sidewalk toward the Police station, [they] . . . kept hitting me.[28]

House finally reached a police officer. "You're the law here," he pleaded. "Why don't you stop this?" He received no answer.[29]

In the meantime Roberts ordered the URW men to surrender and agreed to lead them out of the office. At the top of the stairs, a man hit him in the

[25] "Statement of F. H. DeBerry," NLRB Papers, RG 25, Box 214, Case 149.

[26] "Statement of J. D. House," June 30, 1936, NLRB Papers, RG 25, Box 214, Case 149; George B. Roberts to Robert Wohlforth, n.d., George B. Roberts Papers, Wayne State University, Detroit.

[27] "Statement of E. L. Gray," June 27, 1936, NLRB Papers, RG 25, Box 214, Case 149.

[28] House, "Experiences in Gadsden."

[29] NLRB, *Decisions and Orders*, p. 347.

face. Others pushed and kicked him down the stairs. At the bottom, several men kicked him in the head and back. Two men held him while others punched him in the face.[30] Other atttackers broke the glasses of Stanley Edwards, who followed. Thompson was unscathed until he emerged from the building. Then someone shouted, "That is one of these sons of bitches," and several men knocked him to the ground. He tried to run but was knocked down again.[31] Holmes was also attacked as he left the building. When Lesley reached the stairs a member of the mob addressed him: "Well, are you going to get out of town? . . . You big son-of-a-bitch, you had better get out and stay out."[32] The man did not hit him. The other organizers were not physically assaulted. One Local 12 member asked if he could remain in town with his family. "Just do the best you can," replied a member of the mob. "I will see Mr. Bottoms and talk to him and see what he says."[33]

By the time the battered organizers arrived in Birmingham, Cowherd had already initiated a second wave of appeals and protests. In response Labor Secretary Perkins promised a new investigation and John L. Lewis spoke to Governor Graves, who made "all kinds of promises."[34] NLRB and LaFollette committee officials added more charges to their case against Goodyear, and the Birmingham and Akron papers cooperated with front-page coverage. Photos showing Roberts' swollen face, the organizers' dispirited looks, and the wrecked URW office underlined the destructive power of the Gadsden mob.[35] At a tumultuous armory rally on June 28, Dalrymple made his first public appearance since his beating. Responding to rumors of reprisals against nonunion employees, he called on the workers to "forget the spirit of revenge . . . and concentrate on organizing Gadsden."[36]

Amid the general uproar, two features of the Tolson Building incident attracted little notice. The first was the systematic pattern of the violence. Government investigators thoroughly documented the roles of Craigmile, Bottoms, Leath, and other Gadsden officials, eliminating any doubt about the contrived and premeditated character of the incident. But they overlooked a related feature of the rioters' plan. On the afternoon of the riot, a Local 12 member went to the police for protection. They told him, "There

[30] Roberts to Wohlforth, n.d., Roberts Papers.

[31] "Statement of W. W. Thompson."

[32] "Statement of C. D. Lesley," June 27, 1936, NLRB Papers, RG 25, Box 214, Case 149.

[33] Statement of E. C. Ledlow, n.d., NLRB Papers, RG 25, Box 214, Case 149.

[34] CIO Executive Board, Minutes, July 2, 1936, Katherine Ellickson Papers, Reel 1, Franklin D. Roosevelt Library, Hyde Park, N.Y.

[35] *Birmingham Age-Herald*, June 26–30, 1936; *Birmingham Post*, June 26–30, 1936; *ATP*, June 26, 1936; *ABJ*, June 25, 1936.

[36] *ABJ*, June 29, 1936.

ain't nobody going to bother you; they are just after the other fellows, after those Yankees.'' Sheriff Leath, standing nearby, repeated this assurance.[37] For once the sheriff's word was good. Except for Gray and Holmes, who were union officers, the Gadsden men were not harmed. All of them remained in the Gadsden area and lived peacefully after June 25.

More intriguing was the treatment of the Akron men. Roberts and House were beaten savagely, like Dalrymple; Thompson was hit only after he reached the street. Edwards received a few minor blows and the other Akron organizers were not touched. Several of them attributed their good luck to their local ties. Lester Thomas explained:

I am a local boy raised thirty miles from [Gadsden], and some of them knew me and probably had orders not to hit me because public sentiment would be against them. So they shoved me out of the way. . . . [One attacker] says ''We don't want to hurt you.''[38]

Edwards believed he escaped harm because of the interest in Roberts. Lesley told a similar story. On emerging from the building, he took off his hat ''and just started walking down the street. Nobody made any attempt to bother me.'' He speculated that the Goodyear men did not recognize him because he wasn't wearing his glasses. Boyle admitted that he was ''not even as much as shoved.''[39]

These distinctions did not go unnoticed in union circles. URW leaders, already suspicious of Lesley and Boyle because of their roles in the sitdowns, became doubly concerned after the Tolson Building incident. Garnet Patterson, at that time the chief NLRB investigator in the Goodyear case, wrote that ''two of the men suspected by the union . . . were organizers in Gadsden . . . and didn't get a scratch. This may be mere coincidence, but it may be what is suspected.''[40] Thompson was more explicit. In the organizers' official report and in other letters, he observed that ''Foreman . . . escaped untouched, so did Lesley, Boyle and Thomas.'' The reason, he added, with a note of bitterness, ''was that when the crowd took after [him], they forgot about Boyle, Lesley and Thomas, who followed [him] out of the office and thus escaped.'' Characterizing them as the ''four Musketeers and fair-haired Goodyear boys,'' he wrote that ''the laugh is that the Goodyear boys came out unharmed. Lesley, Boyle, Thomas and Foreman will have big tales to tell about how close they came to getting their

---

[37] ''Statement by Hugh Milam,'' June 30, 1936, NLRB Papers, RG 25, Box 214, Case 149.

[38] ''Statement of Lester Thomas,'' n.d., NLRB Papers, RG 25, Box 214, Case 149.

[39] ''Statement of Stanley Edwards,'' ''Statement of C. D. Lesley,'' and ''Statement of W. Boyle,'' June 27, 1936, NLRB Papers, RG 25, Box 214, Case 149.

[40] Patterson to Fahy, July 20, 1936, NLRB Papers, Case 8-C-33.

hair mussed."[41] Thompson's accusations may in fact have saved Lesley and Boyle. When his statements became known, the Goodyear local charged him with libel under the URW constitution and the executive board voted to oust him. Shortly afterward Dalrymple appointed Lesley to the International staff. The issue of his and Boyle's loyalty never arose again.

The furor following the Tolson Building incident obscured a second major point, the failure of the southern strategy. Far from reviving Local 12 and industrial unionism in Gadsden, the URW campaign destroyed what remained of the locals. Even Governor Graves warned URW leaders not to send organizers to Gadsden in the near future. House, Thompson, and Foreman remained in Birmingham after the riot, working with Cowherd and maintaining the illusion of a continuing effort. But by early July even this gesture seemed futile and they returned to Akron.[42]

Cumberland, Maryland

URW organizing campaigns in eastern and midwestern towns during 1936 and 1937 seldom matched the drama of the Akron and Gadsden struggles, but they provide a valuable perspective on the process of union growth during the climactic months of the economic recovery. The URW effort at Kelly-Springfield, the best-documented of these campaigns, supplies a useful counterweight to the images associated with Akron and Gadsden. In the months after the Goodyear takeover, Kelly-Springfield managers adopted the parent company's anti-union policies; union officials likewise saw the Kelly-Springfield purchase as part of the industry's decentralization strategy. Conflict was inevitable. But the Cumberland struggles were inconclusive and unsatisfying. By the spring of 1937 the local was larger and better established, but the URW had made little progress toward containing the centrifugal forces that threatened all of its post-1935 victories.

Goodyear executives confronted a more complex situation in Cumberland than in Gadsden. L. A. Hurley, manager of interplant relations, wrote that "all of the business people and the better" element in the city were "very well pleased" with the company's plans to increase production and "wholeheartedly opposed [to] agitators from the outside."[43] Moreover, in Mayor Thomas W. Koon the company had an invaluable ally at city hall. Koon may not have been as bold as C. Nelson Sparks or the Gadsden city commissioners, but he made no secret of his bias. Yet the mayor did not have a free hand. A minority in the city council was pro-union, and even

---

[41] Quoted in S. Edwards, C. Lesley, L. Thomas, J. Foreman, W. Boyle, and F. Grillo to Dalrymple, July 13, 1936, Roberts File, URW Archives.

[42] *ABJ*, June 30, 1936; *ATP*, July 3, 1936.

[43] U.S. Senate, "Violations of Free Speech," pp. 3207, 16900.

Koon's allies could not afford to overlook the city's substantial population of miners, railroad employees, textile workers, and other union members. Many Cumberland citizens were sympathetic to both Goodyear and the union and opposed public policies that aided one side over the other.

Union leaders also faced a complex and difficult situation, an outgrowth, ironically, of the FLU presence in Cumberland before 1936. Long years of struggle had created a corps of bitter, defensive union officers, preoccupied with the company's "ruthless destruction of human liberties" and the reemployment of union members who had been unjustly laid off.[44] Their approach risked alienating the hundreds of new employees hired in 1935 and 1936 who were unfamiliar with the local's earlier struggles and interested primarily in improved wages and working conditions.

URW leaders closely followed the fortunes of the Cumberland local because of the plant's size and strategic position in the Goodyear system. Dalrymple and House spoke there in January 1936, and on March 16, after the appearance of the Law and Order League in Akron, Dalrymple ordered Local 26 leaders to present "a set of demands" to the Kelly-Springfield management and "if not accepted, immediately prepare to strike the plant."[45] Union records provide no indication of any action before Dalrymple countermanded the order on March 21. During April and May, Burns and John Marchiando, a new organizer, spoke at Cumberland rallies and Roberts helped resolve several grievances. This activity challenged Local 26 to more energetic efforts and the plant managers to a test of wills.

Goodyear managers threw down the gauntlet in early June by discharging James M. Reed and Minnie Rank, veteran employees and outspoken union activists. Their move, which they refused to explain, outraged the local leaders. A week later, after Dalrymple's beating in Gadsden, they warned Mayor Koon that six hundred Akron workers were coming to Cumberland to close the plant. The mayor pledged to keep the plant open and prepared a plan to deputize citizens. The threatened invasion, which never occurred, "create[d] an angry feeling among the citizens towards the union."[46] When the local passed a strike vote several days later, company executives persuaded the mayor to appoint a citizens committee to conduct a plant referendum on the question, "Do you want to strike—Yes or No." Koon ordered the committee to work in secret. However, Local 26 leaders found out about the vote and spent the rest of the night preparing. In the morning they picketed the gates and urged workers not to vote. Sixty-five employees abstained. The others voted 1,053 to 132 against a strike. James

[44] J. E. Reed to Maryland State Commissioner of Labor, June 30, 1936, FMCS Papers, RG 280, File 182/1586.

[45] Dalrymple to H. T. Wilson, March 16, 1936, Local 26 File, URW Archives.

[46] Smith to Kerwin, July 7, 1936.

Reed charged that "company officials are trying to make another Gadsden out of Cumberland."[47]

The lopsided outcome nevertheless shocked URW leaders. Already reeling from the Gadsden debacle, they now faced the prospect of another disaster. When Local 26 officers inquired about a sympathy strike in Akron if they went out, Burns, still acting-president, and Marchiando rushed to Cumberland. For a week they worked feverishly to avert a walkout. On July 6 they assured a Labor Department conciliator that they would not "permit a strike" and would "pacify some of the workers" by hiring Reed and Rank as organizers and filing NLRB charges against Goodyear.[48]

In the following months relations between Goodyear and Local 26 remained tense. The company blocked the NLRB investigation with an injunction and encouraged the formation of the Kelly-Springfield Employees Protective Association, which opposed "outside aid and influence."[49] Local union leaders continued to demand the reinstatement of Reed and Rank and contract negotiations. They got nowhere. When they finally called a strike on August 22, their prospects appeared to be very poor. Yet the walkout proved to be surprisingly effective. William Carney, now on the CIO payroll, arrived on Sunday, August 23, with pledges of financial assistance and other aid. Together with the local leaders, he organized picket teams, set up a large tent to serve as a commissary, and prepared signs. Carney's most important contribution, however, was to reformulate the local's demands. Besides the customary call for reinstatements, he persuaded the local leaders to ask for wage parity with Akron and six-hour shifts.[50] These demands, more attuned to the interests of Kelly workers than the old cry for reinstatements, buoyed the members' morale and attracted wide support.

Equally helpful was the heavy-handed behavior of Goodyear officials. Kelly-Springfield president Edmund S. Burke announced that the plant would remain open and the leader of the Employees Protective Association indicated that he would cross the picket line.[51] On Monday morning city police guarded the gates while perhaps 50 percent of the first-shift workers entered, including many from outlying areas who had not known about the strike. Pickets jeered but were "good natured." They became less agreeable on Tuesday, when nonunion employees arrived on buses and spent the day building fences and erecting searchlights. At 3:00 P.M., when the buses emerged, strikers showered them with rocks. The police responded with

[47] Ibid.; *Cumberland Evening Times*, June 17, 1936.

[48] Smith to Kerwin, July 7, 1936.

[49] *Cumberland Sunday Times*, July 12, 1936.

[50] *Cumberland Evening Times*, Aug. 24, 27, 1936.

[51] *ABJ*, Aug. 24, 1936.

tear gas. At the 11:00 P.M. shift change nonunion workers ran a "gauntlet" of rock-throwing pickets, and the police again fired gas bombs to disperse them. Burke closed the plant, and the Allegheny Trades Council, the powerful AFL central body, demanded state intervention. Governor Harry W. Nice rejected Goodyear appeals for troops and inspected the strike site with the local state senator, a CIO organizer. At Nice's request, Burke announced that the plant would not reopen. The governor was "greatly encouraged."[52]

For the next four days company and union negotiators worked out the details of a settlement. Burke finally agreed to reinstate "certain" laid-off workers, consider a wage increase, and disavow the Employees Protective Association. The union agreed to ban sit-downs. Allan Haywood arrived at the crucial moment to help Carney sell the agreement at a ratification meeting on September 1. Reed and Rank did not object, though they were not specifically mentioned. Afterward a parade and much "shouting and cheering and singing" informed Cumberland citizens of the workers' "victory."[53]

Although the September 1 agreement had little effect on the operation of the plant, it seemed to say, like the Akron Goodyear agreement, that the balance of power had shifted, that workers could influence the management of industry. Thanks to Carney, the local also appeared in a better light. Many employees who had shunned it in the past now joined. Union committees became "active in each department . . . ironing out complaints."[54] Burke agreed to a small wage increase in October. Yet a familiar problem also appeared: the rhetoric of the strike had cast the workers' economic plight in bold relief and raised expectations. Why shouldn't Kelly workers have the same benefits as Akron workers? The modest character of the 1936 agreement became increasingly apparent. By January 1937, a government investigator reported the "utmost bitterness" among the Kelly employees.[55]

The discontent took a familiar form. Despite the agreement, sit-downs began in the late fall. None of them was "of a serious nature" though production was "somewhat curtailed."[56] Early in January, for example, forty truck-tire builders refused to work from 11:00 P.M. to 6:00 A.M. to protest the discharge of a fellow builder for making a defective tire. The sit-down "was marked by perfect discipline, order, and . . . staunch and grim determination." By morning company officials had agreed to reinstate

---

[52] *Cumberland Evening Times*, Aug. 24, 26, 1936; J. E. O'Conner to Kerwin, Aug. 26, Sept. 2, 1936, FMCS Papers, RG 280, File 182/1586; *ABJ*, Aug. 27, 1936.

[53] *Cumberland Evening Times*, Aug. 31, Sept. 1, 2, 1936; *ABJ*, Sept. 1, 1936.

[54] *URW* 1 (Nov. 1936): 5.

[55] Arthur C. Hungerford to FMCS, Jan. 25, 1937, FMCS Papers, RG 280, File 182/1586.

[56] *Cumberland Evening Times*, Jan. 20, 1937.

the man and to discharge workers "only in extreme cases." A tire builder boasted that he was "beginning to feel like a human being."[57]

Given this atmosphere, it was only a matter of time before the workers revived the wage issue. On January 15, 1937, tire builders on the afternoon and evening shifts requested new time studies of all their rates, which was tantamount to demanding a general wage increase. On January 19, the night-shift tire builders repeated the request. When company officials rejected it they refused to work. Soon other departments had to shut down, and at 6:00 A.M., the superintendent closed the plant. The tire builders and their allies, three hundred to four hundred in all, remained in the factory. More than one hundred of them stayed for fifteen days.

Carney again directed the strike. "Keep them in there until a better wage is granted," he insisted, "or there will be sit-downs every week from now on." A union resolution in favor of the sit-down won overwhelmingly; the vote was 397 to 6 at the union hall and 118 to 3 in the plant. For those on the outside, the biggest job was supplying the strikers. They prepared meals "which were taken to the plant gate and passed to the men."[58] Inside the plant the men formed a "semi-military organization" with a leader and "corps of assistants." They spent most of their time "reading, playing games, visiting and telling tall stories. Two radios blare constantly throughout the day and evening. An orchestra, consisting of a guitar, banjo and mouth harp furnished occasional programs."[59]

After prolonged and often bitter negotiations, Haywood and Burke concluded a new agreement on February 3. The strikers agreed to return to work while union and company officials discussed new base rates and the reinstatement of Reed and Rank. If the negotiations were not completed within three weeks, the union was free to strike again. The talks resulted in modest wage increases, an informal system of seniority within departments, and the reemployment of Reed, Rank, and other union members furloughed in 1935. The workers responded enthusiastically. In February alone, the local initiated four hundred new members; by April, it claimed 96 percent of the Kelly employees. The handful of holdouts would be "cast aside and thrown into the scrap heap."[60] An NLRB election eight months later confirmed that 77 percent of Kelly workers favored the URW. Though Kelly-Springfield managers remained as "stubborn as a mule," they could hardly deny the local's power.[61]

[57] *The Rubberneck*, Jan. 1937.

[58] *Cumberland Evening Times*, Jan. 23, 1937.

[59] *The Rubberneck*, Feb. 2, 1937.

[60] *URW* 2 (April 1937): 2.

[61] *URW* 2 (Aug. 1937): 1; ibid. (Dec. 1937): 1; Local 26, Minutes, Executive Board, April 7, 1936, Local 26 File; *Cumberland Evening Times*, Aug. 13, 1937.

For Dalrymple and the URW officers there was less reason for celebration. The Kelly-Springfield settlements of September 1936 and February 1937 enhanced the local's stature but did not demonstrate that the URW was necessary or inevitable. To those familiar with the Akron upheavals, the Cumberland situation looked distressingly similar. Worker militancy, not the URW, had proven inescapable; the union remained a suspect entity. A determined Goodyear management could still hope to escape a long-term accommodation. Indeed, within six months it began to shift original-equipment orders from Cumberland to a new plant in Jackson, Michigan. By the end of the year, employment had declined to one-half the 1936 peak, and Cumberland began to look more and more like Akron.[62]

OTHER COMMUNITIES

"There was a period," recalled Rex Murray of the months between the Goodyear strike and the recession of 1937, when the URW "could have organized a vast majority of the . . . industry. But we missed the boat. Things changed after."[63] Gadsden and Cumberland were the ends of a spectrum of challenges that union leaders faced during the final months of the recovery. Each factory and town were different, but the URW "missed the boat" essentially for the same reasons AFL organizers failed between 1933 and 1935. Employers remained obdurate, the labor movement was too weak to provide effective assistance, and civic leaders valued industrial growth above other goals, including social harmony and peace.

The rubber industry's one notable "progressive" employer, the U.S. Rubber Company, continued its conciliatory approach to the URW and the CIO after 1935. Cyrus Ching, now a vice-president, seemingly had more influence than ever. In his memoirs, he recalled that "about once a week or more frequently for about six months, the chairman of . . . our Board [Francis Davis] would call me up and say, 'Donaldson Brown [representative of the du Pont interests] is going to call you . . . .' And he would call me at home. We'd talk and argue for sometimes longer than an hour . . . and he tried to convince me that we were wrong in . . . trying to get along with the union."[64] The key words were "talk and argue." Ching had to listen but he did not have to agree. He retained substantial antonomy, probably for two reasons. The first was personal. He was a seasoned executive, a survivor of the housecleaning that followed Davis's arrival and, by his own admission, a wily bureaucrat. The second was economic. Ching was undoubtedly sincere when he advocated a liberal approach to the URW, but

[62] *ABJ*, Nov. 23, 1937.

[63] Rex Murray, interview with author, Sept. 19, 1972.

[64] Cyrus Ching, Oral History Memoir, Columbia University, 3: 377.

his convictions hardly opened the floodgates to Carney or Lesley; quite the opposite. Until late 1937 U.S. Rubber had fewer URW members than the other integrated companies. Ching's central achievement was to foster a reputation as an enlightened manager and simultaneously keep the URW at arm's length. Davis, Brown, and the du Ponts must have been impressed.

Although the evidence is distressingly incomplete, it suggests that Ching's policies contributed substantially to the URW's problems. By eliminating the rhetoric of labor-management conflict, the company's "progressive" approach often made the organizer's job more difficult. Wages and working conditions in U.S. Rubber plants were similar to wages and working conditions at Goodyear or Goodrich plants, but the atmosphere was different. Local unions became strong in U.S. Rubber plants only where a coterie of activists believed, like Ching, that unions were good for their own sake.

The experiences of URW locals in the Los Angeles and Detroit tire plants illustrate the effects of the Ching approach. Los Angeles was notoriously open shop; Detroit, at least after 1933, was pro-union. Yet Local 44 remained the strongest of the Los Angeles locals, while Local 101, chartered only in 1937, was the least successful of the potentially large URW locals. Local 44's growth was due mostly to Herbert Wilson and twenty or so other activists, concentrated in the curing department. Despite Wilson's presence—or possibly because of it—the union had trouble attracting the all-important tire builders. They were "prima donnas" who wanted "to run things" and talked about forming a separate union. Only when the local elected a tire-builder vice-president did they participate.[65] In contrast, U.S. Rubber officials were exceedingly cooperative. They abolished the Factory Council after the URW won an NLRB election in late 1936 and seemed "almost happy" to work with Wilson and his lieutenants, perhaps because the union officers in turn were cooperative. The union did more "to keep the people regimented than the company could."[66] The Samson situation was evidence that a "progressive" relationship paid dividends for both sides.

In Detroit, the company was so accommodating that the workers saw no reason to abandon the Factory Council, formed in 1933. Prodded by Burns, who had visited the plant and learned about the "merry-go-round" and other labor-saving innovations, Dalrymple sent Carney in the fall of 1936. Carney reported that the plant was "one of the hardest nuts to crack in the entire industry."[67] Ching thought otherwise. He began to worry about sit-downs or other disruptive actions that might imperil the company's recov-

[65] George Crawford, interview with author, Aug. 17, 1977.

[66] *URW* 1 (Sept. 1936): 5; George Crawford interview.

[67] *SCLN* 14 (Dec. 30, 1936): 1; *ABJ*, Sept. 16, 1936.

ery. Finally, "out of a clear sky," he called Dalrymple. He complained that if he "didn't know any more about organizing the employees of the United States Rubber Company than you do," he would "quit the job." At his suggestion they met in Pittsburgh on May 11 and talked for nearly twelve hours. Ching promised to "put no obstacles" in Dalrymple's way, providing he guaranteed that the "union officers who were elected locally were responsible people."[68] He then called the Detroit plant manager to set up a meeting with Dalrymple. From that point, Local 101 grew rapidly. At the time of the Pittsburgh meeting, it had only a few hundred members and faced a serious challenge from the company union. By the end of the summer, it had grown to two thousand four hundred members and by early 1938, to five thousand. "Relations with the company," the local secretary reported, "have been progressing smoothly with . . . much evidence of mutual advantage."[69]

The other Los Angeles locals confronted more traditional problems. Goodrich Local 43 was involved in "just a big scrap constantly."[70] Bob Roberts, the International representative in California after mid-1936, described the conflict as a "bitter struggle."[71] Union sympathizers at the Goodyear plant, where the local had expired in 1935, faced hostile managers as well as an Industrial Assembly and its successor, the Goodyear Employees Association. They believed company officials were ready to use "every other means" except violence. Several of them were fired in late 1936. When Goodyear textile workers organized and demanded wages comparable to the rubber workers', the company closed the mill and shifted production to Georgia. The wage demand was the "breaking point."[72] Firestone unionists fared no better. Company hostility and the discharge of leaders like "Red" Humphreys and Ed Barnes forced them underground and frightened away most prospective members. At the end of 1936 the Goodyear and Firestone plants remained essentially unorganized.

The sense of "labor on the march" and Roberts's presence brought important changes in the spring of 1937. Besides experience and oratorical skills, Roberts provided the beleaguered California outposts with a tangible link to the remote International. His support and encouragement helped Local 43 defeat an independent union in an NLRB election and aided Goodyear workers in forming Local 131. Roberts's strategy at Goodyear was to recruit Industrial Assembly leaders such as George Burdon, a popular,

[68] Ching, Oral History Memoir, 1: 20, 3: 347.

[69] *URW* 3 (Jan. 1938): 5; ibid. (Feb. 1938): 1.

[70] Floyd Gartrell, interview with author, Aug. 15, 1977.

[71] George B. Roberts, Speech, n.d., Roberts Papers, Box 2.

[72] Sherman Hardaway, interview with author, Dec. 14, 1977; Edward Barnes, interview with author, Dec. 14, 1977; Hugh Allen, *The House of Goodyear* (Akron, 1949), p. 352.

charismatic individual known for his theatrical performances. By late 1936 Roberts had won over Burdon. Together, they attracted others. By May 1937, Local 131 could count forty to fifty activists, the type "that spread out and engulfed the rest of the people." After considering a strike "to head off the organizing activities" of the Employees Association, Local 131 leaders demanded an NLRB election.[73] In September, they won a narrow victory and became, like the Local 2 and 26 officers, temporarily dominant but insecure. By that time only Firestone Local 100, which Roberts had hoped would become "the largest Rubber Local on the West Coast," had failed to live up to its potential.[74]

In Kitchener, Ontario, the "Akron of Canada," and the neighboring communities where U.S. manufacturers had located to avoid Canadian tariffs, union progress also depended on local conditions. Before 1936 the only organizations were local and ephemeral. Mill-room workers at the Firestone plant in Hamilton had organized in 1935, for example, but faced insurmountable obstacles: a hostile management, a company union, and an indifferent URW.[75] In November 1936, Haywood visited Kitchener and found that a group at Merchants Rubber, U.S. Rubber's Canadian footwear subsidiary, had been meeting secretly since May and wanted a charter. Employees at the nearby Goodrich factory were also interested. Dalrymple sent Lesley to help them. The former sit-down leader proceeded with uncharacteristic subtlety:

A joint meeting of the Merchants and Goodrich workers was arranged secretly. Eighty workers were expected. At the last moment the meeting was switched from the hall originally scheduled. Two Goodrich foremen waited in the cold . . . in vain to see which workers went to the meeting. While the foremen shivered in the cold, ninety workers . . . listened to the story of the Goodyear strike.[76]

Both locals grew rapidly. After a sit-down at the Goodrich plant on March 23, Lesley led a ten-day conventional strike that resulted in a substantial wage increase and a promise of consultations before layoffs. The Goodrich strike was a "turning point" in the history of the Canadian locals.[77]

In the other plants, however, the URW made little immediate progress. After Firestone workers held an open meeting, "members of the new union

---

[73] Sherman Hardaway interview; Edward Barnes interview; Towne Nylander to NLRB, June 22, 1937, NLRB Papers, RG 25, Case 11-R-169.

[74] Ralph Clark, interview with author, Aug. 16, 1977; George B. Roberts, Speech, Roberts Papers.

[75] "A Brief History of Local 113," p. 5, Local 113 File, URW Archives.

[76] URW 2 (Feb.1937): 9; Kim Adair, Peter Pautler, David Strang, "The U.R.W.A. and the Struggle for Union Recognition: 1937–39," in Terry Copp. ed, Industrial Unionism in Kitchener 1937–47 (Olora, Ontario, 1976), p. 2.

[77] ABJ, March 25, April 3, 1937; Adair, Pautler, Strang, "The U.R.W.A.," p. 5.

were fired out of hand."[78] In June, workers at the Seiberling plant in Toronto struck after the company discharged all of the new union's officers. Fifty men picketed for more than three months before admitting defeat.[79] In September at the Kaufman Company, a large independent footwear manufacturer, members of newly formed Local 88 struck to protest discrimination against union members. After more than a month and no sign of a settlement, the provincial minister of labour virtually forced the company to accept an agreement that included a seniority plan. The strike was a "shattering defeat" for the union.[80]

The URW made rapid gains in eastern footwear and mechanical goods plants as the International's finances improved and Burns hired more organizers. Marchiando, the most important of the new organizers, found that many eastern rubber workers were eager to join, provided there was no danger of reprisals. For a large number, the union became a "way of life."[81] By early 1937 the URW had new strongholds at Gilmer Belt in Philadelphia, American Hard Rubber in Butler, New Jersey, and Hodgman Rubber in Framingham, Massachusetts. Of special significance was Trenton. When Burns and Marchiando appeared there in late 1936, rumors spread that they had been involved in the failed 1933 effort and the Trenton workers proved "hard to approach." Once they convinced the workers that the rumors were false, they found a receptive audience.[82] In April Marchiando led employees of the Thermoid Company, the largest Trenton firm, in a four-week strike. Despite an injunction, an aggressive state police contingent, and a tear gas attack by local police, the strikers prevented anyone from entering the plant. The management finally conceded higher wages, more generous overtime pay, vacations, and a formal grievance procedure.[83]

Despite gains in Trenton and other eastern cities, the URW triumph was far from complete. The Naugatuck local remained small and the Armstrong Tire local, in West Haven, Connecticut, collapsed completely in the face of managerial opposition. Most workers at the Goodrich Hood plant favored an independent union. Worse still, the AFL began to organize rubber

[78] "Brief History of Local 113," p. 6.
[79] "Report of General President S. H. Dalrymple," in *Report of Officers to 2nd Annual Convention, U.R.W. of A., Sept. 12th to 18th, 1937, Akron, Ohio* (Akron, 1937), p. 16.
[80] N. H. Eagle, interview with author, March 14, 1974; *SCLN*, Nov. 5, 1937; Adair, Pautler, Strang, "The U.R.W.A.," pp. 12–13.
[81] John Marchiando, interview with author, Dec. 22, 1977.
[82] "Report of Vice President" in *Report, 1937*, p. 17; Harmon Splitter, interview with author, Aug. 16, 1977.
[83] *URW* 2 (Feb. 1937): 3; ibid. (April 1937): 1; ibid. (June 1937): 2.

workers in eastern cities, foreshadowing a problem that would haunt the URW for the rest of the decade.

In the Midwest the sense of "labor on the march" had reached even the smallest Ohio or Indiana hamlet by mid-1936. URW organizers revived Local 3 at Ohio Rubber and established locals at Inland Rubber in Dayton; at Republic Rubber in Youngstown, which had previously employed thugs to keep the union out; and at Bowling Green Rubber, where UAW members from the nearby Toledo Chevrolet plant helped. Union representatives in Chicago organized a Goodyear warehouse and established a local at the Dryden Rubber Company despite opposition from a company union and "lots of intimidation among the girl workers by foreladies."[84] When Dalrymple and Roberts distributed copies of the *United Rubber Worker* at the gates of the Johnson Rubber Company in May 1936, Johnson executives "peeped out of the window in amazement" at their temerity.[85]

When their employers were not sufficiently accommodating, midwestern rubber workers often adopted the militant techniques of the Akron tire builders. In March 1936, when the general manager of the Seiberling Company in Barberton reduced wages, members of Local 18 struck. Dalrymple negotiated an agreement rescinding the cut, but the workers refused to return to their jobs until they had "a signed agreement that . . . no other wage cut would be put into effect until the committee had first been notified."[86] Three months later, Seiberling employees sat down for seven hours to gain the reinstatement of a woman who had been fired for arguing with her foreman. In August they struck for ten days to win a 10-percent wage increase, and in April 1937, to win another increase. In August 1937 they struck for five weeks to protest the discharge of two union activists. Eagle finally negotiated a settlement that featured "an arbitration plan" that removed the supervisors' power to discipline workers.[87]

Local 14 members at La Crosse Rubber Mills, a footwear manufacturer in La Crosse, Wisconsin, also became more assertive. Though organized since the NRA period, they had not been secure enough to confront the management. Several sit-downs in the summer of 1936 increased their confidence and in early 1937, Local 14 president Floyd Robinson launched a campaign against an independent union that the company favored. On January 12, probably by prearrangement, union members in the mill and cutting rooms sat down to protest the presence of nonunion employees. At

---

[84] *ABJ*, Aug. 10, 1936; *URW* 2 (Feb. 1937): 10; ibid. (March 1937): 5; ibid. (June 1937): 5; Harley C. Anthony, interview with author, April 11, 1972.

[85] *URW* 1 (May 1936): 1.

[86] Dalrymple to W. H. Chapman, March 6, 1936, Local 26 File.

[87] *ATP*, June 15, 16, 1936; *ABJ*, April 17, Sept. 2, 3, 27, 1936; "Report of General President S. H. Dalrymple," in *Report, 1937*, p. 7.

least two hundred of them remained inside for five days, until Robinson and organizer Charles Lanning decided to evacuate the plant and begin negotiations.[88] For five more weeks company and union negotiators argued over the union demand for exclusive representation. Only after the strikers broke up a meeting called by the independent union to approve a company peace plan did the management agree to an NLRB representation election. On February 26 Local 14 won, 712 to 435. After that, the negotiations progressed rapidly. An agreement ratified on March 3 made the URW the exclusive bargaining agent.[89]

There were, finally, a handful of midwestern Gadsdens where no amount of assistance or militancy could overcome the opposition of local employers and their allies. One was Norwalk, Ohio, where activists at tiny Maple City Rubber Company organized twenty-five of thirty-six employees and demanded a written agreement in September 1936. The managers refused and Haywood and Eagle failed to change their minds. In early October, when the Maple City employees struck, the company obtained an injunction against mass picketing and encouraged the police to arrest union activists. Lesley was charged with using profane language, and Eagle, with throwing a tomato. Dalrymple feared that the company's strategy was to have all the pickets arrested and then hire nonunion workers. Norwalk was "a second Gadsden, only of a different nature."[90] After several confrontations between pickets and police, the county prosecutor ordered the plant closed.[91] The company held out for another month before accepting a compromise settlement that did not include recognition or a contract.

Equally hostile was Noblesville, Indiana, where the Schacht Rubber Company began to make automobile parts after the owners secretly sold out to Firestone. When the workers organized and obtained a URW charter in the summer of 1937, William Schacht, the manager, became alarmed. He fired local activists, including John Harnish, the union president. "When the union would hold meetings, Mr. Schacht would drive his large automobile up in front of the meeting place . . . [and] his foreman, Mr. Pollock, would parade up and down in front of the meeting hall."[92] When Floyd Robinson, now a URW organizer, arrived to help the local, Schacht employees searched his hotel room. After several meetings with Robinson, Schacht agreed to post a memorandum spelling out certain changes in com-

---

[88] *La Crosse Tribune*, Jan. 15, 1937; *URW* 2 (Feb. 1937): 7.

[89] *La Crosse Tribune*, March 4, 1937; *URW* 2 (March 1937): 1.

[90] "Report of General President," in *Report, 1937*, p. 16; *ABJ*, Oct. 2, 1936; Dalrymple to Brophy, Oct. 7, 1936, CIO Papers, URW file.

[91] *ABJ*, Oct. 23, 1936.

[92] Colonel C. Sawyer, "Conference Memoir," Dec. 7, 1937, NLRB Papers, RG 25, Box 214, Case 149.

pany policy, including wage increases. But the memorandum mysteriously disappeared and Schacht refused to honor its provisions. Pleading the loss of a Ford contract, he then laid off half the employees, including a large percentage of the local's recruits.[93] Schacht himself became inaccessible. By the end of 1937, the Schacht workers were demoralized and the URW had little to show for its efforts.

The closest northern parallel to Gadsden, ironically, may have been Jackson, Michigan, a comparatively strong union town. Goodyear purchased an abandoned auto parts plant there in late 1936, and, in emulation of U.S. Rubber, created a specialized, technologically advanced factory devoted to original-equipment production. When it opened in June 1937, the Jackson plant was supposedly "the most modern and efficient tire factory in America."[94] Most of the supervisors and a large Flying Squadron contingent came from Akron. Many anti-union workers also transferred to Jackson. The company introduced its characteristic personnel program.

In August, when Goodyear held an "open house" for local citizens, Lesley and two officers from Local 101 in Detroit appeared. As they toured the factory, a number of the Akron men recognized them. When they emerged, several workers, including a Goodyear policeman, attacked them, beating Lesley on the head and face.[95] The local newspaper refused to cover the incident and Jackson city officials, delighted with the new plant, were unsympathetic. After six months of effort the URW still had no local in Jackson.

GADSDEN, 1937

The obstacles to URW progress, apparent in every area at the height of the sit-down era, were nowhere clearer than in Gadsden. In the months after the Tolson Building riot, the URW had every advantage it enjoyed in Akron, Cumberland, and Los Angeles: an expanding economy, generous assistance from state and federal authorities, a core of courageous activists, and the resources of the burgeoning labor movement. Yet these assets were no match for a hostile management, an anti-union group committed to violence, and an intimidated local government.

The first harbinger of disaster was the fate of Grady Cleere, whose contacts with the Akron organizers in June 1936 became known to Self and Bottoms through an informer. The following September, when Cleere attended a Labor Day rally in Birmingham and talked with several CIO officers, a "friend" reported him to Self and Bottoms again. When Cleere

[93] *URW* 2 (June 1937): 7.
[94] Allen, *House of Goodyear*, p. 362.
[95] *URW* 2 (Aug. 1937): 1.

returned to Gadsden, Self called him in. "The heat is on," Self told him, "and you had better not go back to the Goodyear. Those boys have already been telling me they were going to get you." When Cleere replied that he could defend himself, Self added that "a dead man is no good . . . you won't be safe at home or on the streets of Gadsden. . . . If I was you I would pick up and leave."[96] Shaken, Cleere decided to quit his job. But he did not "pick up and leave." He contacted URW leaders and provided them with a detailed account of the Gadsden anti-union conspiracy. His "conversion" was the one positive result of the southern strategy.

One day in late 1936, Cleere noticed that Self's car was following him. Fearing an attack, he sought refuge in the law office where his wife Mildred still worked. As the Cleeres watched from an upstairs window, Self and several other men waited on the sidewalk below, one of them with a pistol in each hand. Sheriff Leath lounged nearby. Escaping via a back door, Cleere fled to his brother-in-law's house where he hid until union officials arranged for the state police to drive him to Birmingham.[97] Cleere stayed briefly with union associates in Alabama and Georgia and then went to Akron, where he found a job at the Seiberling plant. Mildred Cleere remained at her job in Gadsden until April 1937, paying off debts. She found it "quite difficult to stay here and work. . . . All of the officials of this town . . . are bitter towards Grady."[98] When Dalrymple found her a secretarial job in Akron, she too left Gadsden. The Cleeres' flight was a lesson for other Gadsden workers.

For a brief period the Gadsden unionists were more fortunate. Zella Morgan wrote on January 1, 1937 that "the members are in higher spirits now than they have been since they were put out."[99] After the Jones & Laughlin decision in April, Goodyear abolished the Industrial Assembly and reinstated the union members laid off in June 1936. Local leaders believed that "this move . . . makes an opening for us." They urged members to "come out in the open with their organizing" and persuaded Dalrymple to employ a temporary organizer, Firestone employee and Gadsden native B. T. Garner.[100] The local had several well-attended meetings in April and May.

However, they were not the only Goodyear employees who became more active. On April 19, after Plant Manager Michaels met with the Industrial Assembly for the last time, most of the representatives reassembled at the Goodyear golf course to form the Etowah Rubber Workers Organization. Their goal was "to get ahead of this damned c.i.o." For several days,

[96] NLRB Hearing, pp. 2720–21, NLRB Papers, RG 25, Box 214, Case 149.
[97] Ibid., pp. 2729–36; Mildred Cleere Neill, interview with author, June 27, 1976, differs on some details.
[98] Mrs. L. G. Cleere to Dalrymple, March 24, 1937, Local 12 File, URW Archives.
[99] Zella Morgan to Dalrymple, Jan. 1, 1937, Local 12 File.
[100] Morgan to Dalrymple, April 20, 1937, Local 12 File.

ERWO men went "from machine to machine with membership cards and pencils in their hands." On April 24 they held a mass meeting to adopt a constitution and on May 4 asked for recognition, claiming one thousand two hundred members out of one thousand five hundred employees. Michaels agreed to post a notice recognizing the EWRO as the bargaining agent for its members.[101]

Competition between Local 12 and the ERWO soon led to new outbreaks of violence. On May 19 a group of ERWO members attacked J. O. Glenn outside his house for wearing a badge that mocked the ERWO. On May 31, Jimmy Karam, one of the most feared of the "thugs," drove his car into an automobile carrying several union members and then threatened the occupants with a shotgun. When a city policeman threatened to arrest Karam, Sheriff Leath waved him away, explaining that Karam was doing "private" work for him. On June 7, a group of men savagely beat union member B. E. Cleveland in the Goodyear parking lot, supposedly for insulting several women. On June 9 Karam and Self met Garner in a restaurant and implied they would murder him. A week later Speedy Brock and Leon Long, ERWO activists, confronted J. L. Miller, a Local 12 member, at his house. Brock held a gun while Long attacked Miller. When Miller fought back, "knocked Long into the bathtub [and] turned scalding hot water . . . on him," Brock fled up a flight of stairs and jumped out a second-story window.[102]

These were the most notable incidents in a wave of labor violence that crested in the summer of 1937. Besides the Local 12 resurgence, the Steel Workers Organizing Committee had launched an organizing campaign at Gulf States that produced more threats and beatings. AFL members were also targets for the first time. A group of blacks, apparently working for Self, abducted Andrew Brown, a black Hod Carriers organizer, beat him, and left him by the side of the road. When local police found him, they called a doctor who was a member of the city commission and whose treatment consisted of asking Brown if he was a CIO organizer, if he "had been to Russia," and if he "had read the propaganda of the Communists."[103] Several weeks later, another group of men attacked Ollie Walls, a molder. Sheriff Leath was apologetic. "God Damn the C.I.O.," he explained. "I like the molders here pretty good, but God Damn the C.I.O."[104] The "sit-

---

[101] NLRB, *Decisions and Orders*, pp. 382–85. "Report on Conditions, Goodyear Plant, Gadsden, Alabama," n.d., Local 12 File; *ABJ*, Sept. 1, 1937.

[102] NLRB, *Decisions and Orders*, pp. 292–97; B. T. Garner to Dalrymple, June 16, 1937, Local 12 File.

[103] See "Report of Citizens Committee on Gadsden, Alabama" (Birmingham, 1937), pp. 9–22, 31; Yelverton Cowherd to Dalrymple, May 19, 1937, NLRB Papers, RG 25, Box 214, Case 149.

[104] "Report of Citizens Committee," p. 25.

uation in Gadsden," concluded Charles N. Feidelson, an NLRB investigator, bordered on "a state of war."[105]

Yet none of the incidents in 1937 occurred in the Goodyear plant or was
directly linked to the company. When Holmes and other Local 12 activists
returned to work in May, Craigmile warned ERWO members that union
members were not to be harmed. On several occasions Goodyear supervisors stopped ERWO men from assaulting Local 12 members. A foreman's
intervention, for example, forced ERWO men to go to Glenn's house and
beat him there.[106] Goodyear officials nevertheless continued to oppose Local 12 by every other means. Beginning in May, they discharged twenty-
one union members and demoted two others. With two exceptions, the unfortunate employees had all joined Local 12 in the spring of 1937. Some of
them may have been punished for other reasons, but the timing could hardly
have appeared coincidental to union members or prospective members.

As the anti-union campaign increased in intensity, the prospects of a
major clash between the two camps grew. When Glenn appeared at a union
meeting after his beating, Local 12 members became "enraged" and "tore
up furniture" to make weapons. By late May many union supporters carried guns, and when Cowherd or Garner visited Gadsden, they traveled
with four to six armed bodyguards. Union men talked vaguely about killing
Karam, who apparently believed he was in danger and left for California.
NLRB investigators later concluded that most of the talk of a union counterattack was an ERWO effort to discredit Local 12. In fact, union members
were not "guilty of any acts of violence or threats thereof in Gadsden."[107]

In any case, the violence subsided in late June. Whether the calm was
due to the prospect of retaliation or the decline of the union, the fate of
Local 12 was unmistakable. Garner acknowledged in early June that the
"membership drive has almost stopped."[108] President Cecil Holmes reported ten days later that "the members have become very much discouraged."[109] The firings were probably more demoralizing than the beatings.
Local 12 leaders assured recruits that the federal government and the URW
would help them if they were fired, but Dalrymple refused to honor their
promises because of his meager resources and concern that they might take
undue advantage of such assistance. The government was quick to investigate but slow to offer substantive help. The victims of 1937 did not regain
their jobs or lost wages until 1940 or later.

In desperation, Holmes and other union leaders played their only ace, an

---

[105] Charles Feidelson to Benedict Wolf, June 1, 1937, Feidelson to Fahy, June 19, 1937,
NLRB Papers, RG 25, Box 214, Case 149.

[106] NLRB, Decisions and Orders, p. 373; "Report of Citizens Committee," p. 18.

[107] NLRB, Decisions and Orders, pp. 402–406.

[108] Garner to Dalrymple, June 8, 1937, Local 12 File.

[109] C. S. Holmes to Dalrymple, June 19, 1937, Local 12 File.

appeal to public opinion. With the help of the local CLU, they organized a citizens' inquiry into labor violence in Gadsden in early July. Prominent southern liberals conducted hearings and published a report that detailed many of the beatings. The NLRB was their other hope. During board hearings on the Gadsden violence, which began in Gadsden on August 19 and continued, with several interruptions, for nearly four months, Cowherd continually pressured government attorneys for more charges and a tougher, anti-Goodyear stand. At one point, he accused the regional director, Mortimer Kollender, of being "buffaloed into an attitude of greater leniency towards the company than should be extended" and threatened to complain to Dalrymple and John L. Lewis. Kollender replied that his role prevented him from adopting a more accusatory stance.[110]

As Cowherd probably feared, the union won nearly all the battles but lost the war. The hearings lived up to URW expectations, with graphic accounts of beatings, admissions of complicity by ERWO members, and Cleere's portrayal of the inner workings of the anti-union group. But a sated public no longer found narratives of union struggles as appetizing as it had a year before. The spread of the sit-down movement, the great auto and steel strikes, and the return of hard times in mid-1937 put the problems of Local 12 in a new and less favorable perspective. The escalation of labor-management conflict in 1936 and 1937 also clogged the NLRB, permitting Goodyear to delay action by drawing out the hearings. Kollender wrote that the company and its exceedingly long-winded local attorney, Col. O. R. Hood, were "putting on the most fulsome defense," which was "designed to embarrass and discredit the Board and its agents."[111]

The company's strategy was to disassociate itself from the violence, portray union members as irresponsible individuals, and suggest that Gadsden was beyond the pale of conventional civilities. A long stream of company witnesses testified to the violent intentions of Local 12 members. Self added a recital of Cleere's criminal associations, and Hood insisted that the hearing officer go to Atlanta, where one of Cleere's friends, serving a prison term, provided additional evidence of his misdeeds. Amid the welter of accusations and rebuttal, the union charges lost much of their original potency. By December, when the hearings finally ended, nearly everyone associated with them was exhausted and dissatisfied. James S. Jackson of the *Akron Beacon Journal* visited Gadsden in November and found that "the town is thoroughly tired of the labor board hearings."[112]

As if to confirm this judgment, the end of the hearings marked the start of a new wave of attacks on union members. On January 5, 1938, a group

[110] Kollender to Fahy, Sept. 25, 1937, NLRB Papers, RG 25, Box 214, Case 149.
[111] Ibid.
[112] *ABJ*, Nov. 22, 1937. Also see NLRB, *Decisions and Orders*, pp. 310–11.

of ERWO members assaulted four union men as they passed the plant office and waylaid Loui Allen as he emerged from the shower in the locker room. Holmes was also there:

[Allen] came to me in the locker room just about [k]nocked out. Just then about five men came up to my back and hit me over the head with a blackjack. I got hold of a mill knife and struck at the leader of the bunch and he ran. I followed him out in the lobby . . . where I caught this man and cut him two or three places . . . while this mob beat me from behind. [A. C.] Michaels came out at this point and it all stopped. . . . I told him that he could stop this if he wanted to, but about all he would say is that it was a very unfortunate situation.[113]

Other incidents followed during the spring of 1938. Finally convinced that they had no choice but to abandon their jobs or the union, one hundred Local 12 members voted on May 15 to stay away from the plant until they were assured protection. Approximately sixty of them carried out their threat. After a week, they were discharged and replaced. For the time being, the union defeat in Gadsden was complete.

One final event provided an epitaph for the southern strategy. Cleere, in Akron since late 1936, lost his job in the layoffs of late 1937 and another job at the U.S. Rubber plant in Detroit in early 1938. Returning to Akron, he became a guard at an illegal gambling club in the nearby community of Boston Heights. He was sitting in an automobile outside the club on the morning of July 7 when he was shot and killed. Another guard claimed that he had accidentally committed suicide while playing russian roulette. The sheriff accepted this explanation over the protests of Mildred Cleere and URW leaders, who insisted that he had been murdered because of his Gadsden associations and testimony. Noting the sheriff's perfunctory investigation, the club owner's underworld ties, and rumors that Goodyear police officials had been watching Cleere, they demanded a thorough investigation. The sheriff reopened the case but only succeeded in showing how incompetently he had handled the original inquiry. A URW call for an NLRB investigation brought no response.[114] Lacking additional evidence, union leaders were helpless. For Akron and Gadsden unionists, and for larger groups of prospective members, North and South, Cleere's death became a warning of the hazards of union membership. By the summer of 1938 few rubber workers needed an additional reminder.

[113] Holmes to Dalrymple, n.d., Local 12 File.

[114] *ATP*, July 7, 8, 1938; *ABJ*, July 7, 8, Oct. 28, 1938; S. Denlinger to J. W. Madden, Aug. 24, 1938, Local 12 File.

CHAPTER TEN

Setbacks, 1937–1938

A FORMER Indiana college student and public school teacher, Leland S. Buckmaster (1894–1967) was probably the best prepared of all URW leaders for the more threatening environment of 1938.[1] Together with a successful career as a tire builder, Buckmaster's education won him the respect and envy of Firestone workers. So, too, did a candor that often bordered on bluntness. As union president, he could point to other achievements: a disciplined local, the industry's most important contract, and a solid turnout for Patterson in 1937. But would his background and experience make a difference as Firestone and the other integrated firms "decentralized" to low-wage, nonunion communities and a severe recession devastated the Akron labor force? Buckmaster's problems, symptomatic of the problems of many local leaders after 1937, raised another, more fundamental question: Would the labor movement of the 1930s be any more durable than its predecessors?

Goodyear in Turmoil

The Akron crisis had its roots in the labor-management turmoil of the NRA years, the URW resurgence of 1936, and the sit-down movement. The cumulative effects were a perception of the city as antibusiness and a move among executives of the integrated firms to decentralize. Union leaders often noted that the large companies had bought or built plants in Los Angeles, Gadsden, and Watertown long before the appearance of the FLUS or the URW. They neglected to add that the pre-Depression acquisitions had not affected the competitiveness or market position of the Akron factories; indeed, the Akron plants had increased their share of total output. The new or expanded plants of the 1930s, at Cumberland, Gadsden, Jackson, Oaks, Memphis, and other cities, were, however, substitutes for the Akron plants. No one blamed the workers exclusively, but no one doubted the link between labor militancy and decentralization. "Never," summarized one observer, "has an industry had the unwisdom of over-centralization called so forcibly to its attention and never has an industry reacted so promptly."[2] A

[1] Gary M. Fink, ed. *Biographical Dictionary of American Labor* (Westport, 1984), p. 134.
[2] Charles B. Coates, "Boomerang in Akron," *Factory Management and Maintenance* 96 (1938): 40.

more sober assessment concluded that union-related turmoil accelerated the decentralization process by five years.[3]

If the sit-downs had been the only problem, Akron's prospects would have improved in 1937 as they became less frequent and disruptive. But two other factors also worked against the city. The first was a growing wage premium. To combat the URW and the sit-downs, the manufacturers had again changed policies in 1936 and granted across-the-board wage increases in May and February 1937. By October 1936 Akron tire workers averaged $.96 per hour and by February 1937, $1.04 per hour. At the beginning of 1937 their rates were 9 to 17 percent higher than the hourly averages of printers, petroleum refinery workers, and auto workers, the highest-paid groups of factory employees.[4] More important, they were 51 percent higher than the average of tire workers outside Akron and Detroit by March 1937.[5] In the mechanical goods departments, the Akron premium was even greater and more threatening because of the labor-intensive character of production.[6] In 1936 Goodyear moved its heel and sole departments to Windsor, Vermont. In 1937 the other Akron manufacturers moved some or all of their mechanical goods production to other, nonunion communities: Goodrich, to Cadillac, Michigan; General Tire, to Wabash, Indiana; and Firestone, to Noblesville, Indiana, and Fall River, Massachusetts. By the end of 1937 Goodrich was the only Akron firm with a substantial mechanical goods operation in Akron.

The second factor was a shift in demand. Tires, like rubber boots and shoes, were familiar products by the 1930s; the expansion of the mid-1930s was impressive only because of the low production levels of the early 1930s. Save for the introduction of rubber-tired farm machinery, it reflected the recovery of the automobile industry. By contrast the expansion of mechanical goods production was based on new products like sponge rubber and insulated cable. In dollar terms, the industry as a whole grew by 42 percent between 1933 and 1937; tires were up 32 percent; boots and shoes, 26 percent; and mechanical goods, 123 percent.[7] This shift contributed to the reinvigoration of U.S. Rubber and the expansion of many of the small companies. It also encouraged the tire firms to diversify their product

[3] *ABJ*, Dec. 16, 1937.

[4] Federal Housing Administration, "Akron, Ohio, Housing Market Analysis" (Washington, 1938), p. 230.

[5] John Dean Gaffey, *The Productivity of Labor in the Rubber Tire Manufacturing Industry* (New York, 1940), p. 172.

[6] Ibid., p. 170.

[7] FHA, "Akron, Ohio, Housing," p. 205; K. E. Knorr, *World Rubber and Its Regulation* (Palo Alto, 1946), p. 48.

lines and divert investment into growth areas, which meant the outlying plants.

By mid-1937 the social costs of these changes were substantial. Decentralization, the end of the Goodyear-Sears tie (which the FTC suit had forced in 1936), and other business developments had eliminated eleven thousand to thirteen thousand jobs in Akron tire plants. Other losses in mechanical goods and the knowledge that the losses were permanent forced local residents to resign themselves to an adjustment period of "several years, perhaps . . . a decade."[8] What they did not anticipate, however, was an additional, devastating blow in the form of a major cyclical downturn. The collapse of the economy in late 1937 marked the beginning of a recession "without precedent in American history."[9] Between May 1937 and June 1938 national income fell by 13 percent, industrial production decreased by 33 percent, and durable goods production declined by 50 percent. Manufacturing employment declined by 23 percent and payrolls, by 35 percent. Unemployment rose from seven to more than ten million.[10] The decline of the rubber industry exceeded the averages. In early 1937 the tire industry had experienced a brief inflationary spiral, as manufacturers passed on escalating rubber and labor costs to consumers. The first signs of trouble appeared in April, when crude rubber prices broke, and in May, when production declined. In July a severe "contraction" began.[11] A sharp drop in auto purchases reduced the demand for tires, sponge rubber, and various hard-rubber products while a more gradual decline in incomes curtailed the sale of consumer products. The federal government's unemployment census of November 1937 reported 15,000 unemployed and 8,000 partially employed Akron residents, and 5,000 others who worked on government relief projects.[12] Workers and union leaders faced conditions reminiscent of the early 1930s.

There was one major difference: the unions now had sufficient power to influence the retrenchment process. This role, one of the obvious benefits of a union presence, forced union leaders and workers to confront painful choices. How would they balance wages and jobs? If reductions had to be made, how would they decide which workers would lose their jobs? Their

[8] FHA, "Akron, Ohio, Housing," pp. 95, 116.

[9] Kenneth D. Roose, *The Economics of Recession and Revival: An Interpretation of 1937–38* (New Haven, 1954), p. 3. This statement probably exaggerates the degree of decline. See Stanley Lebergott, *The Americans: An Economic Record* (New York, 1984), p. 396.

[10] Roose, *The Economics of Recession*, p. 55.

[11] Federal Reserve Board, Fourth District, *Monthly Business Review*, vol. 19, Feb. 27, March 31, May 31, June 30, and Aug. 31, 1937, all p. 4.

[12] FHA, "Akron, Ohio, Housing," p. 94.

responses, formulated in the course of a new round of upheavals, illustrated the possibilities and limits of the union role.

Local 2 members were the first to confront these issues. In June, Goodyear officials informed House that declining sales necessitated a reduction in the labor force. They gave the union the choice of reduced hours or layoffs. Local 2 officers were unable to reach a consensus and authorized an election, which resulted in a narrow 3,047 to 2,711 decision for shorter hours.[13] The issue had split the union, with high-seniority workers, who generally favored layoffs, playing the role of the Industrial Assembly partisans of 1935.[14] As business conditions worsened and the workweek declined to as little as twelve hours in some departments, Slusser asked House for another union decision. The local leaders protested that employees in Gadsden and Los Angeles were working forty hours per week and declined to act until the forthcoming NLRB election strengthened their hand.[15] After the election they again delayed, hoping to include provisions on work sharing and layoffs in a written contract. By September they still had taken no action.

Tensions between company and union officials increased in September and October as the impasse continued and economic conditions worsened. Slusser exacerbated these problems by using his authority to wage a vendetta against House and the Local 2 leaders. He told Robert W. Bruere, a Labor Department conciliator, that he wanted revenge for what the union had done in 1936.[16] In his mind, Local 2 was inextricably associated with the end of the Horatio Alger story that had been his career. The appointment of Edwin J. Thomas as executive vice-president in November 1937 only heightened his bitterness.

In early September, Slusser signaled his new aggressiveness with several provocative actions. For example, he suggested that the company might conduct its own poll, since the union refused to choose between reduced hours and layoffs. Later, when the local finally agreed to the layoff of one thousand seven hundred workers who had been hired in the summer of 1936, he insisted that Flying Squadron members be exempted. After many anxious deliberations and threats of a strike vote, he changed his mind and agreed to include squadron men in the layoff. On October 6 he met union officials and the new NLRB regional director, James P. Miller, and agreed

[13] *ABJ*, June 12, 19, 28, 1937; *SCLN*, June 25, 1937.

[14] Alfred Winslow Jones, *Life, Liberty, and Property: A Story of Conflict and a Measurement of Conflicting Rights* (Philadelphia, 1941), p. 111.

[15] Local 2, Minutes, Membership Meeting, Aug. 8, 1937, Local 2 Archives, Local 2 offices, Akron, Ohio; *ABJ*, June 28, Aug. 6, 1937.

[16] Robert W. Bruere to J. R. Steelman, Oct. 22, 1937, Federal Mediation and Conciliation Service Papers, RG 280, File 182/1010, National Archives.

to post a memorandum citing the reasons for the reductions. Union leaders believed that the memorandum would help placate the workers about to be furloughed. Again, Slusser tried to undercut them by delaying the posting for nearly a week.[17] As a result, a meeting of Local 2 members on October 10 "threatened on a number of occasions to get out of hand." Dalrymple, Denlinger, and local vice-president Ralph Turner (House was ill and unable to attend) narrowly averted a strike vote.

Adding to the unrest was a new policy on grievances. Goodyear executives, Bruere reported;

have recently adopted a policy . . . of refusing to make a record of their detailed agreements arrived at by joint committees, etc. The burden of complaint on the part of committeemen . . . was that no sooner have they reached an agreement with one executive than another would nullify it and that Slusser . . . would agree with them when with them but would reverse himself on appeal from minor executives. All agreements have come to be less than scraps of paper since they are verbal only and repudiated at will.[18]

Slusser exacerbated tensions in the following weeks. On October 14 he announced that Goodyear would furlough an additional one thousand six hundred workers from the tire and tube division in order to give the remaining employees twenty-four hours of work per week. He limited the reduction to the one division, which meant some long-service workers would be included. After several days of anxious negotiations, and repeated threats of a strike vote, he relented and canceled the layoff notice. Shortly afterward he wrote a government official that "we are working along very well with the union committees and . . . are not anticipating any particular trouble."[19] On November 15, without any advance notice, he reinstated the order; on November 18 he rejected union requests for another postponement.

After receiving Slusser's decision on November 18, the local officers met through the afternoon and evening to formulate a response. Convinced that his real objective was to undermine the union, they decided not to send out the notices of a strike vote that the union constitution required. When House emerged from the meeting at 10:00 P.M. and announced a membership meeting for the following Sunday, the workers in the union hall roared their approval. When he added a warning against any "premature steps" there was silence "save for a few scattered hand claps."[20]

[17] *ABJ*, Sept. 10, 11, 14, 20, Oct. 1, 7, 1937; Local 2, Minutes, Membership Meeting, Sept. 19, Oct. 3, 1937, Local 2 Archives.

[18] Bruere to Steelman, Oct. 9, 1937, FMCS Papers, RG 280, File 182/1010.

[19] Slusser to Bruere, Oct. 26, 1937, FMCS Papers, RG 280, File 182/1010. Also see Local 2, Minutes, Executive Board Meeting, Oct. 14, 1937, Local 2 Archives.

[20] *ABJ*, Nov. 19, 1937.

As soon as the union committee had left Slusser's office, he had ordered plant officials to post the layoff notices. Word of the action had spread rapidly. By evening, "east Akron seethed with unrest. Little groups of men gathered in cafes and restaurants and drug stores. . . . Rumors of rank and file plans to close the plants at midnight spread throughout the city." Despite the opposition of union leaders, "the grapevine carried a message to third shift men to stay in the plant and join the fourth shift men when they came on at 12." When House learned of the plan shortly after 10:00 P.M. he called Slusser to appeal for a postponement of the layoff. Slusser again refused. Two hours later, a Plant 2 tire room committeeman "rose at the stroke of midnight, read a list of the workers who were to be . . . laid off, gave the years of service of each man, then demanded: 'What are we going to do about it?' " The answer was apparently unanimous: "Shut down the plant. We'll sit!" Within a few minutes the protest had "paralyzed the entire Goodyear operation."[21] The last of the great sit-downs of the 1930s had begun.

For a day and a half thousands of men occupied the plants. On Thursday night about five hundred strikers remained in Plant 2 and seven hundred stayed in Plant 1. By late Friday their ranks had swelled to nearly four thousand. Many of them, veterans of earlier sit-downs, came with food and decks of cards. Plant 1 workers organized a bingo game and a checker tournament. Periodically, groups of men would parade from department to department "clapping their hands in rhythm and singing marching songs." Though the cafeterias remained open, many strikers ordered sandwiches from neighborhood restaurants, which friends passed through windows. Reporters estimated that local cafes sold two thousand sandwiches "to go" Friday night.[22]

In the meantime union officials worked anxiously to devise an agreement before the Sunday meeting. House and Slusser met shortly after midnight but made no progress. Slusser announced afterward that "the layoff order stands. . . . They can sit down from now until the Fourth of July if they want to."[23] House then called Miller, who promised to come to Akron, and later ordered the evacuation of the plants as a conciliatory gesture. By Saturday morning all of the strikers had gone home. Newspaper stories that Governor Davey had ordered the National Guard to mobilize "caused much uneasiness," but there were no other demonstrations.[24]

[21] Ibid.

[22] *ATP*, Nov. 20, 1937.

[23] *ABJ*, Nov. 19, 1937.

[24] J. P. Miller to National Labor Relations Board, n.d., National Labor Relations Board Papers, RG 25, Box 350, Folder 8, Case 8-C-378, National Archives. Slusser told Miller that he had requested troops.

At a meeting between union and Goodyear officials Saturday evening, Miller listed eight points that summarized the workers' grievances and asked both sides to discuss them. By 2:00 A.M. a compromise statement was ready. The union representatives agreed to layoffs by departments provided that no one with more than ten years' service was furloughed. Slusser in turn permitted tire workers who could perform other jobs to replace less senior employees, "as fast as they can be absorbed without disrupting the efficiency of the group affected." He also agreed to treat squadron members like other employees, recall workers by seniority when the workweek exceeded thirty hours, and give the Akron plants "a proportionate share of all business." When he left before the official statement was ready and Climer refused to sign in his place, Miller signed for all the participants.[25] Local 2 leaders agreed to present the agreement to the union meeting Sunday afternoon.

The Goodyear workers who packed the armory on Sunday were "grim, tight lipped," and ready for a strike vote. House, looking worn and haggard after three days of ceaseless activity, read the agreement and moved its adoption. Dalrymple stressed the importance of "the safe and sane method of settling these difficulties." Several disgruntled workers then called for a strike to "prove to 'em this time we mean business," and William Carney, still a Local 2 member, moved a strike vote. House ruled the motion out of order, on the grounds the twenty-four-hour notice had not been given. One reporter compared the reaction to "the explosion of a bomb." Amid shouts and boos, critics accused the officers of "deliberate trickery." More than three hours of rancorous debate followed. When House finally called for a vote on the original motion, a greatly reduced crowd approved the Miller agreement by a vote of 1,492 to 822.[26]

The following day, when Goodyear employees reported for work, police officers equipped with riot clubs, tear gas guns, and sawed-off shotguns guarded the plant gates. National Guard representatives waited nearby. Workers greeted their potential adversaries with "jeers, hand waves and a few hostile growls." Mayor Schroy, who had earlier promised to keep the plants open, pledged to work for additional WPA funds to aid the unemployed. Slusser appeared at the Plant 1 gate at 6:00 A.M. Expressing pleasure with the outcome of the dispute, he promised his "full cooperation with Mr. House and union leaders in working out any remaining misunderstand-

[25] "Miller Agreement," Nov. 21, 1937, FMCS Papers, RG 280, File 196/3061; Miller to NLRB, n.d., NLRB Papers, RG 25, Box 350, Folder 8, Case 8-C-378.

[26] ABJ, Nov. 22, 1937; ATP, Nov. 22, 1937; Local 2, Minutes, Membership Meeting, Nov. 21, 1937, Local 2 Archives.

15. *Whitey Lloyd, Leland Buckmaster and Garnet Patterson,*
photographed in the 1940's. United Rubber Workers Archives.

ings.''[27] The next day he wrote to Miller, indicating that he would not ad-
here to the November 20 agreement after January 1, 1938.[28]

FIRESTONE AND GOODRICH

Goodyear's traditional opposition to "outside" unions and Slusser's personal vindictiveness could not obscure the more fundamental fact that the
balance between management and labor had changed. Decentralization and
recession had undermined the economic basis of union growth, making the
survival of the labor movement in the rubber industry an issue for the first
time since the crisis of 1935.

The plight of Local 7 was the best example of the unions' new vulnerability. In 1936 and 1937, the Firestone local had been distinguished for its
leadership and cohesion. Yet by the spring of 1938 it faced the ultimate
humiliation: the loss of its right to represent Firestone employees to an independent union that everyone acknowledged was a hasty reincarnation of
the Employees' Conference Plan. Donald Anthony, a University of Akron

[27] *ABJ*, Nov. 22, 1937; *ATP*, Nov. 22, 1937.
[28] J. P. Miller to C. Slusser, Nov. 24, 1937, in Local 2, Minutes, Executive Board, Local
2 Archives.

economist who followed the industry closely, supplied the authoritative contemporary explanation for what happened:

First of all, after an agreement was reached many workers lost interest in the union. . . . Then in the late summer of 1937 came the sudden and sharp business depression. Dues collections slumped badly . . . and many of the most aggressive unionists were laid off. . . . Since a large number of the shop committeemen were in this group, the grievance machinery of the union was badly disrupted, in some departments completely destroyed. Many of those laid off blamed the union for their plight. Union leadership was unable to cope adequately with the problem.[29]

Anthony's analysis appears flawed in several respects. It makes no effort to square the workers' apparent complacency with the local's other achievements in 1937. Nor does it distinguish between the effects of the recession and the results of Firestone's aggressive decentralization policy. During the recovery period the company had expanded its product line to serve its network of company-owned stores; most of these items and a growing proportion of Firestone tires, rims, and other traditional products were made outside Akron in low-wage, nonunion communities. Besides the Memphis tire plant, destined to be the largest non-Akron tire factory by the end of the decade, Firestone added substantial operations in Noblesville and Fall River. It also cut back its Akron operations far more sharply than Goodyear or Goodrich. At the time of the 1937 strike its Akron labor force had been approximately 10,500. A year later it was about 6,000, or 40 percent less.[30] During the same period Goodyear laid off slightly more than 20 percent of its Akron employees.

In any case Firestone employees apparently "blamed the union for their plight." Did they also blame the company? Apparently not in the sense that Goodyear employees blamed Slusser. There were no sit-downs or other protests at Firestone during the winter and spring of 1938. Buckmaster had done his work well. But his leadership could not offset the city's reputation, the higher costs of Akron labor, or, most of all, the flexibility of the integrated firms. Labor peace and stability alone would not save the Akron plants.

Nor did Buckmaster's approach dissuade some unhappy employees from proposing a more generous accommodation. In late December Robert Denholm, a former president of the company union, and other employees organized the Firestone Employees' Protective Association, an independent union dedicated to fostering better relations with the company and preserv-

---

[29] Donald Anthony, "Rubber Products," in Harry A. Millis and Others, *How Collective Bargaining Works* (New York, 1942), p. 653.

[30] Harold S. Roberts, *The Rubber Workers: Labor Organization and Collective Bargaining in the Rubber Industry* (New York, 1944), p. 166.

ing jobs "by encouraging increased production in Akron."[31] By the end of January the group claimed nearly seven hundred members. Contemporary observers believed that the association drew most of its support from veteran employees, including a small group that had always opposed the URW and a larger number whose seniority protected them from layoffs. They found common cause in opposition to the local's work-sharing policies, a desire to protect their jobs, and a belief that URW dues were too high. A conflict between tire and nontire workers may also have been involved; Denholm and other officers of the organization were all from nontire departments. In February Denholm stepped aside in favor of F. A. McDonald, a tire worker whom Local 7 leaders accused of being his puppet.[32]

By late February the association's threat was so serious that Local 7 leaders asked for an immediate NLRB election. They acknowledged that additional layoffs would probably weaken the local further in the spring. The NLRB cooperated by designating the January 3 payroll as the voter list, which permitted one thousand laid-off workers to vote. Both sides sponsored meetings, rallies, and radio speeches. Black workers were a special target. Buckmaster professed optimism throughout the contest. On the eve of the election he predicted that Local 7 would win by a 5 or 10 to 1 majority. The actual tally on March 30 was 3,696 to 2,546, a humiliating and near disastrous result for the union. The local's total was 58 percent of the votes cast but only 49 percent of the January 3 labor force. Though Buckmaster charged that many supervisors voted illegally, swelling the association vote, he could not explain the local's comparatively meager total.[33]

Buckmaster and the local officers immediately resumed negotiations with Murphy, and six weeks later concluded a contract that differed little from the 1937 document. The union won a more generous vacation plan and minor changes in the seniority system. In exchange it reaffirmed its opposition to strikes and sit-downs and accepted an "escape clause" that allowed either side to reopen negotiations on any provision with ten days' notice.[34] Potentially the most important item in the document, the escape clause raised the possibility of a substantial wage reduction.

Local 5's problems began in mid-February 1938 with an item in the employee newspaper and an advance copy of a speech T. G. Graham was to deliver to the Akron Ministerial Association. The newspaper article bemoaned the city's decline as a manufacturing center. Graham's text was more specific: he asked for a substantial wage reduction and assurances of

[31] *ABJ*, Jan. 31, 1938.
[32] *ABJ*, Feb. 19, March 28, 1938.
[33] *ABJ*, Feb. 24, March 24, 28, 30, 1938; *SCLN*, March 4, 1938.
[34] *ABJ*, May 16, 1938.

efficient operations; otherwise Goodrich would reduce its Akron operations by 50 percent and abolish five thousand jobs. The ministers "found it so laden with dynamite" that they canceled their meeting and informed Local 5 leaders, which was Graham's intention.[35] Apparently he had concluded that his only hope for a positive response was to go over the heads of Callahan and the local leaders and publicize the severity of the company's troubles.

Graham soon found allies. The heads of the chamber of commerce, the Greater Akron Association, and various merchants' organizations pledged their support. Mayor Schroy was officially noncommittal but privately as vocal as any of the business leaders. He had good reason for anxiety; as the threat became known, the city's credit rating plunged. The skepticism that had greeted the Goodyear demand for the eight-hour day in 1935 was nowhere evident in 1938. By mid-March, Chappell believed there was a good chance that Local 5 leaders, and possibly other union officers, would be "run out of town."[36]

Union leaders understood that the sit-downs and job losses had put them at loggerheads with most community groups and increased their vulnerability to attack. Essentially they faced two choices, both undesirable. They could make concessions on wages and hours until the economy improved and they had organized the outlying plants. This approach might be costly; it would blur the distinction between the URW and the independent unions and alienate the militants. The alternative was to hold the line and look for allies elsewhere. This choice placed fewer immediate demands on them and appealed to the militants, but it involved risks, including the risk of extinction if they misjudged the strength of the decentralization movement.

In resisting any irrevocable decision URW leaders essentially opted for the second choice. They were wary of complex strategies, hostile to any approach that required them to sacrifice key objectives, and hopeful that the federal government might somehow help. They turned "to any and every agency which may supply aid, or a face-saving device."[37] Dalrymple called the assistant secretary of labor on March 8 and asked for the appointment of an investigative body "to see if the demands made by the company are justified."[38] He and Local 5 leaders also appealed to the NLRB, the La Follette committee, Congress, and President Roosevelt. Labor Department officials, their preferred allies, were reluctant to become involved. Chap-

[35] *ABJ*, Feb. 17, March 5, 1938; Address by T. G. Graham, Feb. 16, 1938, FMCS Papers, RG 280, File 199/1326.

[36] Carl R. Schedler to Steelman, April 7, 1938, FMCS Papers, RG 280, File 195/336; Chappell to Steelman, March 20, 1938, FMCS Papers, RG 280, File 199/1316.

[37] Chappell to Steelman, March 12, 1938, FMCS Papers, RG 280, File 199/1326.

[38] Mr. McLaughlin to Steelman, March 8, 1938 FMCS Papers, RG 280, File 199/1326.

pell believed they ought to avoid a role that was inherently partisan.[39] James Miller, intent on enhancing the NLRB's reputation and his own stature as an industrial peacemaker, was more amenable to union appeals. By playing off the two agencies; URW leaders were ultimately able to have their investigation. In the meantime they stalled.

The immediate issue in the dispute was Graham's demand for an employee vote. On March 9 he submitted a detailed statement of his proposal and asked union leaders to schedule an election. He demanded wage reductions of 13 to 17 percent for men and 13 to 14 percent for women, a flexible workday with an eight-hour maximum, and assurances that the employees would operate new machinery efficiently. In return he pledged to sign a union contract, spend $1.5 million on plant modernization, and halt decentralization for six months. He released his plan to the newspapers on March 12, forcing the union to act. Local 5 leaders decided to hold departmental meetings, a mass rally on Saturday, March 20, and an election on March 21. Callahan attacked the plan in a radio address, signaling the union's opposition.[40]

For the next week the URW waged a propaganda war against a variety of small business groups, led by the chamber of commerce and the Greater Akron Association. Union leaders tried to convince their constituents that the Graham plan was a "smokescreen" for attacking Local 5. They argued that decentralization was inevitable and that lower wages would only mean lower incomes. The merchants, joined at the end of the week by the *Akron Beacon Journal*, countered that a wage reduction would actually increase earnings and that the loss of five thousand jobs would devastate the city. Fearing that union leaders would manipulate the election to defeat the Graham plan, they asked Secretary Perkins to insist on a delay until the Labor Department, or some other government agency, could guarantee a fair and impartial vote of all Goodrich employees.[41]

URW leaders also "got the jitters as the time for the election drew near."[42] On Friday, March 19, Callahan warned that he might call off the election if outside pressures "became too great."[43] The next morning, before the rally, he and the URW officers met and decided to cancel the election. Burns provided the official rationale, a supposed request from the Labor Department. At the end of the rally Callahan announced that the union would defer to the government and cancel the vote. Labor Department officials, who had made no such request, were taken aback. Goodrich

---

[39] Chappell to Steelman, March 9, 1938, FMCS Papers, RG 280, File 199/1326.

[40] *ABJ*, March 12, 1938.

[41] *ABJ*, March 17, 18, 1938.

[42] Chappell to Steelman, March 20, 1938, FMCS Papers, RG 280, File 199/1326.

[43] *ABJ*, March 20, 1938.

employees, apart from the union activists, were also upset and "anxious to know where they stand."[44]

For the next month union leaders played on Miller's ambitions to pressure the Labor Department and keep Goodrich at bay. When Graham, in exasperation, withdrew his wage reduction plan on April 11, Burns persuaded Miller to insist that Isador Lubin of the Bureau of Labor Statistics or some prominent member of Lubin's staff make an immediate study of Akron wages. Lubin could hardly refuse.[45] Miller also pressured Graham to resume negotiations on everything except the wage issue. Graham reluctantly agreed to another delay.

URW leaders had more trouble with the merchants. On April 20, a group of them confronted Callahan and the local negotiating committee as they emerged from Graham's office. When the union men refused to debate, the merchants followed them to the International offices where Callahan was attending a meeting of the executive board. The angry exchanges that followed emphasized the unionists' isolation. That evening, at a Local 5 rally, Dalrymple spoke of a local "war" against organized labor, and Wilmer Tate characterized the merchants as "lousy little nincompoops" organized in a "Fascist chamber of commerce."[46] The following day the gulf between the workers and the city's "middlemen" became greater than at any time since the waning days of the 1913 strike. After Graham told a delegation from the chamber of commerce that he had to have an answer from the union within a week, merchants anxiously called on Callahan. He refused to see them or to offer any hint of flexibility.[47]

The dispute itself was closer to resolution than the bitter words of April 20 and 21 suggested. In the first place, Graham's deadline was probably fictitious; he did not mention it again or repeat his warnings. Second, A. R. Hinrichs, the Labor Department investigator, arrived and began his study. Supposedly analyzing Goodrich wage data, he devoted most of his time to promoting a negotiated settlement. He did not know "if [he could] get them together," but hoped to get "preliminary figures to make [a] case" for revision "look reasonable." The "union attitude," he added, "seems to be one of looking for a way out."[48] By Friday, April 22, he had

[44] Chappell to Steelman, March 20, 1938, and Harold B. Harpham to Frances Perkins, March 24, 1938, FMCS Papers, RG 280, File 199/1326; Whiting Williams to Clients, April 1, 1938, Whiting Williams Papers, Box 4, Folder 1, Western Reserve Historical Society Library, Cleveland. *ABJ*, March 21, 1938.

[45] Memorandum for the Record, April 14, 1938, FMCS Papers, RG 280, File 199/1326.

[46] *ATP*, April 21, 1938; *ABJ*, April 21, 1938; Dalrymple to Steelman, April 22, 1938, FMCS Papers, RG 280, File 199/1326.

[47] *ABJ*, April 23, 1938.

[48] A. F. Hinrichs to Steelman, April 21, 1938, FMCS Papers, RG 280, File 195/336.

recalculated Graham's original proposal and decided it would mean an average cut of only 12 percent for men, which "will be some help to the union in case they decide to accept cuts." He also offered to issue a statement that the reductions were "revisions and do not call for further cuts by other companies."[49] To permit union leaders to blame Washington, he invited them to confer with Labor Department officials in the capital on Sunday, April 24. For nearly twelve hours they discussed "the Akron situation and the question of 'what next?' " As the union men departed, they promised "to make a sincere effort to reach a satisfactory conclusion within the next very few days."[50] Hinrichs told reporters he expected a settlement very soon.

For several days this prediction seemed accurate. Graham indicated informally that Goodrich would take no "precipitate action" as long as the talks held "the promise of some satisfactory settlement."[51] On Tuesday, Callahan reported that the negotiations were "going along splendidly." He had submitted a union wage proposal and hoped for an agreement in the "near future."[52] The union wage plan, based on the Washington discussions, provided for a 10 percent reduction and a number of safeguards for Goodrich workers, including a pledge not to decentralize for two years. Callahan was undoubtedly surprised when Graham refused to accept either the wage proposal or the safeguards, declaring that the rates he proposed on March 9 were "the most liberal" he could offer. After conferring with Dalrymple, the local executive board decided to submit a 12 percent wage reduction to a ratification vote. Callahan refused to indicate whether Local 5 leaders would endorse the agreement, but his comments left little doubt about their hostility.[53]

Official antipathy to the agreement became more pronounced in the following days. At an April 30 membership meeting, Harley Anthony and a dozen activists spoke against the agreement; only one man favored it. He was "booed and jeered and finally . . . escorted from the hall under protection of committeemen."[54] At the May 4 ratification meeting, Callahan distributed a statement indicating how much the workers would lose under the new rates and read telegrams from other unions opposing wage cuts.

[49] Steelman, "Memorandum for the Record," April 22, 1938, FMCS Papers, RG 280, File 195/336.

[50] Steelman, "Memorandum for the Record," April 24, 1938, FMCS Papers, RG 280, File 195/336.

[51] ABJ, April 25, 1938.

[52] Steelman, "Memorandum for the Record," April 26, 1938, FMCS Papers, RG 280, File 195/336.

[53] ATP, April 27, 28, 29, 1938; ABJ, April 27, 29, 30, 1938.

[54] ABJ, May 2, 1938.

After reviewing the provisions of the contract, he warned that the flexible workday could presage a return to the eight-hour day. When asked if he recommended the contract, he answered, "Hell no!" His response evoked cries of "Let's vote." When a worker moved to reject the contract, "a mighty cheer went up." "Those hands came up like grass on a lawn," a local officer recalled. The final result was 2,251 to 239 for rejection.[55] The total was only 35 percent of the Goodrich labor force and 30 percent of the Local 5 vote in the August 1937 NLRB election.

The May 4 vote produced virtually no public response. The merchants had already concluded that Callahan and a few hundred militants were committed to a policy of rule or ruin. Their actions doomed the "crucial battle to keep Akron from becoming a branch plant town."[56] Government officials were equally pessimistic. Even the usually ebullient Miller spurned Dalrymple's appeals for a new initiative. The Labor Department released Hinrichs's report but it was a "dud." Local readers discovered "very little" that they did not "already know."[57] The only unanswered questions were when the company would announce its plans and where it would locate its new plant.

A handful of Goodrich workers rebelled. In early May a small group of nonunion employees organized the Goodrich Protective Association, an independent union modeled after the dissident Goodyear and Firestone organizations, and called a meeting for May 11 at a local church. Of the one hundred workers who attended, three-quarters or more were Local 5 activists. O. H. Wilt, one of the organizers, presided, and the heads of the other independent unions spoke. At one point, Joe Feineisen, a Local 5 officer, interrupted with a question about decentralization. When Wilt attacked the union, Callahan, sitting inconspicuously at the back, jumped to his feet and for half an hour attacked "two-by-four company unions," financiers "controlling large industries," and other enemies.[58] Unionists excoriated Wilt, who soon left. Local 5 members elected Feineisen president of the protective association.

In this volatile atmosphere only a spark was needed for an explosion. On May 15, Goodrich executives announced the layoff of twenty-five electricians, including some long-service workers. Callahan asked Graham to reconsider and warned that if he refused, "we might shut the plant down." Graham declined to revoke the order and on May 19 workers in the tire-building and -curing rooms "started throwing electric power switches in protest." The sit-down lasted until the end of the shift when the strikers

---

[55] *ATP*, May 4, 1938; *ABJ*, May 5, 1938.

[56] Coates, "Boomerang in Akron," p. 43.

[57] *ATP*, May 14, 1938.

[58] *ATP*, May 12, 1938.

marched out, recruited some incoming night-shift workers, and formed a picket line. Within an hour, virtually the entire complex had closed. By morning pickets standing "arm to arm" blocked the gates. It was the first Goodrich picket line since the early 1920s. Callahan announced that "since we've been forced to go the limit, we'll have to sit down and negotiate some sort of signed agreement before this strike can be settled."[59]

That afternoon one thousand seven hundred Goodrich unionists crowded the local hall to hear Callahan call for a continuation of the strike until the company signed a contract. He asked for a vote of confidence and received a "roar of approval." The strike broke the tension of the three-month dispute. Callahan reflected the spirit of the meeting. "It's not a strike," he proclaimed afterward, "just a holiday. . . . The men aren't getting enough work to matter anyhow and the company hasn't got any orders to fill."[60]

Remarkably, the negotiations between Callahan and Graham focused almost exclusively on vacation pay, which the company proposed to abolish in lieu of a wage cut. At one point Graham offered to give the workers tires rather than money, and pickets' signs soon read "For sale, vacation tires."[61] Finally Graham compromised on one-half the previous vacation rate. The contract retained the existing pay schedule, provided for a flexible thirty- to thirty-six-hour workweek, spelled out grievance procedures and seniority rights, and banned sit-downs. It was to last six months. More than four thousand five hundred Goodrich workers attended the ratification meeting on May 26 and voted overwhelmingly to return to their jobs. Graham's apparent indifference to the wage issue encouraged some observers to speculate that his ultimatums had been an elaborate bluff. They were probably right in the sense that he, like Litchfield, was now uncertain of his ability to introduce fundamental changes in the Akron plant. But they were unaware of a trip by Whiting Williams, Graham's private social analyst, to Clarksville, Tennessee, a few days later.[62]

Conflict at Goodyear, 1938

The Firestone and Goodrich approach—a contract coupled with decentralization—was less palatable to Goodyear executives. Their resistance was partly personal; Litchfield and Slusser, at least, had a larger emotional stake in a union-free environment and the Akron complex than their counterparts at the other companies. They were also sensitive to two business consider-

[59] *ABJ*, May 20, 1938; *ATP*, May 20, 1938.

[60] *ABJ*, May 21, 1938.

[61] *ATP*, May 23, 1938.

[62] Jones, *Life, Liberty, and Property*, p. 44; Williams to Graham, June 25, 1938, William Papers, Box 4, Folder 1.

ations. The first was the growth of the mechanical goods market and the comeback of U.S. Rubber, which threatened to surpass Goodyear in total sales by 1938. A successful response would require new products, aggressive marketing, and flexibility. The second was the alarming erosion in the competitiveness of the Akron plants. Labor productivity had fallen for the first time in 1936 and had risen little, if at all, in 1937. A leading student of the industry reported that it was "impossible for any company to introduce a new labor saving machine."[63] And despite the cooperative approach of the URW, many union members were equally vigorous in opposing time studies and other activities that they equated with "speedups." The company's history of rate cutting now haunted it. To most executives, these problems were the best argument for a smaller, not a larger, union role.

In November 1937 Goodyear began a program of "supervisional conferences" that addressed the problem of declining efficiency. Over the next six months, eight series of meetings brought together executives and first-line supervisors. The first series, devoted to the supervisors' complaints, produced wide-ranging discussions of the rising tensions between the foremen and personnel experts. The foremen were virtually unanimous in blaming the personnel department for the plant's troubles. The Labor Division "unload[ed] unsuitable men" on them, made it impossible "to get rid of men that are no good," and promoted a "peace at any price policy." The supervisors suggested various changes: "make each foreman responsible for his own department"; restore discipline; "restrict employees from promiscuously going up the line"; and provide "less welfare work." Slusser provided the executives' official response. Admitting that Goodyear was "not out of [the] woods yet," he proposed to turn back the clock a decade or more. "Management [would] put department foremen in complete charge." With new powers, they would be able to resolve disputes on the shop floor and curtail the role of the personnel specialists.[64]

Another series of meetings explored ways to regain the workers' confidence. Supervisors charged that the Industrial Assembly had become "too political," that the executives had erred in trying to restore the eight-hour day in 1935, and that the Stahl-Mate Club had had "poor leadership." They proposed more guaranteed piece rates and a renewed emphasis on merit in layoffs and rehiring. The latter elicited a pledge from Slusser:

It has always been Goodyear's policy to reward merit. . . . During the past two years we have witnessed a deviation from this policy toward straight seniority. The future trend will be to return to our old established policy.

[63] Anthony, "Rubber Products," p. 662.
[64] Supervisory Conference, Nov. 1937, NLRB Papers, Box 350, Folder 8, Case 8-C-378.

The consensus that emerged from these and other discussions was that "Supervision must take leadership and get the workmen to come to them."[65]

After November 1937 Goodyear foremen became more aggressive, and relations between the company and Local 2 deteriorated rapidly. The most frequent source of conflict was the provision in the Miller agreement that permitted laid-off workers to replace employees with less service in other departments. Supervisors in nontire departments fought the provision because it forced them to accept new and less experienced workers. One foreman told workers that "if it was up to him he wouldn't lay off a man" but union committeemen "were pushing him so hard that he had to lay them off." The superintendent of the mechanical goods division announced that he would retain all current employees if it were not for the "pressure brought to bear by the union." His statements provoked a barrage of complaints to union leaders.[66] Of nearly five hundred meetings between the Local 2 grievance committee and Goodyear managers in the six months following the Miller agreement, approximately half involved seniority issues.[67]

Other points of contention included production standards, hours, and wages. Foremen urged workers to "break limits," and many employees found the temptation to increase their earnings irresistible.[68] Their actions led to rate cuts, since the company was slow to implement its guarantee plan. Slusser was responsible for other provocations. In January he increased the workday in some departments to $6\frac{1}{4}$ hours or $6\frac{1}{2}$ hours, ostensibly as an economy move. Local 2 leaders condemned the new schedule as a "speedup" and promised "to use all methods . . . to fight this issue." When they protested to Climer they received a lecture on differences in production costs between Akron, Los Angeles, and Gadsden. They then sponsored a series of radio programs to "notify the public of . . . the unreliability of those with whom we have to deal" and appealed to the NLRB.[69] Miller and his staff investigated but could find little evidence of Wagner Act violations. They advised both sides to negotiate a contract.

Most troubling of all was the executives' evident disinterest in the contract negotiations. At the time of the NLRB election, Local 2 leaders had taken a contract for granted. The layoffs stalled negotiations during the fall and Slusser and Climer showed no interest in reviving them in the spring.

[65] Ibid.

[66] Miller, "Notes on Conference Held Feb. 23, 1938," NLRB Papers, RG 25, Box 350, Folder 8.

[67] Plant Legislative Committee Meetings with Management, NLRB Papers, RG 25, Box 350, Folder 8.

[68] Local 2, Minutes, Executive Board, Dec. 14, 1937, Local 2 Archives.

[69] C. E. Smith to Slusser, Jan. 28, 1938, NLRB Papers, RG 25, Box 350, Folder 8; Local 2, Minutes, Executive Board, Jan. 11, 1938, Local 2 Archives; *ABJ*, Feb. 12, 1938.

The union negotiators appealed to Litchfield in late April but he refused to meet them.[70] By May, Local 2 was no closer to a contract than it had been the previous summer.

Despite widespread antipathy toward Slusser and the supervisors, Goodyear workers increasingly blamed the union for their difficulties. The local's membership fell from a high of 10,300 in July 1937 to 8,500 in May 1938, but less than 1,000 members were in good standing by the later date.[71] Equally telling was the growth of two groups that advocated substantially different approaches to the company. The first was the Goodyear Employees Association, which claimed a growing number of veteran workers, including many former Industrial Assembly activists. In February 1938, the association announced its intention to seek a new NLRB election. As the recession worsened and the backlog of grievances increased, its threat became more realistic. By the summer, association leaders were confident they could defeat Local 2.[72]

The second and more immediate challenge came from a group of activist committeemen led by C. V. Wheeler, a mechanical goods worker who had been elected to the local executive board in 1937. These "hotheads" had no precise membership or program, apart from a determination to fight the company by any means, including a strike. As the union declined, their influence increased. Although there was only one sit-down between November and May, no one doubted that the "hotheads" would command a large following under the right circumstances.

In April 1938, a major dispute began when company officials announced plans to transfer employees to a new line of tires. They agreed to recognize service in making assignments but selected men who were all former supervisors, squadron members, Industrial Assembly officers, or ex-union members. The union charged favoritism and demanded a conference. Climer met them several times between May 17 and May 24 (Slusser had left for another sanitarium stay) and agreed to reply to six general complaints they raised. After the meeting on May 24, he conferred with Walter Taag, an NLRB investigator, who expressed his belief that "the only solution . . . was a signed agreement with Local #2."[73] When the union officers returned on May 25, Climer mentioned Taag's suggestion and talked generally about a contract before agreeing to call House in the afternoon with a reply to the six grievances. When he did not call by 3:00 P.M., House decided to leave for Cumberland, Maryland, where he was to talk to Cumberland and Gadsden unionists about a national Goodyear contract. Aware

[70] Local 2, Minutes, Membership Meeting, May 8, 1938, Local 2 Archives.

[71] Local 2, Membership Record, Local 2 Archives.

[72] Goodyear Employees Association, Membership Meeting, June 3, 1938, NLRB Papers, RG 25, Box 1879, File 1578.

[73] Taag to Miller, May 24, 1938, NLRB Papers, RG 25, Box 350.

of rumors that the workers would try to close the plant that night, he told local vice-president Charles Skinner and other officers to "keep the goddamn plant going no matter what."[74]

The stalemate continued on May 26. Climer refused to make any statement on the six points for at least another day and added that "he had no authority to sign agreements." The union men "stalked out of the office," promising to take the issue to the members.[75] Climer later told Taag that he could not reply without approval from Litchfield, who was traveling in Europe and could not be reached until the next day.[76] The Local 2 executive board met in the afternoon, discussed the conferences, and agreed that Climer's references to a contract were "just another attempt to stall and evade the issue." The members agreed to call a meeting of Goodyear committeemen that evening and to buy radio time to discuss the six-point proposal and conditions in the plant. Afterward, they admitted "off the record" that they would strike.[77]

With Skinner presiding, the committeemen met at 7:00 P.M. Amid cries of "shut her down," A. A. Wilson summarized the negotiations. Before he had finished, several men arrived with reports that trucks were loading office supplies and tires at the plant. At this news "a spontaneous movement spread throughout the hall to go to the gates and keep the vans inside."[78] By 8:30 pickets guarded the gates.

In the aftermath of what would be "the bloodiest labor battle in Akron's history," these events took on special meaning. On May 30 the local publicly charged that:

Certain facts . . . indicate that the strike itself was the result of a deliberate campaign to draw the union into an open fight under unfavorable conditions. . . . This campaign took the lines of provocation within the factory by stalling on grievance settlements. . . . It took the line within the union of fanning the flames of unrest. . . . This work was carried on undercover within the union by labor spies, whose tactics were such as to mislead many honest union men.[79]

House later recalled a different conspiracy. He believed that a combination of "hotheads" and "opportunists" took advantage of his absence to engineer the strike. He was "quite sure" that he was one of their targets.[80] The

[74] John D. House, interview with author, May 26, 1976; *ATP*, May 27, 1938; *ABJ*, May 28, 1938.

[75] Local 2, Minutes, Executive Board, May 27, 1938, Local 2 Archives; Negotiations, May 26, 1938, NLRB Papers, RG 25, Box 350.

[76] Taag, Memorandum, May 26, 1938, NLRB Papers, RG 25, Box 250.

[77] *ABJ*, May 27, 1938.

[78] *ATP*, May 27, 1938.

[79] News Release, May 30, 1938, NLRB Papers, RG 25, Box 350; *ABJ*, May 31, 1938.

[80] John D. House, interview with author, April 18, 1972.

union never disclosed its "facts," and House, unpopular among the "hot-heads," also had many supporters, including Skinner, Wilson, and most of the officers who were in control of the meeting. The official account may be the best explanation of the events that followed. The move to picket the plant, according to the local's minutes, was an "eruption of long held suspense and dissatisfaction."[81]

From 8:30 until 10:00 P.M. or slightly later, the picketing was peaceful. When police arrived in force about 9:00 there were only thirty-five or forty union members at Goodyear, many of them committeemen who had come from the union meeting. At Plant 3, fifteen trucks, loaded with tires, waited inside the gate. At about 10:00 P.M. the police opened the gate and the trucks drove into a "barrage of rocks." When they had passed, the officer in charge asked if anyone wanted to go in to work. A half dozen men entered, unmolested.[82]

By 11:00 more than one thousand pickets and spectators had gathered in front of Plant 1. Some milled around the gate; others crowded the sidewalk in front of Goodyear Hall, across the street. When a group in the back of the crowd began to chant "Let's go, let's go," the police formed a line and forced the crowd back. At 11:30 a dozen plant guards, out of sight of the crowd, put on gas masks and readied guns and gas cartridges. At approximately the same time a hundred union men formed a chain picket line and marched in a circle, shouting "Close the plant! Keep 'em out!" A few minutes later the officer in charge ordered his men to clear the area around the gate. The police drew their night sticks and started to push the crowd back. Apparently a rubber worker struck one of them. The police retaliated. "They asked for it, goddamit, now let 'em have it," shouted the officer in charge.[83]

The police began to "swing their sticks at the men nearest them." Pickets and spectators ran and the police followed, hitting anyone they caught. Bodies soon littered the street and the steps of the Goodyear State Bank, next to Goodyear Hall. A policeman tripped and fell. Several men kicked him. Others threw bricks at the police. A police lieutenant ordered: "Bring on the gas." The Goodyear police rushed out of the gate and began to fire tear gas shells. The crowd dispersed quickly:

Blood streamed from the faces and heads of many seen leaving the scene of the first gas attack. . . . Cartridges from the tear gas guns shattered the windows of nearby stores. The gas lay like fog over the entire district.[84]

[81] Local 2, Minutes, Executive Board, May 27, 1938, Local 2 Archives.

[82] *ATP*, May 27, 1938.

[83] *ABJ*, May 27, 1938. Also John Kumpel, interview with author, Oct. 25, 1972.

[84] *ATP*, May 27, 1938. Also A. A. Wilson, interview with author; *ABJ*, May 27, 1938.

The officers divided into groups and drove the "jeering, taunting" crowd west on Market Street and east on Goodyear Boulevard. Several officers stopped to fire tear gas at workers who pelted them from the roofs of buildings. Other officers fired their revolvers at workers or chased them through the east Akron cemetery, using tear gas to drive them from hiding places behind tombstones. The Local 2 hall, adjacent to the cemetery, became the center of the conflict. Seventy-five to one hundred workers, advancing in "guerilla-like sorties, hurling rocks and iron bolts," kept the officers at bay for nearly two hours. The police vented their anger by firing "volley after volley of tear gas" through the first-floor windows. An awning on the building caught fire. George Milliron, a prominent committeeman, called Taag to ask for help. He could only speak for a few seconds because of the gas. When a man tried to escape by automobile, an officer smashed his windshield. "I'm just trying to get home," he protested. "The war's on, get out of here!" the officer shouted, while other policemen "beat on the car with their night sticks."[85] After more than an hour of arguments and protests, Denlinger prevailed on the police to let him escort the last dozen union men out of the wrecked hall.

By early morning the violence subsided. The police righted a patrol car that had been overturned and a motorman returned to the streetcar he had abandoned in the middle of Market Street. Union men transported injured colleagues to the hospital or to their homes. Goodyear officials announced that the plant would remain open. Police and National Guard observers began to prepare for the 6:00 A.M. shift change. To nearly everyone's surprise there were no further incidents. A Goodyear representative claimed that three-quarters of the first-shift employees reported for work.

During the day the conflict took other forms. With House again at their head, Local 2 leaders opted to mobilize the local labor movement and work for a negotiated agreement. At their invitation, representatives of seventy-five CIO and AFL unions threatened a general strike if National Guard troops appeared or if the company provoked additional violence. In a radio broadcast, Grillo asked his listeners to call Mayor Schroy and tell him "you want him to be mayor of Akron and not a Charlie McCarthy for Goodyear."[86] Burns demanded that Roosevelt intervene. The next day, at an outdoor rally at city hall, Grillo and Burns were so vituperative that Schroy threatened to arrest them for inciting a riot.[87]

In the meantime Miller and Chappell negotiated a formal truce. Goodyear officials announced that the plants would close for the Memorial Day

[85] *ABJ*, May 27, 1938; *ATP*, May 27, 1938; Taag, Memorandum, May 26, 1938.

[86] *ABJ*, May 28, 1938.

[87] *ATP*, May 29, 1938; *ABJ*, May 30, 1938.

holiday, and Miller arranged a negotiating session for Saturday, May 28. He expressed confidence that the strike would be settled before work resumed on Tuesday. When the Saturday meeting resulted only in an agreement to meet again on Monday, dangerously close to the end of the holiday, House asked Chappell to see E. J. Thomas. Chappell subsequently won Thomas's pledge "to meet with his committee before the conference on Monday and to earnestly endeavor to work out a proposal . . . which could be the basis of at least a temporary agreement."[88]

The negotiators met twice on Monday with more positive results. Climer volunteered to return the tire builders to their original jobs because "production requirements [had] changed." He also drew up a detailed list of guidelines to cover transfers and agreed to reconsider grievances that involved violations of the guidelines. According to Local 2 leaders, he made a "verbal pledge" to negotiate a contract and wage adjustment.[89] Though "not entirely satisfied," union officials were "surprised at the change in the company's attitude." They believed they could "sell" the agreement at a membership meeting scheduled for the armory that evening.[90] As a precaution they persuaded Haywood to come from New York for the meeting. His endorsement would "go a long way" toward convincing skeptical rubber workers. In their speeches that evening House, Burns, and others described the agreement as a victory. They cited the company's concessions and Climer's "promise" of a contract. After Haywood endorsed their efforts, three thousand members voted "not too enthusiastically" to accept the agreement.[91]

The settlement nevertheless left a substantial reservoir of ill-feeling. The union's May 30 statement, noted earlier, was unprecedented in its bitterness. Goodyear officials described the union charges as "too ridiculous to be considered by any sane person."[92] They were also "irate" over union boasts of concessions and the "promise" of a contract. A city council meeting on May 31 degenerated into a shouting match between Schroy and Virginia Etheridge, who wanted to invite the La Follette Committee to investigate a purported Schroy-Davey conspiracy. Davey himself, in the midst of a heated and ultimately unsuccessful primary campaign, left little doubt that he wanted to send the National Guard.[93] Whether Schroy would

[88] Chappell to Steelman, May 31, 1938, FMCS Papers, RG 280, File 199/1891.

[89] Fred Climer to House, May 30, 1938, NLRB Papers, RG 25, Box 350; *ABJ*, May 31, 1938.

[90] Chappell to Steelman, May 31, 1938, FMCS Papers, RG 280, File 199/1891.

[91] *ATP*, May 31, 1938.

[92] *ABJ*, May 31, 1938.

[93] *ABJ*, June 7, 1938; *ATP*, June 6, 1938.

have cooperated if there had been more violence is unclear, but the Mayor's pro-Goodyear posture was an indicator of URW isolation.

The riot also severely embarrassed Dalrymple and the International. Coming little more than a week after the Goodrich settlement, it inevitably raised new doubts about the credibility of the URW. The International Executive Board's subsequent condemnation of Local 5 and Local 2 only underlined its powerlessness. The riot raised similar questions about Local 2, especially when members of the local executive board publicly criticized House for his unwillingness to force a showdown. The *Akron Beacon Journal* probably summarized the prevailing view when it attacked the "manifestly inadequate leadership" of the URW.[94]

The Goodyear management reforms, which had sparked the original conflict, were the key to the long and ultimately fruitless negotiations that followed the May 30 settlement. Harold S. Roberts described the talks in detail and concluded that the company's strategy was simply to stall as long as possible.[95] The minutes of the negotiating sessions and the correspondence of government officials suggest a more complex pattern. The amiable Climer, who favored a working relationship with the local, was unfailingly cooperative. House recalled that their relations during that period were "excellent . . . sensible, businesslike" and without "acrimony."[96] Instead of stalling, Climer continually pushed Slusser and Litchfield for faster decisions, more flexibility, and greater authority for himself. His ally was Executive Vice-President Thomas. Neither man was a Cyrus Ching, but both shared Ching's conviction that the union could be managed. Opposing them were Slusser and others who associated union power with the sit-downs. Litchfield shared Slusser's bias but was concerned primarily with restoring the competitiveness of the Akron plant.

In early June Litchfield told reporters he would sign a union contract if "that contract is one under which the company can live."[97] He did not specify the conditions, but Climer quickly supplied the missing information. At the first formal session, on June 20, he insisted on discussing layoffs and then announced the company's intention to furlough one thousand seven hundred workers in order to raise the workweek to twenty-four hours. Later he explained that "some time we are going to have a wage cut and . . . we should prepare for it by giving people longer hours." He also wanted to discharge laid-off workers after a year, since "there were certain people that [the company] did not want ever to hire back." Company executives, he explained, "were primarily interested in getting the Akron

[94] *ATP*, June 3, 1938; *ABJ*, June 1, 7, 1938.
[95] Roberts, *Rubber Workers*, pp. 240–45.
[96] John D. House interview, April 18, 1972.
[97] *ABJ*, June 9, 1938.

plant on a basis whereby it could compete with outside plants and get some of the business back to Akron."[98] Union negotiators demanded that the company wait until the contract had been completed. Climer refused. By early July, with the layoff order in effect, the negotiations were on the verge of collapse. Union leaders believed that the executives were determined to break the morale of union members.[99]

As soon as the layoff was completed, Climer became more conciliatory. Even House, bitter over the layoffs, acknowledged that the negotiations were "simmering along."[100] In late July and early August the negotiators reached agreements on hours, vacations, layoff procedures, transfers, and the status of apprentices and squadron members—all without serious problems. By August 12 the only remaining issues were wages, the length of the recall period, and an arbitration procedure. Climer agreed to arrange a meeting with "upper management" to discuss these issues. On August 15 the negotiators spent the afternoon reviewing the entire agreement.

At the next meeting, on August 17, Climer announced that he "would still have trouble selling [the] proposed agreement to management." He added that Goodyear executives "desired to deal on top of the table" but believed a wage reduction and a return to the eight-hour day were "inevitable," despite union opposition. On Litchfield's order he proposed to suspend the talks until Labor Day, when "the Union would be advised . . . what additional 'bugs' management had found in the agreement."[101] Union negotiators protested in vain.

In September, company negotiators demanded changes that would permit wage reductions and a return to the eight-hour day. The union representatives offered counterproposals and the talks continued until mid-October when Climer again requested time to confer with "upper management." He did not reply for a month, presumably because Litchfield was preoccupied with other matters. Finally the union negotiators persuaded him to arrange a conference with Litchfield and Thomas. When Litchfield indicated that the talks seemed to be stalemated over wages and hours, House expressed a willingness to proceed. Litchfield then "suggested that the negotiations be resumed." Thomas seconded him. The negotiators met periodically for several weeks without resolving the differences. When the union representatives asked for the company's "final proposal," Climer again asked for time to confer with Litchfield. At the

[98] Negotiations, June 21, 28, 29, 1938, NLRB Papers, RG 25, Box 350.

[99] Chappell, "Progress Report," July 12, 1938, FMCS Papers, RG 280, File 199/1891.

[100] Chappell, "Progress Report," July 14, 1938, and Chappell to Steelman, July 20, 1938, FMCS Papers, RG 280, File 199/1891.

[101] Negotiations, Aug. 17, 1938, NLRB Papers, RG 25, Box 350.

next session, on December 14, Climer announced that he would incorporate the points they had agreed to in the plant manual but that "the company contemplated a broad program of modernization at the Akron factories and did not want to be encumbered by hard and fast rules."[102]

A Goodyear official later told Denlinger that Litchfield viewed the agreement as a "binding marriage contract" and did not want to "get married."[103] By December, with the economy improving, the wage and hours issues had become passé. The key was whether a "binding marriage" to Local 2 would help or hinder the modernization program. Litchfield obviously had concluded that it would hurt. He was also alert to the growing strength of the Goodyear Employees Association, which by late 1938 exceeded Local 2 in paid-up memberships.[104] Though he must have realized it had little prospect of officially displacing Local 2, its presence was a reminder that Goodyear workers were not a monolith and that an agreement with any group would not necessarily end the conflicts that had divided the labor force for five and a half years.

The collapse of the Goodyear negotiations was the last important event in the cycle of union expansion and decline that had started with the economic revival of 1933. Thanks to the peculiar conditions of the early 1930s, the labor movement of the 1930s had become far more powerful and acceptable than ever before. Because of that experience and the contracts that most of the Akron locals had concluded by 1938, it retained more power than any of its predecessors. Yet the price of that achievement was high. For the first time since the turn of the century the upturn of the business cycle did not promise more jobs. Akron union leaders acknowledged that their "primary" task was "to enable labor to adjust itself to steadily shrinking job opportunities with a minimum of human suffering . . . discrimination or favoritism."[105]

---

[102] "Continuation of the Story of Collective Bargaining," pp. 19–20, NLRB Papers, RG 25, Box 350.

[103] *ABJ*, Dec. 15, 1938.

[104] Whiting Williams to Clients, June 2, 1938, Williams Papers, Box 4, Folder 1.

[105] Anthony, "Rubber Products," p. 658.

CHAPTER ELEVEN

Stagnation and Rebirth, 1938–1941

OF THE URW leaders who emerged in the aftermath of the catalytic events of 1933–1935, none was more intriguing or influential than George Bass (1903–1970), a Tennessean who came to Akron in the late 1910s and spent his career in the Goodrich mechanical goods department. Though his public persona in the 1940s would be of a large, loud, and patently ambitious labor boss, he played no significant role in the FLU until 1935.[1] In the following years he became increasingly prominent as a negotiator and a factional leader in Local 5. By 1939 he dominated the union; by 1940, he was president. As the deepening shadows of war created new opportunities for American unions, Bass expanded his political base, became the champion of the Akron militants, and used his power to challenge Dalrymple. His rise symbolized the emergence of a new generation of union officers, more diverse in occupational origins, more comfortable at the bargaining table, and more alert to the possibilities of the new era of prosperity and government controls.

INTERNATIONAL UNION POLITICS

The rapid decline of the Big Three locals and the Akron labor movement in late 1937 and 1938 forced the International officers to reconsider their ties to the industry's traditional core. If they could no longer count on the Akron locals, what choices did they have? They could wed themselves to the CIO as the steelworkers, textile workers, and others had done, or they could look to the non-Akron locals, especially to the flourishing U.S. Rubber organizations. Their decision was comparatively easy. Despite their admiration for Lewis and Haywood, they had no intention of surrendering their independence or opening the door to another Claherty. Until the end of 1940 they spurned most outside aid and strengthened their ties with the non-Akron locals.

During the sit-down era, when the URW's non-Akron membership first became substantial, the International staff had gradually expanded. The new men were respected local union officers like Harry Eagle, Harley Anthony, O. H. Bosley, Rex Murray, and Floyd Robinson, who subscribed

[1] *Who's Who in Labor* (New York, 1946), p. 18.

to the values of local autonomy and self-reliance and avoided actions that might encroach on the locals' authority. Dalrymple's personal style was the final guarantee of a nonassertive bureaucracy. He typically spurned the trappings of authority and devoted much of his time to local union services.[2] One consequence of this approach was the persistence of strong local union identities. Another was the absence of checks and balances that might have reduced the likelihood of financial irregularity and scandal. Local 25 nearly collapsed after Secretary-Treasurer Frank J. Sheehan looted the treasury. Local 2, Local 26, and Local 44 suffered lesser disasters. In 1937 the executive board hired Harman Splitter, treasurer of Luzerne Rubber Local 69, as an assistant for local union finances. For two years he "couldn't keep up" with the embezzlements.[3]

By mid-1937 the URW had recruited the "cream of the crop" and faced the necessity of more concerted and costly efforts if it hoped to organize the 60 percent of American and Canadian rubber workers who remained outside the union.[4] Anticipating this burden, the International officers asked the 1937 convention to increase the monthly per capita tax from thirty-seven to forty-two cents of the dollar dues payment. Their request precipitated a surprisingly heated debate and sharp divisions. On the one side were Akron-oriented local leaders: the Local 5 contingent, some Local 2 and Local 9 officers, and the Seiberling Local 18 delegates. Except for the Local 2 delegates, they represented secure organizations with extensive recreation and welfare programs that they hesitated to compromise in exchange for a vague hedge against decentralization. They were also wary of the International; they disliked Burns, distrusted Eagle and his leftist followers, and worried that Dalrymple was losing touch with his roots. On the other side were delegates who took a more expansive view: the International officers, who tended to equate success with membership growth; Buckmaster and most Local 7 leaders, who feared more decentralization; and other Akron representatives who worried about the city's decline. Delegates from U.S. Rubber and the many isolated locals, who had a direct stake in a larger International presence, also supported the increase.

Callahan and Buckmaster led their respective sides in 1937. The former emphasized the hardships the locals would face if they had to pay more to the International. Buckmaster countered with a plea to "think not in terms

---

[2] "Report of General President S. H. Dalrymple," in *Report of Officers to 2nd Annual Convention, U.R.W. of A., Sept. 12th to 18th, 1937, Akron, Ohio* (Akron, 1937), p. 13; "Report of General President S. H. Dalrymple," in *Report of General Executive Board, Sept. 19, 1938* (Akron, 1938), p. 12.

[3] Harmon Splitter, interview with author, Aug. 16, 1977.

[4] See Finance Committee Report, April 22, 1937, in General Executive Board, Minutes, United Rubber Workers Archives, URW offices, Akron, Ohio.

of local unions but in terms of the International union.'' Otherwise, he insisted, ''this International is going to be on the downgrade. It is going to be wrecked.''[5] Dalrymple and Burns strongly supported him. After a ''bitter'' debate, the delegates voted for the officers' position by a 60- to 40-percent margin, just short of the two-thirds required to ratify a constitutional amendment. A ''hopeless deadlock'' followed. Callahan finally called for a recess, caucused with his delegates, and agreed to a forty-cent per capita tax, which the convention adopted.[6]

During the following months the recession undermined most of the URW's post-1935 gains. By the end of the year, 20 percent of URW members were unemployed; by February 1938, 25 percent were jobless; and by the summer, more than one-third were out of work.[7] Many others worked part-time. By early 1938 the International faced a mounting deficit, despite the per capita tax increase. In April it reduced salaries, closed district offices, forced organizers to operate out of their homes, and curtailed expense allowances. By summer these measures had produced ''quite satisfactory results,'' though not a balanced budget.[8] From a peak of sixteen organizers in early 1938, the staff declined to ten by the end of the year. Even a full complement would have had trouble during the recession, but the International's plight ensured that the URW became a union ''on the downgrade.''

At the September 1938 convention, the Akron-oriented delegates inadvertently revived the tensions of 1937. Led by Callahan and Bass, they tried to purge the left-wing element on the executive board by banning organizers, a restriction that would eliminate Eagle, Camelio, and, ironically, John Marchiando, a frequent critic of the leftists who was little-known in Akron. The Local 5 leaders found allies among the U.S. Rubber delegates, who outnumbered the Akron Big Three delegates but had no representatives on the executive board. In the debate Bass argued that his goal was simply to eliminate conflicts of interest. Burns and Buckmaster, leading the opposition, accused him of conspiring to manipulate the convention. Robert Hill, of U.S. Rubber Local 101, seemed to confirm this charge by boasting that the U.S. Rubber delegates would vote as a bloc. The deciding factor was apparently the conviction of many delegates from isolated locals that the organizers gave them a voice in executive board deliberations, and the restriction lost. The Akron and U.S. Rubber leaders nevertheless achieved their major objective; they elected C. V. Wheeler of Local 2, Scott Fries of

[5] *Proceedings of the Second Convention of the United Rubber Workers of America, September 12 to 20, 1937* (Akron, 1937), pp. 285, 288.

[6] *ABJ*, Sept. 20, 1937.

[7] *Report of the General Executive Board, Sept. 19, 1938*, p. 4.

[8] General Executive Board, Minutes, Jan. 25, 1938, Finance Committee Report, April 21, 1938, and Finance Committee Report, July 18, 1938, URW Archives.

U.S. Rubber Local 65 in Mishawaka, and G. T. Palmer of Local 18 in Barberton to the board in place of Eagle, Camelio, and Marchiando.[9]

By mid-1939 the International was still unable to mount a major organizing effort and an impatient Dalrymple decided to appeal for another increase in the per capita tax. Despite the lingering effects of the recession, he believed that he could win if he capitalized on the resentment of the non-Akron delegates. The 1938 purge had eliminated two non-Akron board members at a time when the non-Akron locals were becoming increasingly important. The U.S. Rubber locals, led by Local 101 officials, were especially agitated.

The tax increase overshadowed all other issues in 1939. Callahan led the opposition, calling for a one-time assessment of one dollar per member to finance an organizing campaign in 1940. Bass seconded his plea. The union needed "men who will go out and get the members in and make them pay up" rather than more burdens. Dalrymple was unusually outspoken in arguing for a permanent increase. He was "sick and tired of calling upon our progressive members to . . . donate [and allowing] those who don't wish to donate to go free." Buckmaster supported him. The first vote, on a five-cent increase, was overwhelmingly negative. A second vote, on a three-cent increase, won the support of a majority of the delegates, including most of the U.S. Rubber representatives, but failed to obtain the required two-thirds margin.[10] Burns's announcement that the executive board would ask for an assessment finally settled the issue.

When the tax question had been resolved, the non-Akron locals joined forces to take control of the executive board. They pushed through a resolution expanding the board from six to eight and then defeated all the Akron nominees except Callahan, Buckmaster, and the martyred Eagle. In their places they elected Camelio; the presidents of the Detroit, Los Angeles, and Eau Claire U.S. Rubber locals; and a Trenton delegate, leaving little doubt about the impact of decentralization and recession on the internal politics of the URW.[11]

The assessment produced only $20,000, exactly half of which came from six U.S. Rubber locals. The Akron locals contributed $3,500, including $1,487 from Local 5, $1,000 from Local 7, and $6.00 from Local 2. Only Local 18, with a $1,028 contribution, responded enthusiastically.[12] Dalrymple hired Robert Hill to organize the Jackson, Michigan, Goodyear fac-

[9] *Proceedings*, 1938, pp. 170–74, 235; *ABJ*, Sept. 23, 1938.

[10] *Proceedings*, 1939, pp. 153, 155, 161, 166–67, 170–71.

[11] Ibid., p. 206.

[12] Report of General Secretary Treasurer, in *Report of Officers to the Sixth Annual Convention Convened at Indianapolis, Indiana, Sept. 15, 1941, United Rubber Workers of America* (Akron, 1941), p. 100.

tory and H. R. Lloyd to organize three Dayton, Ohio, plants. Locals 5 and 101 also sent members to organize the Hood plant in Watertown and the U.S. Rubber plant in Providence, despite the misgivings of the International officers. By the summer of 1940 the fund was exhausted and the officers, impressed with "the gravity of the situation," began to reconsider their original plan.[13] Dalrymple conceded that "we still have with us . . . our number-one problem that we had five years ago—the organization of the unorganized."[14]

CONTINUED DECLINE IN AKRON

Ultimately the turmoil in the URW reflected the problems of the Akron locals, which continued to struggle with the effects of the sit-down era and the recession. One measure of their faltering influence was the collapse of two institutions that had previously extended their authority outside the factory. The breakup of the Central Labor Union was especially painful. The Trades and Labor Assembly became the personal fiefdom of H. A. Bradley, who used it to attack the CIO, while the Industrial Union Council became a center of political intrigue. James Keller, the Akron Communist leader, was "smart enough to wrangle his henchmen into key positions" in the IUC. By vociferously attacking critics as "fascists" or "red baiters," they were able to silence union leaders who disliked them.[15] Since their main interest was the promotion of Popular Front causes that the CIO also supported, the easy course was to disregard them. When that proved impossible the CIO suffered. In early 1939 Callahan clashed with the Communists on several issues. Shortly afterward he announced his candidacy for the IUC presidency to succeed Wilmer Tate, whose failing health was forcing his retirement. In response Keller organized a meeting to plot Callahan's defeat and supposedly to "ban other Local #5 delegates from election to any office."[16] The Communists threw their support to H. R. Lloyd and packed the election meeting, giving Lloyd an easy victory. Callahan was so disgusted that he refused to run again when revelations of the plot forced a new election. Lloyd won by one vote over a little-known opponent. The incident alienated the Local 5 leaders and discredited the IUC.[17]

[13] General Executive Board, Minutes, Jan. 26, July 19, 1940, URW Archives.

[14] Report of the General Executive Board, in *Reports of President S. H. Dalrymple, Vice President T. F. Burns and General Executive Board, 5th Annual Convention, United Rubber Workers of America, Detroit, Michigan, September 16, 1940*, p. 6.

[15] *ABJ*, Feb. 26, 1939; Alfred Winslow Jones, *Life, Liberty, and Property: A Story of Conflict and a Measurement of Conflicting Rights* (Philadelphia, 1941), 302.

[16] Local 5, Minutes, March 5, 1939, Local 5 Archives, Local 5 offices, Akron, Ohio.

[17] *SCLN*, Jan. 13, Feb. 17, 1939.

Labor's Non-Partisan League was at first more fortunate. In 1938, the state and local organizations played a leading role in Charles Sawyer's overwhelming victory over Governor Davey in the Democratic primary. Chairman M. R. Crouch was especially pleased at their success in winning black voters, despite substantial wooing by the Davey forces.[18] The league also helped the Democrats take Summit County by a large margin in the general election. By early 1939 Crouch was looking forward to another local campaign, with labor-backed candidates contesting for the mayor's office, council seats, and the board of education.

Then problems appeared. Crouch, who worked for the WPA, had to give up his post because of federal legislation that prohibited partisan activity by government employees. His resignation in favor of Frank Grillo removed the last tenuous tie between the league and the AFL. The league campaign also suffered from dissension. Unable to recruit an attractive mayoral candidate, Grillo at last turned to Wilford B. Bixler, a little-known state representative. Rubber worker votes probably accounted for Bixler's narrow victory in the primary, but he and Grillo soon parted ways and ran separate campaigns in the general election. The relations between Grillo and Ben Graves, Ralph Turner, and Virginia Etheridge, the labor victors in 1937, were not much better. In November, Bixler lost to Schroy by a large margin, and Graves, Turner, and Etheridge won easily. Even Grillo did not claim that the league or the unions had affected the outcome.[19]

In the tire plants the news was not uniformly bad. Mohawk, Seiberling, and General Tire, which produced for the replacement market, suffered far less than the Big Three in 1937 and 1938. They laid off a lower proportion of their employees, worked longer hours, and, after mid-1938, enjoyed a modest "boom." Their relations with their employees were also harmonious. The Mohawk local requested and received a written contract in 1936. The General and Seiberling locals, buoyed by the trend toward formal contracts at the Big Three, asked for formal written agreements in 1938. The Seiberling negotiations, completed with a minimum of difficulty and publicity in early February 1939, provided for existing wage rates and other features of the status quo.[20]

The General Tire negotiations were longer and much less harmonious. They began in October 1938 and proceeded smoothly until the union demanded a union shop. Months of "fruitless negotiation" followed and led the workers' tempers to rise. In late February Local 9 president Ray A. Sullivan barely averted a wildcat strike. A more serious incident began on

[18] *SCLN*, Aug. 19, 1938.

[19] *ABJ*, Aug. 9, Nov. 12, 1939.

[20] Federal Reserve Board, Fourth District, *Monthly Business Review* 20 (Sept 30, 1938): 3–4; *ABJ*, Feb. 9, 1939; *SCLN*, Feb. 10, 1939.

May 19, when many truck-tire builders stopped work to protest a rate cut and Industrial Relations manager Herman Barnes ordered them out of the plant. Sullivan described the incident as a "lockout" and told reporters that the company had cut rates several times in recent months.[21] His statements enraged the paternalistic O'Neil, who suspended all negotiations until Sullivan issued a public apology. Sullivan refused. The local took a strike vote on May 28 but, under pressure from Dalrymple, agreed to postpone any action. Barnes held out for another week, then did an about-face and presented a detailed response to the union's most recent contract proposal. Two days of discussions produced an agreement. Local 9 members voted to accept the contract on June 11, 1939.[22]

The General Tire contract restored the company's reputation for liberality. Together with formal recognition, seniority by department, paid vacations, the six-hour day and thirty-six-hour week, it committed the company to existing piece rates. With guaranteed rates and the union to back them, the employees had a powerful incentive to increase output. As a result, their wages, already among the highest in the industry, became, in Sullivan's words, "ridiculous."[23]

During the spring of 1939 the condition of the automobile industry and the large tire manufacturers began to improve, producing the first signs of an Akron revival. By March, the rubber industry was "in a much better position than for some time."[24] Domestic demand continued to grow through the spring and summer, and the outbreak of World War II in Europe created an additional stimulus. By the fall, the prospect of a new war-related boom encouraged talk of expansion. At an elaborate celebration commemorating the centenary of Charles Goodyear's invention of vulcanization, Goodyear executives had already spelled out their plans. They promised "further mechanization and conveyorization," efforts to "shorten the cycle from raw materials to finished products," and machinery that would put the Akron complex "on a par with the most modern Goodyear factory anywhere."[25] Firestone, General Tire, and the smaller companies also pledged new investments in their Akron plants. The major question mark was Goodrich, which, by virtue of its slowness to decentralize, had again become the city's largest employer, next to the WPA. Good-

[21] *ABJ*, May 21, 1939.

[22] David T. Roadley, "Progress Report," May 27, 1939, and "Union Statement," FMCS Papers, RG 280, File 199/5371.

[23] "Synopsis of Agreement," Federal Mediation and Conciliation Service Papers, RG 280, File 199/3745, National Archives; Ray A. Sullivan, interview with author, July 21, 1982.

[24] Federal Reserve Board, Fourth District, *Monthly Business Review* 21 (March 31, 1939): 4.

[25] *ABJ*, Feb. 24, 1939.

rich announced the opening of a mechanical goods factory in Clarksville, Tennessee, in May 1939, but for various reasons, including a management succession crisis, scrapped plans for a southern tire plant.[26]

For the large Akron locals the revival was hardly a panacea. The Big Three began to increase hours and call back workers in the fall of 1938 but the gains were modest. Goodrich, for example, rehired one thousand six hundred workers during the fall and winter, but still had four thousand four hundred on layoff in February 1939. Firestone employment was stagnant and Goodyear had fewer employees during the first half of 1939 than during most of 1938.[27] The Goodrich and Firestone contracts, which expired in early 1939, posed additional challenges. When Firestone executives suggested an extension of the 1938 agreement, Buckmaster and the local executive board, still worried about the employees' association, readily agreed. They were happy to have a contract in any form.[28]

Local 5 officers faced even greater uncertainty, given the company's lackluster performance. At least they did not have to worry about the protective association, which had never overcome its birth pangs and had attracted only a handful of members.[29] At the beginning of the negotiations, in November 1938, Graham expressed a willingness to renew the contract if the union agreed to "a reasonable flexibility of hours." He conceded existing wage levels and the six-hour day. Local 5 representatives, led by Bass, pushed for additional concessions, including higher vacation pay. In the course of one rancorous session, Bass threatened to scrap the contract and "run wild again as we did before." Graham "boiled over" at this remark.[30] In early January, the talks temporarily broke down:

Mr. Graham lost his temper in one instance and said he was getting damned disgusted with trying to negotiate . . . and spending so much time and not being able to accomplish anything. . . . Mr. Graham said he never would negotiate another agreement with [the union]. . . . The Company talked about throwing out the entire agreement.[31]

After acknowledging that they were "almost hopelessly deadlocked," the negotiators devised satisfactory compromises on most issues. The union negotiators claimed eighteen improvements, but their principal achievement was the contract itself. After "sharp debate," the local ratified the agreement on February 26.[32]

[26] *ABJ*, Feb. 26, 1939; Jones, *Life, Liberty, and Property*, p. 44.
[27] Employment File, Goodyear Archives.
[28] *ABJ*, April 5, 1939; *SCLN*, April 7, 1939.
[29] Goodrich Employees' Association, Minutes, Nov. 1938, Local 5 Archives.
[30] Local 5, Minutes, Nov. 25, 1938, Feb. 28, 1939, Local 5 Archives.
[31] Ibid., Jan. 3, 1939.
[32] Ibid., Feb. 6, 8, 28, 1939.

The perils of not having a contract were abundantly clear at Goodyear, where Local 2 faced a hostile management and a rival union of uncertain but substantial size. After December 1938, when Climer broke off negotiations, House and the local officers had few options. A strike was hardly feasible, since they had less than two thousand paid-up members and little hope of aid from the International or the other Akron locals. After visiting Akron in December 1938, Allan Haywood reported that they were "very much in the position of a stepchild as far as the International was concerned." Dalrymple was "leaving House and his local to paddle their own canoe."[33] The only other possibility was a renewed appeal to the NLRB. The local had filed several charges and House believed it "had the goods on" the company.[34] The danger, in the words of Labor Department conciliator P. W. Chappell, no friend of the NLRB, was that the local would "allow the matter to drag along in hopes that eventually the NLRB will take some action."[35]

By the end of 1938 URW leaders had concluded that the Cleveland NLRB office was a weak and unreliable ally, and perhaps not an ally at all. Two incidents had raised serious doubts about the leadership of James P. Miller, the director. In April 1938, Thomas Burns became aware of rumors that the H. A. McGrath Detective Agency, long active in industrial espionage, had agents in the NLRB office. Burns notified Heber Blankenhorn, an investigator for the La Follette Committee and the NLRB. Blankenhorn was unable to identify the spy, but obtained Miller's admission that he, too, suspected leaks but had done nothing.[36] Several months later, during the tense Goodyear negotiations, Goodyear lawyers forced Miller to admit that he had received and acknowledged Slusser's letter disavowing the "Miller agreement" after January 1, 1938. Burns, shocked at the disclosure, wrote that it produced a "very strong suspicion that the union was kept in ignorance . . . deliberately." The incident "robbed us of any confidence we might have in Miller."[37] When Miller then refused to act on House's charges, Denlinger complained to the NLRB so vigorously that board officials agreed to remove Miller from the case. They fired him in May 1939, supposedly for accepting favors from outside attorneys. Miller claimed that

[33] P. W. Chappell to John R. Steelman, Jan. 6, 1939, FMCS Papers, RG 280, File 199/1891. Also John D. House, interviews with author, April 15, May 1, 1972.

[34] John D. House interviews.

[35] Chappell to Steelman, Jan. 6, 1939, FMCS Papers, RG 280, File 199/1891.

[36] Thomas F. Burns to Heber Blankenhorn, April 26, 1938, and Blankenhorn to Burns, May 6, June 1, 1938, National Labor Relations Board Papers, RG 25, Case VIII-C-378, National Archives.

[37] Burns to Blankenhorn, June 2, 1938, NLRB Papers, RG 25, Case VIII-C-378.

he was dismissed for enforcing the law impartially. He told congressional investigators that the charges against Goodyear were weak.[38]

In mid-January 1939, NLRB attorney Max Johnstone and a team of investigators arrived in Akron to take over the case. For four months they worked furiously to construct an "air tight" presentation. With Denlinger's help, they reviewed thousands of incidents and interviewed five hundred employees. The case became "unwieldy from sheer volume." Nevertheless, it showed "an overwhelming amount of general coercion and intimidation." House reported in mid-March that it was "developing beautifully." He anticipated "an early and victorious hearing."[39]

The hearings began in late May 1939, continued intermittently for almost a year, and demonstrated that union hopes for government assistance were misplaced. Goodyear attorneys had learned the fundamentals of New Deal labor law in 1936 and had honed their skills in Gadsden during 1937. Led by Lisle M. Buckingham, they sought to show that the company had adhered to the letter of the law and that Local 2 members were responsible for most of the turmoil. For every union charge, they were ready with a countercharge; for every witness who accused the company of intimidation, they presented another witness who accused the union. Belligerent and obstructive, Buckingham managed to turn Johnstone and Denlinger against trial examiner Tilford E. Dudley before finally paralyzing the proceedings with appeals to the courts.

At first, the hearings attracted considerable interest among union members and the public. House was the first witness, and his account of the events of 1937 and 1938 and Buckingham's aggressive cross-examination were good theater. Denlinger added to the drama by interrupting the hearings with a request for more contract negotiations.[40] But after these preliminaries, the hearings bogged down. Lawyers and procedural issues played a larger role, and the purpose of the proceedings became less clear. By fall, the sessions had degenerated into a shouting match between Buckingham, Johnstone, and Denlinger. In early October, Johnstone and Denlinger charged that Dudley's rulings favored the company, precipitating a two-month delay while NLRB investigators cleared Dudley of wrongdoing. In January 1940, shortly after the hearings resumed, Denlinger demanded

[38] Local 2, Minutes, Executive Board, Dec. 9, 1938, and Minutes, Membership Meeting, Dec. 11, 1938, Local 2 Archives, Local 2 offices, Akron, Ohio; *ABJ*, Dec. 18, 1939.

[39] Meeting in House's Office, Jan. 19, 1939, NLRB Papers, RG 25, Box 351, Case 8-C-378; Local 2, Minutes, Membership Meeting, March 12, 1939, Local 2 Archives.

[40] Local 2, Minutes, Membership Meeting, June 11, 1939, Local 2 Archives; *ABJ*, June 13, 1939; Harold S. Roberts, *The Rubber Workers: Labor Organization and Collective Bargaining in the Rubber Industry* (New York, 1944), pp. 246–47.

more records from the company, giving Buckingham an opportunity to appeal to the courts.

The collapse of the NLRB case was almost as damaging to Local 2 as the Gadsden hearings had been to Local 12. As the prospects of meaningful government intervention faded, the local's membership fell from a total of 6,000 in January 1939 to 2,800 in December (with only a handful paying dues) at the same time the Goodyear labor force grew from 8,300 to nearly 10,000. In December, House won reelection over Secretary C. E. Smith, a leader of the "hot heads," by 285 votes to 236.[41] The local's decline had a similar effect on the Goodyear Employees Association, as anti-union workers concluded that an organization was unnecessary. By the summer of 1939 the association was hardly more popular than Local 2.

Finally, a disastrous strike at General Tire in the spring of 1940 underlined the plight of the once-formidable Akron unions. Two problems led to the debacle. The first was a provision of the 1939 contract that called for the resolution of grievances within ten days. In practice, negotiations often continued for months. By the spring of 1940, many workers had concluded that the company was stalling in order to escape the rate guarantee and pressured union officers for a strike vote. The second problem was Joseph Childs, the new local president. Young, attractive, and self-assured, Childs was ill-prepared for the events of March and April. Rather than resisting the pressures of his position, he succumbed to them.

The immediate issue was Childs's job. In mid-March, the company posted a proposed rate for a new truck tire built on a drum-type machine. Childs and other tire builders considered the rate too low and objected. They received little satisfaction. When they went to the head of the time study department, for example, they were told that he "did not have time to go into discussion of the rate." The superintendent called the rate "effective and permanent" and scheduled production for April 8.[42] Though many tire builders were angry, they did not envision any immediate action. Local vice-president W. K. Prather, who worked in the same department on a different shift, was not even aware of the dispute. Nor was there any mention of the controversy at the monthly membership meeting on April 7. However, when Childs arrived at 6:00 A.M. on April 8, he refused to work on the new tire and told other union members in the department to put away their tools. When the superintendent arrived, he insisted that Childs and the others return to work before he would consider their grievance. Again Childs declined. The dispute soon brought the plant to a standstill.[43]

---

[41] Local 2, Membership Record, Local 2 Archives.

[42] "Union's Statement," FMCS Papers, RG 280, File 199/5371.

[43] Testimony of W. K. Prather, May 22, 1940, in Hearings before Bureau of Unemployment Compensation, pp. 20–23, 27–28, 39, NLRB Papers, RG 25, Case VIII-C-716.

For the next two days, the local executive board met in "almost continuous session."[44] Though Childs was unable to explain why he had called the men out, he persuaded the board to support a strike because of the unresolved grievances, the managers' antagonistic manner, and the widespread belief that the company was trying to reduce wages. On April 10 the members voted to strike, and six days later the International, confronted with a fait accompli, added its reluctant approval. Most observers agreed that the real issue was "an accumulation of unadjusted grievances of long standing" and that the executives would act quickly to resolve them.[45]

The optimists did not give sufficient weight to two other factors. General Tire executives emphasized privately that they had "enough materials in their warehouses to last for six months" and were "unconcerned how long this drags out." They also hoped to discipline the local and reclaim some of their former powers. Whether they actually hoped to break the union and discard the contract is uncertain; probably there was no consensus. Labor Department conciliator David T. Roadley reported on April 17 that the company "does not intend to settle" the dispute and "will wait for a backto-work movement."[46] In contacts with union officials, O'Neil was characteristically affable and conciliatory; Barnes and the plant executives were much tougher and refused to negotiate until the men honored their contract and returned to work.

In the meantime, they kept the plant open. Supervisors gathered at the gates in the morning to shout encouragement to returning employees. By April 21, they were able to resume production. Roadley reported that the company had been "receiving raw materials right along and [is] shipping tires to customers. There is no incentive . . . to settle this strike except upon their own terms. The strike has been anything but effective."[47]

The defections compelled union leaders to become more forceful. On the morning of April 22, they mobilized seven hundred pickets and formed a chain picket line in front of the main gate. Police broke up the demonstration and escorted nonstrikers into the plant to choruses of "boos, whistles and cries of 'scab.' "[48] On succeeding days a large contingent of police appeared each morning to clear the gate area. Thwarted and seemingly powerless, some of the strikers embarked on a month-long reign of terror against the nonstrikers. They threw rocks and tear gas through windows

[44] *ABJ*, April 10, 1940.

[45] Roadley to Steelman, April 11, 1940, FMCS Papers, RG 280, File 199/5371.

[46] Memorandum for the Record, April 16, 1940, and Roadley to Steelman, April 17, 1940, FMCS Papers, RG 280, File 199/5371.

[47] Steelman, "Memorandum," April 24, 1940, and Roadley, "Progress Report," May 8, 1940, FMCS Papers, RG 280, File 199/5371.

[48] *ABJ*, April 22, 1940.

and planted bombs outside a half dozen houses, causing varying degrees of damage. Childs accused the nonstrikers of contriving the bombings, but few people took his charges seriously. Denlinger told an NLRB official that union men were at fault and that he would refuse to defend them if they were caught. He was "blue about the whole situation."[49] In earlier Akron disputes, there had been riots, beatings, shootings, and occasional bombings but never a sustained campaign of terror. The violence "unquestionably" hurt the union.[50]

After five weeks, the union was in disarray and no closer to a settlement than it had been in mid-April. Dalrymple began to worry about its future. On May 14, he told one observer that if the members did not settle quickly, "he was going to personally call the membership together and . . . ask them to return to work, in order to preserve the Local Union."[51] He did not intervene, presumably because Childs convinced him that mass picketing and an appeal to the NLRB would force the company to capitulate. The strike continued for another month, with more attacks on nonstrikers and more activity in the plant. The company refused to negotiate or to commit itself to a new contract. The local union held out, but at mounting costs.

In June, the prospects of a settlement brightened as the strikers exhausted their savings, and the company, having underestimated the strength of the recovery, found its supply of tires severely depleted. Labor Department officials sent Francis J. Haas, a well-known mediator and Roman Catholic priest who, they hoped, would be able to influence the devoutly Catholic O'Neil. Haas conducted marathon sessions on June 8 and 9 but failed to persuade O'Neil "to meet the union at any time."[52] He returned a week later with a compromise plan similar to one Roadley had proposed in April. This time he reported some progress. After several more days of conferences, he persuaded both sides to authorize their attorneys to negotiate a new contract, after which the workers would return to their jobs and union and company negotiators would take up the unsettled grievances. With Haas presiding, Denlinger and the company attorney completed their deliberations in less than a week. The new contract provided more generous vacation pay and a detailed procedure for settling grievances; otherwise, it was identical to the 1939 pact. At the June 25 ratification meeting, critics complained that the agreement left "us just where we were when we

---

[49] Louis Plost to Oscar S. Smith, June 17, 1940, NLRB Papers, RG 25, Case VIII-C-716.

[50] *ABJ*, May 5, 1940.

[51] Roadley, "Progress Report," May 14, 1940, FMCS Papers, RG 280, File 199/5371. Three members of the International Executive Board independently considered some form of intervention (Roadley, "Memorandum for the Record," May 31, 1940, FMCS Papers, RG 280, File 199/5371).

[52] Smith to Plost, June 10, 1940, NLRB Papers, RG 25, Case VIII-C-716.

started'' and ''cheers and boos'' greeted union officers. Finally, the strikers voted 548 to 119 to accept the contract and return to their jobs. In Sullivan's language, they ''crawled back.''[53]

The next day, General Tire announced a major expansion of its plant, citing the ''assurance of uninterrupted production.'' O'Neil confidently argued that the '' 'old Akron' had come back . . . it is a 'ghost town' no more.''[54] Local citizens were overjoyed; it was the largest single investment since 1929 and evidence of renewed confidence in the city and its workers. But it also obscured the serious effects of the strike. O'Neil's biographer wrote that he ''never again'' felt the ''same easy natural camaraderie with his workers.''[55] The paternalism that had survived the 1934 strike, the sit-down era, and the recession years died in 1940, along with the image of ''responsible'' unionism at General Tire. The workers faced more immediate and more tangible problems. Eleven weeks without paychecks left them in a ''very embarrassing financial situation,'' as Dalrymple delicately phrased it. Local 9 had only fifteen paid-up members at the end of June.[56] It had suffered the most serious strike defeat of any Akron local since the formation of the URW. In November, Sullivan handily defeated Childs for the union presidency.

PROGRESS IN OUTLYING COMMUNITIES

In February 1940 the International officers published a brief, celebratory report on their stewardship. They listed 27 locals with union shop contracts and 26 with 100 percent membership; nearly half of the 117 URW locals, they boasted, represented all of the workers in a particular plant.[57] Yet there was another, less hopeful side to the data. Of the locals with union shop contracts, only the tiny Denman Tire organization was a tire workers' union. The locals with 100 percent membership included Seiberling Local 18, Mohawk Local 8, Pennsylvania Tire Local 22, and the U.S. Rubber locals at Eau Claire, Los Angeles, Mishawaka, and Indianapolis; the others were small and obscure. Except for the U.S. Rubber plants, none of the industry giants appeared in either group. But in terms of potential members, the small businesses were an even greater challenge. The locals with union

---

[53] F. J. Haas to Steelman, June 17, 1940, FMCS Papers, RG 280, File 199/5371; Ray A. Sullivan interview; *ABJ*, June 26, 1940.

[54] *ABJ*, June 26, 1940.

[55] Dennis J. O'Neil, *A Whale of A Territory: The Story of Bill O'Neil* (New York, 1966), p. 112.

[56] Sherman H. Dalrymple to President, Local 2, July 2, 1940, Local 2, Minutes, Executive Board, Local 2 Archives; Sullivan interview.

[57] *URW* 5 (Feb. 1940): 1.

shop agreements or 100 percent membership represented only 9 percent of the rubber factories in the U.S. and Canada. All 117 locals represented only 19 percent of the plants and 43 percent of the 133,000 U.S. and Canadian rubber workers. The other 478 unorganized plants were nearly all small.[58]

The most striking URW success story of the late 1930s was the union's close and comfortable relationship with U.S. Rubber. Dalrymple and Ching got along well together, as did many of the local leaders and their management counterparts. Glenn Gann, president of Detroit Local 101, reported that "relations with the company have been progressing smoothly, with little hint of disturbance and much evidence of mutual advantage."[59] When Herbert Wilson and the Local 44 officers asked for a union security agreement in late 1938, Samson executives explained that they opposed a formal union shop "because of the anti-union sentiment of certain customers" but were "willing to have a 100 percent union shop" and would cooperate "with the union to get it."[60] By mid-1939, the local had a de facto union shop.

The International officers and staff overlooked few opportunities to praise Ching and his "progressive" policies. Even Eagle waxed eloquent on the virtues of U.S. Rubber.[61] Of special interest to URW leaders was the company's robust growth, which provided jobs and proof that union contracts were not a harbinger of decline. URW leaders took special delight when U.S. Rubber's sales temporarily passed Goodyear's. What they tended to forget was that Ching's goal was not to promote the URW but to contain a development that he considered inevitable. As a result, they had little trouble in U.S. Rubber's tire plants, which Ching considered vulnerable, but found the footwear and mechanical goods factories as inaccessible as the anti-union firms.

The record is sketchy, but it suggests two kinds of obstacles—the company's liberal wage and benefit policy and divisions among the workers. In the late 1930s, the URW hierarchy was still identifiably midwestern and Anglo-Saxon, a fact that the presence of Burns, Camelio, Marchiando, and, after the mini-revolt of 1939, a more heterogeneous International Executive Board only partly mitigated.[62] The major unorganized U.S. Rubber

[58] U.S. Department of Commerce, Bureau of the Census, *16th Census of the U.S.: 1940, Manufactures, 1939*, vol. 2, pt. 2, p. 17.

[59] *URW* 3 (Feb. 1938): 1.

[60] Local 44, Minutes, Nov. 6, 1938, Local 44 Archives.

[61] Local 44, Minutes, Oct. 15, 1939, Local 44 Archives.

[62] Another possible problem, never mentioned in the documents, was the absence of special appeals to women workers. The International had no women organizers after 1935, though Margaret Cowger of Oak Rubber in Ravenna, Ohio, worked part-time in several Ohio campaigns.

plants, at Providence, Naugatuck, and Passaic, employed large numbers of east European immigrants and their children. Differences in style and accent were not insurmountable, but they kept the URW off balance. Prospective members were often suspicious and strongly tempted to join rival AFL organizations that were locally based and untarred with the brush of CIO radicalism.

At the giant Naugatuck boot and shoe plant, Local 45 grew slowly and fitfully despite a benign management and a substantial commitment of URW resources. Workers in the boot room, all male and comparatively well paid, began to organize in 1937. By early 1938, they were strong enough to negotiate a set of "working rules" that amounted to a departmental contract. But they were unable to extend their influence because the women workers, a large majority of the total, remained "wishy-washy" or hostile to the union.[63] By 1939 the International officers were concerned about the local's lack of progress and the appearance of an independent union. Burns recruited an activist Roman Catholic priest to quiet the fears of some workers and encouraged a merger of the two organizations. After talks with the plant managers, he got "an acceptable recognition statement." By the end of the year, many workers "figured it was time"; unions were "getting powerful."[64] Still there were many who refused to join and others who held out for an AFL union. A formal contract remained almost two years in the future.

The URW had even less success at Providence. Local 66, chartered in 1937, was moribund by 1939 when an AFL campaign attracted approximately one thousand members. In response Burns launched an emergency effort to "rebuild Local 66." However, when he inspected the local's records, he discovered that he had been "misinformed" about the Providence local's strength; only eighteen of the plant's two thousand workers were URW members. Faced with an immediate NLRB election, the International officers in desperation asked the NLRB to declare U.S. Rubber a single bargaining unit.[65] AFL attorneys had little difficulty showing that the Providence managers were in charge of the negotiations, and the board rejected the URW request in early 1940. Though URW organizers made good use of the delay caused by the hearings, they could not offset the federal labor union's initial advantage. On March 6, 1940, the AFL won the representation election, 1,120 votes to 711.[66]

---

[63] "Points Covered in the Seniority Discussion," Feb. 10, 11, 1938, Local 45 File, URW Archives; George Froelich, interview with author, Jan. 11, 1978.

[64] "Report of Thomas F. Burns," in *Report of Officers, Fourth Convention, United Rubber Workers of America, La Crosse, Wisconsin, Week of September 11, 1939*, p. 3; George Froelich interview.

[65] "Report of Thomas F. Burns," in *Reports*, 1940, pp. 1–2.

[66] "Proceedings," NLRB Case R 1669-1770-1771, NLRB Papers, RG 25, Box 217.

At Passaic, the only union organization in the 1930s was a local of the International Brotherhood of Electrical Workers, which recruited a dozen electricians. Despite the efforts of Marchiando, Carney, and others, the URW was unable to attract enough supporters to charter a local until 1941.

At Hood Rubber, the other large eastern plant, the URW fared only marginally better. A local chartered in May 1937 attracted only forty of the four thousand employees and soon foundered. When the Supreme Court upheld the Wagner Act, the leaders of the well-established company union reorganized as an independent union and enlisted three thousand five hundred members. The URW protested to the NLRB, which investigated and charged the company with interference in August 1939. By that time, the independent union had given way to an AFL federal local, which demanded an NLRB election. The AFL request prompted URW leaders to launch another last-minute URW organizing campaign, even though the URW had "absolutely no membership" at the plant and many workers indicated "very strong opposition to any type of union."[67] On March 15 the AFL local received 1,560 votes; "no organization," 666; the Arrow Protective Association (a remnant of the independent union), 501; and the URW, 189. Burns blamed the outcome on the management and the NLRB, but the truth was that he and his colleagues had misjudged the Hood workers.[68]

As the economy improved, the tire plants again became the most attractive URW targets. In Los Angeles, Goodrich Local 43 leaders became bolder after May 1938, when the company signed the Akron contract. "We wore a button and spoke loudly and we didn't mind challenging them any place, anywhere," recalled one local officer.[69] In January 1939, when the company posted a three-shift, eight-hour schedule, the workers voted to declare a "holiday" that lasted nearly three weeks. The management finally agreed to a formal contract that included the six-hour day. In the following months Goodyear Local 131 leaders began to demand a similar agreement. By spring of 1940, they had won concessions on a number of points but not the six-hour day. That was the "sore point" that ultimately stalled the talks.[70] Firestone unionists had no less difficulty. Their NLRB charges, filed in March 1937, resulted in a March 1940 decision ordering the company to withdraw recognition from an independent union and reinstate six discharged URW members. Despite more "layoffs, intimidation, and coercion," Local 100 won a May 1940 NLRB election victory and negotiated an agreement that included the eight-hour day and forty-hour

[67] *URW* 5 (Jan. 1940): 1; "Report of Thomas F. Burns," in *Reports*, 1940, pp. 2–3.

[68] Roberts, *Rubber Workers*, p. 292. Also see Thomas M. Finn, "Final Report," Aug. 12, 1940, FMCS Papers, RG 280, File 196/2108.

[69] Floyd Gartrell, interview with author, Aug. 15, 1977.

[70] *URW* 5 (May 1940): 5.

week. Given the hostility of Firestone officials, it was a milestone, however small.[71]

At Armstrong Tire, the principal beneficiary of the cancellation of the Goodyear-Sears contract, prosperity did not translate automatically into a union presence. In 1937 organizer Herbert Dawson formed a local that died with the first company threats. Despite wages that were half the Akron level and "horrible" working conditions, there was no other union activity until late 1938, when an AFL representative contacted several of the men who had been active in the short-lived URW local and undertook a vigorous and successful campaign. He found the managers still "very much opposed to a union" and unwilling to talk until he filed for an NLRB election.[72] Even then, he was unable to wring meaningful concessions. By the end of 1940, many Armstrong union members were unhappy with both the company and the AFL.

The pattern in other eastern tire plants was similar. A few Dunlop Tire workers organized in 1937 to win seniority rights but retreated when the foremen threatened to discharge them. The local's URW charter lapsed in 1938 and was not revived until mid-1940, when the International sent an organizer to Buffalo.[73] Workers at Lee Tire and the Goodrich Oaks plant, both near Philadelphia, were no more active, at least in part because of community hostility.[74]

Goodyear tire workers in Cumberland, Jackson, and Gadsden were more militant but hardly more successful. Despite losing hundreds of members, Local 26 was able to enforce the 1937 seniority agreement during the lay-offs of 1937 and 1938. In May 1938, following conferences with John House and representatives of the Gadsden local, President Charles Eline called for a formal contract. When Kelly-Springfield officials stalled, he launched a vigorous membership campaign. "Shift meetings, department meetings, division meetings and all kinds of meetings followed."[75] In mid-November, these activities led to a scuffle in the tire room, the suspension of a union member, and a week-long "holiday." After the workers returned, Local 26 leaders continued to meet company officials through the spring of 1939. Their demands for the six-hour day and wage parity with

---

[71] Roberts, *Rubber Workers*, pp. 277–78; *URW*, 5 (May 1940): 5; Edward Barnes, interview with author, Dec. 14, 1977.

[72] Francis Quinn, interview with author, Jan. 11, 1978; James J. Clerkin to Frank P. Fenton, Feb. 2, 1941, AFL Papers, Local 22343 Correspondence, State Historical Society of Wisconsin, Madison.

[73] "A History of Unionism at Dunlop Tire and Rubber" (unpublished paper in author's possession), p. 3; *URW* 5 (Aug. 1940): 5.

[74] *ABJ*, Nov. 26, 1937.

[75] *URW* 3 (March 1938): 1; ibid. (June 1938): 2; ibid. (July 1938): 1; ibid. (Nov. 1938): 2; ibid. (April 1939): 1; Local 26, Minutes, Executive Board, May 26, 1938, Local 26 Archives.

Akron ultimately resulted in an impasse and an end to URW hopes for a Goodyear breakthrough. By 1940 the local had regained most of its membership, but was no closer to a contract than it had been in 1937.

Union sympathizers in Jackson made even less headway during the recovery period. Not until the fall of 1939 could they report enough interest to persuade Dalrymple to send O. H. Bosley to direct a formal campaign. The day after Bosley's arrival several workers offered to take him to a meeting of prospective members. They drove him to an isolated spot on the edge of town, beat him, and left him "almost unconscious on [the] highway."[76] He was incapacitated for three weeks. Only in mid-1940 did Robert L. Hill begin a third and ultimately more successful effort to organize the Jackson plant.

In Gadsden the Local 12 "holiday" of May 1938 removed the last vestige of union influence from the Gadsden plant and imposed a formidable burden on the International. When Dalrymple was unable to persuade the men to return to work, he appealed to the NLRB. The results were no more satisfactory than the results of earlier appeals. In November, the NLRB issued a preliminary decision upholding the union charges, but Holmes, now on the URW payroll, reported that Goodyear officials had been "busy . . . telling the employees that it will take from two to three years for it to go through the courts."[77] In April 1940, Dalrymple and Denlinger scheduled a mass meeting in Gadsden only to discover that the Gadsden commissioners had canceled their meeting permit at the last minute. Dalrymple reluctantly concluded that the URW had no chance until the NLRB enforced its decision.[78]

By that time the URW faced a second major southern challenge in Memphis, where the new Firestone facility was almost twice as large as the Gadsden plant. Firestone managers had selected Memphis for its cheap labor and anti-union tradition and found a valuable ally in the Ed Crump political machine, which dominated Memphis civic life in the late 1930s. Crump's coalition of business interests and AFL unions had no room for outside unionists, especially those committed to raising wages or mixing the races. UAW organizers who tried to enlist workers in the city's Ford plant were severely beaten in 1937, and local authorities did not hide their belief that a similar fate awaited other CIO representatives.[79] From the URW

[76] N. H. Eagle to W. Liller, Oct. 1, 1940, FMCS Papers, RG 280, File 196/3061; Oliver H. Bosley, interview with author, Oct. 23, 1973.

[77] Holmes to Dalrymple, Nov. 7, 1939, Local 12 File, URW Archives.

[78] Dalrymple to Holmes, Dec. 1, 1939, Local 12 File.

[79] Roger Biles, "Ed Crump Versus the Unions: The Labor Movement in Memphis During the 1930's," *Labor History* 25 (1984): 540, 544–45; *ABJ*, Nov. 18, 1937.

perspective, the only substantial difference between Gadsden and Memphis was the absence of an active "independent" union in the Firestone plant.

Burns visited Memphis in the fall of 1939 and confirmed that Firestone paid tire workers as little as twenty-five cents per hour and apparently discharged employees whose wages exceeded forty-five cents per hour. The potential for organization was substantial.[80] On the other hand, the Firestone labor force included a high proportion of black workers, and any effort to recruit them would likely lead to racial conflict. Because of the International's financial disarray, Dalrymple was unable to act until the summer of 1940, when he appointed George Bass as a special organizer. The Local 5 activist's Tennessee heritage, leadership skills, and ill-disguised efforts to undermine Callahan were all factors in his selection.

Bass arrived on August 8, 1940, and spent several weeks familiarizing himself with the area. On August 22, he notified the police of his intentions and asked for protection. The next night a Firestone supervisor and approximately twenty men appeared at his hotel, threatened him with knives and clubs, and tried to force their way into his room. The following day, when he rented an apartment, he received more warnings. Later, when he, a lawyer, and another union man left the apartment and got into his car, some twenty men armed with "poles, blackjacks, and rubber hoses" surrounded them. While Bass and his companions sat helplessly inside, the men overturned the car, broke the windows, jabbed them "through the windows with two-by-fours," and tried to set the car on fire. Bass finally freed himself from the wrecked vehicle by kicking the door open. In the meantime the police arrived and the men dispersed. When the lawyer referred to the attackers as a "bunch of 'S-B-s,' " the police arrested him for profanity and held him in jail until the next day.[81]

Three days later Bass informed the police that he would distribute flyers at the plant and again requested protection. The results were similar. As he and several other union men approached the gate, a foreman and fifty to sixty workers armed with clubs and other weapons emerged. The supervisor pointed at them and said, "Get them two SBs," and the men gave Bass and another union man "good beatings." Bass's wounds provided him with an aura of martyrdom that all but ensured his accession to the Local 5 presidency in November.[82]

Thereafter the focus of the anti-union effort changed. The threats and violence, reported in detail in the local press, stopped abruptly, and AFL organizers, condemning the URW's interracial approach, began to organize

[80] "Report of Thomas F. Burns," in *Report*, 1939, pp. 1–2.

[81] V. C. Finch, "Special Report," Sept. 6, 1940, FMCS Papers, RG 280, File 196/3125; *Memphis Commercial Appeal*, Aug. 24, 27, 28, 1940.

[82] Ibid. Also see Roberts, *Rubber Workers*, p. 186.

white Firestone employees. By early December, they claimed one thousand two hundred members and demanded recognition. When Firestone executives insisted on dealing with both unions until the NLRB had certified one of them, the workers became impatient. On December 4, when the superintendent shifted a group of tire builders from day to piece rates, the leaders of the federal local called a strike meeting. Rejecting the counsel of Lev Loring, a building trades leader and Crump ally, they walked out and formed a picket line. Loring later confronted union president Lesley Goings and the pickets and "criticized the men bitterly." His comments made them "so mad that they threatened to upset Loring's car right on the street in front of the Firestone plant." Loring then retreated to city hall. Shortly afterward the mayor, police chief, and sheriff issued a statement attacking Goings as an ex-convict and demanded a change in the union's leadership. Goings resigned.[83]

These events gave the URW an opening. Grillo and Denlinger arrived on December 7, contacted the Firestone attorney, and urged the company not to make concessions to the strikers. "We pointed out . . . the difficulties that arise for companies . . . when minorities are permitted to take this kind of action and the action results in . . . concessions," Denlinger reported. The plant manager later thanked him for the "timely message," which had come "at the psychological moment" in the negotiations.[84] The men returned to work with no concessions and the federal local in disarray. Two weeks later the AFL won the NLRB election by a narrow margin, reflecting the racial division in the plant. URW leaders were encouraged. Local 186 remained intact and continued to attack the federal union, particularly after the AFL officers signed a contract that did not satisfy the suddenly militant Firestone employees.[85] Compared with the Gadsden efforts, the Memphis campaign had been reasonably peaceful, inexpensive, and successful. It underlined the original potential of the southern strategy.

In small nontire plants, URW fortunes varied markedly by region. In eastern factories, organizers had to overcome worker apathy and suspicion, manifested in hostility to any union or a preference for the AFL.[86] In the Midwest and West, on the other hand, employer opposition continued to be the most serious barrier to organization. Despite the changing political complexion of the midwestern states, union sympathizers at Faultless Rubber in Ashland, at Maple City Rubber in Norwalk, and at Pioneer Rubber in Willard, Ohio, were only marginally more secure than they had been in

[83] Stanley Denlinger to Dalrymple, Dec. 11, 1940, FMCS Papers, RG 280, File 199/6048.

[84] Ibid.

[85] E. C. Hodges to William Green, March 17, 1941, American Federation of Labor Papers, Local 22456 Correspondence, State Historical Society of Wisconsin, Madison.

[86] "History of Local 83," Local 83 File, URW Archives.

1933 or 1935. An informal alliance between the Schacht Company and Noblesville's elected officials made Harley Anthony and Floyd Robinson the town's most harassed residents for nearly four years.[87] The mayor of St. Marys, Ohio, site of a new Goodyear plant, publicly dreaded "the thought of what might happen" if CIO organizers "try to come in."[88]

At the Ohio and Barr companies, which had figured prominently in the AFL organizing campaign of 1934 and 1935, URW organizers faced more difficulties. When Rex Murray led a new campaign at Ohio Rubber in early 1938, the company stalled but did not attack the union. Murray responded by pressuring the NLRB for action on the case that had grown out of the violent 1935 strike. For more than a year the union received little satisfaction from the company or the government. In November 1938, Local 3 members sat down briefly to protest a wage cut and in February 1939 took a one-day "vacation" to underline their demand for a wage increase. Finally, in August 1939, the NLRB ordered the reinstatement of seventeen union members discharged in 1935. Three months later the union won a representation election and demanded a written contract. Once more the company delayed. The negotiations were not completed until the summer of 1940.[89]

Barr Rubber also persisted in its hard-line approach. Barr managers signed a union contract in 1937 but demanded sweeping concessions when local union leaders asked to renew it in 1938. After six months of futile negotiations, the local requested Bosley's help. He found "the membership . . . very much discouraged and . . . dues . . . falling off rapidly." After two months of additional negotiations an agreement seemed imminent and he left, only to return in June at reports of new conflicts and a strike vote. When the company abruptly demanded an NLRB vote before it would continue the talks, the local "had no alternative other than to call a strike."[90]

The Barr strike lasted from June 24 to September 7 and featured constant friction between pickets and police. By mid-July, with negotiations deadlocked and police harassment increasing, Bosley was afraid that strikers "would take matters into their own hands." He called for help from other CIO unions in the Sandusky area, but a disastrous parade and rally only encouraged the company to reopen. On August 30 "the entire city police force and several deputy sheriffs," armed "with tear gas, guns, and black-

---

[87] Harley C. Anthony, interview with author, April 11, 1972; *URW* 2 (Aug. 1937): 8, (Nov. 1937): 1, 4 (Feb. 1939): 1.

[88] *ABJ*, Nov. 19, 1939; Eagle to Liller, Oct. 1, 1940, FMCS Papers, RG 280, File 196/3061.

[89] Walter E. Taag, Memorandum, July 21, 1938, NLRB Papers, RG 25, Case VIII-C-33; *URW* 4 (Nov. 1939): 6; ibid. 5 (July 1940): 1; *ABJ*, Feb. 7, 1938.

[90] O. H. Bosley to Dalrymple, Sept. 10, 1939, Local 28 File, URW Archives.

jacks,'' escorted workers to the plant gate. Thereafter the strike declined rapidly. On September 6, for example, eighty-five workers, including twenty-six union members, crossed the picket line. Only twelve pickets confronted them.[91] Bosley had little choice but to advise the remaining members to return to work.

WAR AND REVIVAL

The factors that contained the union impulse during the years of recession and recovery—the decline of the Akron tire plants, the generally hostile environment elsewhere, and the antagonistic role of the AFL—were much less influential after the summer of 1940 because of the coming of World War II and the American preparedness effort. During the eighteen months that preceded Pearl Harbor, all of the integrated companies and large factories and many of the small firms became government contractors. By the summer of 1941, most of them devoted a quarter or more of their time and resources to war production. For them, the war boom meant profits and regulations; for workers it meant labor market conditions reminiscent of the 1910s; and for the URW, it meant a new era of opportunity.

Two effects of the war boom illustrated its pervasive influence. First, military demand, coupled with the ''cautious and faltering'' policies of the Rubber Reserve, the government agency charged with stockpiling natural rubber, greatly accelerated the shift from tire to mechanical goods production. By mid-1941, rubber manufacturers made gas masks, life rafts, linings for airplane fuel tanks, barrage balloons, and parts for military vehicles, as well as various nonrubber products. Goodyear converted its largely unused Akron blimp plant into an aircraft factory that eventually became the city's largest employer. Firestone became a major producer of antiaircraft guns and clips for machine gun bullets. In contrast, tire production languished, largely because the rubber shortage forced the Office of Production Management to discourage civilian output in 1940 and to curtail it in 1941. As the pace of mobilization increased, tire manufacturers often laid off workers because of material shortages.[92]

Second, the new demand, largely for the types of goods that had been made in outlying communities, revived the great Akron factories. The per-

[91] Bosley to Dalrymple, Sept. 10, 1939, Local 28 File.

[92] Nelson Lichtenstein, *Labor's War at Home: The CIO in World War II* (Cambridge, 1982), pp. 44–46; William M. Tuttle, Jr., ''The Birth of an Industry: The Synthetic Rubber 'Mess' in World War II,'' *Technology and Culture* 22 (1981): 39; Hugh Allen, *The House of Goodyear: Fifty Years of Men and Industry* (Akron, 1949), pp. 485–511; Alfred Lief, *The Firestone Story: A History of the Firestone Tire & Rubber Company* (New York, 1951), pp. 257–69; *ABJ*, May 8, 1941.

missive policies of the military procurement agencies removed the economic constraints that had doomed nontire production in Akron during the 1930s. By May 1941, Akron mechanical goods plants operated twenty-four hours a day, seven days a week, while tire plants remained on two or three six-hour shifts, five days a week. Federal Reserve statistics provide another measure of the change. In 1939 Akron area tire output grew more rapidly than department store sales in eight of ten months surveyed. In 1940, department store sales grew faster than tire production in six of eleven months; and in 1941, in ten of eleven months.[93] Akron boosters rejoiced because the war created possibilities for "newer and more diversified type[s] of industrial production" that would be less subject to the "peaks and valleys" of the tire industry.[94]

The war boom also tipped the labor market balance in favor of workers and created an atmosphere that militated against traditional anti-union tactics. One of the most sensitive measures of the change was the increase in total union membership, which exceeded one million in 1940–1941, more than in any comparable prior period except the sit-down years. The CIO efforts were particularly contentious, accounting for most of the record strike total in 1941. The URW was an exception to this pattern. It recruited proportionately twice as many members as the labor movement as a whole, but its successes were also unusually peaceful. For the first time in the industry's history, an upsurge in union activity was not accompanied by social upheaval.

Thomas Burns could take most of the responsibility for this change. In September 1940 he requested a leave of absence to join Sidney Hillman's staff at the OPM, where he finally gained the status and influence he had sought since 1933. Although he worked in Washington, he remained on the International Executive Board and became a vigorous promoter of government policy. His most important contribution came in April 1941, when he submitted a resolution to support the defense effort and the Roosevelt administration's no-strike policy. He also proposed that the International refuse to sanction any strike until an organizer and the Conciliation Service had failed to resolve the dispute. Grillo seconded the resolution and it passed, apparently without dissent.[95] The antistrike policy helped make the industry an anomaly during the months that preceded Pearl Harbor and further shifted the balance of power within the union toward the International and the non-Akron locals. Generally compliant employers obscured these

[93] Federal Reserve Board, Fourth District, *Monthly Business Review* 21–23 (1939–1941).
[94] *ABJ*, July 11, 1941.
[95] General Executive Board, Minutes, April 10, 1941, URW Archives.

effects in 1941, but the Burns resolution remained an alien and potentially threatening innovation for the decentralized URW.

For URW leaders the most pressing problem of 1940 was not the threat of strikes but the decline of the union's foothold in the Goodyear plants, most notably in Akron. As unemployment declined and URW finances improved, an effort to revive Local 2 was obviously in order. Most observers believed that the union's formidable problems, including a leadership divided between the House and "hothead" factions, made a revival unlikely without outside help. The failure of a visit by William Carney, now CIO regional director in New Jersey, to "crystallize the enthusiasm" of the members underlined the seriousness of the situation.[96] Yet the International officers hesitated, unable to view the Goodyear local with the same detachment with which they viewed the Hood or the Memphis local. Eagle finally forced the issue by proposing to take over Local 2. Aware that he was an anathema to both factions and to many uncommitted union members, the International Executive Board turned in desperation to the CIO. Dalrymple talked to Haywood when he appeared at a General Tire strike rally and won a pledge of assistance. In early May 1940, Haywood sent Robert J. Davidson, an organizer who had directed campaigns among glass workers and General Motors employees.[97]

Davidson devised a strategy that differed markedly from the course House had emphasized since 1935. He abandoned the NLRB case, made no effort to negotiate a contract, and stressed "the necessity of first organizing the unorganized." To help him, he appointed a strategy committee and an organizer's committee, both carefully balanced between the House and "hothead" factions. Union meetings turned into "reorganization" meetings and "many members volunteered to assist in contact work." By August, the local boasted thirty to fifty reinstatements per day. In September, Dalrymple reported a thousand reinstatements and a "goodly number of new members."[98]

Davidson's success was a powerful argument for an expanded campaign, financed by an increase in the per capita tax. By the summer of 1940, the International officers were committed to a permanent, mandatory increase. They asked the locals not to instruct their delegates to the 1940 convention and provided organizers with voluminous instructions for answering op-

[96] William Carney to C. E. Smith, April 3, 1940, Local 2 Archives. Carney died several months later.

[97] General Executive Board, Minutes, April 18, 1940, URW Archives; John D. House, interview with author, March 12, 1975; *ABJ*, April 22, 1940; "Report of President S. H. Dalrymple," in *Reports*, 1940, p. 33.

[98] Local 2, Minutes, Membership Meeting, April 30, May 29, June 16, 1940, Local 2 Archives; *URW* 5 (Aug. 1940): 1; "Report of Dalrymple," 1940, p. 33.

ponents. To underline the urgency of the situation, they laid off five of the special organizers they had hired with the voluntary fund.[99] Their reports and speeches to the convention were a litany of failure due to inadequate finances. Dalrymple characterized the voluntary fund as "inadequate and unsatisfactory" and predicted continued stagnation unless the International had more money. Though the Akron locals, including Local 2, led the opposition, the officers' careful preparations created "a high degree of interest." After a prolonged debate, the delegates turned down a dues increase but voted to raise the per capita tax from forty to forty-five cents. They also adopted a resolution specifying Goodyear as the union's "No. 1 problem."[100]

In the following months, Dalrymple hired organizers and planned an extensive campaign but did nothing about the "No. 1 problem." He admitted his reluctance to throw good money after bad. "It will be necessary that we have the support of the CIO," he wrote, and he called on Haywood for at least two additional organizers.[101] Sensing opportunity in the war boom, Haywood responded enthusiastically. He proposed a joint URW-CIO Goodyear campaign under Davidson, offered the services of Davidson, Harry Doll, and F. J. Michael, and authorized a salary for a fourth organizer. There is no evidence that Dalrymple or other URW leaders objected to the outsiders or to the dilution of their influence, presumably because of their sense of frustration and trust in Haywood. Dalrymple contributed Robert Hill and Cecil Holmes, who were already working with the locals in Jackson and Gadsden; Joseph Emmons; and Roberts, whose independence, geographical isolation, and strong following among the California locals had soured his relations with the International officers.[102]

The fourth CIO organizer was a now-unemployed John House. The Local 2 revival had strengthened the "hotheads," who became more outspoken in their attacks on the officers. By late 1940 House was isolated, much like Callahan. In the local union elections of November 1940, he lost to C. V. Wheeler, 174 votes to 392.[103] Haywood immediately appointed him to Davidson's staff.

Most of the campaigns were surprisingly successful. Thousands of

[99] General Executive Board, Minutes, July 17, 19, 1940, URW Archives.

[100] "Report of General Executive Board," in *Reports*, 1940, pp. 6–7; "Report of S. H. Dalrymple," in *Reports*, 1940, pp. 6–7; *Proceedings*, 1940, 171–72; *ABJ*, Sept. 18, 21, 1940.

[101] Dalrymple to Haywood, Nov. 30, 1940, Congress of Industrial Organizations Papers, URW file, Catholic University, Washington.

[102] "Report of General President," in *Report*, 1941, p. 24.

[103] A. A. Wilson interview; Local 2, Minutes, Membership Meeting, Dec. 8, 15, 1940, Local 2 Archives.

Goodyear workers, including many who had been hostile to the URW, cast their lot with the URW locals. Apart from the booming economy, two other developments probably influenced their decision. First, the renewed aggressiveness of the CIO gave the URW-CIO effort an aura of inevitability reminiscent of "labor on the march." While the 1941 campaign was systematic rather than militant, businesslike rather than tumultuous, the sense of momentum was similar. The second factor was the company's reaction. The aggressively anti-union tactics characteristic of the Slusser era gave way to a more "realistic" approach under Thomas, who was appointed president in August 1940. Plant managers understood that their prime responsibility was to meet production schedules, not fight the URW.[104]

Thus local conditions became all-important. The Los Angeles workers were "really going forward by the end of 1940." Though the plant manager granted a wage increase in early February 1941, they used it to their advantage.[105] Jackson unionists showed similar "spirit and drive," and in St. Marys, where "it would have been suicide to even talk union" as late as mid-1940, the workers were "really talking union."[106] In Akron, union veterans detected the "old spirit around the hall [with] seven meetings going on at one time," and voluntary organizers "going out and doing a good job."[107] The initial breakthrough came, ironically, at Bowmanville, Ontario, which Davidson and Dalrymple had overlooked. The Canadian workers were unhappy with their wages and confident that the booming economy ensured them against reprisals. By the end of 1940, 90 percent of them had joined the local, which operated "in full view of the public."[108] After several months of negotiations, the Bowmanville officers signed the first major Goodyear contract in February 1941.

Even in Gadsden there were signs of change. As opportunities for military contracts increased, the city's anti-union reputation became a serious liability. In 1940 Sidney Hillman personally vetoed OPM plans for a large artillery-shell plant in Gadsden, explaining that he would not assist any city that he could not visit. Gadsden city officials were shocked; their accommodating approach to industry now threatened thousands of jobs. At the

[104] See Howell John Harris, *The Right to Manage: Industrial Relations Policies of American Business in the 1940's* (Madison, 1982), pp. 37–44, for the triumph of this approach in industry generally. Also see Lichtenstein, *Labor's War at Home*, pp. 36–53; Paul A. C. Koistinen, *The Military-Industrial Complex: A Historical Perspective* (New York, 1980), pp. 68–96; Joel Seidman, *American Labor from Defense to Reconversion* (New York, 1953), pp. 20–73.

[105] Robert J. Davidson to House, Feb. 6, 1941, John D. House Papers, University of Akron; District 5 Council, Minutes, Feb. 3, 1941, Local 44 Archives.

[106] Davidson to House, Feb. 6, 1941, House Papers.

[107] Davidson to House, Jan. 27, 1941, House Papers.

[108] *URW* 5 (Dec. 1940): 1.

behest of their congressman, they adopted a resolution welcoming outsiders and guaranteeing their safety. Hillman relented and the city got its plant.[109]

Gadsden's change of policy removed the biggest obstacle to union growth. The Steel Workers Organizing Committee, active in Gadsden since 1939, had a large and active local at the Gulf States plant by the end of 1940. The growing union presence also forced opponents to be more circumspect. Holmes reported that Goodyear supervisors and Etowah Rubber Workers Organization members "still spy on us but we don't have any of that rough stuff."[110] When House arrived in 1941, he and Holmes had reason to believe that the worst had passed.

Their plan was to recruit as many new members as possible while Denlinger, Dalrymple, and, if necessary, the CIO, pressured the NLRB to act. Given the vivid memories of 1936 and 1937, the first goal largely depended on the second. The NLRB, however, was uncooperative. After the preliminary ruling of the board in November 1939, and the final judgment in March 1940, the company made no effort to comply and the NLRB took no action, despite URW pressure. When the loquacious Colonel Hood proposed an out-of-court settlement, board attorneys agreed to cooperate, in effect delaying any action until 1941. For several months it appeared that a satisfactory solution might still be possible. At a conference in February, the Goodyear attorneys asked for information about individual workers and promised an offer in the near future. URW leaders remained hopeful.[111]

In the meantime, House and Holmes waited. They rented a hall, contacted former members, and hoped for action on the NLRB charges. By the end of January, they had a half dozen members in the plant in addition to thirty or more former Goodyear employees. House wrote bravely that "the only thing we have to worry about is . . . a sort of hopelessness that is awfully hard to dispel."[112] As the union grew, however, more traditional obstacles began to appear. When House spoke at a public meeting, fifty hostile ERWO members interrupted his remarks to advise him "not to 'mess' around."[113] When he and Holmes distributed literature at the plant gate on February 12, the head watchman appeared and ordered them to stop. As they argued, a group of men gathered at the factory entrance and approached them. House and Holmes left immediately and reported the inci-

[109] John Kenneth Galbraith, *A Life in Our Times* (Boston, 1981), pp. 112–13.

[110] Holmes to Dalrymple, Dec. 1, 1939, Feb. 16, July 13, 1940, Local 12 File; *Gadsden Times*, Feb. 15, 1940.

[111] Winthrop A. Johns, Memo, Feb. 1, 1940, and Johns to Dalrymple, Feb. 20, 1941, NLRB Papers, RG 25, Box 421; Davidson to House, Feb. 6, 1941, House Papers.

[112] House to Davidson, Jan. 18, 1941, House Papers.

[113] House to Davidson, Feb. 1, 1941, House Papers.

dent to the police and sheriff. On February 18, House was working alone in the union office when five men entered; they approached him and asked about joining the union. As he started to answer, they pulled out clubs and blackjacks and struck him repeatedly on the head, neck, and shoulders. Stunned and bleeding, he fell to the floor and feigned unconsciousness. His wounds required eighty-six stitches, a week in the hospital, and a month of inactivity.[114]

The attack was the turning point in the Gadsden campaign. When union protests to local and federal government authorities produced only promises of more investigations, the anti-union militants became more active. On March 28, when House, Holmes, and several Local 12 members distributed flyers at the plant, fifty to sixty men rushed out of the factory and struck several of them before they could escape. On another occasion, twenty-five to thirty ERWO men surrounded a union member, called him "all sorts of vile names," and threatened to "beat him up."[115] Incidents like these brought the organizing campaign to a halt. One member said he was "God Damn tired of being treated like a nigger after twelve years of service with the company."[116] By mid-June, only the unemployed members remained. Their prospects were little better, since the Goodyear offer was so meager that the union representatives rejected it. Due to a "long, unexpected delay," the NLRB did not present the Gadsden case to the circuit court of appeals until May 1942.[117]

By July 1941 Davidson was ready to concede defeat. To "continue pouring money into that situation seems to be just like pouring it down a sewer," he concluded, and ordered House to Jackson, where the union campaign was progressing rapidly.[118] A year later, when both the Steelworkers and Textile Workers had large and successful locals in Gadsden, CIO representatives criticized Dalrymple for not reestablishing the Goodyear local. No charges made him angrier, but Dalrymple refused to resume the Gadsden campaign until 1943.[119]

[114] House to Davidson, Feb. 8, 1941, in Daniel Nelson, ed., "A CIO Organizer in Alabama, 1941," *Labor History* 18 (1977): 576–77; *Birmingham Age-Herald*, Feb. 19, 20, 1941; L. S. Buckmaster to Franklin D. Roosevelt, Feb. 22, 1941, Local 12 File; *URW* 6 (March 1941): 8.

[115] House to Davidson, June 10, 1941, House Papers.

[116] House to Davidson, June 12, 1941, House Papers.

[117] Buckmaster to Holmes, Dec. 2, 1941, and Stanley Denlinger to Dalrymple, May 8, 1942, Local 12 File. Goodyear settled in late 1942.

[118] Davidson to House, July 16, 1941, House Papers.

[119] Noel R. Beddow to Philip Murray, Sept. 12, 1942, and Beddow to Dalrymple, July 25, 1942, Local 12 File; Buckmaster to Allan Haywood, April 13, 1943, URW file, CIO Papers; Sherman H. Dalrymple, interview with Joe Glazer, April 2, 1955.

By the time House left Gadsden, the URW-CIO effort had attained many of its other objectives. Locals 2 and 26 had negotiated wage increases; Local 2 had also won the reinstatement of eighty-seven militants who had been blacklisted during the layoffs of 1937–1938. Local 131 had doubled in size, and Local 185 had gained from the collapse of an independent union in early 1941. Even in St. Marys, where many workers were teen-agers who lived with their parents on farms or in outlying villages, Local 200 had a substantial membership in the curing department. According to Davidson and Dalrymple, Goodyear executives encouraged workers to form an independent union, an AFL local, and a "vigilante" organization, without success. Apart from Gadsden, the only URW setback was in Windsor, where company threats to close the plant so frightened local residents that union sympathizers refused to form a local.[120]

In March, Davidson called a conference of representatives from the Goodyear locals to formulate contract demands. Meeting at the Portage Hotel in Akron on May 17–18, they heard Haywood, Davidson, and Dalrymple call for "real cooperation" because the "interests of national defense" required unity. Goodyear executives and workers were "in the same business and the success of that business is vital to all."[121] Intended to reassure Litchfield and Thomas, these statements also had an immediate objective: a national contract, similar to the agreements the UAW and SWOC had recently negotiated with General Motors and U.S. Steel. The idea of a national agreement was particularly attractive in outlying plants, where workers viewed Akron wage levels with a mixture of awe and envy. As the president of Local 26 later recalled, "the hope of a National contract . . . has been almost solely instrumental in building our organization to the present peak."[122] The conference authorized Davidson and Dalrymple to open negotiations with the company on a national agreement. On May 20, Dalrymple asked Thomas to set a meeting date.

Sometime during the next week, a second important conference determined the fate of the URW initiative. When Dalrymple's letter arrived, Litchfield's initial reaction was to dismiss it. Thomas took a different approach. When he and Litchfield discussed the union proposal, he talked about the government's growing role in the economy, the union's NLRB election victories, and the reports from Jackson and St. Marys that the union would probably win there too. He urged Litchfield to wash his hands

[120] Davidson to House, April 19, 1941, House Papers; Dalrymple to Haywood, March 31, 1941, CIO Papers, URW file; Davidson to House, March 25, 1941, House Papers; John D. House, "Birth of a Union" (typescript), pp. 87–89.

[121] "Goodyear Conference Policy Statement," May 19, 1941, NLRB Papers, RG 25, Box 1578, Case VIII-C-378; *ABJ*, May 19, 1941.

[122] Raymond C. Burkhart to Dalrymple, July 15, 1941, Local 26 Archives.

of labor relations. He did not say he would agree to a contract, only that he would consider all options. Litchfield finally agreed.[123]

Dalrymple, Davidson, and Climer met twice in late May. On both occasions, the union leaders asked for a national agreement and Climer refused, though he did agree to a meeting with "upper management." When Dalrymple and Davidson presented their plan to Litchfield, Thomas, and Climer, the executives "took a very definite position against such joint negotiations," but "did agree . . . to start negotiations in all plants" where the URW had won an NLRB election. Whether or not Dalrymple and Davidson had anticipated this decision, they gladly accepted it, and the national agreement of 1941 went the way of its predecessors. Thomas and Climer then raised the question of the Local 2 NLRB charges. Davidson agreed to negotiate the cases of individuals along with other issues and to drop the other charges. It was the executives' "definite commitment" that mattered.[124]

On May 27, Davidson ordered the organizers in Akron, Cumberland, Los Angeles, and Jackson to negotiate an immediate wage increase. They were to insist on a written, signed statement and to indicate that this was the "first step" toward a comprehensive contract. Wheeler and the Local 2 officers found Climer as agreeable as ever. After several proposals and counterproposals, they concluded that "he had gone as far as he could" and accepted a 7 to 8 percent increase, about three quarters of what they had originally asked. On June 15, Local 2 members enthusiastically approved the agreement. Davidson and Wheeler predicted that it would lead to a contract "within a short time."[125]

Negotiations resumed on July 11 and continued through the summer. Climer agreed to restore the seniority of workers laid off in 1937, eliminating an issue that dated from the "Miller" agreement. The other points of contention were more mundane: a union security clause, restrictions on the Flying Squadron, and a method of calculating overtime favorable to the workers. On two occasions the Local 2 rank and file rejected a contract without these provisions. Wheeler finally worked out a compromise. The local abandoned its demands in return for concessions on overtime, which seemed more likely to be important in the future. The negotiators signed the agreement on September 28, though minor disagreements and an understanding among the Goodyear locals to defer formal acceptance until all negotiations were complete postponed final ratification until October 28.

The other Goodyear locals had similar experiences. The Cumberland and

---

[123] Edwin J. Thomas, interview with author, Aug. 6, 1982.

[124] Dalrymple, Davidson to Organizers, June 27, 1941, House Papers.

[125] *ABJ*, June 16, 1941; Fred Climer to C. V. Wheeler, June 13, 1941, CIO Papers.

Los Angeles locals approved contracts in early October; the Jackson local won an NLRB election on September 11 and began contract negotiations in October. Local 200 in St. Marys struck for a wage increase in mid-July, survived an attack led by local merchants, and won a compromise settlement. By the fall the local claimed a majority of the employees and began to prepare for an NLRB election. Dalrymple and Davidson heralded a "new era" of "responsible cooperation between labor and management." The URW, they argued, had at last proven that it was "a responsible stable organization that is here to stay."[126]

Though the Goodyear campaign was the most celebrated aspect of the URW revival, it was only one feature of a phenomenon that quietly transformed the industry. Between June 30, 1940, and June 30, 1941, the URW grew from 55,000 to 75,000 members, or half of all rubber workers, and by December 1941, to 93,000 members or 63 percent of all rubber workers. It organized many of the remaining Big Three plants, including the Clarksville, Tennessee, and Cadillac, Michigan, Goodrich factories; the St. Marys Goodyear factory; and the Naugatuck, Passaic, and Woonsocket U.S. Rubber plants. It won NLRB elections at Schacht Rubber in Noblesville, Faultless Rubber in Ashland, and Gates Rubber in Denver, long an anti-union bastion in the West. It also revived defunct locals at Mansfield Tire, Dunlop Tire, and Inland Rubber. When URW campaigns failed, as they did in Providence, Memphis, and, of course, Gadsden, union officials turned to other targets. With so many opportunities, it was easier to wait until the workers became dissatisfied with the AFL or the absence of systematic grievance or bargaining procedures.[127] By the end of the year, the new, more humdrum march of the URW seemed inexorable.

In this environment, union leaders quickly routinized the organizing process. By 1941, Eagle, Marchiando, Bosley, and other URW veterans had been involved in dozens of similar campaigns and knew what workers and employers were likely to accept. Their appeal was to the workers' self-interest and their goal was an NLRB election, not a strike. By 1941, Robert Cruden routinely worked with the organizing staff, preparing newspaper ads, pamphlets, and, in many cases, a local union newspaper that appeared at the crucial stages of a campaign. The papers, Cruden boasted, "met with an excellent response."[128]

The workers also viewed URW efforts in businesslike terms, joining or rejoining because the union seemed an appropriate vehicle for asserting

[126] *URW* 6 (Oct. 1941): 1.

[127] Exceptions were small groups of skilled tradesmen at B. F. Goodrich in Akron (1939), at the U.S. Rubber plants in Indianapolis and in Naugatuck (1941) who switched from the URW to the AFL.

[128] "Report of General President," in *Reports*, 1941, p. 18.

their claims on a growing economy. They expected results and had little patience with union officials who did not satisfy their expectations. The General Tire strike cost Joe Childs the Local 9 presidency in November 1940, and a similar fiasco destroyed AFL federal Local 22343 at Armstrong Tire a few months later. Even successful negotiators had difficulty selling agreements to their constituents. A hard-pressed AFL organizer in Providence pleaded with William Green to pressure the Labor Department to arrange a favorable contract. "Our entire future in the rubber industry," he pleaded, "depends on some sort of decent wage increase being granted here."[129] Local 7 negotiators had to submit three contract proposals before winning the workers' approval. And even Bass, who seldom misjudged his constituents, reported in May 1941 that he had never seen "our people in a state of mind as they are today in regard to wages."[130] The coming of the war had created a mood reminiscent of 1913 or 1919.

By the eve of Pearl Harbor, then, the dilemmas characteristic of the late 1930s were not as pressing as they had been in the spring of 1940. It became easy to see the years 1937 to 1940 as an aberration and to argue that the events of 1940 and 1941 marked a resumption of the expansion of the mid-1930s. The obvious flaw in this interpretation was the unusual pattern of union growth after the spring of 1940. Less evident was the changing character of the industry and the URW. A year later, when Bass and the Akron militants revived the sit-down movement to press their demands against the manufacturers, the government, and, increasingly, the International, their actions sparked a prolonged, bitter struggle with Dalrymple, Buckmaster (who succeeded Burns in 1942), and their non-Akron allies for control of the union. By the time the officers had consolidated their position (ultimately, in 1948), the opportunities of the early war period were a dim memory and the specter of decentralization had reemerged. The rebellion of the Akron militants was a fitting sequel to the story of a generation of workers who came of age with the automobile, found material success in the Rubber City, and took advantage of the opportunities of the 1930s to build a labor organization of unprecedented influence. Even the world war could not wholly obscure the heritage of the mass production era.

[129] John J. Murphy to William Green, March 31, 1941, AFL Papers, Local 22014 Correspondence.

[130] Meeting with Management, May 15, 1941, Local 5 Archives.

The Rubber Workers in Retrospect

THE ACTIVITIES of Dalrymple, House, Buckmaster, and others featured in these essays will stand as examples of the human drama that figures so prominently in the history of organized labor, but they also help to explain what is arguably the most important development in twentieth-century American labor history: the rise of mass production unionism. The tire workers' experiences were not interchangeable with those of auto workers or steelworkers, but their environment was sufficiently similar to distinguish them from the majority of employees in manufacturing (including mechanical goods and rubber boot and shoe workers before the 1930s) and to make their activities pertinent to an understanding of the larger phenomenon.

In the rubber industry, as in automobile and steel manufacture, the new technology redefined the character of the business firm and the labor force, and the options available to employers. The stark contrast between the vertically integrated big business of the 1920s and the more characteristic rubber manufacturing firm of either 1900 or 1940 leaves little doubt about the significance of what had happened. On the shop floor, mass production transformed the semiskilled tire builders and pit workers into strategic machine operators, comparable to other workers who were becoming the targets of the labor movement, and gave them a common source of grievance in the industrial engineers and their techniques. The persistence of rate cutting meant that the animosity that had marked the earlier relationship between the foreman and the workers also characterized the relationship between the plant bureaucracy, centered in the personnel department, and the workers. The mass production factory was neither as smooth-running nor as peaceful as its popular image implies.

By the 1920s the physical elite was no longer indispensable, but tire building and curing continued to be hard work and most of the strapping young men of the 1910s remained. Confident of their own abilities and skeptical of outsiders, they created a union that impressed observers like Adolph Germer and Allan Haywood as excessively decentralized and "chaotic." Still, their experiences illuminated the obstacles that all mass production workers confronted when they tried to build durable labor organizations. The most obvious of those was the leadership of the labor movement. It is sufficient to compare the contributions of Cal Wyatt, Wil-

liam Green, and Coleman Claherty (or Marguerite Prevey and the Wobblies) with those of Germer, Haywood, and Robert Davidson to understand
why the AFL had difficulties and why the CIO excited such high expectations. Less evident was another factor. Before 1933, aspiring union leaders
seldom had time to perfect their organizations before their employers counterattacked. The New Deal, on the other hand, gave union leaders in the
larger plants opportunities to develop their skills, define their goals and
tactics, and clarify their relations with the AFL before they faced the most
demanding tests. That hiatus did not ensure a permanent union presence
but it did create possibilities that had not existed before.

Rubber workers, no less than other union groups, had to overcome internal divisions in order to survive and succeed. Their most serious internal
problem, once Claherty had departed, was not a clash of ideologies or egos
but the distinction between Akron and non-Akron workers. The size and
character of the Akron labor force, and the presence of many strong-
minded individuals among the activists there, were sources of both strength
and difficulty. The Akron unionists created and sustained the URW, but they
also ensured that geographical rivalries would characterize its politics in
the late 1930s and especially in the 1940s.

Finally, the industry is the necessary starting point for an understanding
of what the workers hoped to do for themselves. If their methods seemed
radical to their neighbors, their ends, like the ends of most industrial workers of their era, were conservative. Their organizations were a threat to the
manufacturers not because they promised change but because they demanded a commitment to the status quo, including the blunders and miscalculations of the past. They hoped to raise wages, for example, but were
far more determined to defend existing rates against cuts. At Firestone in
1913, Goodrich in 1922, General Tire in 1934, Firestone in 1936, Goodyear in 1936 and 1938, Goodrich in 1938, and General Tire in 1940, to cite
only the most notable examples, they vigorously opposed wage reductions.
The prospect of a longer working day in the 1930s caused similar opposition.

Other worker goals of the 1930s also had deep roots in the industry's
past. Career employment and its corollary, the seniority principle, were
originally products of the manufacturers' commitment to personnel management. There were of course differences in emphasis: the manufacturers
assumed that dedicated employees would gravitate to the best jobs and opposed formal procedures to spell out the process or to create entitlements,
while their employees, chastened by the Depression, demanded the strict
application of the seniority principle.[1] The union veto of "speed up" tac-

---

[1] For a more extended treatment of the seniority issue see Ronald Schatz, *The Electrical*

tics, in the form of piece-rate limits, sit-downs, attacks on rate setters, and opposition to technological innovation were likewise extensions of earlier activities. Even the emergence of the union as a "way of life" was not unprecedented. The Industrial Assembly, the Factory Councils, and the Hood Rubber Company union were durable workers' organizations that fostered an "ethic of solidarity" equal to the attachment of the most dedicated unionists to the AFL and URW.[2] Until mid-1940, they and their "independent" heirs held their ground against URW organizations in virtually all of the plants where they operated.

More surprising was the continued failure of the URW to translate the workers' collective power into a larger role in civic affairs. The disappointing union performances in the 1937 and 1939 Akron municipal elections were not aberrations. In 1941, for example, the mayoral election proceeded "without outstanding issues or incident," and reminded observers of the elections of the late 1920s and early 1930s. The hated Schroy went down to defeat, but only because thousands of his erstwhile supporters stayed away from the polls. The decline in voter turnout, almost equal to the difference between Schroy's 1937 and 1941 tallies, strongly suggested that he was no longer perceived as a necessary bulwark against the URW. The "listless and uneventful" campaign was a fitting introduction to a new era of politics in which union power, while substantial, would not provoke the hopes or fears of 1937.[3]

More important for the future was the failure of URW leaders to address the challenge of decentralization.[4] In retrospect, it is clear that decentralization was the great industrial innovation of the late 1930s, one that would ultimately destroy the jobs of the Akron and Los Angeles rubber workers.[5] Dalrymple, Burns, and the local officers understood this danger but were uncertain about what they could or should do. The obvious solutions—a more accommodating approach in Akron, a more aggressive effort on the

---

Workers: A History of Labor at General Electric and Westinghouse, 1923–1960 (Urbana, 1983), pp. 106–109, and Sanford M. Jacoby, *Employing Bureaucracy: Managers, Unions, and the Transformation of Work in American History, 1900–1945* (New York, 1985), pp. 242–43.

[2] Gregory Clark, "Authority and Efficiency: The Labor Market and the Managerial Revolution in the Late Nineteenth Century," *Journal of Economic History* 44 (1984): 1976.

[3] *ABJ*, Nov. 2, 4, 1941. Also see James Caldwell Foster, *The Union Politic: The CIO Political Action Committee* (Columbia, 1975), for CIO political strategies.

[4] John D. House strongly disagreed with this statement and noted that URW leaders promoted legislation to restrict plant movements and tried to win nationwide bargaining contracts with Goodyear and other companies. In my opinion there is no inconsistency between House's statement and this paragraph.

[5] See Charles Jeszeck, "Plant Dispersion and Collective Bargaining in the Rubber Tire Industry" (Ph.D. diss., University of California, Berkeley, 1982).

industry's frontiers, or some combination of the two—were as unpleasant to contemplate as decentralization itself. To alienate the Akron militants or embark on still more expensive and problematic campaigns in the South or West would have required a commitment to the future at least as bold as the manufacturers'. The International officers' political alliance with the outlying locals and partnership with the federal government were haphazard and ultimately inadequate substitutes.

By 1941, the legacy of the 1880s had ceased to play an important role in the rubber industry or in most of American industry. The divorce between mass production and the labor movement had ended, and the industrial unions that had been the principal agents of that change, like the URW, were as well established, as effective, and at least as well led as the most formidable organizations of the traditional labor movement. This achievement became apparent only in the months immediately preceding Pearl Harbor and surprised many people, including many union leaders, but it was due only in part to the opportunities of the war boom. It also reflected the activities of Marguerite Prevey, Clifton Slusser, Wilmer Tate, and the men who created the unions of the 1930s and the thousands of individuals who participated in them. Their legacy would prove to be as durable and, in some respects, as controversial as the legacy of the earlier period had been.

ALTHOUGH the rubber workers appear briefly in most labor histories of the 1930's and tangentially in the many histories of the industry and its major firms, they have been the subject of only one extended account, Harold S. Roberts's *The Rubber Workers* (1944). A competent, scholarly study, based in part on materials collected while the author was an investigator for the National Labor Relations Board, *The Rubber Workers* was a model for its time. Perhaps because it is so detailed or because Roberts wore his biases so unmistakably on his sleeve, it had virtually no impact on subsequent scholarship. It is now badly out of date. I have relied on it sparingly, preferring instead to reconstruct the history of the rubber workers from original sources.

The most useful of those sources are the case files of the Federal Mediation and Conciliation Service and the NLRB available at the National Archives. For studies of industrial conflict, the records of these agencies are invaluable. Somewhat less important and infinitely more difficult to use, are the records of the United Rubber Workers and its various locals, located in the nooks and crannies of union halls. The other indispensable source, the papers of the American Federation of Labor at the State Historical Society of Wisconsin, are easily accessible and exceedingly well managed. The surviving records of the Firestone, Goodyear, and Goodrich companies (listed in the order of their volume and importance) will soon be available to researchers at the American History Research Center at the University of Akron, together with several related private manuscript collections and the notes, interview tapes, and transcripts that I accumulated.

Two other related groups of materials were critical to this study. As indicated in the acknowledgments, I benefited from the recollections of approximately a score of workers and other participants. Their reminiscences filled important gaps and provided essential details. When used in combination with other data, they provided a dimension to the story that will soon be impossible to recapture. Newspapers are the other vital source for any twentieth-century social history. The Akron newspapers, including the publications of the URW and the Central Labor Union, are exceedingly rich. There is a Works Progress Administration index to the *Akron Beacon Journal* for the 1920s and 1930s, but it is of little value for the latter decade, when labor stories were front-page news almost every day. The newspapers of the many smaller communities that are featured in this account are likewise important repositories of information about strikes, negotiations, and other newsworthy events.

Several published works, apart from the Roberts book, deserve mention. Alfred W. Jones's *Life, Liberty and Property* (1941), a penetrating study of Akron in the late 1930s, is a little-known, community survey, comparable in many respects to the famous Middletown books. It provides a telling snapshot of a midwestern city on the eve of World War II. Among the company histories, Glenn Babcock's *History of the United States Rubber Company* (1966) is equally noteworthy and equally obscure. Regrettably, the company destroyed most of its records after Babcock completed his research, greatly complicating the work of any historian of the footwear and mechanical goods industries. The many fine scholarly books that have appeared in recent years on subjects pertaining to this account are acknowledged in the footnotes.

Library of Congress Cataloging-in-Publication Data

Nelson, Daniel, 1941–
American rubber workers & organized labor, 1900-1941 / Daniel Nelson.

p. cm.
Bibliography: p.
Includes index.
ISBN 0–691–04752–9 (alk. paper)
1. Trade-unions—Rubber industry workers—United States—History—20th century.   2.
Trade-unions—United States—Organizing—History—20th century.   I. Title.   II. Title:
American rubber workers and organized labor, 1900-1941.

HD6515.R9N45 1988
331.88′1782′0973—dc19   87–35404